With Our Faces to the Foe

A History of the
4th Maine Infantry
In the War of the Rebellion

By
Peter P. Dalton

Union Publishing Company
Union, Maine
04862

ISBN : 0-9642029-6-4

Published By

Union Publishing Company
Union, Maine
04862

Cover Illustration

Franklin's men charging across
the railroad at Fredericksburg

ISBN : 0-9642029-6-4

With Our Faces to the Foe

Foreword

With Our Faces to the Foe
A History of the Fourth Maine Regiment

The annual meeting of the Fourth Maine Regiment and Second Maine Battery Association met in Rockland on September 18, 1894. The members of the Edwin Libby Post, G.A.R., had opened their hall to the members of the association. Today was to mark the 30th anniversary of the regiment's mustering out. It would be a solemn occasion marked by many speeches and tearful moments.

About 11:30 the members departed from Tillson's wharf aboard the steamer Silver Star destined for a clam bake on Hurricane Island. It was from these pebbled shores that the stone had been cut for the 4th' Maine's monument at Gettysburg. As the men ambled about the ship, their thoughts undoubtedly traveled back to a day in June of 1861, when these very same men had departed from Rockland on the Daniel Webster, bound for war. Thirty-three years had passed since that voyage. The memories of that journey, the faces of lost comrades, and the experience of three years in the field, were as indelibly etched in their minds as if the events had unfolded only yesterday.

As the formalities of the meeting were concluded, several of the members of the organization were called upon to address the assembly. Commander Hanson Simmons of the 4th Maine now took his turn. Slowly, but deliberately, he began to speak :

"Of all the days of the year I look forward with anticipation to this the day of our annual reunion. I look forward to it with mingled feelings of pleasure and sadness - with feelings of pleasure at the thought of greeting once more so many of my old comrades, with feelings of sadness at the thought of faces I shall see no more.' I am also deeply affected as I look round upon you here and note the furrows time is making on your brows and as I think how soon we shall all be gone. However we may have differed in the past, it is time we laid aside our differences. The cords that

bind us to each other should and do strengthen with each passing year. I am glad to see so many of you here today, though I miss many who have been wont to meet with us. I hope to live to meet you many times in the near future, though conscious that you will be fewer still in number every time we come together. And now good bye till we meet again."

Such were the experiences these men had shared in war, that no single force of nature, or man, could split these bonds asunder. The strength of their resolutions had been set from the very beginning, for before there was a military draft, and before there were local, state, and federal bounties of any kind, there had been an all volunteer 4th Maine Regiment.

Colonel Walker later remembered that in the very beginning "there was a meeting of Rockland's citizens on the evening of April 23d. Speeches were made and resolutions passed, and a twenty dollar gold coin was tossed on the floor for the first volunteer.[1] It was picked up by Stephen H. Chapman, who enlisted in my company and acted as orderly sergeant until appointed by Col. Berry as sergeant-major of the regiment. He was a noble man and a true soldier. Had he been spared he would have won an honorable record for our city and state." With this act Chapman had breathed life into an exceptional military entity.

By May 20, 1861, most of the 4th Maine's volunteers had assembled in Rockland. Hiram Berry, who had been elected Colonel of the unit, had received not only four Knox County companies, but also one each from Searsport, Winterport, Wiscasset, and Damariscotta, as well as two from Belfast. In all 1,085 men, including a regimental band, were assembled on a promontory overlooking Rockland. In honor of one of the area's most famous early residents, the encampment which these men created was named Camp Knox. It was a label which they would proudly carry with them throughout the war.[2]

This assemblage of individuals, this "Limerock Regiment", these "Fighting Tigers", would soon earn a reputation as tough combatants, schooled by experience in the art of warfare. Heavily engaged in battle after battle, from First Bull Run to Chesterfield Bridge, the regiment repeatedly

---

[1] C. F. Hodgdon of Rockland offered the twenty-dollar gold piece.

[2] The encampment's name was in honor of Henry Knox of Thomaston, a famous Revolutionary War general.

suffered heavy casualties, many times approaching, and even exceeding, fifty percent. This dedication to duty, and their fearless self sacrifice, though often matched by other Maine units, was seldom exceeded.

It should be noted that a written history of his regiment has been attempted by many. Elijah Walker set his pen to the task near the end of his life in the late 1800's. Unfortunately, much of that history has been lost. Due to the length and depth of this particular study, however, much of the information which has been discovered by this author will undoubtedly require a second volume. The addition of a regimental roster to this book alone would have required an additional hundred pages. It has been decided, therefore, to create a second volume in the years to come, which will include both a regimental roster and Walker's regimental history. The date for this release has not yet been determined but will hopefully appear in the next couple of years.

It should also be noted that the early history of this regiment, as it appears in this record, was written only in part by this author. Sergeant-Major Stephen H. Chapman's newspaper accounts were so well written that it seemed better to repeat it than to try retelling it. The remainder of this history, though, is my own responsibility, written as it was viewed through the eyes of several key witnesses. Additionally, this author would like to extend his sincerest gratitude to the many individuals who have extended aid and assistance. It is sincerely hoped that the end product will prove how valuable the regiment's existence was to the overall war effort. It is also hoped that this regimental history, With Our Faces to the Foe, will prove not only to be a story worth telling, but one worth remembering as well...

The 4th Maine Struggle to Survive in the Devils Den.
July 2, 1863

Far from over the distance
The faltering echoes come.
Of the flying blast of bugles
And the rattling roll of drum.

To the members of the 4th Maine Volunteer Infantry :

May your deeds of courage
And your unfaltering devotion to duty
Be forever remembered.

Peter Dalton

Table Of Contents

Dedication

This is the part of a book seldom read. It is the part of a book that explains why one dedicates seven years of one's spare time to researching this or any topic, and why one feels the need to put the story to paper. For though there are many people who express the desire to write a book, there are so few that actually do it. How many times have I researched and read, and then reread, in order to write a single sentence. Agonized over the composition of a sentence to complete a single paragraph. Each paragraph, a story unto itself, and each chapter, a collection of so many, many stories. The completion of this history always seemed important. Many times it seemed one of the reasons for my existence.

I owe thanks to the values inherited from my father, who himself experienced the terror of war. A man who had landed on the beaches of Normandy, during World War II. A man who had narrowly escaped death when a stray artillery shell had fallen into his foxhole on a cold winter night. Strangely, everyone in the foxhole had been killed, save my father, who only moments before the explosion had been beckoned from the crater by a ghostly female figure. To this day he swears it was his mother, clothed in a flowered dress. After the war he discovered that his mother did indeed own such a gown, but had purchased it only after he had left for war.

I owe what I am to a kind and loving mother, who was always there for me when I needed her. One who helped me raise my own children. One who had herself survived a devastating fire in 1950. A fire that had taken from her all that she had, including her first husband, a mother-in-law and six children. Her husband had thrown her through a window that she might run for help. The act had saved her life. The husband had then proceeded upstairs to try and save the children, only to be overcome by the smoke. Only she survived the tragedy, and yet my mother was the kind of woman who could survive the mental devastation of all this, and still have the courage to start life over again, and give birth to another child. Me.

From all of this death and destruction, here I stand like the phoenix, myself giving birth to this book, and marveling at how, somehow, it has all come to pass. I want to lovingly thank my own wife, Cynthia, who has always shown her own love and special patience with me while I labored away on this book, and to my two children, Laura and Andrea, who I love so very much, and who just thought I was crazy.

Captain, and later, Colonel Elijah Walker

Chapter I

"Go, and God Bless You."

"Trust us, dear friends, if we die, it will be with our faces to the foe. How can one better or more gloriously die than for his country?" SHC

For the United States the Civil War began at 4:30 a.m. on the morning of April 12th when a "dapper, showy Creole from Louisiana named General Pierre Gustave Toutant Beauregard, ordered his men to open up on Fort Sumter" in Charleston harbor. For the men of the Limerock Regiment it began at a citizens meeting on the evening of April 23rd, 1861. Elijah Walker, many years later, recalled that "speeches were made and resolutions passed, and a twenty dollar gold coin was tossed on the floor for the first volunteer. It was picked up by Stephen H. Chapman, who enlisted in my company and acted as orderly sergeant until appointed by Col. Berry as Sergeant-Major of the regiment."[1]

On the morning of the twenty-fourth Elijah Walker met with Major-General Titcomb of Augusta and received "orders for raising troops." Walker was "given blanks" and authorized to enlist a company for ninety days service. "At eleven o'clock a.m. seventy-three names had been signed to the roll. The general then took the roll and would not allow me to make further enlistments as he wanted others to raise companies. Capt. O. J. Conant and Capt. L. D. Carver at once commenced to raise companies." At two o'clock the following order was received :

Headquarters Division
Rockland, April 24, 1861

To Elijah Walker, Recruiting Officer: -

You are hereby ordered to notify and warn the enlisted men by you to meet at the court room in this city at five o'clock this

[1] Walker, History of the 4th Maine Infantry, p. 2.

Colonel, and later, Major-General Hiram G. Berry

afternoon for the purpose of choosing one captain and two lieutenants.

By order of Wm. H. Titcomb,
Major-General.

The 4th Maine Volunteer Militia was, itself, the only infantry organization to be mustered into service in the Rockland area. This is not to say that Rockland men did not serve in other regiments during the American Civil War. This they most certainly did. But this regiment was unique, for it was an all volunteer unit, in so much as it's existence was not a direct result of military conscription. It should also be noted that the men in this unit came, almost exclusively, from Knox, Lincoln, and Waldo Counties. The only other organization which can trace its' roots to the Rockland area is Hall's Second Maine Battery, itself one of the most distinguished artillery units to fight in the war.

The field staff of the regiment included several notable and able leaders, but it was Hiram Berry that was given overall command of the unit. Berry had been the originator, and leader, of a militia unit called the Rockland Guards. Additionally, Mr. Berry had been the first to offer his services to the State of Maine when hostilities broke out between North and South. Though not a West Point graduate, he was a natural choice for the Colonelcy of the fourth. His leadership abilities were, indeed, impressive, a fact which was soon recognized by the Union Army, where he was promoted to the rank of Brigadier General, and, later, Major General, and given charge of his own division.

The regiment gathered at Camp Knox in Rockland on May 8, 1861, and drilled for a month before being mustered into federal service by Captain Thomas Hight of the United States Dragoons, on June 15, 1861. As the men assembled on the heights above town Colonel Berry designed a simple set of rules under which the regiment was to operate, a copy of which may be seen in this chapter. This was organizational paperwork, but it was a major part of his new job. Berry would become very skilled at instituting order and discipline among his men.[2]

---

[2] Walker, History of Fourth Maine Infantry, Special Collections U.M.O., p. 3.

RULES OF CAMP KNOX.

Ordered by Col. Berry, commanding:

Each captain will divide his company into squads of four (4) equal parts, and each so divided will be placed under charge of sergeant and corporal, two of which squads will be placed under charge of a lieutenant.

Each lieutenant will divide his squad into messes of six each, and order each mess to choose a head, and messes will be formed in squads of three each, making 18 in a squad; each squad will be placed under charge of sergeant and corporal; two of such squads will be held under each lieutenant.

Each company will detail two men daily to cook, and distribute to the several messes the food for the day, and such men will be relieved from drill and guard duty for the day.

Sergeants and corporals will be held responsible for the cleanliness of camps, arms, mess-dishes, and for the general cleanliness and good order of the several squads.

Breakfast hour, 7 o'clock, A. M.; dinner, 12 M.; supper, 6 P. M.

At sunrise the camp gun will be discharged under the order of the officer of guard. The companies will be formed immediately, roll call and parade under 1st sergeant, after which the camps will be put in order and all made clean. Soldiers will attend to such duties after roll call and dismissal as are necessary to cleanliness previous to 1-4 hour before breakfast.

At 8 o'clock company drill under company officers.

Line will be formed at 10 o'clock.

At 1.30 o'clock P. M. company drill under company officers.

At 3 o'clock P. M. line formed.

At 7 o'clock P. M. roll call.

By order of commandant,

HIRAM G. BERRY.

Berry's Rules of Camp Knox

At the organizational meeting in April the enlistees were informed that their term was to be three months. About mid-May the term was changed to two years. A few days later, at morning roll, Colonel Berry addressed the troops and stated to them "that no troops would be mustered for two years, and for those that were not willing to be mustered for three years to step to the front and give up their guns and equipments." All but two agreed to the three year enlistment term. The rest were sworn into service on June 15th. These terms were understood by most, but not by all.[3]

It should be noted that in addition to the men, three women from Rockland had also tendered their services to the Fourth. These included Mrs. Ruth S. Mayhew, Miss Orissa A. Packard, and Miss Jennie Grafton. Of the three none actually departed with the regiment. Mrs. Mayhew and Miss Packard would, eventually, serve as nurses in the "Maine Camp and Hospital Association of Portland" along side the famous Mrs. Charles A. L. Sampson.[4]

Sunday, June 16th, religious services were performed by the local Methodist minister. Following this event swords were presented to the Rockland company officers. Elijah Walker was so moved as to give a speech in which he gratefully accepted the weapons which had been procured by the subscription of the citizens of Rockland. He pledged that the weapons would "only be drawn in defense of our country...and against rebels and traitors who have threatened our country and insulted our flag...", all of which was done amidst wild cheering and applause.[5]

Early on Monday morning, the 17th of June, reveille sounded early. It was exactly four a. m. The day had finally come for these Maine men to depart for war, and it was an event of major historical significance for the City of Rockland. The departure, itself, is descriptively captured by the Rockland Gazette and presented in their June 20, 1861, issue. It is presented here, in its' entirety, for your consideration.

DEPARTURE OF THE FOURTH REGIMENT

[3] Ibid., p. 2.
[4] Maine Adjutant General Report, 1864-5, Vol I, pp. 118-119
[5] Walker, op. cit., pp. 3-4.

Photo showing the original Camp Knox in Rockland.

Rockland celebrated the anniversary of the battle of Bunker Hill, on Monday, by sending forth her sons to sacrifice on the altar of their country their lives, if need be, to defend the holy legacy which the fathers made like sacrifice to win.

On Saturday the troops were inspected and mustered into the service of the United States by Captain Charles Hight. On Sunday evening knapsacks were packed, as well as camp equipage and baggage, and each soldier received one day's rations. On Monday morning the reveille sounded at four o'clock, and the soldiers took their last breakfast in Camp Knox at five o'clock. The men in each company were subsequently divided into squads, and at the proper time proceeded to lower and pack their tents. After the cords had been all unfastened and pegs taken up, at the tap of the drum all the tents were simultaneously lowered to the ground, every man cheering as the tents came down.

The camp grounds were thronged with thousands of people of this and surrounding towns during the morning. Many were light hearted and gay, enjoying the beautiful morning and the varying scene before them; but many were sad and weeping, and the bright day was to them, doubtless, one of the saddest which had ever dawned. Many were there to take a sad leave of husbands, sons, and brothers, whom they might never see again, and yet perhaps there were few of these wives and mothers and sisters who were not ready to say, with a true devotion to their country's cause, "Go, and God bless you!" Among the many young faces we met as we walked through the field, there were not a few cheeks wet with tears and eyes red with weeping. Among the soldiers there were fewer moist eyes, but perhaps not, on that account, fewer feeling hearts. Most of the men appeared very cheerful, many of them merry, and a few poor fellows, it made us sad to see, were drunken - conquered by their worst enemy, before they had fired a gun. Many were serious and thoughtful, but all ready to go to their work with stout arms and brave hearts.

The Adjutant began to form the regimental line at a little past eight o'clock, and when all was ready, the regiment took up its' line of march at a little past nine. First, the crowds on foot and lines of carriages came pouring down Middle Street, and then the platoons

Rockland Gazette.

VOL. 16. ROCKLAND, MAINE, THURSDAY, JUNE 27, 1861. NO. 27.

Fourth Regiment of M. V. M.

Rockland Gazette on Day of Departure of the 4th Maine

of our brave soldiery appeared, their bright bayonets flashing in the morning sun. The whole route of march was densely thronged with people, and we have never seen our streets so filled before. The sides of Main Street, through the center of the city, were lined by a dense mass of people, every window along the street was occupied, and carriages stood in all the avenues looking on the street. At Main Street the troops were joined by the Rockland Band, in full uniform, who accompanied them through to Washington The regiment bore on the march a white banner, bearing the inscription, "From the Home of Knox," and when the head of the column had arrived opposite the Kimball Block, a halt was made, and Major General Titcomb presented to Col. Berry, for the regiment, a small silk banner, bearing the arms and motto of the State of Maine. The troops were then greeted with enthusiastic cheers by the throng of citizens, which were heartily returned by the soldiers, when the column moved forward again at a quick march, directly to Atlantic Wharf, where the steamer Daniel Webster, which had come down from Bangor on Sunday, was waiting to receive them.

The wharf, with the ground, sheds, buildings, and shipping in the vicinity was densely thronged with spectators to witness the embarkation. Probably not less than eight or ten thousand people were assembled in the vicinity of the wharf. The troops were embarked in order, each company going on board and taking the position previously assigned to it by the Colonel's special order. During the embarkation a salute was fired from two or three small pieces of cannon on board the ship Alice Thorndike, lying at the wharf.

When the troops were all embarked, Major Gen. Titcomb addressed the citizens assembled on the wharf in some patriotic and stirring remarks fitted to the occasion, when three times three hearty cheers were given for the Fourth Regiment, which were returned by the soldiers, and the boat moved away, the band playing, handkerchief waving, hearts throbbing and tears falling, as she bore our brave volunteers away to the soldiers work.

General Titcomb accompanies the regiment as far as New York. The Webster arrived in Portland at a little past four o'clock, where the troops were received by the city authorities and escorted by the Fifth Regiment. They were quartered at the New City Hall on

The steamer Daniel Webster whisked the 4th Maine off to war in June Of 1861. Later the Daniel Webster became a hospital ship.

Monday night, and left for Boston, in good spirits, at 7 1-2 o'clock on Tuesday morning. They arrive in New York this (Wednesday) morning, by the Fall River route from Boston. The horses, tents, camp equipage, and baggage went direct to Boston, by the Sanford, on Monday night, in charge of a guard detailed for the purpose.

And so our brave volunteers have left us. May the God of our fathers have them in his care, make them true patriot soldiers, return them again to their homes and loved ones, and make those they leave behind ready, when duty calls, to follow them in defense of our flag and country.

Rockland Gazette : June 20, 1861.

The departure of these soldiers was, without doubt, one of the most significant events ever to take place in the history of the town of Rockand. Even Governor Washburn could not resist the temptation to review the regiment, which he did on the Saturday prior to their departure. He made an address to the assembled troops, stating his pleasure over their appearance. The Gazette was led to believe that he had complimented the men as being "the best looking body of troops Maine has yet sent to the service."

In the Thursday, June 27 issue of the Rockland Gazette there is conspicuously very little said about the progress of the Fourth Maine. The paper took the occasion to list a complete roll of the membership of the regiment. The newspaper's correspondent is mentioned, once again, as Sergeant Major S. H. Chapman. The only other consideration given to the theme is an article reproduced from the Boston Herald.

THE KNOX REGIMENT

"The Cadets escorted the regiment to the Common, where the afternoon was passed away very pleasantly by means of a collation, the joint production of the regimental Quartermaster and the City of Boston, music and fun. - This was the merriest lot of men we have

Ruth Mayhew offered her services as a nurse to the 4th Maine Infantry as they went off to war. Only later, at the time of the Battle of Gettysburg, would she join the war effort.

seen on the Common since the war commenced. - They were continually at some "rough and tumble" games which neither fatigued them or the thousands of laughing spectators.

Nearly every company had a wag who kept them in good humor. The lower part of the Common was closed off for their accommodation, and those who had friends inside or favor at the gateways were admitted. Outside there were thousands enjoying the fashionable amusement of the time - a military display. This is getting to be an everyday affair, and fashionable audiences flock to the Common as they do in the season thereof to balls and the opera. The Common never looked better than in its elegant June dress this year, but the carpet of green on the hills and parade ground is worn gravel bare by the great audiences of late. The Maine boys stacked their arms on Charles Street Mall, and the Cadets kept guard for them while they ate and rested.

The Brigade Band was out with the Cadets, and together with the Rockland Band which accompanied the Maine Regiment, they issued some good notes to pay the visitors for their trouble. They were better than the Confederate bands. It was enough to make a man wish to "go for a soldier" - all the pretty faces and the music. There were whole troops of Maine girls about cheering the soldiers and making them more unhappy when they left. A soldiers life is not always gay, but these boys were bound to go in and enjoy it as it comes.

The moments flew away, and at six o'clock the regiment was assembled and fell into columns by platoons, and marched through Beacon, Park, Tremont, Winter, Summer streets, Harrison Avenue, and so on to Old Colony Depot, where a train of twenty cars was filled. - Here the jocularity continued. John Keller, of Company B., made himself the centre of an audience wherever he moved. He was a rare wag, and his grimaces will be remembered for a long time. He kept the whole company and a crowd of outsiders, "in a roar." We should be sorry to see his name among the dead or missing, for he is better than a medicine chest in a company.

The train started out without incident at 7:22 o'clock, amid a volley of cheers, the last of which was for the Boston ladies, from the soldiers.

So endeth the fourth lesson of Maine for the Union. Four thousand of her hearty sons have gone forward, every one of them anxious to see a rebel."

Boston Globe : No Date

The next issue of the Rockland Gazette came out on Thursday July 4th. The paper is buzzing with reports of military activity in northern Virginia near Manassas Junction. There is rumor from a citizen of Alexandria, who had just escaped from the area, of a gathering of over 20,000 soldiers and numerous artillery batteries. At this early date nobody is yet aware that a great battle will take place near this insignificant hamlet, called Manassas, along a minor stream called Bull Run. The stage, however, is being set.

In the July 4th edition, the date set for the celebration of the United States' own anniversary of freedom, the probability of a major battle appears imminent. The overwhelming sentiment, however, is that the war will be short and that the Confederate Capital will once again be in Union hands within the month. Mr. Chapman gives us now a first installment on his unique style of reporting. The following article was written on June 23rd, but did not reach the newspaper until the following week. We will examine Chapman's words and compare his literary style with that of the other two journalists whose writings have already appeared in this story.

On Thursday, June 20, 1861, another announcement appeared in the Rockland Gazette...one which, up to this point we have ignored. The history of the Fourth Maine Infantry will at this point receive the temporary voice of one of its members in the recounting of its history. After reading

Our Army Correspondence

We are pleased to inform our readers that our able correspondent "S.H.C.," an officer in the fourth regiment, will furnish the Gazette with a regular correspondence, keeping our readers informed of the position, movements, health and fortunes of our volunteers, and of other matters of interest. These letters will necessarily be of interest

Post war photo of Edwin Libby.

to the friends and families of our soldiers, and to the families of volunteers, or to soldiers who may wish the paper to be sent to their friends, we will make a reduction of one third in our advance price, and send them the Gazette for one year for one dollar, in advance. Thirty or forty copies have already been ordered by soldiers, to be sent to their families.

"S.H.C.", is actually S. H. Chapman. Though Maine State Archival records tell us precious little about him, the one thing that neither official state documents, or the Rockland Gazette tell us is what his first or middle names were. Even his obituary, which appeared in the Gazette, referred to him as either Sergeant Major S. H. Chapman, or as, simply, Mr. Chapman. One can only assume that he is referred to in this manner by his own request. Only very late in our research did we discover that the S. stood for Stephen.

What we know for certain about Mr. Chapman, is that he was born in Jefferson, Maine, in 1826. At the time of his enlistment, he was thirty-five years of age. He was a resident of Rockland, and a teacher. His eyes were blue, his hair and complexion dark, and he was six feet three inches tall.[6]

We know that Mr. Chapman was a patriot. Two weeks before the recruiting office was opened for the Fourth Maine Regiment of Infantry in Rockland, he wrote a letter to the Gazette, while he, himself, was absent from the city, stating that if a company were formed, he wished to become a member. Thus, by his own public statement, he became the first to volunteer his services. When the organizational meeting was held on April 23rd, it was, once again, Stephen Chapman that was first to step forward and join the fledgling regiment. Due, in part, to his energy and dedication, Chapman was made orderly sergeant of Company B, and, shortly thereafter, Sergeant Major of the regiment. This promotion actually placed him fifth in the overall chain of command.[7]

FROM OUR CORRESPONDENT
Camp Knox, Meridan Hill
Washington, D. C., June 23, 1861

[6] Maine State Archives, Soldier Index.
[7] Walker, op. cit., p. 2.

Mr. Editor and Readers of the Gazette : - The promise we made to keep you informed of the movements and camp life of the 4th Regiment of Maine Volunteer Militia, it has been absolutely impossible to keep, for our duties, though humble, have been so arduous that neither night nor day has been available for that purpose. To the many readers of the Gazette who have friends in our regiment the promise is renewed that each week shall furnish them with reliable accounts of our labors. Our records will not be one sided, but truthful.

It is a matter of interest and consequence to their friends to know under what kind of men the soldiers are placed. As to capacity in military science, all the Regimental and Company officers are necessarily a little inefficient, but if we are not hurried into service too soon, no danger from such cause need be feared, if they apply themselves vigorously, as they will, of course. It was quite impossible at the outset to get men for officers who understood tactics.

Officers have much to endure, - to try their patience. Indeed, in our soul, we pity a captain of a company and the colonel of a regiment, - the former has great cares and troubles, - the latter, tenfold more. Men, in their enthusiasm, enlisted with the idea that no restrictions would be imposed upon them, but when they find camp life a little like prison life, they fall to "growling" and blame their officers. But in respect to discipline our men need more to complain of too much liberty, for they enjoy far more than legitimately belongs to them. Good men have been allowed extra opportunities to leave the camp (at Rockand) and due discrimination was not exercised towards worse men.

Parents sometimes - frequently, promise their children what they cannot give, in order to get rid of a present annoyance, - so officers of companies have deceived their men in the same manner. Reasonable men can be dealt with in reason, and will appreciate and abide by what is reasonable, but will not stand it to be insulted by false promises.

We know much of the material of which our regiment is composed, and we candidly believe, we know, it is composed of excellent, honorable, high-minded, patient, brave material.

There are nuisances, drunkards, drones and cowards among us, but such are immensely scarce. We have not a few who "take a little too much" now and then, but who, in other respects are perfect soldiers, - worth, in this trying emergency, a hundred fold more than their "ram rod" opposers at home, - ready to fight to the last drop of blood, for their country, regiment and colonel.

If general expression of people, along our route from home to Washington, was a just criterion, we are a noble regiment. Our men are larger, hardier, braver looking than other troops who have been received here. But let this go for the present, and let us say a word of our journey from Camp Knox in Rockland to our Camp Knox in Washington.

South Carolina seceded December 20, 1860. Fort Sumter was taken April 15, 1861. The President's proclamation was promulgated on the 16th of the same month. First volunteering began in Rockland April 23d, "Camp Knox" was organized May 21, and evacuated June 17th, the anniversary of the Battle of Bunker's Hill. During our stay at Rockland we had many pleasures and annoyances. Companies had been promised this and that thing or kind, and when they could not possibly be procured, dissatisfaction was the result.

In order to get recruits, many promises had been made of Minnie rifles, sword bayonets, pistols, suits of uniform, accoutrements, and support of families, which those who made them, in many cases, knew could never be fulfilled. But the State Government had promised us rifles - in misplaced charity, we suppose they could not be procured. But when the 4th regiment was told that no other regiment from Maine had been supplied with the rifles, we were deceived, for the 1st regiment had and has them.

Well, long, had we talked and conjectured about the time of leaving our State for the seat of war. All wished to get out of Rockland. Some because actual is less painful than anticipated separation from dear wives, children, parents, sweet-hearts and friends. Others because they had been egregiously cheated by unscrupulous, money making, "cheeky" clothes dealers. Others because their natures do not allow them many days in the same place. Others because they desire to have this work of war done with as soon as possible, and some would fain have run away.

We were in Camp Knox about one month. We were fed and generally treated as well as our circumstances should allow us to hope. Mr R. Anderson fed us for a time with good food, neatly and well cooked. His kind heart was always sympathizing with our real or supposed needs. He has many friends in our midst. Give a soldier's love to him for us all, Mr. Editor. The ladies of Rockland, we all say God bless them, and when the 4th of July occurs we shall drink to their and all Maine's daughters health. When in camp and far from home, we think of them with burning tears, - and in battle we will fight the harder as our hearts palpitate, and our arms strengthen, at your loved memory. God bless you. We are braver and better, as we are happier, for you.

The Commissary procured and the Quarter Master dispersed food at Rockland which was good and healthy. Ordinarily, commissaries and quarter masters expect to make money out of their connections with this department, but the writer has his credulity very hardly taxed to believe either Mr. Farwell or Mr. Abbott has done so. Mr. Abbott has worked assiduously, and arduously. He has thus far been a slave to this regiment, and done all in his power for our comfort.

Our tents are the boast of our country and Gen. Cochran is known as their maker. There is now and then a whole souled man who, when he executes a contract with a state even, will do it as if his composition was not the collection of the "scraps, odds and ends" of the devil's workshop. Mr. C. has been here to see us - we shook his honest hand heartily. - Would like to see another contractor come and see us. Gen. Cochran is here trying to induce the War Department to have flies to all the tents, which would add infinitely to the comfort and health of our men.

We may be incapable of fairly judging, but our opinion is that our regiment is peculiarly fortunate in their choice of field officers, - the Colonel, Lieut. Colonel, and Major. Colonel Berry has adorned all the places he has ever been called to fill. He is a man of energy, endurance, stern, unyielding, uncompromising, austere, collected and a thorough disciplinarian. A man's nerve and heart must not be sensitive for a skillful surgeon or commander. He must be able to smother his finer feelings under a sense of duty to his command. Pity and compassion must not mold his conduct, when their exercise would vitiate his camp. Col. Berry is feared, respected and loved. If our first and third Field Officers are occasionally hasty and heated, the calm, cool, serene, easy manners and judgement of out Lieut. Colonel neutralize their influence. We mistake if Lieut. Marshall's composition is not better fitted for the statesman than the warrior, and, too, we need him at every turn, and appreciate his fine, manly, scholarly qualities.

We had a banner and a flag presented us in New York, but for some unaccountable reason, neither Colonel Marshall nor Major Nickerson was called upon to respond in behalf of our regiment, which should have been allowed to exhibit its full proportions, intellectually as well as otherwise. Major Nickerson will make a soldier, - a thorough disciplinarian, - a fighter. - Adjutant Greenhalgh's specialty is thorough drill. His voice is better heard than any on the field, and his commands inspire the men to jump like electrical puppets. The Captains and Lieutenants are among the finest, most gentlemanly persons we have ever met, - always ready to obey and oblige.

We have a few low privates, graduates of Colleges, who stand a good chance of a kick from an ignoramus officer. But there are strange mixtures, - strange bed-fellows, strange everything in this world of ours, - a very good, very desirable world, nevertheless. - We soldier boys must succumb to its demands, - and we are willing to. The boys in our camp would shed their last drop of blood for some of our officers.

The most distressing, heart-rending duty most of us ever did in our lives, was the parting with our friends at Rockland on the 17th of June. For a number of days previous the friends of the men from other cities and towns had been gathering to bid adieu to those it is possible they may never again see. The morning of the 17th was beautiful, and at 4 A. M. every man was roused from his pleasant dreams and slumber by the Drum Major. A hurried and scanty breakfast was taken and at another "tap" every tent was razed to the ground and a wild and enthusiastic "three cheers" and "tiger" celebrated the desired but painful event. It was an interesting contrast and picture. You stand looking at the hundred tents at one moment, the next and every tent is gone, vanished, and instead a mass of men expressing a forced joy at the prospect of parting. Our war materials are soon packed, - the companies are mustered into line, - we march from the field down the hill, through the city to the wharf. We cast our eyes to the friends on the walks who crowd to take a last look at us -perhaps forever - we feel the heart-ache - the tear is coming, - our sternness is failing us, - our weakness appears as we see our darling friends, and wives, and children, with sorrow stricken countenances, and tearful eyes, - the Colonel gives orders of sternness, but we discover the gathering tear, which he cannot with all his forced effort repress, we clasp the wife and child and sister who have placed themselves in position to claim their last favor, we kiss them tenderly, and our dogged fortitude is gone, the tears will do their mission, - we enter the boat and the Major General calls for nine cheers for the noble body of men, which are given with a zeal which cannot be mistaken. We are no cowards, - we did not regret our undertaking, - we should have repeated our patriotic efforts, even at that moment, but it was the most soul-stiring of our lives.

Our passage to Portland was very pleasant, extremely so. We had entered the Webster at precisely 10 o'clock, as the Colonel had ordered, and everything passed off with precision. More anon. S.H.C.

As was reported before, in the Boston Globe, the passage to Boston, at least, had gone smoothly. You must realize, however, that the vast majority of these men bound for war were traveling far beyond the bounds of the world they had known, or even dreamed of. The sense of adventure which they all shared, overshadowed any sense of fear, or doom, which they might have otherwise felt. On the same day that the previous letter had appeared in the Boston Globe an additional installment manifested itself in the Gazette. Once again, the newspaper's correspondent eloquently speaks of the Maine regiment's journey into harms way.

Our Army Correspondence

The Journey to Washington - Fare by the Way - Effects of the March to Camp - the Sick List etc.

Dear Readers:- The weather was beautiful when we left Rockland, and everything tended to make our voyage to Portland pleasant, but our hearts were heavy, - our thoughts behind us, our prospects and fears before, and the pangs at parting were too severe to be transient or fleeting. But the sympathy and tenderness expressed by the immense throng on the wharf lightened and cheered our depressed spirits not a little. Do not suppose that ours was a sorrow occasioned by fear or cowardice,- we have not yet felt either. Our tears, our emotions, our heart attachments showed nothing more than that we are men.

We were just six hours on our passage to Portland land, where we arrived at 4 o'clock P. M. Here we were escorted all over the city, through clouds of dust, enough to suffocate us, to the "City Government House." The Portlanders, or somebody, exhibited their characteristic hospitality by giving us a few tubs of tea and coffee, which we constrained our stomachs to receive against the strongest remonstrances of a hungry appetite. Noble! generous! hospitable! Portlanders! Long may you wave and "wilt!"

At Portland John A. Poland, from Montville, broke his leg, and was left in charge of the city authorities. The Boston papers misstated it to be D. N. Royal, who is well and doing duty.

Tuesday morning, June 18th, at 7 o'clock we gladly entered the cars for Boston. During the passage we were occasionally cheered by men and women, especially by the latter at Kennebunk, where they came along and shook hands with us like a band of loving sisters. Saco and Biddeford appeared as quiet as if every citizen were a secessionist. We understood, however, that usually they manifested much patriotism on such occasions, but not being credited by the newspapers, they had concluded to "dry up." At Newburyport much enthusiasm was exhibited.

At half-past one o'clock, we arrived at the Eastern Depot, Boston, and were conducted by a most beautifully costumed, and excellently drilled company, the Independent Cadets. The people of Boston turned out to cheer us in a manner characteristic of Boston. We were conducted to the Common, where was prepared one of the best dinners ever furnished to a tired and hungry soldiery. There was no waiting, no irregularity, - everything was ready and each company marched directly to its table as readily as if it had been a custom for years. We thought the soldiers and men "took to" this kind of drill more naturally than any other. But all were happy, and the nice bacon, coffee, cakes, and pies were never more useful or acceptable. After dinner, for some reason or another, cigars were extremely plenty, without price, and we noticed one soldier, who was afraid to carry Eastern money to Washington, asking a gentleman to give him gold for his paper. The gentleman could not accommodate him, but offered him the money he needed for present purposes.

After tarrying for most of the afternoon on the Common, and our boys indulging in their peculiar pleasures, tricks and antics, and shaking hands with many of our old friends, with tears in our eyes and sorrow in our hearts, we entered the cars for Fall River. How strong and fast the ties will fasten themselves around such a magnanimous people as the Bostonians. If at Portland we thought ourselves only mean soldiers, at Boston we were elevated to men,- to patriots. We shall never forget the hospitable people of the Athens of America. God bless you Bostonians.

The ebullition of feeling we had witnessed at Boston continued unabated, all along the route to Fall River. Never had we seen, felt, or manifested such enthusiasm as prevailed. Everybody said, or cheered, or waved with handkerchiefs, or hurrahed, or laughed, or shed in tears "God bless and save you, Maine Boys of the 4th regiment." At Fall River the ebullition of feeling was intensified. Ladies were eager to take the hand of the soldiers, and some noble hearted woman, refined and beautiful, said "Let us kiss a soldier," and did. We saw an old, ragged Irishman by the road-side, alternately waving his old hat and crying, - to refuse to respond to such a heart was impossible with us. Was there ever a drop of Irish blood that was not patriotic.

Many of our men and officers were highly incensed at the arrangements they were subjected to on board the Bay State, which conveyed us to New York, and with much reason. But everything can not be the most methodical, when all, officers and men, are "green." We had but little to eat on board the steamer, but bore the privation with creditable patience. During the early part of Wednesday, June 19, we were moving along by Long Island near New York City, where we arrived at 11 o'clock.

The day was hot and we were much fatigued with previous labor, but were able to march with apparent good strength and courage through Broadway to the City Hall Park, where we were presented with a flag and a banner, furnished by the sons and daughters of Maine residing in New York, or its vicinity. We were obliged to wait in front of City Hall for a number of gentlemen to make speeches, while we all waited with patience for their conclusion and dinner. The flag and banner are as perfect as any that was ever made in this country, and we promised our Colonel from the bottom of our hearts that they shall never be disgraced. We will keep that pledge. Rev. I. S. Kalloch responded to the presentation remarks in our behalf, but our wishes and pride would have been indulged had our Lieut. Colonel done that duty.

After these ceremonies were ended, the men were, after much suspense and bothering, conducted into the Park barracks and treated to a lot of swill, which the lankiest hog would refuse to eat. We can hardly believe the same persons furnished this dinner who paid for the officers dinner at the Astor House. However we were as thankful as we could be under the circumstances.

The soldiers strolled about town considerably, and, as they tell us, were treated generously, and in some instances money was refused for little matters they had purchased. Cigars, oranges, &c., were thrown to us liberally as we left, and, withal we were highly pleased with the appearance and hospitality of the New Yorkers.

At 6 P.M. we bid adieu to our Gotham friends, amid wildest congeniality and enthusiasm of officers, men, and citizens , (not caused by whiskey or lager) and took passage in a freight boat for Perth Amboy in New Jersey. When we were half a mile from the pier, it was discovered that Captain Conant and Lieuts. Mitchell and Greenhalgh had been left at Lovejoys, so eleven hundred men and one steam boat were detailed to retake them. (Oh, Lager, where are thy charms?) Our passage to Amboy was extremely pleasant, and all seemed to enjoy the beautiful, placid, scenery of Staten Island, which lay on our left, dressed and reposing in all the charms of rural nature. It was far into the dusky evening when we arrived at the landing, so that we had little opportunity to see what the Jersey Spaniards were doing, but had an immense amount of work to do ourselves. The removing of so much baggage, seventy horses and a thousand troops from a steamer to cars, in the night, is a job of no inferior labor. We should not forget to mention that Lieuts. Greenhalgh and Strickland, and Quartermaster Sergeant Crowell were assiduous, determined and effective in their efforts to forward our camp materials, - they also had the privilege, (being left behind at Philadelphia,) of marching "through Baltimore" with the rear guard.

But we are so far behind in our narrative that we must hasten on. Towards morning the left wing of our regiment arrived at Philadelphia at "early morn," the right having preceded us two or three hours. Here we found the amplest arrangements for accommodating us with a comfortable breakfast of hot coffee, bread and cheese. The Quaker citizens did not make much noise about us, but their hospitality, good feelings and wishes were amply exhibited in their good deeds.

From this place we took the Philadelphia and Baltimore Railroad through the northern part of Delaware, stopping a short time at Wilmington and Newark, where we found nothing but the Union sentiment prevailing, and the Republican flag waving. At Perryville near the mouth of the Susquehanna and on the opposite side of that river from Havre de Grace, we waited a long time for our baggage train to come up, but getting tired of this, we crossed the river to Havre de Grace. At these two places we found United States troops stationed to guard the facilities for passing over the Susquehanna. Soon after leaving those villages, we were supplied with ammunition for our muskets, preparatory to our march through Baltimore. We had little to fear in relation to this part of our journey, but all felt that no confidence could be put in what the Baltimoreans had done a few days previous - they might treat us as they did the Massachusetts Sixth. As we entered the outskirts of the city, the poor, squalid, dirty men, women, children and negros made some demonstrations of approbation. As we passed a machine shop the workmen came out and cheered us, but as we got farther into this brothel of secession, and all else that devilizes human beings, a dogged silence prevailed. Not a cheer, no waving of handkerchiefs , "tigers", no "bully for you." Their appearance indicated their coward and imprisoned sentiments to be, "We would treat you to a volley of brick-bats, stones and abuse were we not afraid of your stalwart,

Chaplin Bernard Chase

daring, well armed men, and General Banks at Fort Henry." Our men (and we can't help thinking our officers) rather wished than dreaded a collision. We were in the rear of the regiment, and, as we passed along, occasionally a gentleman would come to our side and whisper, what he dare not say, words of cheer and encouragement, - wished us well, success, a return to our families, and to believe there are many true Union men in Baltimore.

In good order we again entered the cars and were on our way to Washington, distant thirty-nine miles. Nine miles from Baltimore is the Relay House, which has figured so conspicuously in this war. It is nothing more than a small country hotel in a rural, mountainous region, of the most romantic and picturesque loveliness. We had been here five years before, and never lost the impressions we then received. We cannot describe its loveliness, - but felt our hearts were better for a gaze at the picture, and a kindling sympathy with the people who were reared amid such loveliness. The Sixth Massachusetts Regiment are quartered here, and only too anxious to revisit Baltimore and avenge the blood of their brothers. Nine miles farther on is Annapolis Junction Station. Here, too, a regiment is quartered and all along the road are picket guards.

Thursday, at nine o'clock at night, we arrived at the termination of our journey. We were tired and most of us had eaten nothing for twenty-four hours. We, in our simplicity, had anticipated some kind of reception, - something to show we were wanted, and somebody glad to see us. We did not suppose "Old Honest Abe" was going to come out and invite us to his shanty, nor that General Scott would come and shake us each by the hand. We were not even over ambitious to see either one of them. We did not desire to see the "hub of Washington," Willard's, should be vacated for our benefit. We did not wish to quarter on Washington Monument, in the Great Aqueduct, or under the Potomac. We wanted neither an epic poem, an eulogy, nor the litany read or said over us. We are modest, decent, respectable, common sense human beings, and only and simply wish to be thus considered and treated. We are fighting men, and came here for that purpose. We are the "mud sills, " but, also the muscle, bone, and sinew of Down East. - We dare to and will do and die, - and say that we were treated like a thousand brutes by whoever had the leading string of the treatment we received in being sent into such holes as we occupied in Washington the night we arrived - especially the Belfast City Greys. We, however, express our condign gratitude for the hot coffee and tea furnished for us after all our men were asleep. Our soldiers were so fatigued that no sooner were they on the floor than they were asleep, and one poor fellow, Charles Crowley of Co. I, as he sat in a second story window, dropped to sleep and fell to the ground. He is now on duty again.

Friday morning we were drawn up into line, preparatory to marching to our camping grounds, two miles distant. We had no hot weather in Maine, before we left, so that this, though not as hot as our hottest days in New England, affected us extremely. Hardee's Tactics are adopted so far as movements are concerned (which are quick and rapid) so we were put on our muscle and a "dog trot." By the time we moved a mile the excessive heat so preyed upon the men that they began to drop from the ranks, and throw themselves under the fences, or anywhere out of the oppressive heat. Arriving at the grounds an unfortunate, extra, useless march of a mile was made, in consequence of some misdirection of the guide who was sent to conduct the Colonel. After the regiment finally reached the grove in which we are encamped, and were dismissed, they dropped to the ground like so many rag babies. Some we thought would surely die, but by care they finally revived. More than half the regiment are able to do duty, and many are still suffering from its effects. Your correspondent happened to be a fortunate one, and was able to administer to the wants of others. The effects of this, and eating every kind of trash that has been brought here to sell have given us now (June 26) the number of 127 on the sick list.

None are very sick. Dysentery, measles and bad colds are the principle complaints. Not more than a quarter are in the Hospital, for it is too small to hold more. The 1st Rockland company has eleven sick; 2d do., ten; 3d do., nine and 4th do., fourteen. Belfast Greys have twenty-four; Captain Cunningham fifteen; Captain Bean, ten; Captain Smith, eleven; Searsport Co. has fifteen; and Captain Whitehouse has eight.

Captains Cunningham, Smith, and Burns have been quite unwell. Lieut. Dow of Damariscotta Co., is about returning home, on account of a complaint which had troubled him for years. We are

Captain Edwin M Smith

sorry to have him go, for his modest, retiring, affable manners have endeared him to all who have made his acquaintance. But this is no place for a sick man.

Lieut. Gunn was discharged and left us at Fall River. We expect to hear of him fighting secessionists on his "own hook." He has a liberal soul, and as much "fight" as the next man. We have lieutenants, a bakers dozen of whom would not furnish his equal in what makes a good warrior. The report is that Dr. Banks is not to be our surgeon, &c., which proves that the log-rollers are not all dead. But we are writing too much.

The Rockland Gazette SHC

As seen through the eyes of Sergeant Major Chapman, the journey of the 4th Maine Infantry had ended. The adventure, though, was about to begin. It would not take long to realize that there would be a major confrontation, putting patriotism and idealism to the test. Some of the Maine boys would "see the elephant" and prove their mettle, while others would not. The public cry of "On to Richmond" had imparted an irresistible momentum to the armies of the North and the South. This ninety day war was rapidly coming to a head and these men from the mid-coast region of Maine were destined to play an important role in its outcome.

Chapter 2

"Faces to the Foe"

In the early days of July President Lincoln called a special session of the Thirty-Seventh Congress. In his address to that body he requested the raising of 400,000 new soldiers and the sum of $400,000,000 to make sure that the war would be a short and decisive one. Lincoln stated, "No Compromise in this case could be a cure. No popular government can long survive a marked precedent that those who carry an election can only save the government from immediate destruction by giving up the main point upon which people gave the election. The people will save their government, if the government itself will do its part indifferently well."[1]

It was at this time that Virginia invited the Confederacy to make its capital in Richmond. The Southern States accepted and scheduled its next legislative session to begin there on July 20. Most saw this as a direct challenge to the military power of the federal government. The New York Tribune and Horace Greeley took an editorial stand with the headline:

FORWARD TO RICHMOND! FORWARD TO RICHMOND!
The Rebel Congress Must Not Be
Allowed to Meet There on the
20th of July.

BY THAT DATE THE PLACE MUST BE HELD
BY THE NATIONAL ARMY[2]

On to Richmond became the cry throughout the North. By the time the Fourth Maine arrived in Washington some 35,000 troops had gathered in the area and General Irvin McDowell had been selected as their commander. McDowell had many shortcomings, the most significant of

---

[1] McPherson, Battle Cry of Freedom, p. 321.
[2] Ibid., p. 334.

which was the fact that he had absolutely no field experience. As a result, military discipline was almost totally lacking in the troops.

Over the course of the next several weeks, the Gazette's Correspondent, Stephen H.Chapman, continued to paint a vivid picture of the gathering storm, and the impending chaos. Let us relive these moments, in the words of those that lived it.

Camp Knox, Meridian Hill, Washington, D. C., June 28, 1861

Mr. Editor: - The hill on which our camp is located is thus called because on it, and not far from our quarters, are "stakes and stones" designating the precise point from which longitude is reckoned in the United States. Col. Jameson's quarters of 2d Regiment of Maine are near the stone or longitude monument, but says he hopes to have an increase in his southern latitude soon.

Our tents are pitched in one of the most beautiful groves of chestnut and oak trees, so that we are completely protected by their dense foliage from the intense heat of the sun. - Other regiments are obliged to protect themselves by setting out bushes, as we did in Rockland. We are wonderfully favored in this respect. Our parade, or drill ground is in that part of our quarters which faces the grove, to the South. These grounds are owned by Columbia College, which is located in our front and not far distant. The inmates of this college have had suspicion attached to them as secessionists, and many stories are afloat of their signalizing to the southern generals, by rockets, the number of northern regiments that arrive daily, but we have kept a strict eye to this since our arrival, and seen nothing of the sort. At the Commencement yesterday there were three(!) graduates present, and five absent, commissioned officers in the southern army. The president of the college made some remarks, which were patriotic and Union. Regiments are arriving here daily, almost hourly, and one might as well try to count the lime kilns in Rockland as to count their encampments.

We have often been queried in our mind whether we should, in case of battle, have sufficient, stamina and courage to meet it with calmness and fortitude. Well, the other night about eleven o'clock, a false alarm, (unbeknown to our men or officers) was made from a regiment not far from us, when suddenly our camp was thrown into the wildest fighting fury, on hand in a moment, and apparently glad an opportunity had come for such efforts. The cry was "The secessionists are close upon us," and in a moment nearly every man was in his place and gun in hand, though no one of our field officers had given a single order. Presently we collected our thoughts, reflected, became calm, and found we were "sold." The colonel ordered us to our quarters, with orders not to commit such a premature condition of things till ordered by him. This was not a fight, - it was our "maiden" battle, - but we do claim that we manifested determined courage. You ought to have seen some of our boys as they took their place in line, cool, calm, but fully inspired by the War-God with intensified fight.

Last night, Wednesday, some of our outermost sentinels heard firing not far off, and fearing they might be fired upon, raised the cry of the enemy at hand again, and again most of our companies were "up and dressed" in double quick time. Our major sent us to our quarters at once. The fact is our boys, more than all else, wish to have a fight. The night of our first alarm, one fellow who was sick in the hospital, rushed out at the call, seized his musket and took his place in line determined to have a chance in the fun. But one man fainted, another said he felt dreadfully, and another refused to be waked from his slumbers.

Now dear friends, whose hearts, are out after us, daily, hourly wishing us all the best of blessings, what do you imagine is our first wish as we sit under these shady oaks and view the lovely, flickering stars that shine on you and us, and the silvery moon? It is that we might step in and take supper with you, tarry all night, and eat breakfast with you and return to our duty.

It seems that a Brigadier General is to be elected over our Maine Regiments, and probably Col. Berry of the 4th, or Col. Howard of the 3d will be claimants. We shall be glad of Col. Berry's promotion, but our regiment will suffer proportionally.

Orderly Sergeant Fowler of the Searsport company, has been promoted to a Lieutenantcy; a most worthy and active officer he will make too.

Orderly Sergeant of Company A was yesterday elected second Lieutenant, and a better appointment could not have been made in this camp. The Damariscotta company will elect a successor to Lieutenant Dow, who returns home on account of his health, to-morrow.

Lieutenants Rollins and Randlett are sick. Capt. Smith is now on duty. We have quite a number on the sick list to-day. None are very sick, however.

S.H.C.

Camp Knox, Meridian Hill
Washington, D. C., July 4, 1861

Dear Readers of the Gazette: - We are getting along in our camp, since our last letter, much in the usual way; but, as you may not know, distinctly, what is usual, a few words of information may not be objected to. We Magnify mole-hills into mountains, as we are in humor, much as you do, and everybody, so that every day brings something of great moment, of vital importance to those concerned. If the surgeon hasn't cured every invalid "at sight" - or has not given every fellow, who feigns sickness to avoid work, a certificate to relieve him of drill, - or if soldiers cannot go and come at their pleasure instead of the officers, or an inappreciable trouble is discovered or fancied in quality or quantity of food, - or if it is too hot or too cold, or too wet, or too dry, or too anything, or even too everything, we resort to our inalienable, indefeasible, self-evident, personal, religious, fighting-right, privilege and pleasure of "growling."

But on this glorious Fourth of July, we rise above dust and humility and say we will think, talk, act, be, do, live, die and growl whenever we have the occasion to do either or all, sink or swim, - survive or perish, - Yankee doodle, - Hail Columbia, - Star-spangled Banner, - spread Eagle, E Pluribus Unum, Multum in parvo, non est, Excelsior, Dirigo - there!

"Oh! there's not a thrade that's going.
Worth knowing or showing,
Like that from glory going,
For the bould soldier boy."

But to be candid, we do think our officers "coop" us up a little snug for such chaps as we are, for they well know we need more room than most bodies of men of equal numbers. We wanted a chance to expand our muscles, minds, stomachs, selves on this day specially. Wanted to see General Scott who holds the American Eagle in one hand, American

Flag in the other, and is all powerful to annihilate both and himself in a moment.

Who blames us for wanting to see General Scott? We have temerity, audacity and bravery to dare see Old Honest Abe, for we never did see an honest man, and would like to. We have an ambition to see the homeliest man in our country, and they said, last fall, that he was really that man. Then we desire to see a live President, - all the Lions hereabouts. We want to see the big houses, - the Capitol, so large that having been building sixty years is not yet finished, the White House, about which we have read, heard and believed so much from our infancy up to the palmy days of our patriotism, we wish to gaze upon. We want to see the Smythsonian Institute, the hub around which the American scientific wheel revolves, and in which Prof. Henry is said to make Comets with which to frighten the ignorant and credulous. We want to see the Egyptian mummies, bones skulls, busts, and statues of dead animals and men in the Patent office, where are kept in miniature all the inventions from our earliest ages, useful and useless, from a pin to a steam engine, -from a spinning top to a balloon. We would like to see all these.

But we will be quiet, for our officers know what is best for our health, comfort and usefulness. They think though we are soldiers, we are yet men. We respect, we love most of our officers, and there is no place between the frontier boundaries of secessiondom and pandemonium where we would not follow Col. Berry.

The fatigues of the journey here, the hot weather and sickness since have permanently effected the constitutional health of some of our men who have received certificates of discharge and will immediately return home. These receive three months pay in advance.

Just at dusk the other night we were visited by a tremendous thunder shower. The rain, which came moderately at first, fell in torrents. The men's tents and the hospital were without floors and in ten minutes were flooded, the sacks wet, and in Captain Fuller's Company had two feet of water in which to sleep, swim or play. Necessity knows no laws, - not usually no comforts, - so the Greys put for Columbia College, where they quartered for the night. But we have got to learn grief, and this will do for one lesson. Some of our boys run guard to get down town (Washington), got drunk enough to be ugly and get a good pounding, and run a narrow chance of being stabbed or shot. We shall be lucky if some of the Rockland boys are not murdered before we leave this camp.

One poor fellow of the Third regiment was shot a night or two ago. His friend was on guard, supposed his gun not to be loaded, and as he approached him, he jocosely said, I am a secessionist, when the guard snapped his piece and the charge passed through the largest bone in his thigh, fracturing it dreadfully. The next day the limb was amputated, and soon after he died and his body is buried in the land of the stranger. All this was the result of sheer carelessness.

George Hall, a very worthy young man from Nobleboro', and member of the band, was one afternoon wandering in the woods, in citizens suit, near one of the New York regiments, when they took them into their possession as a secession spy. The matter was all right when one of our officers was sent to vouch for him.

We are about to have a new suit of clothes. They will be of thin blue material, light and comfortable for this climate. They are in camp our now.

Capt. Whitehouse's company are in trouble about a person to fill Lieu. Dow's place. Probably the matter will be best arranged by an appointment by the Colonel. Certainly Capt. W. needs somebody to help him in his arduous duties. The date at the beginning of this letter is nearly worn out, so we will begin anew.

Washington, July 4.

For a number of days the writer has been prostrated by a violent attack of cholera morbus, but this morning, was sufficiently convalescent to pay some attention to the orders of the day as they occurred in this city. We are early awaked this morning by the heavy booming of cannon and beautiful band music from the 3d V.M.M., who are our next neighbors on the right or West.

In our regiment nothing was done by way of celebration. At 8 o'clock we had the pleasure of a first look at Gen. Scott, President Lincoln and other celebrities, on the occasion of the President's review of 20 regiments of New York Troops. A stage was erected, in front of the White House, very like such as we build at home for political stump speaking. It was covered by an American Flag for protection from the sun, and in front marched the numerous regiments of soldiers. Mr. Lincoln stood with his head uncovered, Mr. Seward on his right, hat on, and Gen. Scott sat on his left dressed in a military suit appropriate to his position. All three seemed deeply interested in the scene before them, though more than two hours were required for the purpose.

Our quartermaster, Mr. Abbott, is no stickler for servants, broadcloth, gloves, silk stockings, gold spoons, swell spread or show of any kind, except what is of utility. Soon after our arrival here, he went down to the Quartermaster General's department for something to eat. - The premises were filled with Quartermasters in fine clothes, high dickeys, white gloves, etceteras. Mr. Abbott said, "I want something for my men to eat." The authorities looked at him intently for a moment, probably supposing from his appearance, that he had no business with them and inquired, "Who are you sir?" "I am quartermaster of the 4th Maine regiment and want something for my men to eat," Mr. A. said.

"Stand back, white shirts and silk gloves, and make way for the Quartermaster from Maine." Mr. A. was supplied in preference to them. There are very few hyfalutin gentlemen in the regiments from Maine. They came here to fight, - and to a man, a chance to fight on a big scale is all they want, or will accept to satisfy them for coming so far from their friends and homes.

A quantity of molasses was taken from some rebel vessel and has been distributed to the regiments. We got one half hogshead for our share, and it was acceptable to all of us.

Members of Congress have been very liberal towards us in franking envelopes for our use, especially Hon. E. B. French of Damariscotta. This is about the first good use of franking privilege, of which so much has been said in and out of Congress. Soldiers, with such a favor write oftener to their friends, and thus use up their spare moments to advantage. Allow us to express our thanks to Mr. French through the columns of the Gazette.

If any one shall ask us how Old Abe and General Scott look, we should answer, that every picture ever made of the latter, from a wood cut to an elaborate painting, looks like Scott; and just the contrary is true of the former, Mr. Lincoln. In his face, Mr. Lincoln, somewhat resembles Mayor Wiggin of Rockland, though he is more erect. His hair and whiskers are black, and he at once inspires the beholder with a desire to be better acquainted, - or rather, a feeling that he always has been acquainted. He looks genial, kind, benignant. Comparing his expression of countenance with Mr. Seward's who stood near him, we felt like turning away from the contemplation, for Mr. Seward looks as if his heart might be proportioned to his personal stature.

General Scott is massive in his physical proportions, and follows the universal law of "large bodies move slowly." He looks old, very old we thought. His movements of the head and hands were rapid, but he walks slowly and carefully. He talked a pleasant word or two with common soldiers, who approached the aged hero with reverence and admiration. The days of his earthly pilgrimage are, in all likelihood, few. He is now engaged in the masterpiece of his life. No doubt it will be an honor to the author, the nation, the times and the world.

Not long ago Jeff Davis told the world he would occupy Washington on the 4th of July. He has not been seen here yet, though we hope to see him soon, somewhere.

S.H.C.

Camp Knox, Washington, July 6, 1861.

Our men are somewhat afflicted with the diarrhea, yet there are only four in the hospital at Georgetown from this regiment, and all who are not able to march when we are ordered away, will be sent to Georgetown. We have had only one death. Mr. Joseph L. Hatch, of Company E, belonging in Nobleboro', 18 years of age. He had been sick with the measles and was up and doing well, but took a relapse and died this morning at 7 1/2 o'clock. Young Hatch was one of the worthiest young men in our regiment, and his captain, company comrades and specially his brother are deeply afflicted at their loss. Sufficient money was immediately raised by the deceased's friends to purchase a metallic coffin, and he will be sent home by express.

Major Nickerson has been quite unwell recently, but is now better. The celebrated philanthropist, Miss Dix, paid our sick people a visit the other day.[3] She spoke comforting words, gave good advice about cooking, and said she would see that the hospital was supplied with fans, and also, that skillful cooks were sent up to instruct our men in the art of cooking.

---

[3] Dorothea Dix was a Worcester, Massachusetts, native appointed by Secretary Cameron as Superintendent of Female Nurses in June of 1861. Nurses receiving government pay were appointed by her.

The 3d Maine Regiment are now moving off, and our boys are cabbaging their tent floors with a zeal, to use in their own quarters. This regiment have exchanged their grey suits for blue (as we shall do tomorrow) and as they left us presented a fine martial appearance. Some of their sick are left behind. Capt. Bachelder of Company B, (3d regiment) formerly of Union, a noble fellow and soldier and competent officer, was obliged to tarry on account of ill health.[4] Col. Jameson with the 2d Maine Regiment, is nearer the enemy lines than any of the government army in this vicinity, and is within seven miles of Fairfax Courthouse.[5] - He will probably have a brush with the foe soon, - he was reported to have to-day, but it must be a mistake.

Evening. Our men have been eagerly reading the Gazette correspondence this P.M. and evening. They are also by turns, singing their songs (which to us are beautiful, here) telling stories, talking religion, discussing the comparative merits in boxing or fighting of somebody, talking of home, or expressing their desire to go farther in to the land of "Dixie," where they may have a chance to develop themselves.

S.H.C.

Camp Knox, Washington, 12 M., July 8, 1861.

Orders have just come to us to be ready to leave this lovely grove at 5 P.M., and to have one day's rations with us. Everybody is busy, a little excited, the day is hot, and we shall have a warm day of it. The men are leisurely packing up their knapsacks and the officers stuffing their trunks. To-day there are several reported on the sick list, who will not be able to ride, and will be left in the college near by, which has been fitted up for that purpose by the government. Capt. Conant reports only one man sick to-day, and Capt. Whitehouse the same. Lieut. Hussey has an honorable discharge and returns home. Sergeant Erskine (of Bristol) and private Carlisle (of Boothbay) were appointed Lieutenants by the Colonel this morning. Mr. E. is a very promising young man, a graduate of Bowdoin and will make an excellent officer. Mr. C. will doubtless be a good officer for he has good drilling in the military before. Lieu.

---

[4] Captain Batchelder of the 3rd Maine had a habit of not being attached to the regiment during times of conflict. The one exception was the Battle of Fredericksburg. Following this fight he was tried for cowardice and dismissed from the army.

[5] Captain Jameson was the first Colonel of the 2nd Maine. Following Bull Run he was promoted to Brigadier General. In September, 1862. He became sick, returned home, and died in October.

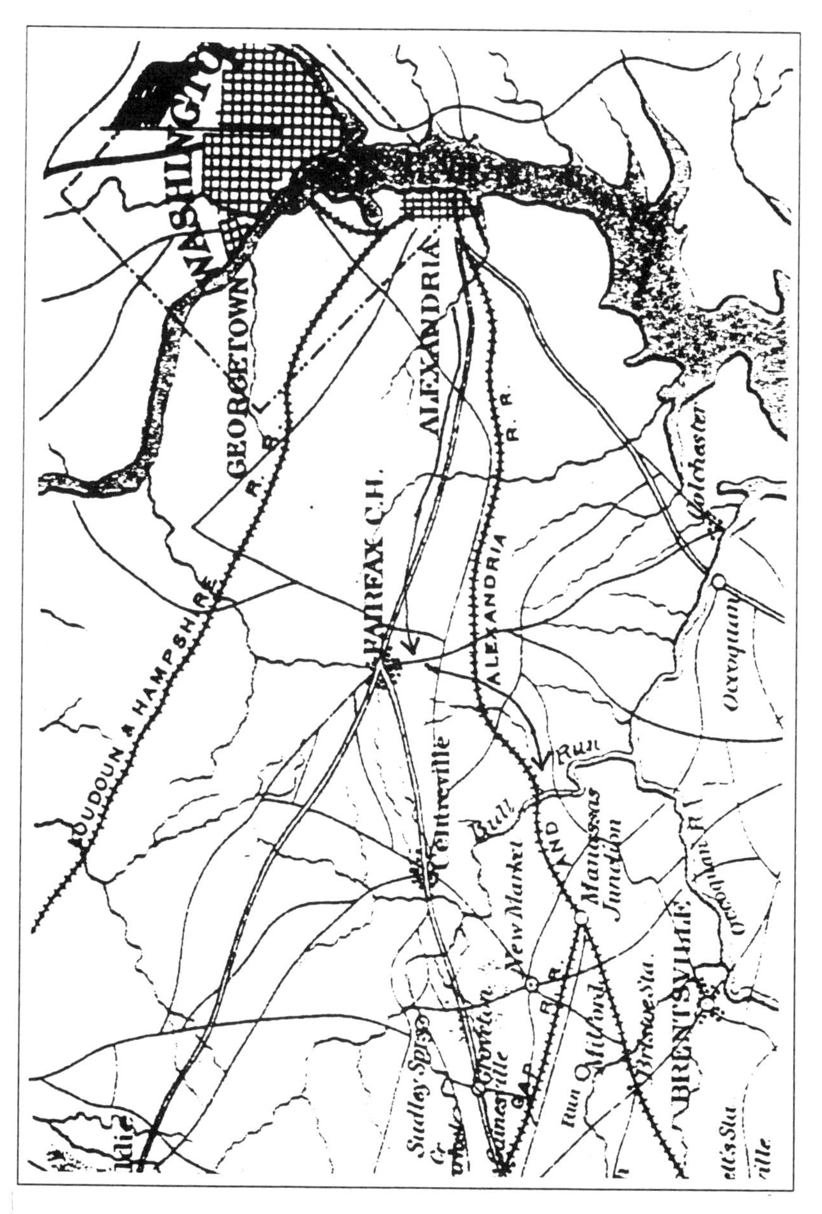

Route of the 4th Maine from Alexandria through Fairfax Court House to Manassas Junction. July 9 - 19, 1861.

a good officer for he has good drilling in the military before. Lieu. Rollins is still quite unwell. We have some pleasant associations in this place. Vice-President Hamlin has made us a call. President Lincoln rode by our camp yesterday and appeared very gracious toward us. Rev. N. Butler preached for us yesterday, and every night the comet has been a pleasing sight, and a subject for the credulous and imaginative to speculate upon. The prevailing opinion among the boys is, that it is a sign of war.

You would hardly know us now, we look so much better with our new suit of blue, and everybody is pleased with it.

The body of young Hatch was sent home this morning by express.

Well after a long time we have a regimental band. The instruments, Cornets, were made in Baltimore and have the rotary valves. Yesterday they played together for the first time in front of the Colonel's tent, and all were surprised at the good time and general efficiency they manifested. Under the direction of their well known leader, Mr. J. F. Singhi of Rockland, we promise ourselves much good music.

Names of the band members: - J. F. Singhi, Leader; G. E. Dyer, G. L. Hall, H. H. Rockwell, F. M. Gilman, O. J. Wells, H. G. Tobbetts, J. Grenen, T. J. Woods, G. W. Burgess, J. Warren, S. Davis, J. Hall, J. H. Havener, J. R. Burpee, J. R. Teague, G. F. Teague, H. M. A. Poor, J. F. Gould, S. K. Whiting, J. R. Skinner, V. Whittier, Mark L. Knowlton.

S.H.C.

Chapman's dialog carries us on a detailed journey through the events which terminate in the Battle of Bull Run. Already we begin to hear the rumblings of the army, as it comes to life, and begins its advance on the 21,000 rebel soldiers under the command of General Beauregard. The novelty of camp life has worn off and the men are itching for what they term, "a real fight." All are anxious to get back to their homes as quickly as possible. Few have a clue to what lies in store for them. Stephen Chapman will now bring us to the brink of battle. It will be the responsibility of others to carry us beyond.

Camp Knox, Alexandria, Va., July 10, 1861.

Mr. Editor: Our last letter left us packing our camp materials on Meridian Hill. At five minutes to four we were ordered to be ready to

Governor Israel Washburn, 1861 to 1862.

lower tents, and at precisely four P.M. our tents fell to the ground amid the tremendous cheers of our regiment. At five we formed into regimental line and took up our march for Alexandria, after distributing twenty rounds of cartridges to each man. We are so anxious to go ahead, to advance south, to do something, that we have no time or fancy for forming attachments for particular localities, so that we are glad to be moving. We have not yet learned to break up camp in a thoroughly military manner, so that our Quartermaster did not find the grounds left in the commendable condition.

Passing down 14th street our men amused themselves with singing "Dixie" and other favorite airs secular and religious. Near "Willards" we put on our military dignity and marched down Pennsylvania Avenue (the finest street in the country) and towards the Capitol. It is only fair self praise to state that our appearance, in every particular, - our stature, soldierly bearing, and regimental marching was more than average, and we believe the Colonel was proud of his regiment. Military gentlemen spoke of us in terms of commendation. We were dressed, in blue, like regulars, and had no knapsacks to uselessly fatigue the men.

9 O'clock P. M., July 10, 1861

We stop our narrative to inform your readers of the scene that is now going on in our camp. We are having a very heavy shower, thunders and lightning's are awful, such a shower as we have not seen in Maine for years. But the mail from Washington arrived an hour ago and a happier set of men can hardly be imagined, than ours who have received letters this evening. The mail was very large, and we have just made a running visit to a number of the tents to witness the joyful countenances. Love of home and friends, - of wives, children, parents, brothers, sisters, and sweethearts, - fills every heart, irradiates every countenance from the highest officer down to the lowest private. Oh! precious letters, what could we do without them. The next best thing to seeing our friends, is hearing from them. In this connection, it is but a merited compliment to express our gratitude to our worthy Chaplain, Rev. Mr. Chase, who has charge of our Post Office arrangements, and who leaves nothing undone, for our accommodation in receiving or dispatching our letters.

We have an Escolapian "war in camp." Dr. Banks, as is well known, is our regimental surgeon, and has proper commission from Gov.

Washburn. Within a few days, Dr. Hunkins of "back of Portland", comes with another commission from our governor, and asks, or commands Dr. Banks "to evacuate," "disperse" or "play second fiddle," - all which the latter disdains to listen to. We hope this war will not be so serious as to provoke either party to make use of professional missiles, or medical bullets, for the result would be serious and fatal beyond doubt. Probably if the Governor would send a few of those Blue-coated boys out here whom he has to do the chores, the matter might be settled amicably. But it is hard to tell why another doctor was sent out here, unless offices are too few for the applicants, and Gov. Washburn thinks our regiment can "carry double." It can of most anything else.

Dr. Banks, in our humble opinion has done as well as any other physician. He has a very large number of cases of dysentery and kindred complaints, some very severe, and he has not lost one. This complaint is rapidly disappearing, and our men are recovering their wonted healthy appearance.

At first medicines were very insufficiently supplied for the surgeons' use and he was obliged to do with what he could get. With one exception our sick have well recovered. - Our sick list is very small, we have very few left in the hospital at Washington, and those are gradually coming back to our camp. Disease is not controlled by the same means, precisely, here as at home, and, besides, every surrounding circumstance is new and different. Any physician would have had the above drawbacks to contend with. This department of the service is all important and should not be trifled with by uneducated, or otherwise unfit men in whatever capacity. We are, duty obliges us to state, in need of some essential change, some important improvements. More interest, more feeling, more care should be manifested towards the sick, and the regiment looks to Dr. Banks for such increased efficiency as the case demands.

At 9 o'clock P. M., (July 8) we were on board two steamers with our camp equipage, and in one hour more landed at Alexandria, on the South side of the Potomac. At 12 our baggage was all discharged and the men distributed here and there, on whatever they could find that would afford a chance for rest and sleep. Though the lodging was on logs, boards, bales of hay or anything or anywhere, we were refreshed by sleep, and at 5 o'clock next morning took up our line of march for our camping ground. Alexandria is under martial law, as it ought to be with its

Postwar photo of Company D's Captain Lorenzo D. Carver.

population of secessionists. As we marched out of the city, we passed in review before the quarters of General Heintzleman, commander of our Division, who it is said, was highly pleased with our appearance.

Alexandria, judging now or long ago, and by whatever standard, is the nearest city in all the South, and in every particular. It is a fitting nursery of secessionists. Secession and its effects are written on everything you see within its borders. Houses deserted, blocks of stores untenanted, grass growing in the streets, and a general appearance of dilapidation, prove it to be worthy of the cause and men its inhabitants have "bowed down to worship."

We are now encamped two miles from the city, and twelve miles from Washington. The 3d Maine Regiment is on our right and the Ellsworth Zouaves, the Scotts Life Guards and other regiments not far from us.

The land rises in modern elevations all around us, and is well cultivated by secessionists though they pretend to be for the Union. The negros tell us that the white folks can't be believed, - they talk secession at home, and when confronted pretend to be Unionists. The negros, probably tell the truth.

We arrived at our present quarters at 6 1/2 and pitched our tents as soon as convenient, though the day was very hot, and some of our tents not on the ground. Not withstanding the thermometer stood 98 above zero, companies B and D (Capt's Walker's and Carver's) were detailed to go out towards the enemies line as a scouting party. They started at 12 1/2 and went nearer to the enemy than any of our troops had been before. They saw nothing of the enemy and after regaling themselves in blackberries and cherries, returned about dusk in a drenching shower of rain, after traveling ten miles.

July 11

Last night about midnight we were aroused from our slumbers to prepare to meet the enemy, who, it was feared, were making their way towards us, but no farther preparations were made than to be already to load if necessary. - The alarm was false.

We are now (8A.M.) making ready to take up our march again before noon toward Mount Vernon, and Richmond. Orders are given to have one days rations cooked, and officers and men are to be allowed to carry only two blankets and one pair of stockings besides what they have on.

The remainder to be brought up by the teams. Our regiment is on the right of the First Brigade of the First Division of the U. S. Army, so we shall have the front of the fighting and first honors. Col. Berry will be in for both and his men will follow him to the bitter end.

Col. Howard is our Brigadier General, a graduate of West Point, thoroughly posted in all that is necessary to be known in this campaign. General Heintzleman, the commander of our Division, is said to be one of the best generals in the Union. You may expect to hear a good report from us. Trust us, dear friends and relatives, if we die it shall be with **our faces to the foe.** We are in good spirits, health and courage. Let all of our friends send letters to Washington as they have, and we shall get them. - We are thankful for all epistolary favors, - they are much comfort to us.

S.H.C.

Camp Knox, July 11.

Mr. Editor. - To-day we have marched by a hard circuitous route of five miles, but actually advanced only three. We are encamped six miles south of Alexandria. We struck our tents this morning about seven, or took up our march about that time. There is not to be long hence, somewhere between here and Richmond, a pitched battle of respectable proportions and which, in all probability, will settle the question of who can fight the best, the southerners or the northerners. These two sections have never been pitted against each other, and all we know of their relative merits is drawn from history, backed up it is true, by recent developments. We of this regiment enlisted to fight if necessary. We have all along been willing to do so, and all now anxious to have a brush with our foe. There are honors too, to be won in this great conflict. Somebody must be the winner, and it is an honorable ambition to be foremost in doing duty. - Our Colonel is desirous that his troops have the first, best and foremost chance at the enemy, and rise or fall as it may happen in the fortunes of war. Hence, we are ahead of other regiments and nearer the enemies line than any other troops. We shall have part in the first battle on this wing of the army, and shall lead in that battle. Who would be a gentleman soldier? Who would be a supernumerary soldier to be called on, only when the meanest troops are acceptable. Wouldn't we be proud of such a position? The truth is Washington is to be protected, and we might have staid on Meridian Hill till September, - gentlemen silk stocking, silver spoon patriots. Col. Berry disdained the idea of coming out here on a fools errand. He came to fight, and his men, almost unanimously, are glad at the opportunity of moving directly south. Some of the commissioned officers think we uselessly hurried South, and that we are to be sacrificed on the altar of some one's personal pride and ambition. The officer, field or company, who has no pride or ambition in this struggle, will have no courage in the trying hour, and rather than expose themselves or their state, had better show the white feather now and then go home.

Our state was disgraced last night by the cowardice of a Captain in the 5th regiment, who was sent to protect and guard a bridge. - During the night he was fired at, by some person, and he ran with his company into Alexandria. No one was hurt and wouldn't have been. He will be Court Marshaled, and undoubtedly shot, or sent home to enjoy his laurels. We believe nearly every man in our regiment would rather be shot than have the contaminating name of cowardice attached to him and his children. We can tell better on a trial of hearts.

On our march to-day the men seemed unusually light hearted, and amused themselves with singing familiar songs, "Dixie" always having the preference. The fore part of the day was beautiful, - not uncomfortably warm, - we rested frequently, - and enjoyed the fine, and sometimes romantic, rural scenery which surrounded us on all sides. Peach, cherry and apple orchards, wheat and corn fields, and comfortable country houses surrounded by beautiful groves whose loveliness and cool shade almost tempted us to steal into their poetic charms. Such rural loveliness and comfort so contrasted with our armed mission, that we could not resist a faint tinge of regret that we were thus cut off from the bowers of ease, and charms of home to engage in what is farthest possible from the other extreme of earthly occupation. But our band played "Hail Columbia," or "America" and we are again at heart-felt ease in our own glorious cause.

It is not a difficult matter to determine who is, or not, a secessionist. Men everywhere and in everything exhibit themselves through their face, and their most trifling actions. Union men may not dare to make much stir about their sentiments, may not dare to boldly cheer us as we move through the country, but no man need try to impose on us his words for his sentiments, while his face gives him the lie. - A blacksmith near to our last encampment pretended to be for the Union, but when our regiment marched by his shop to this place, he never left his anvil nor looked toward us. - But a butcher, standing in his door said by his smiling, joyful face, "God be with you boys."

We arrived on our new grounds, passing on the way a number of regiments of Zouaves and Infantry, at nearly 2 o'clock in the afternoon. We have not teams enough to bring all our camp equipage at once, so that we are obliged to wait for our teams a second or third trip before we can pitch our tents. We have plenty of horses for the purpose but the government has not furnished us with wagons. Tonight a heavy shower of rain fell (we have a shower every afternoon) giving us a good ducking. Finally our tents came, were suddenly put up, and at dark the "camp fires" were ablaze and occupied in preparing a hasty supper.

Some of us contested our stomach with hard bread and water, with less grumbling than a well prepared supper would have elicited at Rockland. We are gradually adapting ourselves to our circumstances, -we find much less fault (even when we might reasonably) than formerly.

This is our fourth encampment. The line of tents is north and south in the direction greatly elevated and the right of the regiment rests on the main road, on the opposite side of which are two companies of Fire Zouaves. When we entered the field, it was occupied by shocks of wheat, owned by a widow lady whose mansion is just over a little brook bordered by heavy trees, to the West of the Camp. This ladies residence is surrounded by a beautiful garden, forest trees and orchards, but suffers a little neglect, as though money or a husband were wanting. It has been suggested that Sentinels be set over the hearts of such of our officers as have no help - meet, for patriotism goes with the heart, and the Brooks company might be wanting a first officer. Perhaps we in our correspondence, claim too much for our men and officers, - we do not mean to. It would be unfair to forget a single merit, or deprive them of a single laurel, and in justice to them and truth we will, with the greatest degree of satisfaction, state, that our Lieutenants unapproachably surpass other officers in the divine art of "playing the agreeable." Let them captivate the Southern hearts, the rest of us will look out for their heads.

Recently our boys have managed by some inconceivable, incomprehensible means to procure a good supply of potatoes, onions and other vegetables for varieties, and their effect on the health of the men is salutary. We manage to buy a little milk now and then but it is very scarce. Blackberries are ripe, and plenty and not injurious to health. We have very little butter, and once in a while we get a few pies and cakes of the negros who come to our camp.

July 12

We have a few reported sick to-day, - and one the less physicians, which may account for it. One smart woman who understands taking care of the sick, with what herbs could be found in any country house chamber, could do more good in our camp, as we have been afflicted with thus far, than all the physicians Gov. Washburn can commission in a week. Were some of the patriotic women, who desired to accompany us, here now, they would be appreciated, respected and loved. How comforting would be the consoling words, kind acts, and pleasant looks of a noble hearted, magnanimous, sympathizing woman, to a sick, homesick soldier. We believe in woman. We love the women. The world were a dark, rayless, cold, worthless, world without them. Take them out of the consideration and nothing is left in the present struggle to buoy up our oft dejected hearts, - nothing left to fight for, nothing to love or cherish. Ask that soldier or officer what causes the sunlight in the heart, that joy in his countenance and he answers, "a letter from my wife." my mother, my sister, my daughter, my friend. Dear ladies who are attached to this regiment (in your affections) let us ask you to remember, and favor us always in this particular.

You seem to hear many most unreasonable yarns about us out here, if we can believe the many letters that we received from friends at home. What we write in these letters is intended to be reliable, and the "ghost" "bear" and "fish stories" you hear of us are false.

This afternoon it is reported that the southern troops have left Fairfax Court House, which has been, of late, the principle point of talk and fear. Capt. Walker and his company has gone on a scouting expedition this afternoon. Col Berry, Adj. Greenhaugh and Capt. Carver accompanying them. All companies are not equally capable of scouting, Co. B. is well fitted for the purpose.

Lieut. Randlett of the Wiscasset company, and Lieut. Rollins of Company C have gone home sick. There have been quite a number of changes among our officers, and before a year must be more. Many men mistook their calling when they entered the army, and have found it so.

Every man's physical or mental organizations will not stand the test of a few months of military life, while some like it better and better.

S.H.C.

The following series of articles appeared in the Rockland Gazette on Thursday July 25, 1861. This was a full four days after the Battle of Bull Run. The results of the battle are reported in a very sketchy, though articulate, fashion. The letters from the correspondent, Stephen Chapman, that appear in the newspaper are dated July 13 and 18. This is an illustration of the time delay in the relaying of information back home. By the time it arrived there, though it might still be interesting to read, it could not possibly contain any information which might be of use to the enemy. Still, the Gazette decided to publish a notice which it had received regarding the government's position on this issue.

Publication of Army Movements.

It is said that the Commander-in-Chief of the Army is about to issue an order to the effect that no officer, non-commissioned officer or private, attached to any division of the forces now in government service, "shall communicate directly or indirectly to any newspaper, or publication, any movement of the army, or of any part or division of it, either before or after such movement shall have taken place." Reporters who have permission to visit inside the lines may speak of movements already made. - But the new edict is supposed to aim at soldiers who write for the press.

The proposed new regulations would soon spell the end of the type of reporting being done by Sergeant-Major Chapman. This would prove extremely tragic, for this was exactly the type of information which was so desperately needed by the friends and families of the Maine soldiers back home. For now at least Mr. Chapman's story continues.

Camp Knox, July 13.

Mr. Editor: We are encamped fifteen miles south of Washington. The first capture of rebels by Maine troops, was made this afternoon by the fourth, and as you can easily guess, by Captain Walker's company, who, with Capt. Conant's command, were detailed by Col. Berry last night for a scouting party, -that is, a party to scour thoroughly a certain section of country to ascertain the sentiment of the planters, and discover and capture, or report any rebel scouts, suspicious persons, or any information of the enemy's approach or location. - Col. Berry gave minute instructions, and directions by plans of the woods they were to explore, and all were put under the command of Major Nickerson who is always ready for any daring enterprise. They started from camp at five in the morning and presently took their route along the Orange and Alexandria railroad, a distance of seven miles, and within three miles of Fairfax Court House, to a little place called Acotinck. Two railroad bridges between here and there have been burnt by the rebels.

Major Nickerson sent a detachment to the right under Lieut. Litchfield of Co. B. and another from Co. C. who were to scour the woods thoroughly. A third were sent along the railroad in the direction of our camp to prevent the enemy from escaping across the road, and were to keep a hailing distance from each other. From a negro, Lieut. Litchfield learned that a number of rebels had been at the house of Mrs. Fitzhue in the morning, and that the notorious Ab. Miners who had been engaged as a spy and in shooting our sentinels, went from her house at ten in the morning. This lady had been in habit of harboring southern troops, though she had protection of Gen. Scott. From this plantation a negro was impressed into service as a guide, and a quantity of bread and milk demanded of Mrs. Fitzhue for the Lieutenant's squad. A mile farther on they fell in with about a dozen Rebel scouts three of whom fell into our hands without resistance. John Butler of Co. B. was the first to seize one of them, running from him a number of rods, putting his hand on his shoulder and very coolly saying "I want you." Corporal Stevens, Sergeant Crocket, Private McKeen, and all did them selves much credit. - The prisoners are smart looking men, and could most likely do their part at fighting. One of them, D. D. Fiquet, is a young lawyer, recently from Harvard Law School, and appears very intelligent. He says he is unfortunate, but will suffer like a soldier. They all say they were treated very kindly by the men who took them and after they were brought into camp. The excitement in our camp was intense when they were marched in.

After being delivered to the Colonel, they were sent to head quarters at Alexandria. - They were then brought before General Heintzleman, and

Captain William A. Barker, Co. H.
(Maine State Archives)

were questioned by Major Nickerson. They seemed at first afraid they were to be hung, for their southern leaders had told them such was the result of being taken prisoners.

They seemed frank and honest in their statements. The Negro says he has been to Manassas Junction and seems to give intelligent answers in relation to what he has seen, and heard.

Statements of D. D. Fiquet, J. S. Walker, and Francis Walker, prisoners of war, taken in arms near Acotink bridge Fairfax County, Virginia, July 13th, 1861.

D. D. Fiquet: I belong to Company H. 3d Regiment Alabama V. M. There were fourteen in our party, Capt. Shelly and a Lieutenant. Our regiment is stationed two miles south of Fairfax Court House, Colonel R. D. Rhodes commanding. The regiment originally consisted of between 1000 and 1100 men, - have been reduced by sickness and otherwise to about 7 or 800. The measles, and dysentery principle diseases. A battery belong to our regiment. Heard it arrived at Manassas Junction. Have been in Virginia about three weeks. Am a native of Alabama. Live in Tuscaloosa. Mustered in on the 17th of May. Came through Richmond and right through to Manassas. Our army has plenty of ammunition.

J. S. Walker: I am a private in the 3d Alabama Regiment. Have been mustered in about two months - mustered in, in Pensacola about the 17th of May for 12 months. About 800 or a 1000 in our regiment. Arms, are rifles, muskets and Springfield muskets of 1843. Plenty of Ammunition. The 6th Alabama regiment is with us, Col Seibels commanding. One regiment on the left of us, stationed two miles from Fairfax Court House, near a brick church. - We came from "Bull Run" through Centreville. Stopped at Manassas a few hours only. There were some troops at Centreville. Have not sent tents back to Manassas. (This question was to ascertain whether they were retreating from Fairfax.) We have no artillery and have heard of none. We do not see newspapers. Saw Baltimore Sun with President's message. I know nothing about Washington. I judge there about 8000 troops at Manassas. Gen Ewell commands our Division. We are for 12 months. Those now arming are for three years.

Francis Wooster: I belong to no regiment, or company. I live about one and a half miles from Bark's Station. Gen. Ewell sent one of his aids for me - took me to the regiment and sent me with these men. We were on our way to Springfield Station (six miles from us) to see if Federal troops are advancing. My brother lives beyond Fairfax Court House. Most of the troops at Fairfax Court House are from South Carolina, - there are five or six regiments. There are two regiments up at Germantown. - There is one near or back of Fairfax Court House and two more near it, I saw eight pieces of artillery. The guns are six pounders, brass. There are entrenchments about it. The Braddock Road is one and a half miles this side of the Court House, and there are entrenchment's right across it one fourth of a mile long. There are breast-works on the turnpike road. The entrenchment's are about breast high. Have seen no long guns. The entrenchment across the Braddock Road is made of Pine trees and earth.

It is probable that the rebels are pretty well prepared for a defense at or near Fairfax Court House, where we hope to try their mettle and ours soon, if Col. Berry can have his advice accepted, and there is little doubt on that point. Col. Berry presented John Butler the rifle which he took, as a reward for taking the first prisoner. John McKeen received the pistol, W. E. Crocket the musket and all received the Colonel's thanks through "sparkling wine," drank to his health, with a soldiers "flow of soul."[6]

S.H.C.

Heights above Fairfax Court House
Thursday July 18, 1861.

Dear Readers: I have only opportunity for a hasty note from this place.

Tuesday, the 16th, our Colonel gave us the order to march at precisely 3 o'clock P. M., and we were on the road to Fairfax with more than twelve thousand troops on our train - destination this place. For a few miles the roads were quite good, and we made rapid progress, but towards nightfall they became muddy, narrow, over, down and around (seldom) steep hills, filing over narrow planks or logs across streams or small rivers, or fording when no other facilities offered. Our march was through miles of scrubby pines and forests of oak, with now and then a dwelling. "To the victor belong the spoils'" and our boys planted themselves on this maxim, and provided themselves with a few pounds on bacon, beans, etc., and added to our number of horses. We went

---

[6] Walker, History of the Fourth Maine Infantry, Special Collections, U.M.O., p. 5.

Lieutenant Gustavus Rundlett, Company G. Resigned from regiment in 1862 (Photo Shore Village Museum)

poorly supplied with rations, and Captain Bean suggested, "If Uncle Sam wont feed us, Aunt Virginia will."

We were rejoiced at the prospect of a fight, which kept up our courage, and occasionally we got up a "traveling concert" of singing and whistling.

We left in camp all our tents, rations, knapsacks, sick men, and the band. During the last two or three hours of the afternoon our march was very slow, not moving more than a few rods at a time, for the nature of the narrow passes would not admit of it.

At 11 o'clock we came to a halt for the night, and in a moment every man was under his blanket, a bush, or anything that affords any protection from the heavy dew. Our rest for a few hours on the hard ground was as sweet as we ever enjoyed. We forgot our fatigue and dreamed of our friends at home.

Early yesterday morning we were again on our march, with at first much better roads, but in the afternoon our advance guard had much labor in clearing the roads of the heavy trees placed across them by the rebels to impede our progress, but they had not seemed to understand the art, and one half of the trees had fallen the wrong way. At half-past one we stopped to dine, on rations that had just arrived by a portion of our train.

After resting for an hour, we were ordered again into line, and were on our march toward Fairfax Court House, distant four miles. On our way we passed in sight of one of the enemies breastworks, just evacuated, which Capt. Walker's company was ordered to visit and sack. They found flour, fresh beef, wines, whiskey, and all the luxuries of a southern camp, and brought them on for our use. At five o'clock P. M. we halted in our present locality for the night, where we heard that our enemies had fled, as usual. But our regiment is ready to march again, so is the mail carrier, and we must close.

S.H.C.

P.S. - Sergeant Havener of Company K., one of the best and most efficient in our regiment, was this morning appointed by Col. Berry to be Second Lieutenant, in place of Lieut. Chase, gone home sick.

Two men in the 5th regiment were shot by their own carelessness yesterday, and at this moment (9 o'clock) a man of that regiment carelessly shot another man, while one of his comrades is being buried.

Lieutenant Kendall Rankin, Company C.
in 1862 (Maine State Archives)

The 5th is becoming very unpopular, and deservedly so. The 4th, and its Colonel stand as well as any from New England.

S.H.C.

Sergeant-Major Chapman had one final correspondence for the Gazette's readers before the Battle of Bull Run. Through Mr. Chapman's eyes and words we have followed the development and maturation of this Maine regiment into a cohesive military unit. These men were proud of themselves and confident that they would perform honorably and courageously in battle when so ordered. Let us take one final look into the mind of a man about to experience that which few could imagine, the indescribable horror of war.

The Rockland Gazette, August 1, 1861

Our Army Correspondence
Camp Knox, Friday evening, July 19th

Dear Readers of the Gazette: Our journey from near Fairfax Court House, to our present encampment, two miles from Manassas Junction, was performed yesterday between 5 and 10 o'clock P. M., in "double quick" march, during intense heat in a heavy shower of rain, through dense woods, over hills, down into vales, and hungry from lack of necessary food for two or three days. We cannot give you particulars of our journey (nor need we) for our camp is busy, getting ready, we suppose, for a battle to-morrow. We had a brigade dress parade tonight, at which Colonel Howard hinted we shall start early to-morrow evening for somewhere, and the chaplain's prayer intimated that there the opposing foes will try their relative strength.

The expanse of fields, now within our view, covered in all directions with United States forces, is truly magnificent, but distressing to behold. We have 50,000 troops without exaggeration, and more are arriving or are on their way. If we fight, it will be the greatest battle our country has ever witnessed, - perhaps the world has.

Our soldiers under General Tyler committed a great blunder yesterday by running into a masked battery. Their loss was twenty-five killed and as many wounded. A New York regiment actually took to their heels and ran. They could not be rallied by their Colonel.

Our men of the Fourth are ready for the encounter if need be. Of course we have some who will falter, whose courage will totter, possibly fail, in the trying hour. This is a serious, momentous, awful occasion. It is a lamentable state of affairs for our country, but a glorious cause to be engaged in. How can one better, or more gloriously die that for his country. - Before you see this, you will have heard of the result. Do not believe all you hear of the sick, or wounded, or killed. Hope for the best, believe nothing until you know it is true, and you will save yourselves much pain and anxiety. - The most unreasonable stories are believed here as well as home. Men have little to do, mentally, than to indulge their imagination and credulity to the fullest extent.

A visitor from Fairfax tells us that that place is totally destroyed. The eighteen or twenty houses are deserted. The Fairfax County News is suddenly discontinued, and the type distributed through the street.

Orderly Sergeant Libby of Company H. was accidentally shot by the carelessness of one of his company. The bullet passed through the large toe of the left foot and fractured the two smallest of his right. All three were amputated by Dr. Banks. This is a serious loss to the company, and Mr. L. regrets very much that he is deprived the privilege of engaging in our first engagement.

S.H.C.

Now, "*on to Richmond.*"

Chapter 3

"Tell My Wife I am Shot - God Bless Her!"

On July 17, 1861, the Union Army under Brigadier General Irvin McDowell, and the men of the 4th Maine, began their march for Centreville. Their journey was highlighted by a spectacular comet, with a trail, splashed across the Ursa Major Constellation, that covered fifty degrees of arc in the evening sky.[1] The troops of the North, as well as the South, saw it as an omen signifying a great victory in battle. Beneath its blazing glory, the men from Maine converged, as the rest of Heintzelman's Division slowly gathered about them. They could see and smell the smoke from the burning bridges over Bull Run. It hung close to the ground and carried with it an evil foreboding of events yet to unfold. Slowly, ever so slowly, the rest of the army assembled, delayed only by their inexperience and a shortage of supply wagons.[2]

The success of McDowell's move on Richmond depended to a great extent on the success of Major General Robert Patterson in the Shenandoah Valley. If he could keep Brigadier General Joseph E. Johnston's army from slipping south and joining up with Brigadier General Pierre G. T. Beauregard, then, surely, McDowell could easily handle his outnumbered opponent. Due to a mix-up in the interpretation of his orders, however, Patterson decided to maneuver in front of his opponent and thus keep him occupied. His efforts failed dismally, and on July 18th and 19th, Johnston began to ship his troops south by rail.

On July 18th, Brigadier General Daniel Tyler's Division entered Centreville. Tyler had determined, based on information obtained locally, that he should shift his troops to the south of town. McDowell's orders specifically stated that he was not to "bring on an engagement." He was only to maintain the impression that he was moving on Manassas. One of Tyler's brigades under the command of Colonel Israel Richardson, moved through the town and on toward Blackburn's

---

[1] Davis, Battle at Bull Run, p. 77.

[2] Ibid., p. 100.

Ford. He took with him two companies of infantry and a squadron of cavalry and ran smack into a large detachment of rebel troops.[3]

Tyler had visions of crossing Bull Run and capturing Manassas in one swift stroke. When Richardson reached the ford and met with rebel opposition, he immediately called up the four remaining regiments under his command, as well as two batteries of artillery. What ensued was a very minor skirmish, but one that necessitated the withdrawal of Union forces. Most of the Confederates involved in this clash called it the Battle of Bull Run, and later named the engagement of the twenty-first, the Battle of Manassas. Regardless, Tyler had done exactly what he had been told not to do. McDowell was furious.[4]

McDowell examined the right flank of the rebel army and decided that the terrain was not favorable for an attack there. He then took an additional day to explore the Confederate left before designing his plan of attack. McDowell's delay would prove costly and would favor the chances of a Confederate victory. By the time Union troops had actually implemented their plan, three full brigades of Johnston's army had already arrived from the Shenandoah Valley and a fourth would soon be on its way.[5]

McDowell had planned a flanking maneuver, deciding to divide his army and send Hunter's and Heintzelman's divisions on a wide sweep to their right. They would begin their deployment at about 2:30 A.M. The divisions would then turn south and roll up the Confederate left flank. The plan was a good one and came within a hair's breath of success.

On the evening before the great "demonstration" the 3rd Brigade's Commander, Oliver Otis Howard, delivered an address to his men. Being a devoutly religious man his "address was a fine sermon, giving us an idea that we should be prepared to die, as no one could tell who would be saved. The sequel proved it was not the most Godly who were saved, but those who had the longest legs, and the best wind...Twilight fades and gives place to the shadows of night and soon nothing is heard but the challenge of the guard and the restless movement of the horses. The army of the Union is at sleep."[6]

---

[3] McPherson, Battle Cry of Freedom, pp. 339-340.
[4] Davis, op. cit., pp. 112-114.
[5] McPherson, op. cit., p. 340.
[6] The Rockland Gazette, May 26, 1891.

General Oliver Otis Howard, then a colonel, commanded the 4th Maine's brigade at Bull Run.

On July 21, exactly on schedule, 10,000 Union troops began to form for the march. Sergeant William Crockett of the 4th Maine recalled "the arrival of an orderly, a few hurried movements, then comes the rat-tat-tat-t-r-r-r-r of the long roll. Now there is haste, every man comes onto his feet. The Union Army is awake and the Union Army looks forward to the west and the coming of the day. For to the west was our foe and the field on which we were to meet our first disaster. My comrade came to me with a drink of brandy which I took; soon it had the desired effect and I was out on my feet; a few moments passed and I was sitting on an empty coffee box, calling the company into line."[7]

Hunter moved his men out along a narrow path that wound two miles north, parallel to Bull Run. The regiments crossed the stream at Sudley Ford and then headed south along the Sudley-Manassas Road. The movement of troops was very slow, due to both the narrowness of the road and the ever increasing heat of the day. Various factors, including a half hour rest at Sudley, delayed the planned assault until about 10:30 A.M. By this point, however, Confederate Colonel Nathan Evans had figured out McDowell's plan and was redeploying his small brigade to counter it.

Meanwhile, Tyler's division was moving along the Warrenton Turnpike on order to make a demonstration at the Stone Bridge. Here he would deploy his troops and guns, and, after the main attack began, join in himself. As we have seen, this feint, which was designed to occupy the rebel army and keep them from noticing the approach of troops on their left flank, had already faltered.[8] The one remaining Union assurance, that Patterson was keeping Johnson's army pinned in the valley, had also failed in its accomplishment. With each passing moment the hope of a decisive victory was rapidly slipping away. Still, if the Union Army could only move quickly enough, victory might still be theirs.

Colonel Oliver Otis Howard of Leeds, Maine, formerly colonel of the 3rd Maine, and now in command of the 3rd Brigade, which included the 3rd, 4th, and 5th Maine Infantry, as well as the 2nd Vermont, began to form his men in the rear of Colonel Cadmus Wilcox's command about 2:30 A.M. The sun had been up for over an

---

[7] Ibid.

[8] Davis, op. cit., p 156.

hour, however, when the brigade began to move. As Howard turned to the right along the narrow road leading to Sudley Springs, McDowell halted them and gave them instructions to wait there until ordered forward. Howard's men were now to act as the reserve on the chance that a suspected rebel attack might materialize on the Union left flank. These regiments could then be used to absorb the shock and plug any holes that might appear.[9]

At 6 A.M., Lieutenant Peter Hanes, situated near the Stone Bridge, fired a thirty pound rifled cannon, which was to serve as the signal for the attack to begin. Four additional artillery batteries, supported by General Tyler's division, soon joined in and began to pound the Confederate positions on the opposite shore. With rebel troops thus occupied, Hunter would now be able to cross unopposed at Sudley Ford and press on to his objective.[10]

Colonel Nathan Evans' troops were on the opposite bank of Bull Run. His command consisted of the 4th South Carolina, 1st Louisiana, a squadron of cavalry, and two guns. As the bombardment continued for more than an hour and a half, Evans' soon began to realize that what was going on in his front was only a feint. At 8:30 A.M., Evans', receiving a report that enemy troops were moving in on their unprotected left flank, positioned four of his companies to face Tyler and took his two small regiments to face the Union advance. This thin gray line, constituting fewer than 1100 rebel soldiers, was all that now stood between McDowell and complete victory.[11]

About 9 A.M. Beauregard realized that he had been outflanked. He ordered Bee, Bartow, and Jackson's brigades to reinforce Evans. In the meantime Evans had placed his troops along Matthew's Hill. On the left he had situated the 4th South Carolina with one gun, and on the right he put the 1st Louisiana, also with one artillery piece. Within fifteen minutes of their arrival the first shots were fired.[12]

The battle surged back and forth along Matthew's Hill for two hours. Forty-five hundred rebels held off half the Union Army until about 11:30 A.M. when they were finally forced to withdraw up the north slope of Henry House Hill. Here, Thomas (soon to be nicknamed

---

[9] Official Records. Series I, Vol II, pp. 417-418.

[10] Davis. op. cit., pp. 163-165.

[11] Ibid.

[12] Ibid., p. 167.

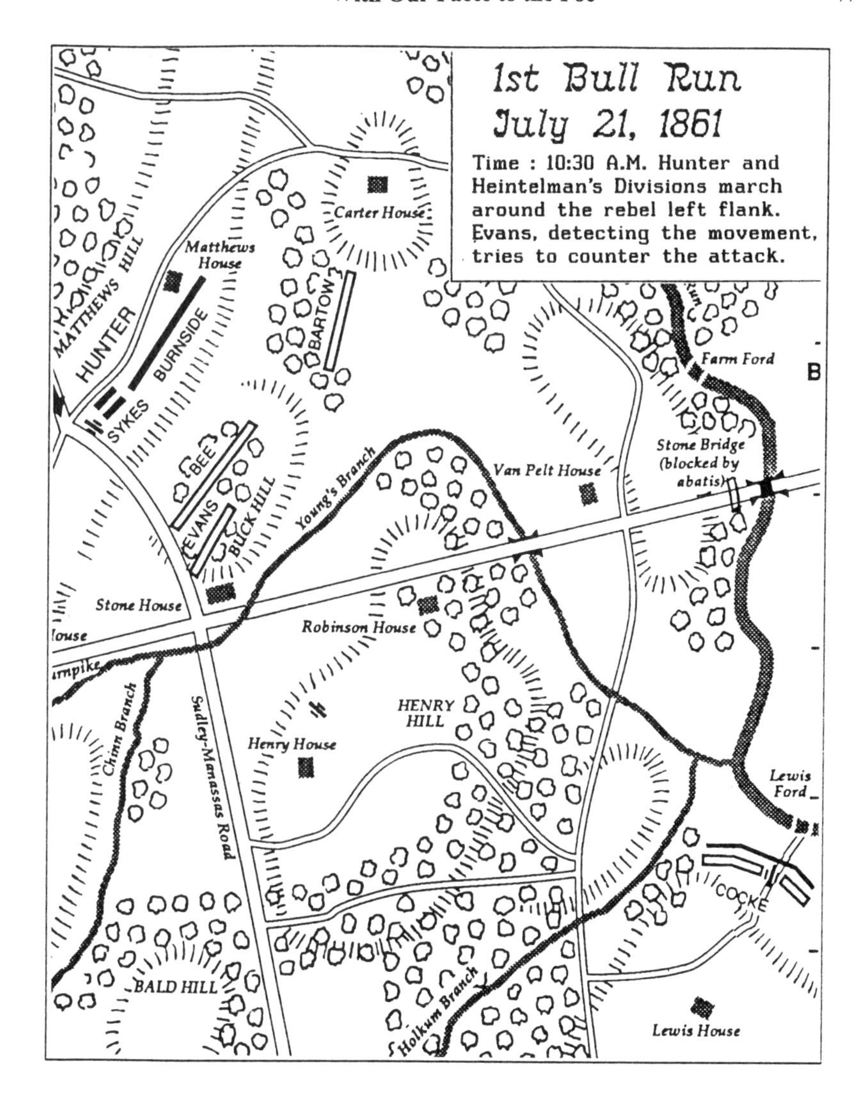
1st Bull Run
July 21, 1861
Time : 10:30 A.M. Hunter and Heintelman's Divisions march around the rebel left flank. Evans, detecting the movement, tries to counter the attack.
Carter House
Matthews House
MATTHEWS HILL
HUNTER
BURNSIDE
SYKES
BARTOW
BEE
EVANS
BUCK HILL
Young's Branch
Van Pelt House
Farm Ford
Stone Bridge (blocked by abatis)
Stone House
Robinson House
HENRY HILL
Henry House
Chinn Branch
Sudley-Manassas Road
Lewis Ford
COCKE
BALD HILL
Holkum Branch
Lewis House

Stonewall) Jackson's three thousand men awaited them. Fortunately, for the southern troops, the Federal attack had been totally disjointed. Had it been otherwise the course of the war might have been much different. It would certainly have been much shorter.[13]

Two of Heintzelman's brigades arrived on the field at about the same time that the Confederates began their retreat up Henry House Hill. As the 1st and 2nd Brigade slowly deployed in the same piece meal fashion as had the other troops, McDowell ordered Griffin's and Rickett's Batteries up Henry House Hill. These two artillery units moved to within a hundred feet of Jackson's line. They were far in advance of the infantry's support and well within range of enemy musket fire.[14]

Despite the lack of friendly infantry support, these two batteries caused havoc in the Confederate lines. Jackson's 33rd Virginia, which had been concealed in the woods, advanced out of its cover seventy yards to the right of the artillery. These soldiers were dressed in blue uniforms, almost indistinguishable from those of many of the Union troops. Though some of the guns were turned and trained upon the advancing lines, fire was ordered withheld until the identity of the infantrymen could be determined.[15] The Virginians leveled their muskets and cut down the artillerymen of Griffin's and Rickett's Batteries. Jackson then ordered a charge to secure them, but before they could be taken they were forced to retreat themselves due to the deadly effect of fire from Brigadier General William B. Franklin's men. All told, these guns would be taken and retaken three times.[16]

Sergeant Crockett recalled the nervous anticipation that afflicted the men under Howard's command as they awaited the order to join the fight. "Here we rested hour, after hour, waiting to be sent into the fight. We could hear the noise of battle, could see the smoke and the movements of troops, pressing forward, far on our left" and still they waited.[17] Presently, they were located at a point south of Sudley Ford, on the near side of Bull Run. It was not until sometime around noon that the brigade quartermaster, Sergeant Burt, who had been out in

---

[13] McPherson, op. cit., p. 341.
[14] Davis, op. cit., p 203.
[15] McPherson, op. cit., p. 341.
[16] Davis, op. cit., p. 418.
[17] The Rockland Gazette, May 26, 1891.

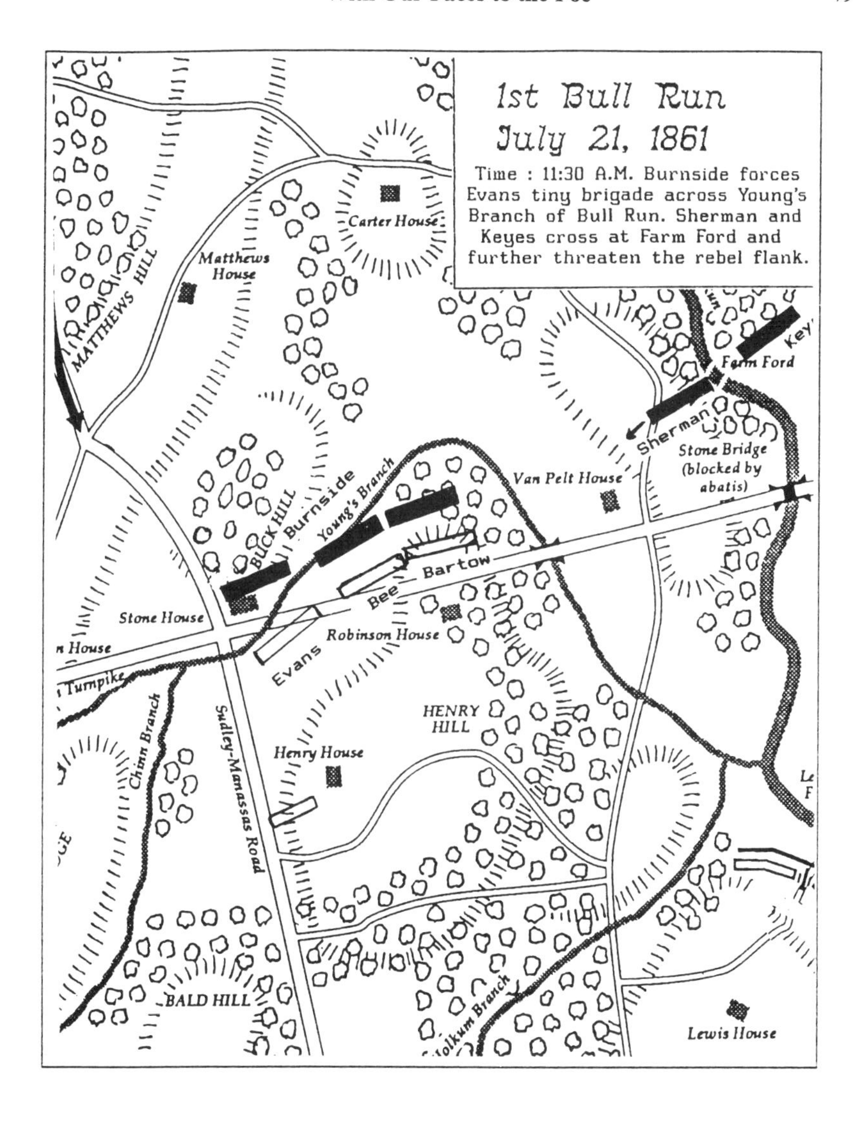
1st Bull Run
July 21, 1861
Time : 11:30 A.M. Burnside forces Evans tiny brigade across Young's Branch of Bull Run. Sherman and Keyes cross at Farm Ford and further threaten the rebel flank.
Carter House
Matthews House
MATTHEWS HILL
Farm Ford
Keyes
Sherman
Stone Bridge (blocked by abatis)
Van Pelt House
BUCK HILL
Burnside
Young's Branch
Bartow
Bee
Stone House
Robinson House
Evans
Turnpike
Chinn Branch
Sudley-Manassas Road
HENRY HILL
Henry House
BALD HILL
Holkum Branch
Lewis House

advance of the Brigade, brought orders from their division commander, Colonel Samuel P. Heintzelman, to advance immediately.

Captain Elijah Walker, captain of company B, later recalled that Colonel Howard yelled: "Forward, double quick." The 4th was on the right with Walker's own Company in the lead. "Next was the brigade commander and staff; then Colonel Berry leading the Fourth Maine and the other three regiments following. Our general was wild with excitement, crying out, 'Double Quick!'"

William Crockett remembered the order, "Double quick, forward march, on, on, up hill, and down in the swamp, through the bush and brush, over farms."[18] Walker further stated that "while miles yet separated us from the foe, he ordered me to deploy a skirmish line 150 yards on both sides of the road. The heat was intense. Forty of my men divested themselves of everything except gun and ammunition and complied with the order, running through brush, bushes and over uneven ground until nearly exhausted. My First Lieutenant fell prostrate.[19] I left the oldest man to care for him and moved on as fast as I could walk. Again the commander came forward, crying out, 'Double-quick!' To this last order I objected, using qualifying words that could be found in the Bible. I hurried forward as fast as was possible and at the same time saved the lives of myself and men."[20]

The 4th Maine was first in the brigade to arrive at Sudley Ford. Writing in 1903, Sergeant William Crockett of company B remembered crossing the stream. "I may have missed the rocky road and steep hills, but certainly not the dust for part of the way. Much of the way led us through swamp land. The sight which came to our inexperienced eyes as we struggled up the bank, to the broad, smooth, green lawn in front of the Sudley Church, after wading the broad, shallow stream will never be forgotten. The beautiful green grass was covered with dead and wounded soldiers and ambulances were arriving in from a long line coming down the hill from the battlefield, which was a few miles distant."[21]

The sight of so much suffering did not delay them in their journey. They marched on about a mile at this blistering pace until they came

---

[18] Ibid.

[19] Walker's First Lieutenant was 35 year old Orrin P. Mitchell of Rockland.

[20] Walker, History of the 4th Maine Regiment. Special Collections, U. M. O., p 6.

[21] The Rockland Gazette. Oct. 20, 1903.

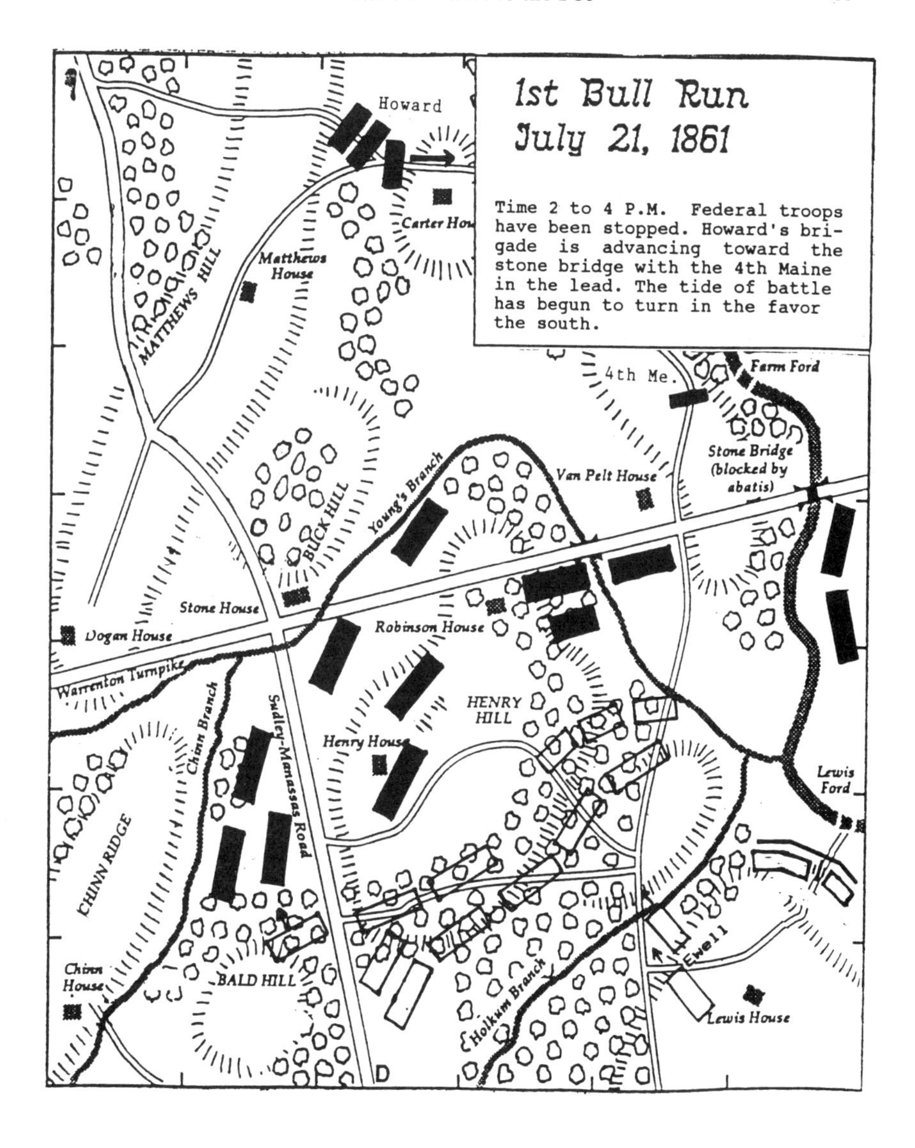
1st Bull Run
July 21, 1861
Time 2 to 4 P.M. Federal troops have been stopped. Howard's brigade is advancing toward the stone bridge with the 4th Maine in the lead. The tide of battle has begun to turn in the favor the south.
Howard
Carter Hou
Matthews House
MATTHEWS HILL
4th Me.
Farm Ford
Stone Bridge (blocked by abatis)
Van Pelt House
Young's Branch
BUCK HILL
Stone House
Dogan House
Warrenton Turnpike
Robinson House
HENRY HILL
Henry House
Chinn Branch
Sudley-Manassas Road
CHINN RIDGE
Chinn House
BALD HILL
Holkum Branch
Ewell
Lewis Ford
Lewis House

upon the rear of their own troops. "We soon arrived at the stone bridge where, standing by the small brook, were our wounded, bleeding soldiers, bathing their wounds until the water ran red with their blood. The brave fellows at the same time were cheering for us to 'go in and finish them,' as they thought they had the rebels nearly subdued. These sights made me feel as Belshazzer as he saw the hand writing on the wall. We were ten or more minutes in advance of the head of the brigade which gave us a chance to take a long breath and prepare for the coming struggle."[22]

"Blood here there and everywhere, staining the dusty road, soaking the beautiful grass and running in streams from the ambulances. A new sight to our boys, a new and trying test, for the nerves of green troops."[23] Sergeant Crockett remembered passing a large grove of trees which contained a large number of New York soldiers. It was the 69th New York and the Ellsworth Zouaves, but here they were, so far from the distant rattle of muskets and the report of the cannon. Crockett recalled that "we had expected great things from these two regiments. As we marched past, there was many comments from them. Some encourage us to 'go on and pitch in and clean them,' etc., etc. Others said, 'It's no use, boys. The things all up, we are beaten.,' etc. But without much bracing we passed on, and into a fight that was already lost to our side."[24]

The heat of the day continued to devastate the regiments. As the men were rushed to the front their commanders forgot to order them to drop their packs and blankets. Overburdened, the men began to fall out. Probably twenty-five percent, or more, never reached the battlefield. Many of the casualties in Howard's Brigade and the 4th Maine were inflicted in this manner.[25]

One member of the Damariscotta Company, in a letter addressed to his wife just two days after the fight, described the forced march in the following terms. "It was quite warm and we had to go at the double quick a part of the way, so that when we arrived at the scene of action we were nearly exhausted. It affected our company so that nearly half of our number fell out by the way before we arrived at the scene of ac-

---

[22] Walker. op. cit.. p. 7.
[23] The Rockland Gazette. May 26, 1891.
[24] The Rockland Gazette. Oct. 20, 1903.
[25] O. R.. op cit.. p. 418.

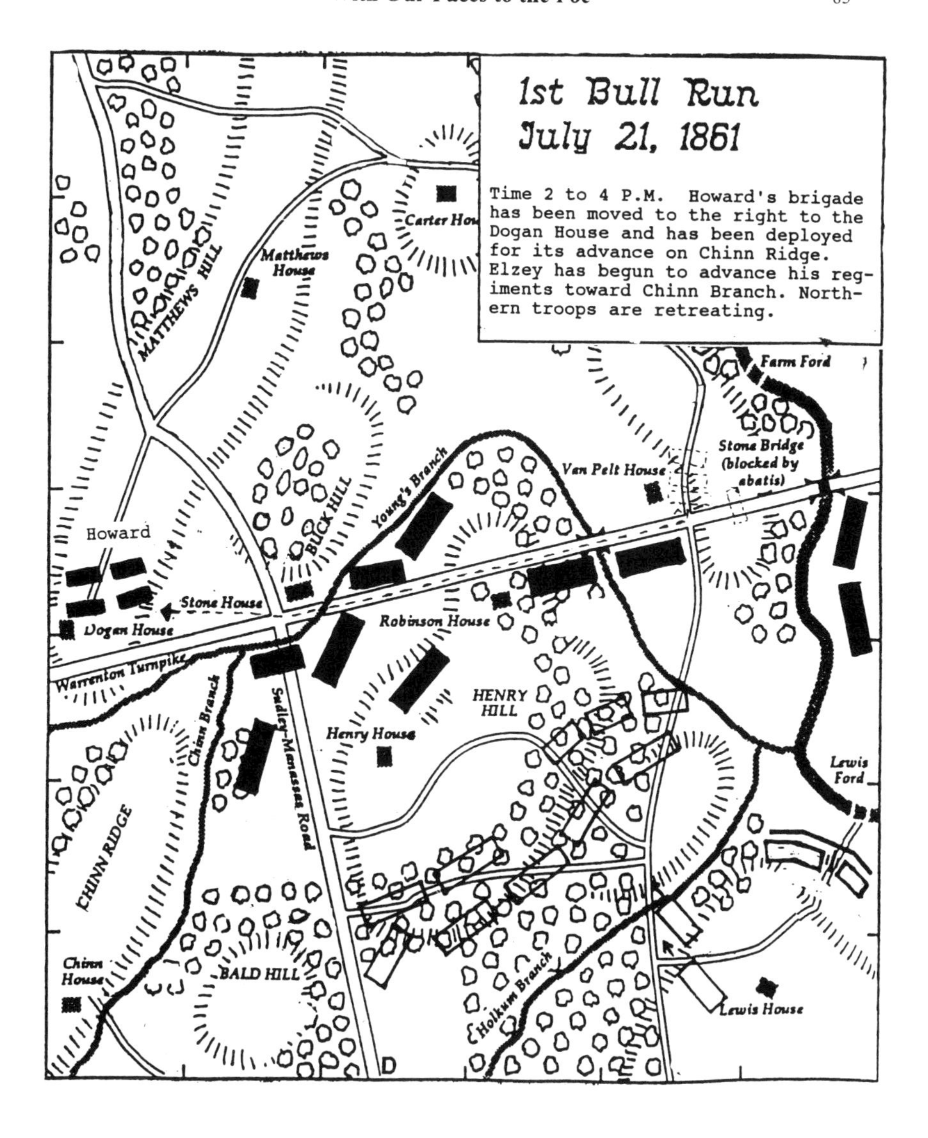
1st Bull Run
July 21, 1861
Time 2 to 4 P.M. Howard's brigade has been moved to the right to the Dogan House and has been deployed for its advance on Chinn Ridge. Elzey has begun to advance his regiments toward Chinn Branch. Northern troops are retreating.
Matthews House
MATTHEWS HILL
Carter House
Farm Ford
Stone Bridge (blocked by abatis)
Van Pelt House
Young's Branch
BUCK HILL
Howard
Stone House
Dogan House
Robinson House
Warrenton Turnpike
Chinn Branch
Sudley-Manassas Road
HENRY HILL
Henry House
Lewis Ford
CHINN RIDGE
Chinn House
BALD HILL
Holkum Branch
Lewis House

tion. When we formed our line of battle and numbered off there were only 42 to fight - among that number was your humble servant."[26]

From here they marched an additional two miles to the right and awaited orders to join the battle. In recollecting the move, Captain Walker later remembered that "it was the first time that cannon - shot and shell - whistled about our heads and passed through our line. Double-quick soon brought us to the edge of the woods, under the brow of the hill and out of range of the enemy's guns."[27]

William Crockett described the event, thusly. "Our company had hardly passed the shelter of the trees, before a cannon shot came whistling through the air, and struck the ground three feet in front of me. Another passed through the ranks as many feet behind. Forward from the rear came a horseman. In a frantic manner he ordered our Captain to double quick the company down the hill, to the shelter of the hill, to the front and left of us. It was done and our brigade came to a halt in the valley where runs the stream, which was said to be red with blood on that day."[28]

"Captain J. B. Frye of McDowell's staff, led the way to the right, across Young's Branch to a hill not far from the Dogan House." Colonel Howard was then ordered to deploy his troops so as to flank the rebels on Henry House Hill and support Ricketts' Battery. The artillery men they had been ordered to support, however, had already met them in retreat as they began their advance. "The six guns of Ricket's' Battery which had fought there were already disabled or lost, and Captain Ricketts' wounded and captured."

Howard formed his men into line along Dogan House Ridge. The 4th Maine was situated on the right and the 2nd Vermont on the left. The order was then given to advance through the woods to the top of the hill. Before moving, Colonel Berry asked Colonel Howard what was expected of them when they got there. Howard responded, "Support the battery." Berry ana Walker obeyed orders, both knowing full well that their mission, as stated, could not possibly be accomplished.[29]

---

[26] Rockland Free Press, July 31, 1861.
[27] Walker, op. cit., p. 7.
[28] Rockland Gazette, May 26, 1891.
[29] Davis, op. cit., p. 220.

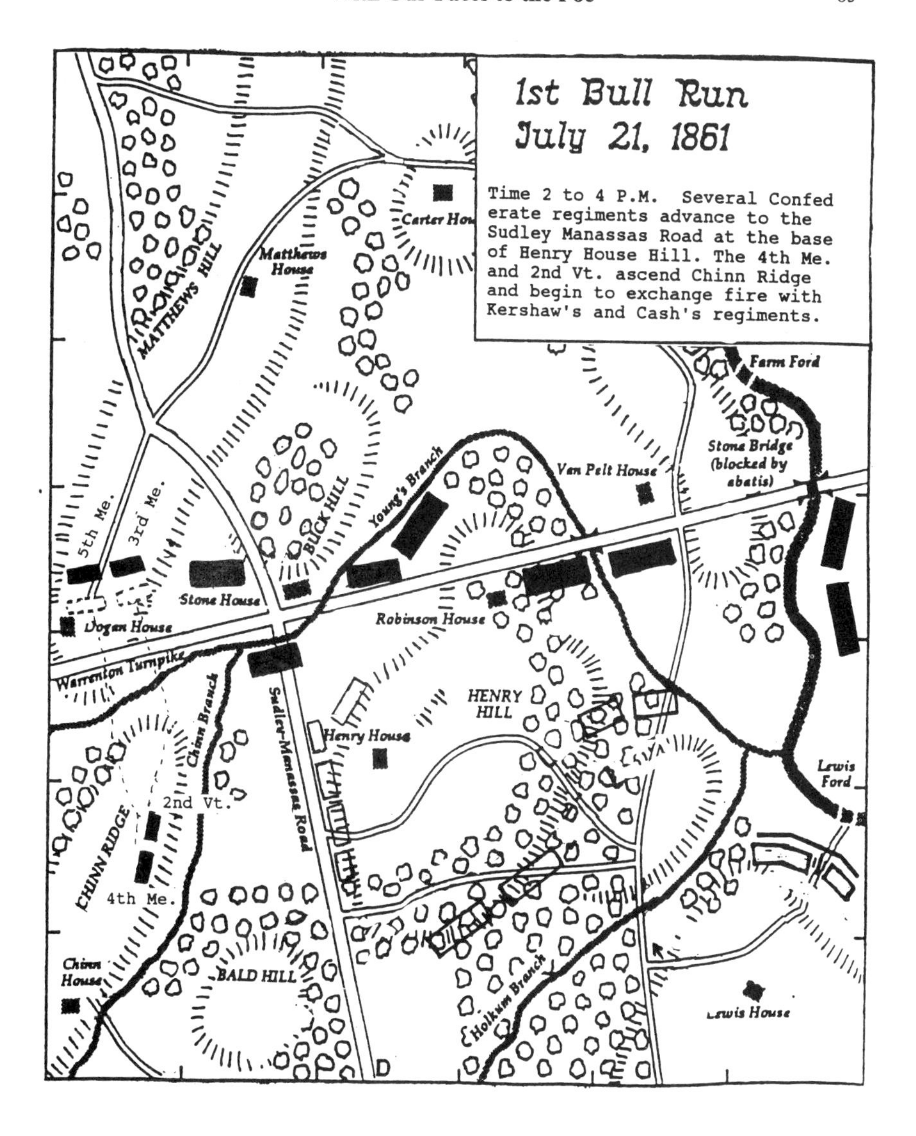
1st Bull Run
July 21, 1861
Time 2 to 4 P.M. Several Confederate regiments advance to the Sudley Manassas Road at the base of Henry House Hill. The 4th Me. and 2nd Vt. ascend Chinn Ridge and begin to exchange fire with Kershaw's and Cash's regiments.
MATTHEWS HILL
Matthews House
Carter House
Farm Ford
Stone Bridge (blocked by abatis)
Van Pelt House
Young's Branch
BUCK HILL
5th Me.
3rd Me.
Stone House
Dogan House
Robinson House
Warrenton Turnpike
Chinn Branch
Sudley-Manassas Road
HENRY HILL
Henry House
Lewis Ford
2nd Vt.
CHINN RIDGE
4th Me.
Chinn House
BALD HILL
Holkum Branch
Lewis House

"'Attention', left face, forward! Up the hill we went, through the woods, out to the brow of the hill, for the purpose of supporting a battery."[30] Howard later remembered watching as his men passed. "I closely observed them. Most were pale and thoughtful. Many looked up into my face and smiled. As soon as it was ready the first line swept up the slope, through a sprinkling of trees, out into an open space on high ground." Here..."we had no battery to support but were thrust into an engagement against Confederate infantry and artillery."[31]

As the Limerock Regiment advanced up Chinn Ridge a couple of Rockland boys recognized Adelbert Ames' familiar face. Though Ames had received a serious wound in the thigh and his clothing had been riddled with bullet holes, he had opted to remain at his post and continue to direct his section of artillery. When the surviving gunners had retreated from Henry House Hill Ames had been left behind. Presently his wanderings had brought him to the area. Two of the 4th Maine's soldiers requested, and were given permission, to remove him from the battlefield. This they did under fire and at extreme risk to themselves. Ames had already earned the Congressional Medal of Honor for his efforts. Following his recovery, he would be appointed Colonel of a soon to be formed Maine regiment, numbered 20th in sequence. His understudy in this new unit was Joshua Lawrence Chamberlain a man who would become one of the Civil War's most famous heroes.[32]

Upon reaching the crest the two New England units began to take small arms fire from two rebel regiments hidden along the western edge of the Sudley Road. The northernmost regiment was the 2nd South Carolina under the command of Colonel Joseph Kershaw, while the southern one was the 8th South Carolina receiving orders from Colonel E. B. C. Cash. The 4th Maine "stood stiff and still, in line receiving a fire from front, and right and left flank, and then we got the order to fire at will. That is all we had to fire at, as far as we could see. 'But the Johnnies were there, you bet.' In the cornfield, in the woods, anywhere they could find shelter, and it was always so, to the end of the rear."[33]

---

[30] Rockland Gazette, May 26, 1891.
[31] Howard, Autobiography of Oliver Otis Howard, pp. 158-159.
[32] Whitman, Maine in the War, pp. 85-86.
[33] Rockland Gazette, May 26, 1891.

Present day photo of the Dogan House at Bull Run.

Present Day photo of the Stone Bridge.

The 4th Maine's return fire must have been totally ineffective. The men were firing smoothbore rifles at unseen targets more than three hundred yards distant. In addition four of Colonel James Kemper's Alexandria Artillery rolled up on their right flank. As the two regiments began to take it on the chin from shot and shell, Howard went back to get his second line. When he reached the remainder of his brigade, however, some of the 5th Maine had already routed away as the result of a stray cannon ball. The 3rd Maine was as yet untouched. Together, he led the remnants forward and joined them with the rest of his command.[34]

Crockett later recalled seeing the deadly rebel guns move into position on their right..."Over the open field, goes a battery from the enemy's left. Our boys fairly scream with excitement. 'They are running! Running! Oh yes! Running to get a good position.' Every horse at a full gallop with belly almost touching the ground. See! they swing into line on the right, the men jump to their work, home goes the little red bag of powder., down goes the shot to meet it; a puff of smoke, a whir-r-r in the air, and the ball strikes just at my feet, I duck my head when Greenbalgh, our adjutant, calls out 'Don't dodge Ned.' Another shot strikes just behind him, he takes a step forward and I reply, 'The same to yourself!'"[35]

As Howard was bringing up the reserves so, too, were the rebels. Kirby Smith's brigade had been among the last of Johnston's forces to arrive by train at Manassas. Smith had trailed after Kershaw, but when Kershaw had turned toward Henry House Hill, Smith had continued straight ahead across the Sudley Road to the top of Bald Hill. When a sudden volley of musketry impacted the regiments, Smith, was struck by a Minie ball in the neck. The wound was serious and command now devolved upon Colonel Arnold Elzey. Elzey was quick to take control and immediately dispatched Beckham's Culpepper Artillery farther to the left near the Chinn House. He then reformed his men into line and moved them down the slopes of Bald Hill to Chinn Run.[36]

Elzey kept his men concealed in the trees facing Chinn Ridge. Spotting Howard's men on the high ground, a mere two hundred yards distant, Elzey first made sure that they were, indeed, Northern troops.

---

[34]Davis, op. cit., p. 219.
[35]Rockland Gazette, May 26, 1891.
[36] Davis, op. cit., p. 219.

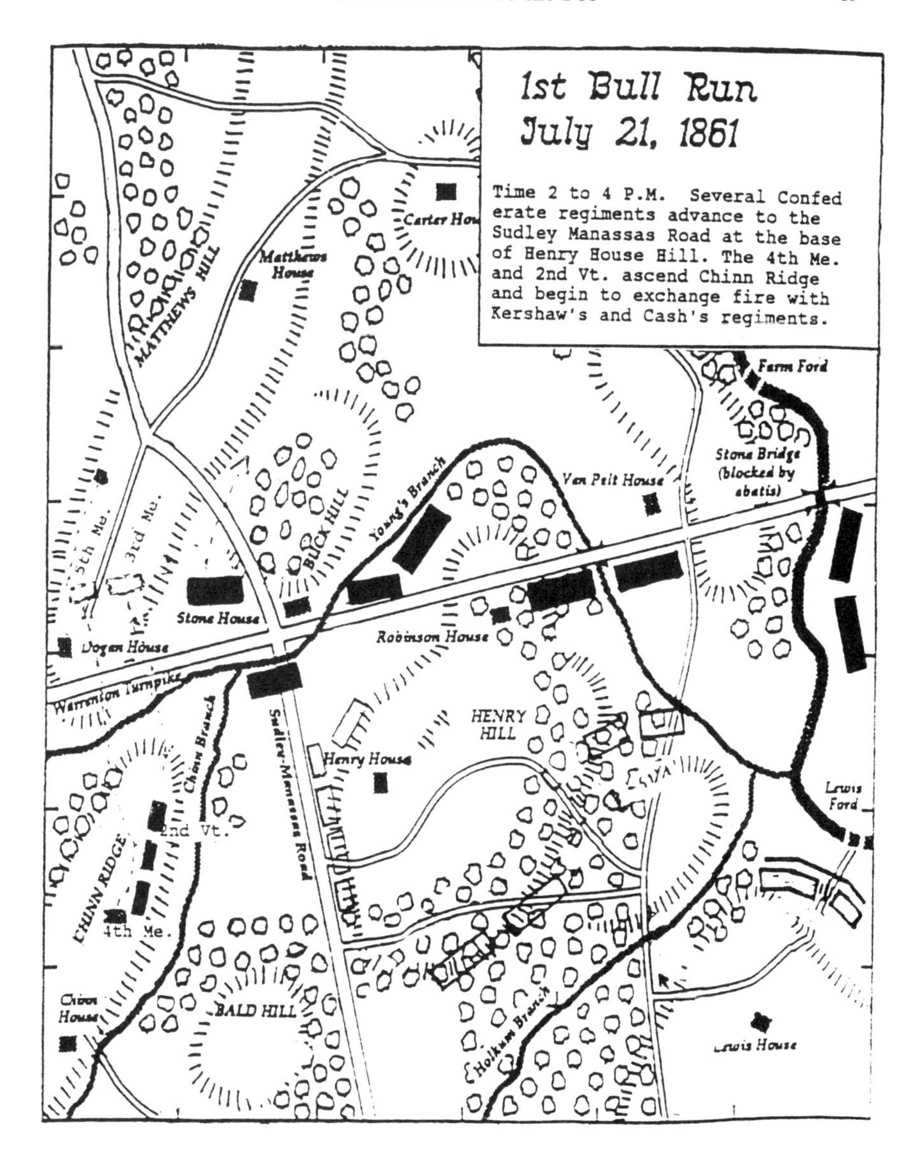
1st Bull Run
July 21, 1861
Time 2 to 4 P.M. Several Confederate regiments advance to the Sudley Manassas Road at the base of Henry House Hill. The 4th Me. and 2nd Vt. ascend Chinn Ridge and begin to exchange fire with Kershaw's and Cash's regiments.
Carter House
Matthews House
MATTHEWS HILL
Farm Ford
Stone Bridge (blocked by abatis)
Van Pelt House
Young's Branch
BUCK HILL
5th Me.
3rd Me.
Stone House
Dogan House
Robinson House
Warrenton Turnpike
Chinn Branch
Sudley-Manassas Road
HENRY HILL
Henry House
2nd Vt.
CHINN RIDGE
4th Me.
Lewis Ford
Chinn House
BALD HILL
Holkum Branch
Lewis House

Positively identifying the Federal flag, Elzey yelled, "Stars and Stripes! Stars and Stripes! Give it to them boys." Smoke and lead erupted from the woods. From Beckham's battery near the Chinn House, rebel shells shrieked through the air, crashing into the rapidly diminishing ranks of blue.[37]

In all of the available accounts of the fighting one single event is noted by each, and that is the death Stephen Chapman. One man remembered him as being nearly cut in two by the impact of a cannon ball. Elijah Walker remembered Chapman as "standing on the left of the regiment, a few paces in front, with a red sash around his body, a man more than six feet high, he was a conspicuous mark for the rebel sharpshooters. He was the first to fall. He was cut down by a rebel bullet."[38]

One of Chapman's fellow comrades rushed to his side as he collapsed. "Tell my wife I am shot - God bless her!" Chapman died in his friends arms. He left behind a wife and five children to mourn his passing. During the retreat his body was, unceremoniously, left behind on the battlefield. Perhaps he would have preferred it this way.

Hiram Berry wrote in a letter to his wife shortly after the battle that "My mind was occupied by my command entirely. Men fell all around me, killed and wounded. The ground was covered with men and horses, some mine and some of other regiments, who had passed over the same ground. Chapman left me only one minute before he was shot. He came for orders to my post by the regimental colors; asked for orders with a smile. I gave them, he extended his hand, we exchanged blessings, he cautioned me against unnecessary exposure, and we parted for the last time. He was shot through the heart immediately upon resuming his post."[39]

Sergeant Crockett remembered that "Splinters began to fly from the tree behind us, we were doing our best with poor guns, and worse powder. Powder that was old enough to be your great grandfather's. Powder that would heat our guns so hot we could only hold them by the straps. Powder that would clog so, it was impossible to get a bullet home."[40]

---

[37] Hennesseee, The First Battle of Bull Run, pp. 111-112.
[38] Walker, op. cit., p 2.
[39] Hiram G. Berry Correspondence, Larry Smith Collection.
[40] Rockland Gazette, May 26, 1891

Battle of Bull Run, July 21, 1861.

Colonel Berry also noted that many of the men "were wild with excitement, discharging their muskets in the air, and in a frantic endeavor to reload, forgetting to cap their pieces." When the men did remember, the sudden discharge would cause the guns barrel to burst. It was a scene of total confusion and death.[41]

One of the members of Company E remembered the terror of the artillery fire and the horrible effect it had upon his company. Yelling to his friend, Private Asa Hall, he screamed, "I bet you wish you were under your mother's bed eating catnip." He later recalled watching as his close friend was torn apart "by a cannon ball, and instantly killed." He also observed Orderly Sergeant, Freeman Hall, and Private Enos Clark, of Damariscotta Mills, fall prey to rebel bullets.[42]

Captain Oliver Conant of Company C wrote, in a letter to his wife on July 23rd, the following description of the combat. " When our brigade arrived we had no batteries to protect us from theirs, which were in the woods, completely masked by woods, and raking us two ways, our forces being in an open field. We having nothing but small arms to use, I think our bullets could harm them but little. My old soldier, whom you have heard me speak of as Sebastopol, had his gun shot in two pieces; he called for another which was handed to him, and he used it through the engagement. Charles (Miller) had his gun shot in two pieces by a cannon shot. Joseph (Shuman) lost his while he was carrying off the dead and wounded."[43]

"Asahel Town of Captain Conant's Company was killed by a shell. B. W. Fletcher of Captain Walker's Company had an arm shot off and his side injured. Lieutenant Clark of Company G, Wiscasset, was killed by the bursting of a shell as he was cheering on his men. Lieutenant W. E. Burgin and D. Blanchard of Company E were wounded. P. Henry Tillson of Thomaston, a member of Company C, and a young man of high character and worth, had both legs shot off by a cannon ball, and expired almost instantly."[44]

"One fine man who was killed, one who not withstanding was a cripple, had come out to do and die for his country, laughingly remarked that unless the rebs were more careful somebody would get

---

[41] O. R., op. cit, p. 418
[42] Rockland Free Press, July 31, 1861.
[43] Ibid.
[44] Ibid.

Frank Nickerson of Swanville distinguished himself at Bull Run and was later promoted to the rank of Brigadier General. (Photo Maine State Archives)

hurt. One youngster had his right arm shot away. I ran to the left of the company where he was, asked quickly if anyone had a bit of string, none was to be had; a glance showed me a silk necktie about his neck, a moment, and two turns of it was about his wounded arm. A splinter from the ground was shoved through the tie, a few turns and the blood is stopped. A word to him, Hold on to this for your life.'"[45]

Colonel Berry went about his business totally indifferent to the danger of his position. As the missiles screamed about him one found its mark in his horse, which fell dead beneath him. Berry's clothing was "riddled with bullets." When the color sergeant went down, the colonel picked up the flag, that it might not trail in the dirt, and carried it throughout the rest of the fight himself.[46]

By the time the 2nd Vermont was ordered to retire, the men of the 4th Maine had fired about twenty to thirty rounds. A private from Damariscotta later recalled that "according to my cartridge box calculation, I fired sixteen rounds at the enemy and escaped without a scratch."[47]

Most of the men discharged their weapons into the woods at the base of the ridge at an enemy they never saw. Years later, a member of the 5th Maine recalled..."we were ordered to fire. Fire at what? About five hundred yards in our front was a belt of woods, though not a Johnny in sight. Into this wood we poured our volleys, though wholly ignorant whether our efforts were of any use or not; but still we worked with a will. Everyone was desirous of doing his whole duty, a special illustration of which was seen in the action of a Captain firing his revolver at a battery *at least three-quarters of a mile distant."*[48]

As the "Green Mountain Boys" began to withdraw to their new reserve position in the rear at the base of the hill, small groups of Maine boys began to follow. Frank Nickerson, the 4th's Major, asked Howard if they had been ordered to retreat. Howard replied by shaking his head that he had not given that command. Major Nickerson, as well as a

[45] Rockland Gazette, May 26, 1891. The quote continues; "He did as directed, was taken prisoner, lived to see the end of the war, and the only time I have seen him since that day was when he thanked me for my kindness. He was selling the picture called the Empty Sleeve. The rebel surgeon told him I had saved his life."

[46] Howard, op. cit., p. 160.

[47] Rockland Free Press, July 31, 1861.

[48] Bicknell, History of the Fifth Maine Regiment, pp. 30-31.

number of the other officers of the regiment, attempted to stem the tide. It was useless though and the attempt was finally aborted. Shortly after, Howard commanded all of his troops to reform in a clump of trees in the valley near Young's Branch.

Colonel, and soon to be General, Oliver Otis Howard took special note of how Frank Nickerson, a lawyer from the small town of Swanville, Maine, had taken charge of his troops under fire. Shortly after the battle Nickerson was promoted to lieutenant colonel of the 4th Maine. In late November, 1861, he was offered the colonelcy of the newly formed 14th Maine Infantry. Later he would command his new regiment in the fighting at Baton Rouge. In March 1863, he was promoted to the rank of brigadier general, and led a brigade, and finally, the 3rd division, XIX Corps, in the fighting around Port Hudson. Frank Nickerson was one of the last Union generals to die, expiring just days before the United States entered World War I.[49]

William Crockett later remembered the order to retreat in the following words. "A few moments we stood this then an orderly from the Gen. rode up and we received orders to fall back. The change which took place in our brigade in a few moments has always seemed strange to me. We had come on the field in good order and had maintained a good line during the disastrous fire we had been subject to. But the moment that the order was received, there ended all form or discipline. It was a mob from that time to the end. Every man for himself. Back over the hill we went with the rebels in quick pursuit, the shot from their battery skimming the hill in very unpleasant style. It was at this point in the fight that one of my comrades was struck by a six pound shot and cut completely in two, the shot passed so near me I was thrown down, and as I fell I saw him fall forward on to his hands. I went to him and asked him to get up and come along. As I took hold of his collar to help him I saw how badly he was hurt. He replied that he could not move, for he felt numb all over. I called to one of the boys to come to my assistance, but before he could get to me, the man was dead. As it was getting uncomfortable in those parts, I took long and rapid steps to remove myself."[50]

When Howard's men disappeared along the top of Chinn Ridge, Elzey ordered his men to charge. Up the hill they went, pausing only

---

[49] Sifakis, Who Was Who in the Civil War. pp. 471-472.

[50] Rockland Gazette, May 26, 1891.

occasionally to paw a handful of blackberries. As they crested the heights they found the ground littered with the dead and dying. As the rebels continued on, their advance was slowed, and eventually halted, by the sporadic fire of Howard's troops in the pine thicket below them.

Suddenly Beckham began, once again, to rain a steady barrage of shell into the pine trees. This time there was no way that Howard could hold the remnants of his brigade together. The New Englanders' joined in the great rout that was already in progress. One of the members of the 5th Maine put it best. "It was everyone for himself, and having a due regard for individuality, each gave special attention to the momentum of his legs."[51]

About 4 P.M., coinciding with the retreat of Howard's brigade, the rebels, newly reinforced with Jubal Early's men, counter-charged, screaming out that soon to be famous rebel yell. Panic seized the northern troops, who, having decided they had had their fill of fighting for one day, began to retreat. The retreat soon became a rout, but the 4th Maine tenaciously held their ground. Several times their line was breached by the retreat of their own cavalry. When finally forced to retire they did so in comparatively good order, helping form the rear guard of the army as they streamed back to Alexandria.[52]

Various members of the regiment characterized the retreat in different ways. Sergeant Crockett called it "a mob of men and horses, fleeing in all directions and a howling enemy in full chase." A member of the regimental band called it "one general stampede, and they did not stop at the old campground, but passed by, which fact led us to believe we were not safe, and had better join the crowd, so each seizing one blanket, our canteens and the instruments, and run for our lives in the direction of this place. We left everything else behind, and joined the rest on the railroad track, arriving here Monday morning. We run about two miles - did not run all the way, but as Dr. Rouse once said, 'It was pretty d--d tall walking.'"[53]

---

[51] Bicknell, op. cit., p. 31.
[52] Gould, Hiram G. Berry, p. 64.
[53] The Rockland Gazette, August 1, 1861.

No 53

Report of Hiram G. Berry, 4th Maine Infantry
HDQRS. FOURTH REGIMENT MAINE VOLUNTEERS
Clermont, Va., July 26, 1861

Sir: I have the honor to report to you my regiment now in quarters at this post. The engagement with the enemy on Sunday, and the long march incident thereto, have exhausted my men, and some time must necessarily elapse before the regiment will be fitted for active duties. As near as can be ascertained, the loss in killed in the engagement at Bull Run consists of two commissioned officers, Lieutenant Clark of Company G., and Lieutenant Burd of Company F. Two commissioned officers wounded, Captain Bean and Lieutenant Huxford. Sergeant Major Chapman killed; twenty-eight privates killed and thirty-three wounded. This indeed has been an unfortunate affair for this regiment.

I herewith hand you a report of wants for regiment, in accordance with order to do so. In doing so, I must beg leave to say that my men have no confidence whatever in the kind of arms with which we are now partially supplied. Had they been properly armed, the result of Sunday's loss would have been somewhat different. It will take some time to bring the regiment up to that state of confidence in the managers of this war that it had prior to last Sunday's affair. I mention these things for the reason that a commander should know all the facts material to the efficiency of his command.

Truly your servant,

H. G. Berry
Colonel Fourth Regiment

Colonel O. O. Howard, Commanding Brigade

The regiment had paid dearly for its moment in history. At Bull Run the 4th lost two commissioned officers, Lieutenant William Clark of Wiscasset and Lieutenant Charles Burd of Company F. Twenty-four enlisted men were killed while twenty-four were wounded. Forty-two of the Maine boys were taken prisoner, nearly all of whom were

1st Lieutenant William Clark aptured at Bull Run. He resigned January 28, 1863 (Larry Smith Collection, Wiscasset)

injured and had to be left behind. In all the regiment suffered sixty-four casualties in but two hours of fighting and maneuvering.[54]

Sometime after the battle, General Beauregard wrote of the attack of Howard's men. In his remarks he states; "It is truly a magnificent, though redoubtable, spectacle as they threw forward in fine style on the broad, general slopes of the ridge occupied by their main line a cloud of skirmishers, preparatory for another attack."[55] When Beauregard ordered his counterattack; "Brigades all along the crest drove against the northerners, down the slope of the plateau, across the valley of Young's Branch, northward and eastward, in a fan shaped phalanx..."[56]

Heintzelman was also a witness to the retreat and later wrote: "such a rout I have never witnessed before, and this soon degenerated still further into a panic. Much excuse can be made for those who fled, as few of the enemy could at any time be seen. Raw troops cannot be expected to stand long against an unseen enemy."[57]

Most of the enlisted men, and even some of the officers, were highly critical of the performance of the army's command structure. A private in Company E wrote home to his wife that "our officers were greatly in error for placing us as they did. By doing as they ordered it exposed us to a crossfire from masked batteries. Great disaffection exists among the men for being used as they were both in and out of the battle. We might have gained this day had we had good management."[58]

Berry summed up the situation well in a letter written to the Governor on July 23rd. "My regiment fought bravely and stood their ground manfully. I have no cause of complaint in that respect. We marched fifty miles without halting except to fight a battle - without sleep also. I have lost everything. Lost one of my horses, the best one - killed. Say to General Titcomb that one of my flags was carried through the fight - the stars and stripes presented in New York. It was riddled with bullets. I have done my best and my whole duty, as I hope. I am sorry indeed to have lost so many, many men in a losing affair. Not less than 3000 killed and wounded on our side and prisoners - say

---

[54] Whitman, Maine in the War, p. 85.
[55] Jones, First Manassas, p. 39.
[56] Ibid. p. 42.
[57] Ibid.
[58] Rockland Free Press, July 31, 1861.

twice as many more of the enemy. The victory was ours up to one half hour of our arrival on the ground. At that time the enemy was reinforced by 17,000 men, and that fact together with the failure of ammunition lost the battle. Our part was to fight, and cover as far as possible the retreat. I am well, but exhausted, and my men are nearly so."[59]

The Gallant Fourth Maine Regiment

Editor of the Washington Star

I have seen no mention in the papers of the Fourth Maine. I suppose it happened from the fact that when this regiment was ordered forward the reporters had left, as in fact up to this time almost all the other forces were in retreat excepting Colonel Howard's Brigade. It has been a noticeable fact that none of this regiment have yet been seen in Washington, city, they have come into Alexandria from the old camp at Centreville, in good order, under command of their officers. This regiment was the last to leave the field, and made, with the 2d Vermont, a desperate charge upon the battery of the enemy, and stood receiving the fire of shot and shell for more than half an hour before being ordered to retreat. The battle had been lost before this, but not withstanding, they were aware of it from the fact that their lines were more than once broken by our own cavalry retreating. It was remarked by those who witnessed it that their lines were more steady than any regiment that had gone before them up the hill. Perhaps this fact might had been earlier known had this regiment chosen Washington for a stand rather than a point nearer the enemy's line.

Respectfully, & C

J.C.N.

The men of the Lime-Rock Valley had seen the elephant. First blood had been drawn. Naturally, it was not to be the last. The engagement had been particularly costly, both to the regiment and to

[59] Gould, op. cit., p. 65.

the folks back home. Almost everybody in the tri-county area knew someone who had been killed, wounded, or captured in the fray. The War Between the States had struck home, very personally, and left an indelible scar. As Berry had said, "The glamour and romance of a soldiers life disappeared after Bull Run. The deadly business of war was now at hand."[60]

[60] Ibid.

Chapter 4

Their Season of Discontent

"The Young Soldier Dying.-"Bring me my knapsack," said a young soldier, who lay sick in one of the hospitals at Washington. "Bring me my knapsack."

"What do you want of your knapsack?" inquired the head lady of the band of nurses.

"I want my knapsack," again said the dying young man. His knapsack was brought to him, and as he took it, his eye gleamed with pleasure, and his face was covered all over with a smile, as he brought out from it his hidden treasures.

"There," said he, "that is the bible from my mother. And this - Washington's farewell address - is the gift of my father. And this," - his voice failed.

The nurse then looked down to see what it was - and there was the face of a beautiful maiden.

"Now," said the dying soldier, "I want you to put all these under my pillow." She did as she was requested, and the poor young man laid him down on them to die, requesting that they should be sent to his parents when he was gone. Calm and joyful was he in dying. It was only going from night to endless day from death to eternal glory. So the young soldier died."[1]

Upon reaching Washington the regiment was forced to set up temporary camp in Alexandria. Colonel Berry's men, battered and shelterless, had suffered greatly following the Battle of Bull Run. Having been scattered to the winds, the fate of many of their comrades was, as yet, unknown. They had slept upon the hard ground without blankets, endured food shortages, the searing rays of the sun and the one hundred degree, plus, temperatures of the Virginia summer. They had marched, and fought, and then they had served as the rear guard for the army while most of the army was running for their lives.

---

[1] Rockland Gazette, August 9, 1861.

On July 24th the Maine regiment went into bivouac at their former camp at Bush Hill. Colonel Berry, in a letter to his wife written on August 10, described the scene in the following words. "We are now encamped on the side of a hill fronting the Turnpike Road leading to Fairfax Court House. Three New Jersey regiments are on our right and the rest of the brigade, the 2d Maine and one Vermont regiment, are on our left. We have a battery of ten-pound rifle cannon in our front, and a cavalry camp in our rear. I should judge by appearances that no move onward would be made for some time to come. Weather is very warm here, thermometer 130 degrees in sun every day and 95 to 105 degrees in the shade. General McDowell called on me yesterday and reviewed the regiment. He complimented me somewhat."[2]

For three weeks they remained here anxiously waiting as the 4th's soldiers straggled back into camp. Many of the men brought back remarkable stories of escape from the hands of the rebels. The wounded of the regiment, those able to return with it, had taken up residence at various hospitals in the Georgetown, Washington and Alexandria area. Some were at the Union sanitarium at Columbia Hospital on Meridian Hill. Some resided at the Third Brigade's General Hospital, and at the City Infirmary on E. Street in Washington. Many would live, and many would die. Many would expire alone, their identities unknown though not forgotten, all so very far from their precious homes and families in the Limerock Valley.

Take for example the case of Lieutenant Robert H. Gray, who "was taken prisoner at Bull Run. He received his wound just before the order came to retreat. On his way to the rear Lieutenant Burgin of the Searsport company found him and bound up his wounded arm, and afterwards sent some men to conduct him to a place of safety. They did not find him, however, as his wound commenced bleeding soon after the Lieutenant left him, and he started for a stream near by for water. Before he reached it he fainted from loss of blood, and on reviving, saw the retreating column of the Union army nearly a mile away. Replenishing his canteen at the brook, he attempted to rejoin his comrades by a short cut, but soon came in view of rebel troops who began firing on him, but he escaped further injury. His wound was so painful that he was indifferent to the danger he run, and continued

---

[2] Gould. Major General Hiram G. Berry, p. 70.

steadily on his course until he had nearly reached his friends, when he beheld the rebel cavalry rapidly approaching. Hastily entering a house which had been converted into a hospital by the Union forces, he lay down among the wounded, and had just made himself comfortable, when the cavalry dashed up, shooting two unwounded men."

"The rebels entered the hospital and proceeded to relieve the wounded of such valuables as they possessed, after which a guard was placed over them and from that time they were prisoners of war. The rebel officers were kind and courteous, but the soldiers used abusive language toward the prisoners. A rebel officer approached Gray and attempted in a pleasant manner to extract information, but it is superfluous to say that he got no satisfaction. The good woman of the house prepared some goose broth for the wounded. The dish was without much salt, and being strongly flavored with the oil of the goose was not a palatable dish for the sick. Gray was seven days in the rebel camp, when his condition becoming intolerable, he determined to escape or die in the attempt. Purloining some biscuit, and secreting bandages and salve about his person to dress his wound, he watched for a favorable opportunity and then made a break for liberty. Enveloped in a rebel blanket which effectually concealed his uniform, he safely passed several rebel officers and shaped his course toward Georgetown. During the first fourteen hours of his journey he was constantly dodging rebel pickets, and on reaching the Potomac River boldly plunged in and by wading and swimming soon reached the opposite side. After being thirty-four hours on the road, he reached Georgetown in an exhausted condition, and suffering from a high fever. Here he received kind care and was sent home on furlough. For gallantry at Bull Run, Gray was promoted to lieutenant. Afterwards he became Captain of Company I, and subsequently was promoted to major."[3]

Then there is the case of Charles O. Fernald of Winterport, whose "fighting was stopped by a cannon ball, which took the clothes clear to my breast, taking it all off but a little skin; then passing through the rear rank it struck a man by the name of Fletcher, just the same as it struck me." In excruciating pain Fernald was forced to complete the amputation of his own crushed arm. His attempted escape from the

[3] Ibid., pp. 73-75.

Manassas Battlefield, however, was foiled by the Confederate Army and he was sent to Libby Prison in Richmond. It was not until October, 1862, that Fernald was finally paroled and allowed to return home. The regiment, not knowing his fate listed him, simply, as killed in action, and that is what his family believed for more than a year.[4]

Other members of the regiment discovered desertion as a means of escaping the horrors of the battlefield. Men like Seth Dickenson of Wiscasset, and George Chatts of Rockland, just plain skedaddled. Chatts was never discharged from the regiment for it was thought he might be a prisoner in Richmond. Records show, however, that he in fact died on December 6, 1861, at Freeport, Maine.

Zathan Berry, a twenty-two year old private from Belfast and a former member of the Belfast City Greys, is reported to have left service on July 21st, 1861. His record in the Maine State Archives states, simply, that he "deserted". His legend, though, asserts that he was not guilty of the charges. The desertion and absence without leave charges, which allegedly occurred between August 12, and August 27, 1861, were not officially removed, however, until December 13, 1886, more than twenty-five years after the fact.

Nearly all of the men's personal effects, and regimental equipment, had been lost in their rapid retreat from the battlefield. Tents, blankets, clothing, and even their weapons were now in the hands of the Confederates. "Great difficulty was experienced in securing supplies for the regiment, which was due partly to the inexperience of the commissary and quartermaster departments, and partly to their incompetency. In his zeal for the welfare of his men, Colonel Berry lodged a complaint against the quartermaster of the brigade, but before the completion of the investigation which the brigade commander ordered to be made, the quartermaster resigned, and thereafter the men were better supplied." [5]

As news of their plight reached families back home, however, the men began to ,receive goods intended for their relief. Nineteenth Century equivalence of care packages were assembled and shipped south to the men of the Limerock Regiment. Within days thirty-three bundles, weighing more than three tons, were collected in Rockland

---

[4] Maine Bugle. Fernald's own remarkable story of survival in Libby prison can be found in its entirety in the appendix of this book.

[5] Ibid., p. 68.

and sent to the 4th Maine. "They were made up of private parcels sent by relatives and friends, packages for general distribution, the gifts of generous citizens, and articles purchased by the committee appointed for that purpose, such as pickles, dry fish, stockings, towels and stationery." The city of Belfast alone sent more than a ton and a half of supplies.[6]

In addition to equipment shortages, the regiment also faced a manpower crisis due primarily to a mix-up that had taken place when the regiment was sworn into service. When the Maine boys joined the unit, they had done so in the mistaken belief that they were a ninety day regiment. An informality, which occurred while they were being mustered into the army led to a very serious misunderstanding. Rather than enlisting for three months, they soon discovered that they had been recruited for three years.

Union and Journal
(Biddeford)
September 27, 1861

MUTINY IN THE FOURTH REGIMENT. - *The mutiny that was reported in one of the Maine regiments was, says the Portland Advertiser, in the Fourth (Rockland) in which the major part of two companies refused duty, and were put under arrest. It is probable that they had been tampered with by secessionists in disguise, with representations that they could be held for three months. Most of the men returned to duty. Some one writes to the Whig that a certain individual has done a great deal to ferment the three months uneasiness in the regiments. Give his name! Let's have it! The same writer also says a leading lawyer who speaks at the meeting for the Union and at another for traitors, is busy sowing tales among the soldiers at Portland. Out with his name!*

The first sign of trouble in the ranks came on the morning of August 12, when Sergeant Libby burst into Captain Walker's tent proclaiming that several of the best men in the company had decided they "were no longer held in the service and refused further duty." Walker immediately reported the situation to Colonel Berry who

---

[6] Whitman, Maine in the War, p. 87.

Nelson Burns, a participant in the 4th Maine revolt, who was transferred to the 38 th New York Infantry.(Photo Burns family of Union, Maine)

became very agitated, and for once in his career could not decide on the proper course of action.

About mid-morning Walker and Berry finally reached a consensus and decided to turn the matter over to their brigade commander. Colonel Howard, in turn, assembled the men and delivered to them a very stern lecture on the consequences of their decision. After a great deal of soul searching all but three of the mutineers agreed to return to duty. Those who persisted were sent to Alexandria's "slave pen" and incarcerated there for three weeks. At the end of that period a court martial was convened, and, in return for their peaceful return to their company, all charges were dropped, not withstanding a severe admonishment by the judge advocate.

Of the three men involved in the incident, Walker later spoke of them as being "amongst the best soldiers in the regiment. I often think of those men. One of them fell at Chantilly,[7] while holding the state flag, one was on the fated steamer that was blown up on the Mississippi, and the third returned to Rockland, minus one of his arms." [8]

The term of service issue continued to be a point of contention. Once again, on September 21st, it seethed to the surface when the men of Company H were ordered to report for picket duty. To a man each of them decided that their term had expired and that they were going home immediately. The message was passed to the regimental adjutant and, then to Colonel Berry. Once again, Berry addressed his men in a vain attempt to convince them of their error. He explained that he had..."done all that could possibly be done to make his men comfortable and contented, and now the men were determined to bring disgrace upon themselves and the regiment, which at this time stood second to none in the division." It was all to no avail, however, as all of his pleading and soul searching did not change a single stubborn Maine mind.[9]

Once again Berry and Walker scratched their heads over a solution to the issue. Walker quipped the opinion that the boys should be turned over to Colonel Sedgwick, the brigade commander. The idea was also expressed that Berry should "put them in the 38th New York.

---

[7] The unidentified man was Francis Whitney of Machias.
[8] Walker, History of the 4th Maine Regiment, p. 8.
[9] Ibid., p. 9.

Old Ward will cook them." "Old Ward" was the severe and rather imposing Colonel John Henry Hobart Ward of New York City. [10] Ward would soon be promoted to command of the brigade which would include the 4th Maine. His true fame, however, would come much later at Spotsylvania where he was relieved of his command, arrested for drunkenness, and later mustered out of service without the benefit of a court-martial.[11]

Colonel Sedgwick had the men quickly assembled and formed into line. He then ordered all those who had refused to do their duty to step forward. In all, ninety-one men, primarily from companies D, G, and H, stepped forward. They were at once arrested by a detachment of the 38th New York Infantry and placed under guard in an open field for the night. The next morning they were escorted to the camp of the 38th New York regiment and assigned to duty with its men.

The mutineers were quickly court-martialed. It was decided that these individuals were to be separated from the rest of the soldiers in their regiment and were never to receive a promotion in rank, even to that of corporal. Company H was dispersed completely, to be replaced in November by a company raised in Bangor and Belfast. Those who had agreed to continue their service were distributed among the other companies of the 4th.

The officers, on the other hand, were now left without men to command. The men were given the option of either resigning or being dismissed as "worthless." Two officers, including 1st Lieutenant John Cobb, and 2nd Lieutenant Beniah Brackley, chose resignation. Captain Burns' on the other hand refused to abdicate and was dishonorably discharged on October 4th.

In his writings following the war, Walker expressed the opinion that... "the assigning of those men to the New York regiment was unlawful and without due authority. Still, it was the best thing for the men that could be done at the time." Walker always believed that the men who "served in the 38th New York was as good material as Maine furnished." They would serve well and prove to be the backbone of the 38th New York.[12]

---

[10] Ibid.

[11] Sifakis, Who was Who in the Civil War, pp. 690-691.

[12] Ibid., p. 10.

Only on one other occasion could I find a reference relating to disciplinary problems in the "Old Fourth Maine." The event occurred shortly after the regimental mutiny, and on a day when Captain Walker was acting officer of the day. On this occasion a single individual from an unnamed company suddenly became "fighting ugly and refused to go to his quarters and keep quiet. Walker tried everything he could think of to quiet him. Finally, in an act of desperation, he bound the soldiers wrists and "tied him to the limb of a tree, and told him he should remain until he would promise to behave himself."[13]

As soon as Walker walked away the man began to scream "blue murder." Colonel Berry instantly went to the man and held him up while someone else cut him down from the tree. He immediately took him back to his own tent and "bathed his wrists expressing for him all the affection of a kind father."[14]

The tables were now abruptly turned. Suddenly Captain Walker became the object of disciplinary action. Berry did not take kindly to what he interpreted as the abuse of authority. The Colonel took Captain Walker aside and gave him a severe verbal tongue lashing. Thirty years later Walker claimed that he never forgot it, a lesson that he carried with him to his grave.

In his memoirs Walker states that : "Had Colonel Berry included in his makeup some of the 'ugly' of General Benjamin Butler, who could without winking more than an eye, take a man from the arms of his wife and hang him, and then as a reward to the widow, get her a clerkship in a government department at Washington, his men would not have been sent to the 38th New York. As a general commanding a brigade or division he had no superior. In those capacities he was not brought into direct contact with the discipline of the men. In actual conflict he was as brave as a tiger. I have seen his sword wave bravely in the smoke of battle. I have seen him weep over his fallen comrades, and almost refuse to be comforted."[15]

On September 24th, 1861, McClellan felt he was ready for a military review of the troops. He believed they were as spit and polish as they would ever be. Politicians turned out en masse to witness the new commander's achievements. The review, itself, took place at Fort

---

[13] Ibid.

[14] Ibid., p. 15.

[15] Gould, op. cit., p. 72.

Franklin along the line of Washington's defenses. As members of the Fourth Maine recounted in their letters home, the whole affair was held in full view of the rebel fort located just across the Potomac on Munson's Hill. Many of the men justifiably wondered for whose benefit the event was really being staged.[16]

General Berry describes the occasion of the review and relates that the ceremony took place "in a large field to the left of Fort Franklin, which was well adapted to the maneuvers of large bodies of troops... The troops to be reviewed numbered between twelve and fifteen thousand, and they made a most impressive spectacle. Gaily dressed officers galloped here and there, and generals of brigade resplendent with gold epaulettes and black plumes rode up and down the lines arranging their men."

"The center of the field was filled with carriages of civilians, who patiently awaited the arrival of the general-in-chief. Soon the booming of cannon on the right announced his approach, and he appeared at the head of a group of horsemen and commenced the review, passing down the line, and raising his hat gracefully as he approached each regiment, whose band played "Hail to the Chief" as he passed."[17]

The members of the 4th Maine recalled that General McClellan "was plainly dressed, and at the review was mounted on a gray horse. He critically examined the 4th Maine, as he passed along its front, and seemed well satisfied with the appearance of the men. After riding along the entire line of horse, foot and artillery, General McClellan took his stand in the center of the field, and each brigade breaking into column of companies, marched in review before him." It was like being inspected by the almighty himself.[18]

On September 30th the regiment was, once again ordered to move camp. The men had become quite comfortable in their old quarters and were very much against the action. Every tent had a wooden floor and each man a berth, each begrudged compliments of the local populace. Most tents had "cane seat chairs and well constructed tables were not uncommon articles." Still, orders were orders, and all of this comfort

---

[16] Whitman, op. cit., p. 92-93.

[17] The Fourth Maine's band was present at the review and though no verification can be found as to whether or not they actually played "Hail to the Chief", it should be assumed that they would not allow themselves to be outdone by other bands.

[18] Gould, op. cit., pp. 76-78.

was left behind. "Baggage packed and regimental line formed, the command 'forward' was given in Colonel Berry's ringing tones, and with the band playing a popular air, the regiment marched down past Fort Ellsworth, then to the right to Happy Valley..."

By the end of the day the regiment reached the site of their new home. The new bivouac was also an extremely good one, situated on high ground overlooking the Potomac and the city of Alexandria near Lawson's Hill and Hunting Creek. General Sedgwich located his brigade headquarters a couple of hundred feet to their front. This was the extreme left of the Army of the Potomac. To anchor the line an imposing set of earthworks was constructed at the top of a rugged hill on their immediate left.[19]

Here the Limerock Regiment was permanently brigaded with the 3rd Maine, and the 38th and 40th New York. The 38th, also known as the 2nd Regiment of Scott Life Guard, was only a two year regiment. When this unit was mustered out of service in June of 1863, the remaining forty Mainers in the New York regiment were transferred back to the 4th Maine, to serve the remainder of their enlistment's. Though the details of their service in the New York regiment is lost to Maine history, the fact that they remained brigaded with the 4th during these two years at least gives us a clue to their ordeal.[20]

Over the ensuing months the regiment remained in camp, drilling and training under the direction of their new army commander, George McClellan. Control of the army had been bestowed upon him at two A.M. on the morning after Bull Run. When he arrived to take command, the troops were "only a mere collection of regiments cowering on the banks of the Potomac." Just sixty days later they would be the "Army of the Potomac". These volunteers, had been transformed into soldiers, trained in military discipline and instilled with a sense of pride in their army.[21]

By mid October it had been determined that the men from the Pine Tree State must, by default, be well skilled in the lumbering trade. On October 22nd Colonel Berry wrote home stating to his wife that his men had just completed "another large fort, making the second one by this brigade, besides cutting down miles of forests, and also heaving up

[19] Ibid., p. 78-79.

[20] Whitman, op. cit., p. 88.

[21] Foote, The Civil War, Vol. I, p. 86.

miles of rifle pits or breastworks." The theory of operation of the army clearly seemed to be the elimination of every tree trunk behind which an enemy soldier could hide.[22]

Once again things began to look up for the regiment. Walker recollected that on November 15th a replacement company finally arrived to fill the void created by the dissolution of Company H. The unit consisted of three officers, led by Captain William Pitcher, 1st Lieutenant Albert Spencer, and 2nd Lieutenant George Bourne. There were also five sergeants, eight corporals, and seventy-five privates. Walker described them as a... "fine body of men and an honorable addition to our Fourth Maine." The addition so enhanced the regiment's complement as to make it the largest unit in the brigade.[23]

Elijah Walker's recollection of the date of the arrival of the replacement company is probably not entirely accurate. On November 15th, General Sedgwick, now Brigade commander, was still so concerned about the size of the 3rd and 4th regiments that he took the time to write a letter concerning the subject to Governor Washburn. In the correspondence he requested that the governor send some 285 replacements for the 3rd and 200 for the 4th. Unfortunately, replacements were more easily requested than obtained.[24]

Shortly after Captain Pitcher's arrival in camp another familiar face appeared. It was Lieutenant Gray returning from Maine following his recuperation from the wound he had received at First Bull Run. Gray had not returned alone, however, but had brought with him twenty-eight of his own recruits who were quickly distributed among each of the companies.[25]

In the waning days of November Sedgwick's brigade was called upon to help in the construction of a major fortification. On an almost daily basis the regiment was ordered to provide some fifty to two hundred men to work on Fort Lyon.[26] The only known photo of a Fourth Maine encampment in the field was taken at this time and is

---

[22] Gould, op. cit., 79-80.
[23] Walker, op. cit., p. 12.
[24] Maine State Archives, Civil War Records.
[25] Gould, op. cit., p. 86.
[26] Walker, op. cit., p. 11.

Libby Prison, home now to several members of the 4th Maine.

displayed on the opposite page. Notice the neat layout of the streets and the fact that Sibley style tents are still in use.[27]

The 4th Maine had an additional problem which annoyed them during the months immediately following Bull Run. In the waning months of 1861 some forty-five men deserted the regiment. More than half of these, twenty-four to be exact, had been members of Companies D and H. Only Companies E and K held perfect records, showing no reported desertions.[28] The reasons the men deserted are not recorded. The justifications, they would have carried with them when they ran. Walker later stated that these men could not..."be governed by military discipline, and some who were disappointed in not receiving promotions skeedaddled. Some skipped to Canada, a number shipped for sea voyages, and others were roving about the country." [29]

Many of these Maine boys must have been as skilled at running as they were at fighting, for, in the regiment's three years of service, not one was ever executed for the offense. Other Maine regiments were not as fortunate, notable among this group being the 4th Maine's sister regiment, the 3rd Maine Infantry. This unit did, indeed, suffer the embarrassment of a military execution of one of it members. Much of this can, most probably, be attributed to luck. It should be noted, however, that many of these men returned to their regiment voluntarily. Many others, of course, were never seen again at all.

There was one notable incident involving desertion which took place on August 7th, 1861. On this occasion Joseph S. Shuman of Waldoboro convinced Emerson Overlock of the same town, and Albert Salisbury of Tremont to go AWOL. Overlock and Emerson always claimed that they did not know where they were going. Once out of camp Shuman headed straight for the rebel lines. Shuman went directly into the rebel ranks, while the other two went directly to Libby Prison. Later the next year the two were exchanged and returned to the regiment. This is the only recorded incident in which a member 4th Maine deserted directly into the Confederate army.[30]

The main enemy for the Civil War soldier was not a rebel bullet. It was disease. On average twice as many soldiers would die of

---

[27] Photo courtesy of Carlisle Barracks
[28] Adjutant General's Report, 1861.
[29] Walker, op. cit., p. 13.
[30] Ibid.

ailments in this war as would die of wounds in combat. Maine, and the 4th Regiment in particular would be well represented in this department. Departures from the regiment for sickness occurred on an almost daily basis; deaths took place weekly. In November and December diphtheria was the major culprit. The epidemic was so bad that, on average, the names of thirty-seven 4th Maine boys could be found on the sick list on any given day.[31]

When Dr. Hunkins was captured at First Bull Run, Governor Washburn responded by sending Dr. Carr to take his place. At the same time Abiel Libby also received a commission as assistant surgeon. By reputation, both were thought of as being very skillful and conscientious surgeons. Fortunately for us, Dr. Libby kept a journal of the events in which he was to take so vital a part. Through his eyes one can begin to see what camp life was like for these soldiers. One can see that life in the army was not all fighting. There was a great deal more to contend with. Though perhaps brave and fearless in combat, it is obvious from Dr. Libby's descriptions that they had their weak, their playful, and their immoral sides as well.[32]

For example, when the doctor speaks of the activities of the regiment on the day after Christmas, the picture which he conveys is not what one might expect on so reverent a day. He states that..."camp was somewhat noisy last night in consequence of drunken soldiers. They had access to whiskey shops yesterday and some of the men drank their fill." So much for the puritan ethic. But then again, these men never knew when they would be called into battle. Many felt they had but a short period into which they had to condense a lifetime of living.[33]

Hiram Berry remembered that it was the "thunder of the cannon on the battlements of Fort Lyon, adjacent to the camp of the 4th Maine, which heralded a 'Merry Christmas' to the gallant soldiers of the Pine Tree State. The day was indeed a merry one to Camp Knox.[34] Thoughtful friends had provided Christmas viands, and all the companies feasted on roast turkey and concomitant luxuries which the

---

[31] Libby, Journal of Abiel Libby, p. 1.
[32] Ibid., p. 90.
[33] Ibid., p. 2.
[34] Camp Knox was the name which the 4th gave to all of their camps and it was done so in honor of their local Revolutionary War hero, Henry Knox.

George French, 4th Maine Sutler (Photo Maine State Archives)

generosity of the company commanders had supplied. So also they had holiday exemption from usual duties, and officers and men gave themselves over to the pleasures of the day unreservedly. The almost summer mildness of the atmosphere gave to the scene a strangeness and an unreality quite unlike the bleak meadows and snow-clad trees and housetops which are associated thoughts of Christmas in the mind of every New Englander."[35]

Just before the New Years the regiment was visited by Vice President Hannibal Hamlin and his wife, as well as Senator Anson Morrill, and Representatives Morell and Rice. A special dress parade was held that the guests might review the troops. All were very impressed with the appearance of the men and congratulated Berry on the exhibition. The dignitaries then dined with the Colonel, and, under his escort, visited the 3rd Maine in their camp as well.

On January 4, 1862, Dr. Libby spoke of the sins of the soldiers. "It is very different from the Sabbaths of our Puritan ancestors. How fallen men become in the army, and how many sins they will commit when they would blush to think of it at home." He then tells a story of how some men of the regiment attempted to blow up the sutler's wagon by filling a canteen with gunpowder and then igniting the fuse. Fortunately the result was disappointing to all but the sutler. The bomb went off, but it did very little damage.

A second story, reported to have occurred at about the same time, involved a soldier who had stolen a shirt. In talking to his other tent mates the man was heard to boast of the quality of the shirt, which he now had in his possession. Later the man discovered that the coveted shirt was his own "which he had washed and hung out and then forgotten." Such was camp life during the winter of 1862.[36]

Several important promotions also took place during the fall and winter months. In September the 4th's Lieutenant-Colonel, Thomas Marshall of Belfast, had been promoted to the Colonelcy of the 7th Maine. Berry wrote that "his lofty character and pleasant ways had endeared him to officers and men alike..." When the regiment learned that he had died of typhus fever a month later on October 25th, the men were in a state of shock. Colonel Berry was moved to issue an order as "a tribute to the dead."

---

[35] Gould, op. cit., p 89.
[36] Libby, op. cit., p3.

**Headquarters 4th Maine Regiment
Camp Knox, October 29, 1861.**

It is with feelings of sorrow and sadness that I announce to this regiment, in an official manner, that an all-wise Providence has thought proper to remove from the scenes of his earthly labor, our late lieutenant-colonel and beloved companion, the Hon. Thomas H. Marshall, colonel of the 7th Regiment Maine Volunteers.

This is indeed sorrowful news to all of us. Colonel Marshall was beloved, respected and honored by all for all his many virtues. As an officer ever faithful, allowing none to excel him in the performance of his duties, in the depth of his patriotism and love of country. In his death the Government has lost a valuable officer; the State he has in part represented in the tented field, an honored son; the 7th Regiment a valued and beloved commander; we with whom he has shared the dangers and privations of a soldier's life, a true and beloved companion and friend; his family; a model husband, son and father. We can only exclaim "Peace to his ashes," all honor to his memory.

Ordered, That the officers of this regiment wear crape on the left arm for a period of thirty days, and that the regimental colors. be hung in black for the same period of time.

H. G. Berry, Colonel. [37]

As we already know Frank Nickerson had been promoted to the rank of colonel in the 14th Maine Infantry. In addition Major Fuller was promoted to lieutenant-colonel, replacing Frank Nickerson and Elijah Walker had been advanced to major. All told, some thirteen recommendations had been submitted to the governor for his approval in November alone. It should be noted that all of the appointees received their commissions.[38]

There was one notable demotion in the regiment. Corporal Alvin D. Burns of Company B, it seems, set himself up in the business of forging passes for both himself and his paying friends. It did not take long, however, for the officers to catch on to his scheme. One frosty November morn Corporal Burns was paraded in front of the regiment.

[37] Gould, op. cit., pp. 81-82.
[38] Walker, op. cit., p. 12.

RECRUITS WANTED

FOR THE

Fourth Maine Regiment

COL. H. G. BERRY, Commanding.

TERM OF ENLISTMENT THREE YEARS. Pay 13 per month, rations and clothing. A Bounty of $100 will be paid at the close of the war. The Regiment is now stationed at Alexandria, Va., about 8 miles from Washington, one of the most healthy locations near the Potomac.

OFFICE—Berry's Block, corner Main and Lime Rock Streets, Up Stairs.

Adjt. J. B. GREENHALGH,

Recruiting Officer.

Feb. 5, 1862

7tf

Colonel Berry had the charges against entrepreneur Burns read to his fellow enlisted men and then had the orderly cut the chevrons from his sleeve. So much for free enterprise.[39]

On January 22, 1862, several members were sent back to Rockland for the express purpose of recruiting replacements for the regiment. Captain Andrew Bean headed up the detachment, which included Lieutenant J. B. Greenhalgh, Sergeant Converse Groves, Sergeant J. T. Gould, Corporal Henry Mitchell and Private Alden Crockett. The men acted aggressively in trying to collect new recruits. They ran ads in the local newspapers, a sample of which is exhibited in this text, and traveled to all of the surrounding communities, stumping for volunteers. The results were somewhat less than impressive.[40]

Meanwhile, back at the front, Major Walker was detailed on January 24th to take a detachment of two hundred and fifty of his own men, along with a company of cavalry, and make a reconnaissance in the direction of the Occoquan River. The force moved..."through woods and Virginia paths for some ten miles, when we came to where we expected to find the enemy's pickets." Some of the 4th's advance skirmishers spotted them and brought the information quickly back to Major Walker.

Orders were quickly barked out. The men quickly rammed home a charge into their Austrian made rifles, and then fixed bayonet. Most of their thoughts probably drifted back now to the events of the previous July. All were fidgeting about, anxiously awaiting the dreaded command. Captain Smith mounted his horse, drew his sword, and, pointing it in the direction of the enemy, yelled "charge". The men flew across the broken ground, determined that they would kill, or capture, all of the rebs that stood between them and Richmond.

These Maine boys were not to be denied. On they rushed, determined to revenge their losses at Bull Run. Like men possessed, these fighting tigers went crashing into the Confederate camp, taking the enemy totally by surprise. The struggle was brief and their subjects quickly subdued. Their prize, was "an old man and woman, a cripple and a fool"...along with several broken down horses. It was not Richmond, but it would have to do.

---

[39] Ibid.

[40] Ibid., p. 13.

This brilliant military victory was not accomplished without casualties. One of the men had actually been quite seriously wounded when a heavy limb from a dead tree had fallen across his head and shoulders. The man had been knocked senseless and required the assistance of several members of the regiment in his safe return to camp.[41]

The 4th now turned and headed down river. After traveling but a short distance, Walker's skirmishers contacted the 37th New York. This unit had been sent to hold a strategic crossroads so that the 4th would not be cut off by rebel troops. The New York boys had become rattled due to an encounter with a band of guerrillas. The colonel of the regiment panicked and sent a message to Colonel Berry stating that his Maine men had been attacked and captured by the enemy. Berry had notified General Heintzelman of the situation. When Major Walker arrived at Pohick Church, however, he found that the whole division had been mobilized in an effort to rescue his command. Walker was shocked to discover what had taken place, especially in light of the fact that he had not even seen an enemy soldier.

While the men had been out on picket, nature chose that moment to send a "cyclone" through the 4th Maine's camp. The twister made "sad havoc with the tents and equipage. Colonel Berry's tent suffered with the others, but being absent in command of the picket, he experience no inconvenience, and the men speedily restored it to its place. The sutler's covered wagon performed a gyration over the tent of the surgeon, Dr. Libby, damaging it somewhat, then speeding away at random, making havoc along its course."

The regiment, finding both the rebel army and the elements of wind and weather allied against them, decided that it might be time to make a course correction in their lives. Five hundred of the nine hundred enlisted men and officers in the unit, at the urging of Chaplain Chase, signed a petition supporting the temperance movement and declared, for the moment at least, that King Alcohol, not Jeff Davis, was public enemy number one. Of course all of this was done with the understanding that priorities could change at any moment, without notice.[42]

---

[41] Ibid., p. 15.
[42] Gould, op. cit., p. 93.

The month also saw the regiment send many of its best men out on detached service. On February 4, 1862, a special order had come down from division headquarters asking for soldiers who had been seamen to volunteer for service in the river gunboat service. As many of the Maine boys had extensive seafaring experience, more than a hundred men volunteered. Some twenty-seven were selected and were reported as being on detached service. Elijah Walker thought that this was an odd classification for the men especially since he could only remember one of them ever returning to the unit. The volunteers were quickly sent away on February 17th, and were for the most part never seen again.[43]

With a couple of minor exceptions, the regiment did not participate in any advances on the enemy until March 9, 1862. Their excursion went extremely well and was very quiet until about one A.M. on the morning of the eleventh. It was just about this time when one of the guards on picket duty was hailed by an approaching stranger. The guard yelled, "Who comes there?" The answer was quickly returned; "I am a woman; don't shoot me." The sentinel quickly took the woman and her "12 or 14 year old son" into custody and delivered them to Captain Carver who was in charge of the line at that point.

Colonel Walker remembered years later that "the new comers' clothing was scant, wet and badly torn. The woman with her boy had forded the river and made her way through the woods to our line, as she dared not follow the road for fear of being overtaken and carried back among the rebels. With needle and thread furnished by a soldier she stitched together her torn outer garment, and the Captain took her before the colonel, whom she informed that the rebels were leaving Ocoquan. The entire Confederate Army was departing, she said, and she had come to apprise us of the retreat. She could not go back, for if they caught her she would be killed. She was loyal, and declared she was rejoiced to once more see the stars and stripes."

Colonel Berry acted quickly on the information they had received. As some of the members of the regiment had been assigned to assist Professor Lowe in his aeronautical experiments, one of the professor's balloons was quickly ordered inflated and about midnight Berry ascended in it to a height of about two thousand feet. From this altitude

---

[43] Walker, op. cit. p. 15.

Berry made "sketches of what was going on..." He then descended and sent his regiment" to the front and captured some of the enemy, and took inhabitants, and got the whole thing so the Army of the Potomac moved the next morning at four o'clock."[44]

Fourth Maine Men Sent on Gunboat Service

Company A	Company F
Augustus Munroe	B. C. Hines
Edward Gray	James Malherin
Company B	**Company H**
William Galland	Manforn Miles
David Lauderback	George Wellington
Francis Whitney	Horatio Alvin
John McKean	**Company I**
Company C	Charles Crowley
Elisha Mills	Allen Dow
John Grant	E. Roberts
Weston Grant	George Kimball
F. G. Mellus	**Company K**
Company D	Charles Welsh
S. J. Needham	George Johnson
Thomas Wyatt	Joseph Guptil
William Norton	G. W. Burgis
Company E	
William Stetson	
Elijah Whitney	

General McClellan was quickly notified by telegraph of the retreat of rebel troops. Colonel Berry ordered Captain Walker, along with two hundred and fifty selected men, to advance immediately on Occoquan Village. Walker remembered that "the night was dark, the roads were narrow and through woods, and the branches of the trees so intermingled above us that we were enshrouded in gloom... At daylight we stood on the bank of the Ocoquan River, opposite Ocoquan Village... I was under positive orders not to cross the river; a few of our

[44] Gould. op. cit. p.103.

men passed to the other side by stepping from stone to stone, but did not go to the village. We returned to our outpost picket reserve, where we took a late breakfast."

On the following morning Walker once again visited Occoquan, this time with a slightly larger force, and quietly slipped across the river and captured the town. "The site of the Confederate camp was plainly marked, but there were few men of any description visible. The contents of the stores were light, and the only thing our men saw, which they fell in love, was tobacco; that was abundant and the owners generously gave the men all they desired. We returned to the outpost, where we had a sup of coffee and some hard bread; then we returned to camp with the regiment."[45]

Abraham Lincoln was greatly impressed with the information that had been supplied by colonel Berry to General McClellan. As the war dragged on the President's impression of Berry continued to grow more and more favorable, fostered by both his deeds, and by the words of Berry's close friend, and associate, Vice President Hannibal Hamlin. In terms of his career prospects, this was an extremely good circle of friends to be associated with.

On March 17, the regiment was moved to Alexandria and from there to Old Point Comfort. The army had been divided into five Corps by order of President Lincoln. General Heintzelman was to be their commander. This action was a sure indicator that the army was about to go into action. McClellan's spring offensive was about to begin. From here the soldiers would embark on their voyage to Fortress Monroe. The Peninsula Campaign was about to begin. The regiment's 'Season of Discontent' was about to end.[46]

---

[45] Op. cit., pp. 16-17.

[46] Whitman, op. cit., p. 92.

Chapter 5

"Instead of driving the rebels, we have been driven."

The army, under McClellan, arrived at Fort Monroe on March 19th. For most of the men the trip down the Potomac was a novel adventure. The troops, along with their weapons and gear, were loaded on the transports. Ships in the Washington Navy Yard fired their guns in salute, while bands played. The ships sailed past Fort Washington, Mount Vernon, and Washington's Tomb. The vessels would travel all night, usually arriving at Fortress Monroe on the early dawn. The men would then disembarked and set about establishing their camps near the fort. Here they sat, the rebels to their front, and their backs to the sea.

Though the 4th had arrived at Fort Monroe at 4 P. M. on March 19th, they did not land until 1 P. M. on the twentieth. The regiment was then marched a distance of about three miles in the midst of a tremendous rainstorm. At the completion of their journey the Maine men found the ground to be too wet and muddy for them to sleep upon. The soldiers then scoured the area for whatever they could find to insulate them from the cold wet earth. They pitched their tents and placed boards or straw down and spread their blankets over them for warmth. It was hard for the men to sleep but "they bore it cheerfully and came out in the morning all right for the most part."

Doctor Libby, on the other hand, found the night's fare to be much more hospitable. The doctor spotted an old mill and in company with the assistant surgeon, Dr. Weiswell, Chaplain Chase, and several others, sought out the structure as protection from the storm. These men soon discovered that the mill was occupied by four families of contrabands. The negros, however, allowed the guests to stay upstairs. While the visitors tried to sleep, the negros held "a lively prayer meeting" downstairs. "They enjoyed it more than we did; for we got no sleep until the meeting closed. In the morning we took breakfast with the contrabands and fared sumptuously. Hoecake, shortbisket, fresh oysters, boiled mackerel, eggs, coffee and sugar formed the amazing menu served by the willing darkies for twenty-five cents."[1]

Camp Near Hampton, Va.,
March 25, 1862.[2]

Having been ordered by the War Department to report for orders to Major-General McClellan, Commander of the Army of the Potomac, it becomes my duty now to take my official leave of this regiment.

I Part with the officers and men composing this command with very much regret. My intercourse with all has been of the most pleasant nature. My friendship for officers, and men alike is one of the strongest ever formed by me. I have every reason to believe that it is more than reciprocated by this entire command. I can only say, may it continue. I shall watch with great interest your future, and judging by the past, I feel assured the 4th Maine will stand second to none during the period of its service. I shall be ever ready to assist whenever and wherever my poor service may avail you. When the time arrives and you are brought face to the foe, remember you carry with you your own reputation and that of your state. Strike, then, with a will, for your country, your God and the right.

If in the discharge of my duty, I have in any way wounded the feelings of any, I beg them to forget. None are perfect and very few have more imperfections than myself.

The duties I have had in organizing, disciplining and drilling a new regiment have not been light. I hope I may have done the service assigned me by His Excellency, the Governor of Maine, passing well; at any rate, I feel I have endeavored to do my duty to you all, by my State and by my country. God bless you all.

On March 20, colonel Berry was promoted to the rank of brigadier general by President Lincoln. Major Elijah Walker, in turn, was advanced to regimental office in his stead. The Rockland Gazette

[1] Libby, Journal of Ariel Libby, p. 8.
[2] Gould, Major General Hiram G. Berry, pp. 104-105.

proclaimed " We are pleased at the promotion...and we believe it an honor justly due to the merits of an able and efficient officer."[3]

Shortly after the announcement of the promotion the sergeants of the regiment ordered a special presentation sword to honor their colonel. It arrived a few days after the 4th Maine left Yorktown and was presented to Berry in a small ceremony a few days later. Sergeant Burpee had the honors. The sword was manufactured by J. H. Caldwell and Company of Philadelphia. The hilt was of solid silver and the blade, made of Domascus steel, was flowered for one third of its length. A small silver plate on the scabbard was inscribed with the words, " Presented to Colonel H. G. Berry, by the sergeants of the 4th Maine Regiment."

Not to be outdone, the officers of the regiment presented him with a service of silver plate. It was made up of seven pieces and cost them about a thousand dollars. Naturally, at this period of time, a thousand dollar gift was extremely extravagant. The silver was similarly inscribed and came to be a very valued possession of General Berry's family after the war.[4]

General Berry's replacement was forty-three year old Elijah Walker. Though at the time of his promotion he had been a resident of Rockland, Walker had actually been born in the town of Union, only a short distance up the St. George River. He had been involved in a coal and lumber venture with Berry before the war, a friendship which quite certainly had not hurt his chances for promotion. Nevertheless, this five foot, six and one-half inch man would have some pretty large shoes to fill.[5]

Dr. Libby reported that on March 25, the brigade surgeon took possession of former President John Tyler's summer residence. He drove out the contrabands who had occupied the dwelling and then hired a man to make the home ready for its new occupants. Once this was completed the doctor then turned the domicile over to General Birney. Shortly after they had settled in, orders arrived insisting that they vacate President Tyler's residence. "They had to leave forthwith and let the gleeful darkies return to clean quarters. And the general and his staff returned to their tents."[6]

---

[3] Rockland Gazette, March 12, 1862.
[4] Rockland Gazette, March, 1862.
[5] Civil War Index Files, Maine State Archives, Augusta.
[6] Libby, op. cit., p. 8.

On April 4th, the army began its' march on Yorktown. The advance was slow, moving but twelve miles and camping at Great Bethel.[7] Next morning the army pushed on to the fortifications at Yorktown itself. The rain had been falling heavily, causing the roads to turn into mire. Artillery pieces sank out of sight, slowing the movement of the Army. The rebel commander, General John Magruder, awaited the advancing Federals in his entrenchments. Magruder had but 11,000 troops. McClellan had more than 60,000.[8]

Headquarters Fourth Maine Vols.,
Camp Knox, near Hampton, Va.,
March 25, 1862
Regimental Order #1 [9]

The Undersigned hereby assumes command of the Fourth Maine Volunteers, until the present held by our late Colonel, Hiram Berry, now relieved from duty with the regiment by a well-earned promotion to a brigadier-generalship.

1. It is not without feelings of diffidence and mistrust in his own ability that he enters upon the duties, and to him unaccustomed duties, about to devolve upon him, particularly when he succeeds such a commander as we have lost. It will lessen his labors much, and he sincerely hopes and expects to have the cordial support of every officer and man in the regiment, on the side of good order and discipline. The standing of the regiment is high - let it lose none of its reputation in our hands.

2. The orders heretofore issued from these headquarters will remain in full force until specially altered or annulled.

Elijah Walker
Commanding Fourth Maine Regiment

Perhaps a note of interest regarding the advance of the regiment. Walker in his memoirs recollected that "we were not in the advance,

---

[7] Actually the name is Big Bethel
[8] McPherson, Battle Cry of Freedom, p. 426.
[9] Walker, op. cit., p. 18.

consequently saw nothing of the enemy. On this march we had one officer wounded; we all thought he must have shot himself." This officer was Lieutenant Otis McGray of Unity. Walker stated that "he soon after became crazy, as he said, and tendered his resignation."[10]

When the men left Hampton in their advance on Yorktown the Maine boys were instructed to prepare three days' rations. As Elijah Walker later stated :" Now, no old campaigner needs to be told that when soldiers start on a march with such a limited supply of subsistence the fare on the third day is not Sybaritic; and as we arrived near Yorktown April 4th, and the army mule teams did not appear for several days, we were very hungry. The soldiers found a bin of corn, over which our brigade commander placed a guard and dealt out the cereal to the men. The boys roasted, boiled and steeped it and it was a meager substitute for nothing. None of the feathered or bristled tribes could be found."

Speaking of the "feathered tribes", the regiment had learned a valuable lesson on this subject just a week earlier while they were still back in Hampton. It seems that "General Heintzleman learned that a large party of soldiers of his command were several miles from camp, making sad havoc among the feathered tribes. He made some rough talk, which I (Walker) happened to overhear, then ordered a guard to every regiment of the division with instructions to arrest every man found with a turkey. Fearing some of our regiment might be among the foraging party, I requested my major, Pitcher, who was acting brigade officer of the day, to look after our men and give them a word of caution. Forty-four men were arrested with turkeys. My men came to camp without turkey or foul of any kind. At night the guard watch was withdrawn and our men found their plunder where they had hidden it. We all dined off turkey the next day and the forty-four who were caught were tried by court-martial and convicted. The general was so fond of turkey that he commuted the sentences."[11]

By the time the 4th Maine reached Yorktown most of the army was already beginning to settle in. The men picked out a suitable encampment within sight of the city. On the ninth they moved to a point in the woods to their left that was closer to the enemy works. Here they stayed, watching Magruder's theatrics, as McClellan brought up his siege artillery. The Mainers spent their time building entrenchments and

---

[10] Ibid., p. 19.
[11] Ibid.

Photo Adjutant and 1st Lieutenant Charles Sawyer. (Photo Maine State Archives)

laying out roads. As the fortifications grew in length, the line that the Union forces occupied grew to span almost twenty miles.

The work was laborious, and the surroundings were very unhealthy. As related by Dr. Libby, the 4th Maine at this time resided on very low swampy ground. Many of the men had begun to get sick and a large number had come under the care of the surgeon. Though oblivious to the apparent causes of their sicknesses, the doctor does make an interesting note. "The men get water by digging about two feet. This water is full of decomposed vegetable matter and is pretty bad stuff." If only he could have comprehended what he was saying; so many lives could have been saved.[12]

Despite the inactivity of the Army of the Potomac, the regiment began to accumulate casualties. On the morning after their arrival the rebs sent over one of their compliments in the form of a fifty or hundred pound shell. The projectile struck one of the rail fences nearby, splintering it into pieces. Private Thomas Snowdeal of Thomaston found himself in the path of one of these wood fragments and was struck in the back. The wound was serious and he died a short time after. Walker recalled "he was a good boy and a fine soldier, and was given a soldier's burial."

Private Johnson Jones was another one of the early victims of the Peninsula Campaign. Jones, a native of Union, was just twenty-one years old. He was a farmer, and, as yet, unmarried. Johnson was not a lucky man, for not long after his arrival in front of Yorktown he became sick. His condition rapidly deteriorated to the point that the field hospital, and Doctor Libby, could no longer take care of him. In late May he was transferred to Washington. On June 6, 1862, however he became a casualty of disease, and war. It might have been dysentery, caused by consumption of contaminated water, or cholera, or even measles that caused his demise. The record is not clear on this point. Johnson Jones was not the first man in the regiment to die of disease, but he was one of the forgotten multitude, and he would certainly not be the last.[13]

While opposing forces sat eyeing each other for a full month, the 4th was involved in just one minor skirmish on April 27th. While on picket duty it had been reported to command that the rebels were advancing. The 37th New York was brought up to the trenches behind the 4th Maine

---

[12] Libby, op. cit., pp. 10-11.
[13] Civil War Files, Maine State Archives, Augusta.

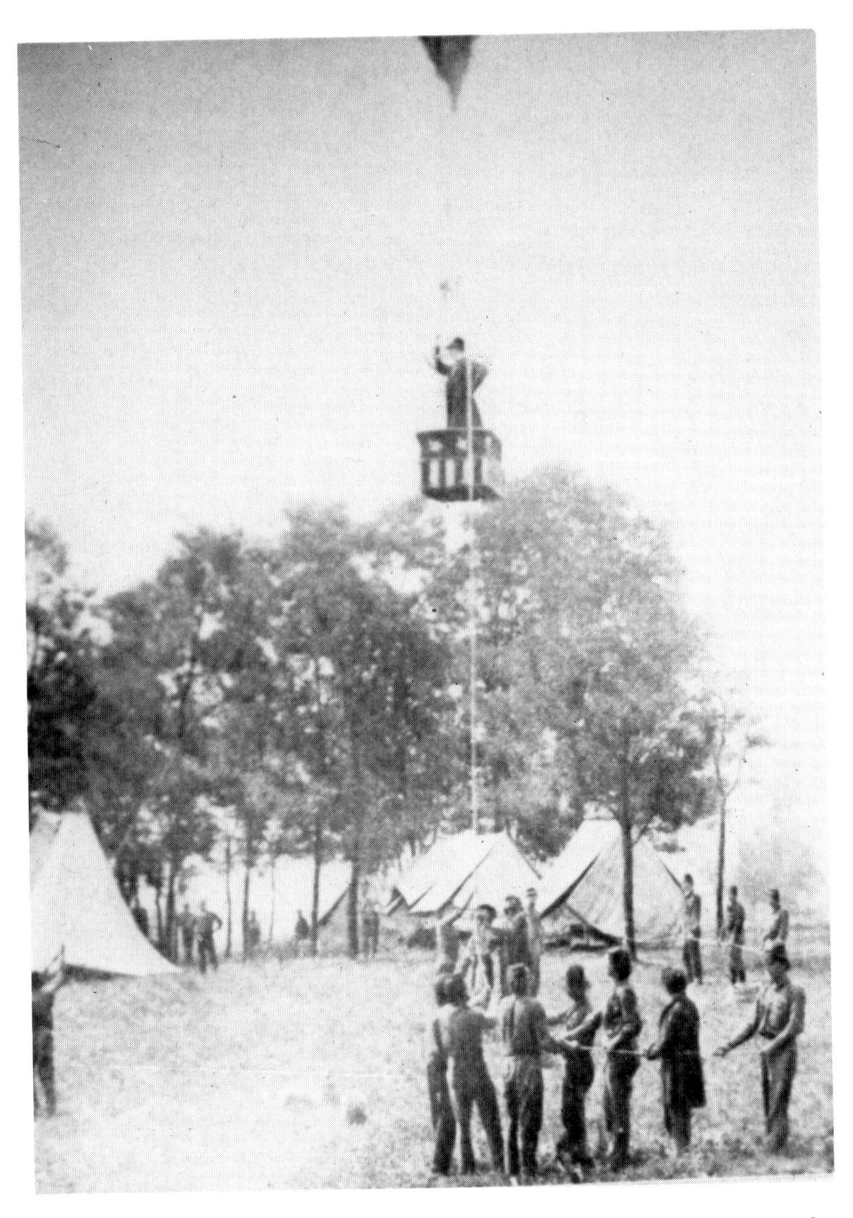

Photo showing, it is assumed, members of the 4th Maine Infantry operating one of Lowes balloons. (Brady Photo)

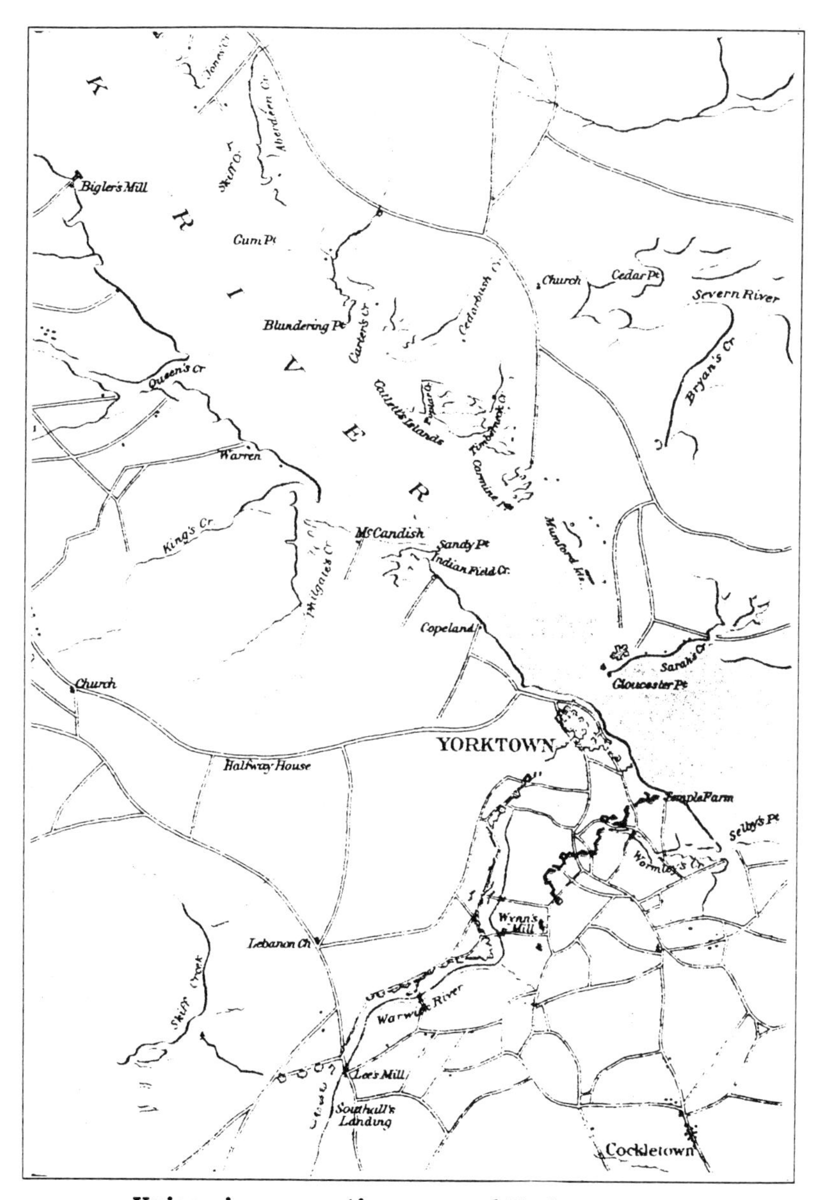

Union siege operations around Yorktown.

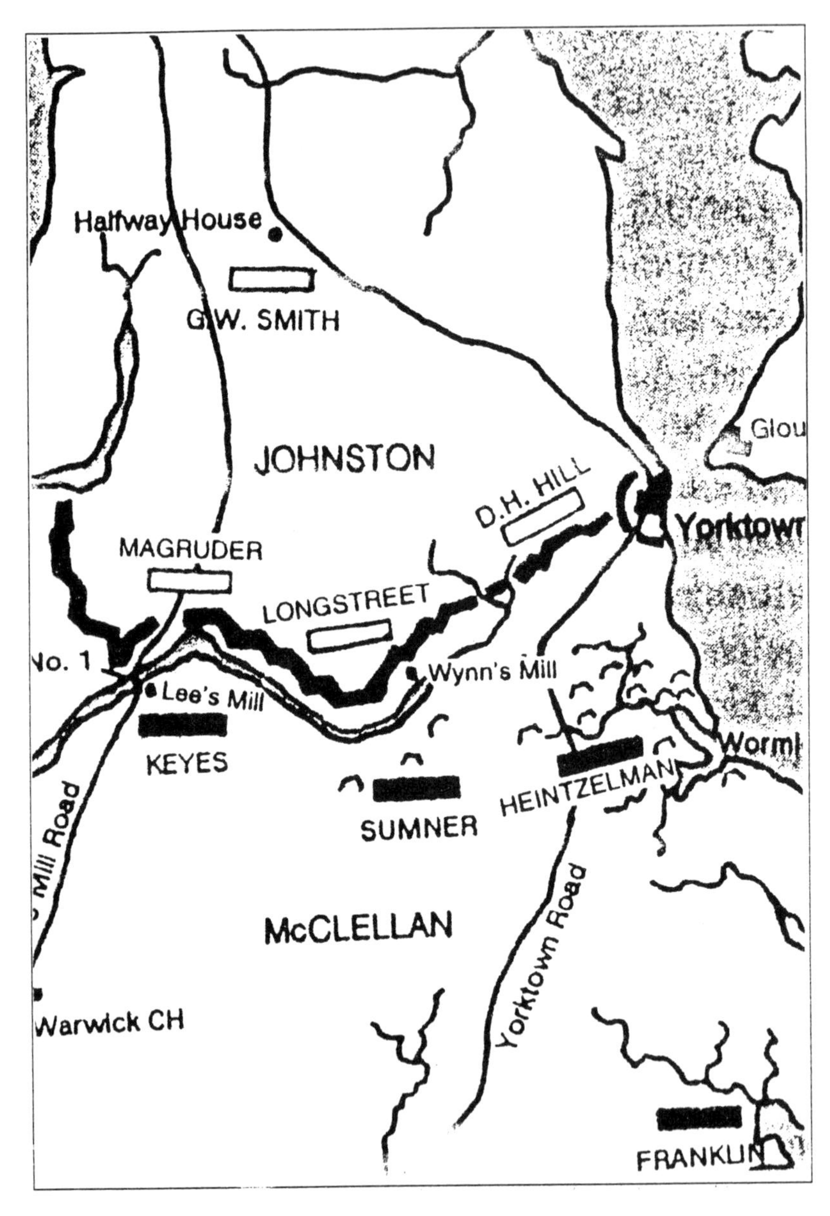

Union and Confederate troop positions at Yorktown.

Once again photo showing members of the 4th Maine Infantry operating one of Lowes balloons. (Brady Photo)

after dark to serve as support. The New York men were not informed that the 4th Maine was entrenched directly in front of them. Being somewhat nervous about their new surroundings, "the Irish regiment began to fire on the troops in their front, not knowing who was there". The Maine regiment hunkered down and resisted the temptation to return fire. The situation was finally resolved, and "As good luck - or bad aim - would have it, not a single man of our force was even scratched."[14]

During the period of the siege of Yorktown the 4th had several visits from some of the state's more prominent citizens. Elijah Walker relates the story of the visit of John Hodsdon, Maine's Adjutant General, to the regiment in late April. General Berry had planned to show their guest the Union lines and then visit the camps of some of the state's other regiments. "While eating dinner and talking of the sights that were to be seen and the Maine soldiers they were to meet, the enemy passed one of their compliments, in the shape of a hundred pound shell, which came crashing through the branches of the trees and exploded within seventy-five feet of where we were sitting. Such little episodes had been far from rare during the last two weeks and we were not disturbed, but the officer from Maine suddenly turned pale, became nervous and looking at the general and myself inquired what it meant. "Oh, that is but a common occurrence," said the general. As soon as the visitor had recovered and became able to talk he said his business at home was of so much importance that he must leave for Fortress Monroe in order to take the boat for Washington that evening. No words from General Berry could persuade him to remain to call on his Maine acquaintances. I never heard that he made the army a second visit."[15]

As mentioned earlier, some of the men in the 4th had become extensively involved with Lowe's Balloon Corps. The project drew the attention of both armies. By the first part of April Professor Lowe was actually operating two balloons, the Intrepid and Constitution. Both, as it would happen, were kept aloft and in flying condition mainly through the efforts of Rockland native Lieutenant Arthur Libby and twenty-eight other 4th Maine boys under his command.[16]

Many Union generals saw great value in Lowe's enterprise and enthusiastically sought out the opportunity to ascend with Professor

---

[14] Libby, op. cit., pp. 13-14.
[15] Walker, op. cit. pp. 20-21.
[16] Ibid. p. 20.

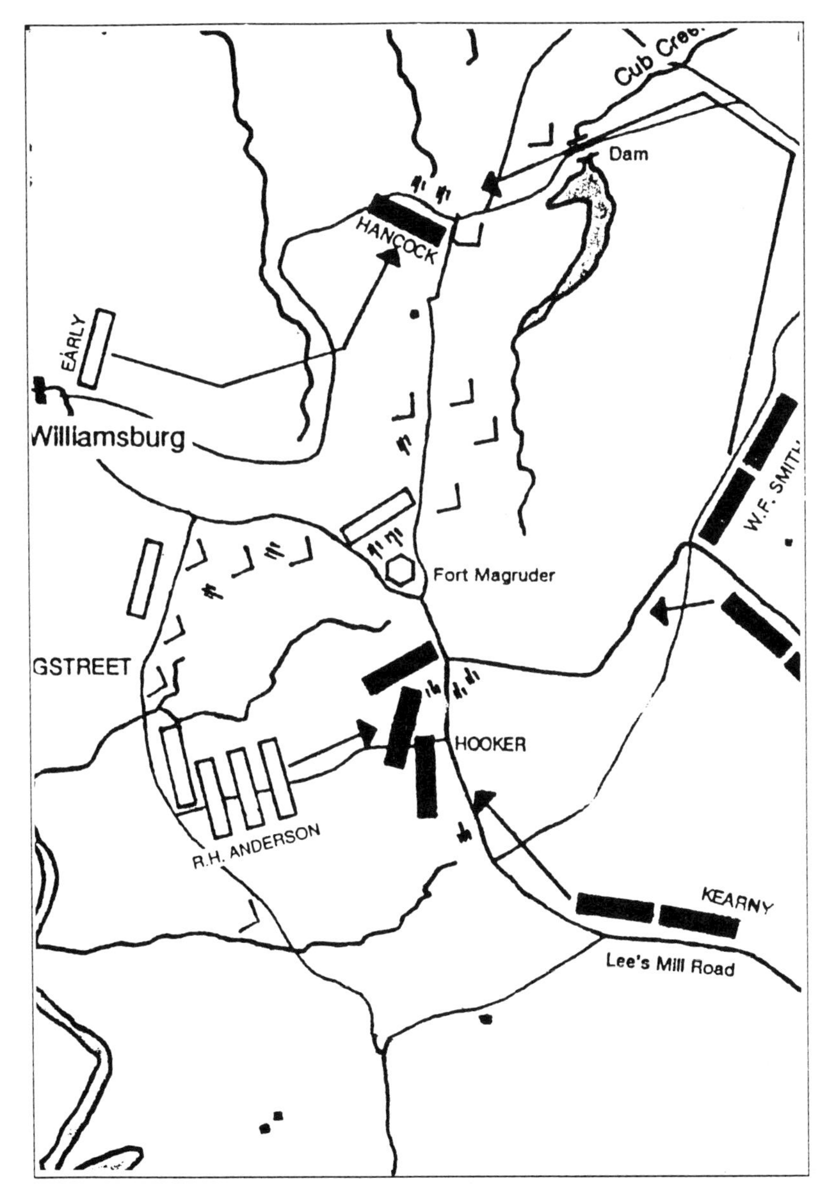

First day of fighting at Williamsburg.

Lowe to observe both troop movements and troop strengths. On April 11, one of McClellan's favorite generals, Fitz John Porter, made an ascension all by himself in the Intrepid. Libby's men, who were in charge of the operation, somehow failed to make sure that the balloon was securely moored. A sudden strong gust of wind caused the airship to break free and Porter was quickly carried out over enemy lines. Adrift in the balloon, Porter was an easy target to enemy artillery and sharpshooters. Fortunately for Porter, though, the wind changed directions and he was pushed back into friendly territory. Porter acted quickly and was able to reach the gas valve and lower both himself, and the airship, safely back to earth. Even professor Lowe admitted that a considerable amount of time passed before any other Union generals took the opportunity to go up with him.[17]

Early on the morning of May 4th George McClellan sent a five word telegram to Secretary of War Edwin Stanton. It stated simply that "Yorktown is in our possession." A short time after he followed this up with the additional declaration that Union forces "have the enemy's heavy guns ammunition camp equipage etc. - hold the entire line of his works which the Engineers report as being very strong. I have thrown all my cavalry and horse artillery in pursuit, supported by infantry."[18]

The 40th New York was sent to take possession of the city. Several of the men in this regiment fell victim to one of the first known uses of land mines, or what were known in the Civil War as torpedoes. Doctor Libby, who had been mustered in as regimental surgeon officially on April 30th, himself had a close call with one of these devices. "I myself, while riding into Yorktown, escaped being blown up by one of those buried torpedoes through the friendly aid of a soldier who having discovered it caught my horse and turned it to one side in the nick of time."[19]

When the Confederates evacuated Yorktown on May 4th, the 4th Maine left their camps that very afternoon in hot pursuit. They followed closely on Magruder's heels, all the way to Williamsburg. When the regiment was within three miles of the Williamsburg battlefield they were ordered to lighten their loads and prepare for the coming fight. The regiment was moved to a place on the extreme left of the line. Here they

---

[17] Sears, To the Gates of Richmond, p. 54.
[18] McClellan, The Civil War Papers of George McClellan, p. 253.
[19] Libby, op. cit., p. 16.

paused as the rebels advanced. The Maine soldiers waited for over an hour in a heavy downpour to be committed to the battle. By the time they were moved to the front, however, the Confederates had called off their attack.[20]

Only the 4th Maine's mutineers, now in the 38th New York, would see action in this fight. For the New York Regiment, overall, this would be their first action. Many of the members of the unit had been frightened about how they would act under fire. The presence of the 4th's several veterans, and the example of their famous leader, General Kearny, certainly did them no harm. Later that very day, Kearny would say to Heintzelman, "General, I can make men follow me to Hell." By the time Kearny would arrive there, however, the path would already be well trampled by these fighting men from Maine.[21]

McClellan's army camped for the night, and early next morning, about five A. M., the 3rd and 4th were ordered out of the woods to form a skirmish line opposite Fort Magruder. Walker recalled that "we were soon on the move, my orders being to go out into the open field. We advanced to the edge of the woods, whence we could see the enemy's cavalry leaving the fort...Generals Heintzelman, Kearney, Jameson and Berry appeared in the field quite a distance to our left. I called to General Berry and asked if I should advance. He replied: 'Yes! Forward Fourth Maine!'"

The 3rd Maine was to act as a reserve as the 4th was ordered to assault the fortification. Walker gave the order. "Charge!" The object of their attack was about a quarter of a mile distant. "Without an alignment every man tried to be the first there." The "Limerock Regiment" climbed the walls of the fortification and planted their colors on the parapets without firing a gun. "The enemy's cavalry made their exit from the fort as we entered it, leaving guns, ammunition, banner, and their dead and wounded; and long before our Brigade Commander with the balance of the troops emerged from the woods the flags of the Fourth Maine waved over Fort Magruder. Only three of the rebel wounded and about eight of their dead had been left behind in the stronghold."[22]

When the Maine boys took possession of the fortification they also took a rebel banner. The flag was made of blue silk, and was three feet

---

[20] Whitman, op. cit., p. 91.

[21] Sears, op. cit., p. 77.

[22] Walker, op. cit., p. 21.

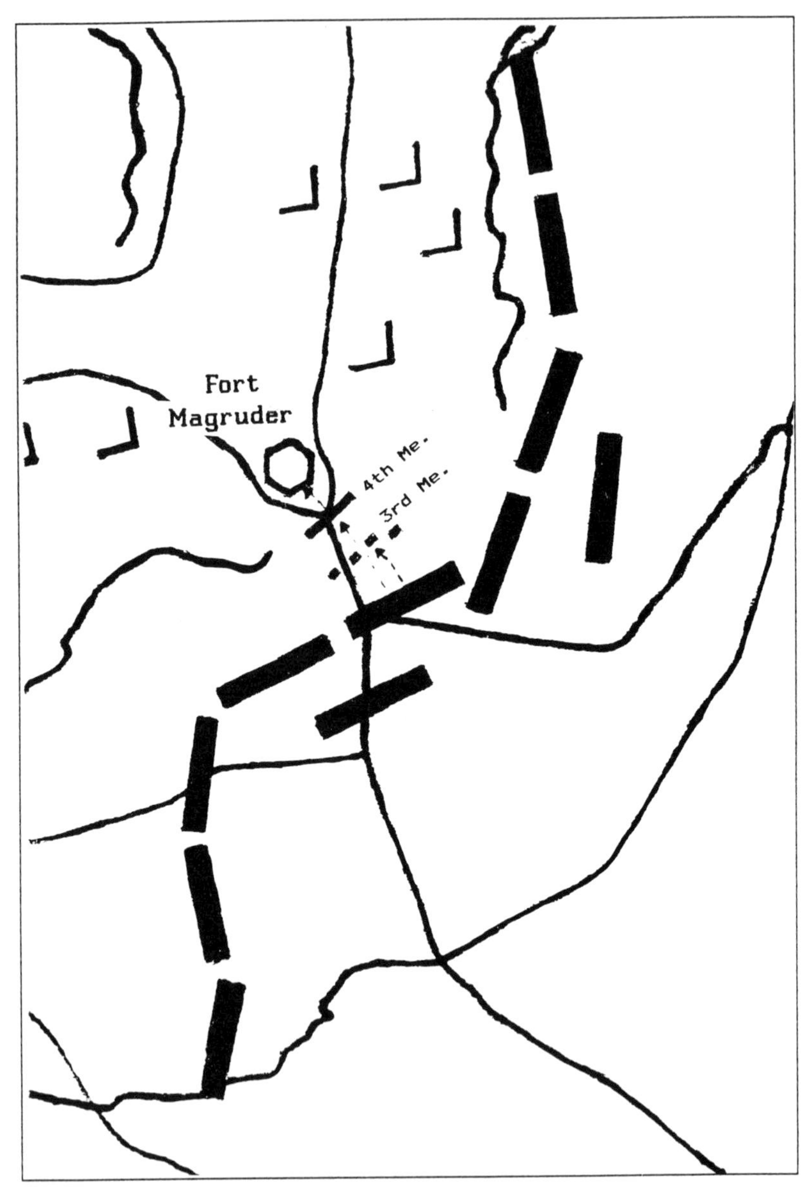

The 3rd Maine acts as skirmishers as the 4th Maine makes a successful solo attack on Fort Magruder.

square. Its borders were embroidered with a fringe of crimson. On one side was a Palmetto tree, encircled by an evil serpent. A crimson belt surrounded this with seven stars upon it and the motto, "Opehusque Parati." In the upper left hand corner was a white crescent. On the reverse of the flag was a laurel wreath, within which was stated:

Pickens Sentinels
Preserve
Southern Institutions
or
Perish With Them
January 10, 1861

Overall, the fighting at Williamsburg had been quite sharp. For the North, it was an impressive victory. For the South, Williamsburg was only a holding action, allowing the main body of rebel troops to escape up the Peninsula to the safety of the Richmond defenses. Johnston lost about 1,700 men, McClellan, 2,200.[23] The 4th Maine had been fortunate as they avoided any injury or loss of life. The 38th New York, however, had been heavily involved in the first day's fighting and many of its Maine natives had fallen.

McClellan's army now began a slow approach on Richmond. The rain was nearly constant, and with the movement of men, armaments, and supply wagons, the roads became impassable. If a unit was able to move two miles in a day, it was only through extraordinary effort that it was accomplished. Every time the troops stopped, they dug themselves in. McClellan, constantly believing that he was outnumbered, moved slowly and cautiously.

On May 29th, the 4th Maine moved to within a short distance of a place on the outskirts of Richmond called Seven Pines. "The Third Corps, now composed of three divisions commanded by Generals Kearny, Hooker, and Casey, was seperated from the other Corps by the river, and it was wise on the part of our Corps commander to move cautiously."[24] The rain was falling heavily, and, as a result, all of the rivers had flooded over their banks. The Chickahominy had risen so high that most of the bridges were washed out, effectively isolating two

---

[23] Wheeler, Sword Over Richmond, p. 160.
[24] Walker, op. cit., p. 23.

Union Corps from the rest of the army. Johnston, being an opportunist, took this occasion to go on the offensive.[25]

At this moment Colonel Walker was serving as division officer of the day. He later recalled that his "principal and most important duty was to look after the outpost picket line, which was nearly two miles to our front, while the Third Division was far in our advance and but a short distance from their outpost videttes." About two in the afternoon, while Walker was returning from camp to the outposts, he ran into General Kearny who inquired if Walker was returning to the outposts. When Walker replied in the affirmative Kearny replied, "That is right." "I want you to remain there all night. See that the men keep a sharp lookout for the enemy; we shall be attacked soon. I have been to the front and our men are all right. Don't let us be surprised. That d----d fool of a Casey is so near his picket line, and his men are lying about so carelessly, he will be surprised. The enemy will be upon him before he knows it."[26]

The Battle of Fair Oaks was for the Confederates," a phenomenally mismanaged battle" according to Edward P.Alexander, Johnston's chief of ordnance.[27] An attack that had been planned for May 31st, at dawn, got delayed until two P. M. Assault columns accidentally mingled with each other on the flooded fields and roads. When the attack was finally executed, the Union left flank was driven back more than a mile. General Keyes' two divisions, under Couch and Casey, were the object of the attack. Greatly outnumbered, they were unable to slow the rebel assault, but were not able to stem it.

General Sumner's II Corps had been pushed up to the bridges over the flooded Chickahominy. Sedgwick's division had gathered at Grapevine bridge, a structure that was twisting and turning in the freshet and threatening to float downstream. Somehow these troops were able to cross, the bridges probably being held in place by the weight of the soldiers themselves. The first of these troops did not arrive on the battlefield until almost 5:30 P. M. The appearance of these troops was effected in the nick of time, saving McClellan from an embarrassing defeat.[28]

---

[25] Whitman, op. cit., p. 92.
[26] Walker, op. cit. p. 23.
[27] McPherson, op. cit., pp. 461-462.
[28] Sears, op. cit., pp. 135-136.

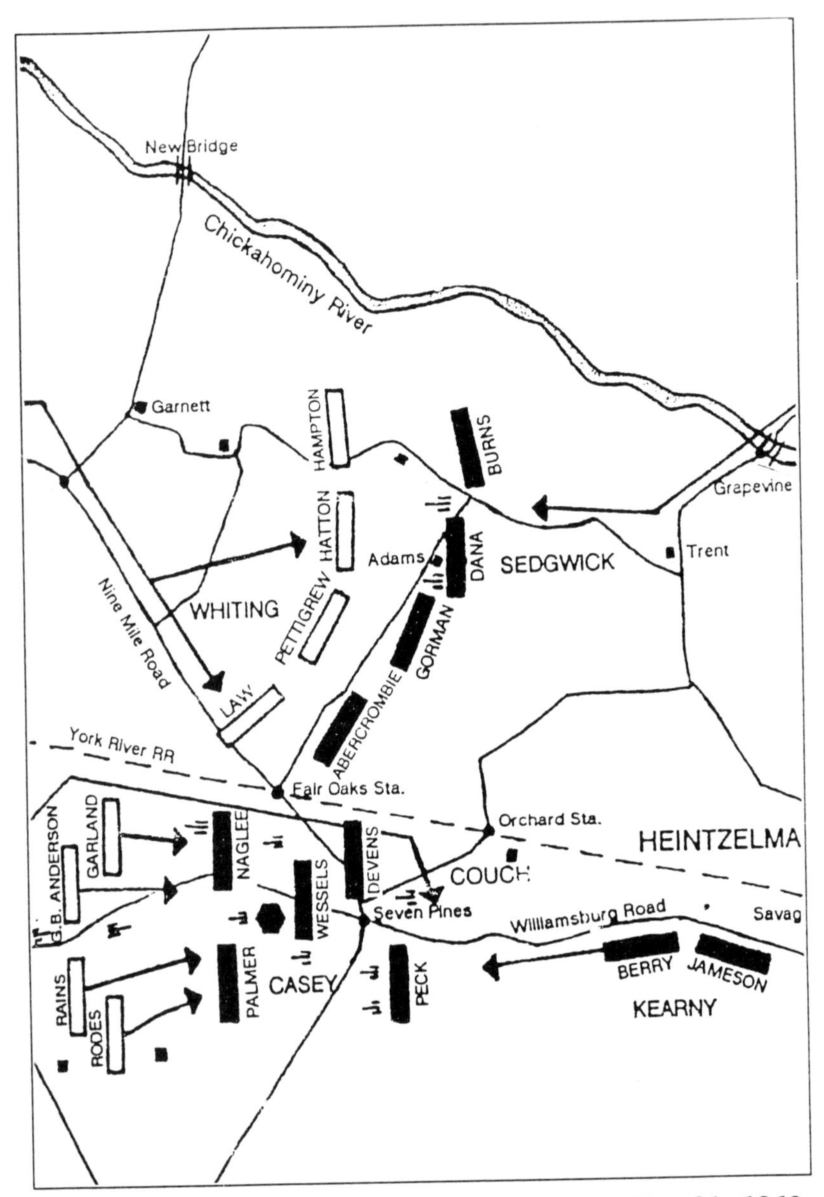

The fighting at Fair Oakes, or Seven Pines, on May 31, 1862. Union forces held the line.

David Birney's second brigade, numbering some thirteen hundred effectives, was summoned to the front at about three P. M. In less than ten minutes the men were on the march. The 4th Maine led off the procession, with the 40th New York, 3rd Maine, and 38th New York following, in that order. Their objective was to be a railroad grade, but before they could reach it, General Kearny rode up and ordered them back to the Williamsburg Road to dig rifle pits that would serve as a second line of defense.[29]

Back at the Williamsburg Road the 40th New York was ordered to occupy the newly constructed defenses. The 3rd Maine and 38th New York were directed to send a number of men out to act as sharpshooters. The soldiers stationed themselves in, and around, a home owned by a Miss Susan Allen. Later this residence would be used as a division hospital. The 4th Maine was ordered to the right of the entrenchments occupied by the 40th New York and formed a line of battle in the woods.[30]

In the official records, while chronicling the activities of his regiment, Colonel Walker states: "While my regiment was advancing in line of battle in the belt of woods occupied by Miss Susan Allen as her residence, I ordered that ten men (one from each company) should proceed some distance to the front to act as scouts." Lieutenant Moses Ford of Company F took a prisoner on his own. As the advance continued the Maine boys found a man "with a gun in one hand and a white handkerchief on a stick in the other, he ordered him to lay down his gun which the man did." The Confederate prisoner turned out to be Colonel Breton of the 6th South Carolina infantry regiment. The scouts also captured a rebel provost guard, consisting of five soldiers, who had been detailed to escort a prisoner back behind the lines. In capturing the rebel detachment they freed the captured Captain John D. McFarland of the 13th Pennsylvania Infantry.[31]

At about 4:30 P. M. Kearny ordered Birney to bring up the 3rd Maine and 38th New York and form them in column of companies along the railroad. General Casey's men had been overrun and it was believed that Kearny's boys were the only hope that the Union army had of plugging the hole. As Casey's men began to retreat through the lines

---

[29] Series I, Vol XI, Part I, Official Records, pp. 851-855.
[30] Ibid.
[31] Ibid., pp. 858-859.

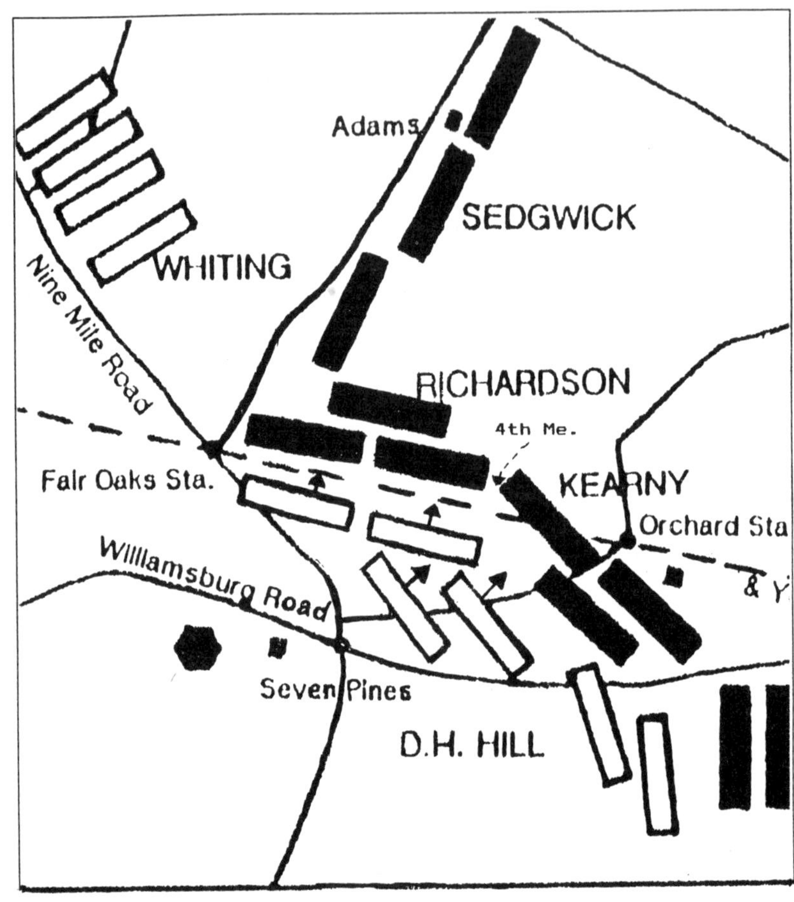

Fighting at Fair Oakes on June 1st. The 4th Maine held the right of Kearny's line near the railroad as shown.

Birney tried, unsuccessfully, to rally them. Fearful that his two regiments might not hold, he ordered the 40th New York and 4th Maine up to reinforce the line. The mobs of routed Union soldiers were so thick that the two regiments had to fix bayonets in order to advance. As the rebels closed in, the fighting became heavy on the brigade's left flank.

Shortly after the shooting began one of Kearny's aides rode up and ordered that Birney return his brigade to the position he had been ordered to hold at three P. M.. Birney then sent a message to Kearny that to obey this order would cause a half mile gap to be created in the line between Sumner's left and Kearny's right. Kearny ordered him to do it anyway. Birney obeyed orders, but before he departed, he sent Major Pitcher with four companies (G, H, I, and K) of the 4th Maine, to the spot where four regiments had once been, and instructed them to hold the position. Meanwhile General Birney rode off ahead of the retreating column to Kearny's tent. Following a brief but heated discussion, Birney was allowed to march his men back to the railroad, a post still considerably in the rear of the 4th Maine's detachment.[32]

About seven A.M. the following morning, June 1st, the Confederates were detected forming on Pitcher's front. General Howard had informed "major Pitcher who had held the advance during the night, with companies G, H, I and K, that he could call in his men and take some rest; that he, Howard, with his brigade, was taking a position in front of the major."[33]

The Captain had proceeded to pull back his pickets and formed his men in rear of a fence that bordered a small "lane a few rods to the left of the railroad, parallel to the rebels." About 7:30 the detachment had just handed out rations and begun to heat coffee, their arms stacked, when Colonel Walker arrived. Walker remembered calling upon "my reserve vocabulary and the men seized their rifles and croched behind a hedge fence not an instant too soon."[34]

Colonel Walker had watched as "the enemy had attacked and driven in the Pennsylvania regiment of General Howard's brigade, on the right and in front of Captain Pitcher's command." He had seen these refugees pass through the ranks of Pitcher's meager detachment "like a flock of sheep with a pack of dogs after them". Close upon their heels came the

---

[32] Ibid. pp, 859-860.
[33] Walker, op. cit., p. 24.
[34] Ibid., p. 861.

pursuing Rebels, firing their weapons and yelling at the top of their lungs all the while.[35]

"The rebels in large numbers came out of the woods within a few rods of us, when a volley from our Austrian rifles put a stop to their further advance." Smoke and lead spewed from their line and cut down the rebs in their tracks. The Confederates were staggered by the blow. The men in the four companies fired better than forty-five rounds apiece. As quickly as it had begun, the assault was broken. As the attackers began to flee the Maine boys jumped over the fence and began a pursuit. At their head was a little known, and never to be heard from again, Belfast man by the name of Private Robert Waterman. The ill-advised counterattack was quickly called off, but not before they had taken more than thirty prisoners.

Walker relates that "in front of where my four left companies fought, thirty-six Confederate dead were buried in one hole, without moving a single body more than ten feet. Our casualties were, Darius Knowles, of Co. I and Agustus Parker of Company F, killed, and seven wounded. We were so fortunate under the circumstances, that I was almost persuaded myself that our mission was to kill, not to be killed; but things changed before the expiration of our service."[36] To their credit, they had been at the right place at the right time, and had, almost by themselves, helped check a major attack. Certainly this was the glory of battle about which Stephen Chapman had spoken of so eloquently.[37]

One of the other casualties of the day had been General David Birney. No, he had not been shot. Rather, he had been arrested by order of General Heintzelman, presumably for the poor handling of his troops during the previous day's fighting. Colonel Hobart Ward was substituted in his stead. A court martial was quickly convened, however, and Birney was directly acquited of all charges and returned to brigade command.

The rebel colonel, who had fallen into the hands of the regiment's skirmishers, was questioned to see if any vital information could be obtained from him. One of the questions asked of him was what the rebels thought of McClellan. The response was not surprising. The colonel stated that they rather liked him, "because he always gives them

---

[35] Walker, op. cit., p. 24.
[36] Ibid.
[37] Whitman, op. cit., p. 93.

plenty of time." The Colonel's statement perfectly characterizes the remainder of the Peninsular Campaign.

Dr. Libby recorded in his diary that General Casey's division had been in the front at the time of the attack on the 30th. It had taken the full brunt of the assault. The fact that they had been able to hold out at all is particularly remarkable, especially in light of the information which Dr. Libby reveals. "Gen. Casey spent last night in our camp. He is an old man that has been stationed at Washington to receive all the raw troops that arrived and form them into brigade after drilling them...Thus the green men in the army were in the front line, which accounts for the way they were surprised in this battle of yesterday."[38]

The regiment returned to the camp that they had occupied before the engagement. During the continuing operations of McClellan's army in front of Richmond they remained on picket duty and helped in the construction of entrenchments. The process was continual as the army inched itself ever closer to Richmond.[39]

During the days prior to the Battle at Fair Oaks, disease had once again raised its ugly head. On average in 1862 a Union soldier was sick about three and a half times a year. The medical director for the Army of the Potomac, Charles Tripler, had decided not to send the majority of the sick back to Washington. Instead, he let these men travel with the army. As a result, the army field medical facilities were already filled to near capacity at the time of the fighting at Fair Oaks. The weaknesses of this arrangement struck home dramatically when thirty-six hundred wounded soldiers were added to the already overburdened hospital system.[40]

Fortunately for the soldiers, the women of the U. S. Sanitary Commission were on the scene to help. These volunteers, which included women from the mid-coast region of Maine, turned out to be the salvation of the Army of the Potomac. As the injured were passed along, many untreated, from hospital camp to hospital camp, the trains eventually wound their way along the rough and rutted tracks to the waiting hospital ships at White House. These men were carried directly on board and attended to immediately by the volunteer nurses and

[38] Libby, op. cit., pp. 21-22.
[39] Whitman, op. cit., p. 93.
[40] Charles Tripler was relieved of his responsibilities shortly after the Peninsula ampaign.

surgeons. The men were washed, their wounds dressed, and their appetites satisfied.[41]

On June 15th, Colonel Walker was again in command of the outpost with the 4th stretched along the outer line of the division's defenses. Walker had "the Thirty-Seventh New York as a reserve, and twenty-five cavalry under the command of a Lieutenant. I was attacked by a large force, which broke through my line, but we drove them back, re-established our line and captured five of the invaders. I had two men wounded, and the lieutenant in command of the cavalry had his horse shot from under him and was himself slightly wounded."[42]

With the passage of command of the Confederate Army to Robert E. Lee, things were about to change. Lee had decided that he must go on the offensive. To do so without some knowledge of the disposition of the Union troops would, however, court disaster. Lee immediately ordered J.E.B. Stuart to select twelve hundred troopers and to undertake a raid to explore around the right flank of McClellan's army. Stuart not only explored the right flank, but also passed completely around the Union army without a casualty. The information that he brought back to Lee would form the basis for the plan of attack in the Seven Days Battles.[43]

On June 23rd, Lee decided to attack McClellan's right flank. Jackson's 18,000 troops were key to the success of the overall campaign. McClellan had anticipated that Stonewall would be called out of the Valley to support Lee in front of Richmond and was not at all surprised to hear of his arrival.[44]

On the morning of June 25th, Heintzelman's corps began their attack on Old Tavern. The brigade, which included the 3rd and 4th Maine, was called out in support of the attack. Though Heintzelman succeeded in reaching his objectives, this would be the only venture undertaken in an attempt to take Richmond. The 4th would skirmish with the rebel army this day, and though they held a difficult position, suffered no injury or loss of life. Little did they know that all that stood between them and the city was 25,000 troops under the command of Generals Magruder and Huger. Basically, all they had to do was walk into Richmond.[45]

---

[41] Sears, op. cit., pp. 147-148.
[42] Walker, op. cit., p. 24.
[43] Ibid., pp. 168-169.
[44] Ibid., pp. 181-182.
[45] Wheeler, op. cit., p. 300.

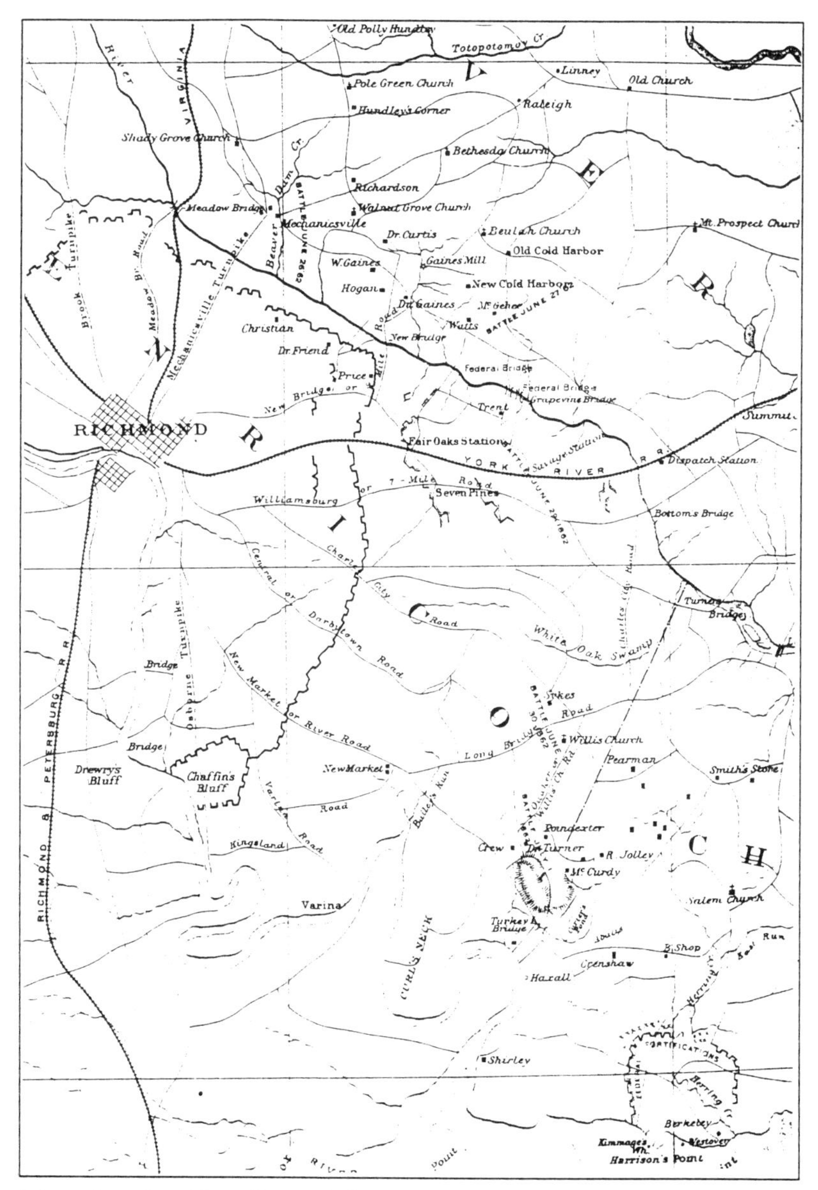

Map showing the sites of the Seven Day's Battles and the route of the Union retreat to Harrison's Point.

Birney speaks "of the high state of discipline evinced by the Fourth Maine and Fortieth New York. They were steady and united." The 3rd Maine, however, had experienced a crisis in command. Lieutenant-Colonel C. A. L. Sampson, who had been in charge of the regiment, had apparently left his post. Though he returned next morning, Brigidier General Birney had felt compelled to place him under arrest.[46]

Meanwhile, Lee marched north and east, around the Union right to a position near Mechanicsville. Here Porter had posted some skirmishers in front of the main body of troops who were in prepared positions at Beaver Dam Creek. Troops under Longstreet and the two Hills lingered all morning for Jackson to attack the Union rear. Tired of waiting, A. P. Hill decided to attack in the hope that Jackson would soon join in. He never did. When the fighting ended 1500 Confederates were dead or wounded. Porter had lost about 360 in this the first of the Seven Day's Battles. This engagement would come to be known as the Battle of Mechanicsville, or Beaver Dam Creek.[47]

Though McClellan's victory had been complete on the 26th, he refrained from going on the offensive. Instead he began to implement his plan of retreat back to the James River and Harrison's Landing. At 3 A.M. Porter was ordered to retreat from his strong position at Beaver Dam Creek, down the Chickahominy to Gaines' Mill. Here he would set up a new line of defenses, preparing once again to meet an expected assult.[48]

The attack that Porter had anticipated on the 27th did not actually begin until two P.M. Once again Jackson was to be a key element in the Confederate assault, but when the shooting began he was not there. Lee's plan had called upon Longstreet to make a feint on the Union left. This he would do. Only later would he turn this bluff into a general assault. The fighting would be extremely intense, with Jackson, half heartedly, joining into the fray about seven P.M. to make the attack general.[49]

Porter's 35,000 troops held 60,000 rebels in check all day. Still, by day's end, the Confederates were able to force a breakthrough in the Union lines. Only by the gallant efforts of rapidly advancing reinforcements was the Union army prevented from being completely

---

[46] Official Records, op. cit., pp. 180-181.
[47] Wheeler, op. cit. p. 300.
[48] Ibid., 302.
[49] Ibid., p. 309.

routed. The North lost 6,800 men, the South 9,000, nearly as many as she had lost in two days of fighting at Shiloh. The battle had lasted just six and a half hours.[50]

During the fighting at Gaines' Mill the 4th Maine had been detached to Jordan's (Jourdan's) Ford, near White Oak Swamp, to build a bridge to assist in the retreat of the army. Birney soon arrived with the rest of the brigade and the men busied themselves in throwing up a barricade. General Kearny appeared next, surveyed the position, and ordered Birney to march south and cross by the lower ford. The 4th was left behind to guard the crossing.[51]

On the 29th, General Kearny asked Walker to examine Fisher's Ford and determine how long it would take to prepare for a crossing there. Walker went and examined the ford and relayed a message to the general that it would take about three hours to get it ready for the passage of infantry. Kearny approved the operation and Walker proceeded to the site with about one-third of his command. Lieutenant-colonel Carver was given command of the detachment and the project.

Upon his return to Jordan's Ford Walker received an inquiry from General Berry as to where the best spot would be for him to cross his brigade. Walker told Berry that Fisher's Ford would be the best, a suggestion that was followed by Berry. "The other two brigades crossed at Jordan's Ford, by means of the bridge we had built, but met the enemy in force and were obliged to re-cross and find a passage several miles down the swamp where our teams were crossing."

"Walker later recalled that "at the Ford some misunderstanding arose between General Kearny and myself, which resulted in his placing me under arrest. He then rode to the front, saw the condition of affairs, returned, came up to me, and extending his only hand acknowledged himself in error and asked me again to take command of my regiment. From that moment, to his death, he was one of my warmest friends. After that incident, had anyone intimated the Fourth Maine was inferior to any regiment in the Corps, what the boys were wont to term 'Kearney's Blessing' would have been vehemently bestowed upon the presumptuous individual."[52]

---

[50] McPherson, op. cit., p. 466.
[51] Official Records, op. cit., p. 181.
[52] Walker, op. cit., p. 26.

Shortly after the departure of the brigade, rebel skirmishers began to probe out the position taken by the Limerock regiment. When Confederate artillery began to appear the 4th fell back across the bridge, setting fire to it as they went. The regiment bivouacked for the night a few rods down the road, concealed as much as possible by the trees. Nervous sentries were posted to watch for the enemy's movements during the night.

Dr. Libby, speaking of the action at Jordan's Ford, states that the 4th was the last unit to cross the bridge. Shortly after, the regiment came to a halt for a brief repose. He goes on to say, "I got some sleep under my ambulance on a landbank. The whole army is hurrying - not towards Richmond - but toward the James. The men are disheartened, feeling that an opportunity to take Richmond had been negligently or stupidly let slip."[53]

As June 30th dawned, bright and clear, the 4th Maine rejoined its brigade on its march to Charles City Cross Roads. Here the regiment was again given responsibility for holding a rear guard position against the Confederate advance. The men became engaged about noon in what would come to be known as the Battle of Glendale.

At Glendale, Lee had planned a three pronged attack on McClellan, who had deployed three corps on a three mile front. Once more Jackson was an integral part of the overall assault, and, once again, he did not make it to the main battle. Only the Confederate right went into action this day. Though Robinson's brigade of Kearny's division would be impacted by Longstreet's assault, Birney, with the 4th Maine in tow, would see very little action. The Confederates would achieve a breakthrough in the Union center, but this would be quickly patched up by elements of the II Corps.[54]

As recollected by Elijah Walker, the 4th Maine was sent to the front to act as a skirmish line. "With Gen. Berry I spent most of the first part of the day examining the grounds, blocking the roads to prevent the approach of artillery, etc. About 1:30 P.M. we discovered a road some distance to the left of out line as then formed. 'This is the place they will endeavor to get through,' said Gen. Berry, 'I will have my brigade and Thompson's battery here at once.' "Gen. Berry, with his brigade and the

---

[53] Libby, op. cit., p. 25-26.
[54] Sears, op. cit., p. 302.

battery, moved to the spot he had indicated, arriving in time to check the enemy's advance, which was in strong force."[55]

It was about 3:30 P. M. when the rebs made their attack down the Charles City Road on Slocum's left and Berry's front. By 5:30 P. M. McCall had also become involved. As the Confederates began to take advantage of the crack in the center of the Union line, General Hooker began to move his division to the right. This sudden movement, unexpected by the enemy, caused the Confederate attack to become momentarily stalled.[56]

Walker remembered that he and his men were on "the right of Birney's brigade and joined the left of Berry's brigade and had an exceptionally good chance to see the attack made by Magruder's troops. Of all the fighting I ever witnessed this was about the most desperate. The enemy hurled their legions upon that small brigade and Thompson's battery, taking two of the latter's guns. They had not gone far with them, however, when a regiment led by Lieutenant Greenhalgh retook them and put them in place. The second charge of the rebel hosts resulted in the capture of one gun, but the captors were quickly put to flight by a regiment of Michigan men, and the gun was returned to its position."

"Dead and dying Confederates lay in piles within a few feet of Thompson's brass Napoleon guns. Gen. Berry was in the thickest of the fray, directing every move with coolness and judgment. Gens Heintzelman and Kearney arrived soon after the contest commenced. Whatever credit may be due elsewhere, it is undeniable that the hardest fighting in that particular locality was done by Berry's brigade and Thompson's battery."[57]

Finally, Kearny's division was attacked on its left flank at about four P. M. The rebel forces attacked in a column, "about 200 paces wide ... with a determination and vigor and in such masses as I had never witnessed." The assault was repulsed by rapid, and heavy, volleys from Kearny's troops, and by a desperate charge made by the 63rd Pennsylvania Infantry and a small number of men from the 37th New York Volunteers. The slaughter was appalling.

The brigade "held a long line some two miles in extent, connecting with Slocum's Division." Most of the time the 4th, along with the rest of

---

[55] Walker, op. cit. p. 27.
[56] Official records, op. cit., p. 182.
[57] Walker, op. cit., p. 27.

the brigade, were lightly involved in skirmishing with the enemy, even though the battle itself raged fiercely all about them. About eleven that evening General Birney was ordered to withdraw his men to a position along the James River. This he did "within 100 yards of the enemy's pickets, in such a long line and dark night through a dense woods and tangled copse, was no light undertaking."[58] The Maine men remained in their positions until about two A.M. and then followed acting, once again, as a rear guard in the retreat of the brigade. The regiment's losses in the fight were very minor.

While this was taking place all was being prepared for the grand finale on a elevation just to the south. McClellan's army had moved to a strongly defended position at a place called Malvern Hill. Here Union troops were dug in on an elevated ridge with artillery placed such that it swept every inch of the ground before them. The Maine regiment was assigned the task of providing support to a battery of guns. Shortly after their arrival a major artillery duel erupted. Union gunboats along the James River joined in with their own deadly song.[59]

Jackson was given the left, Magruder and Huger the right. Longstreet and A. P. Hill acted as the reserve. Lee believed that this attack would be his last chance to shatter the Northern army. Further, he believed that his offensive would be successful because McClellan's army had become demoralized. The assault began late in the afternoon and was nothing short of murder. The repeated attacks staggered Lee's army, leaving him dangerously vulnerable for a counterattack which, of course, never materialized.[60]

Early on the morning of July 1st, Birney marched his men to Turkey Island Bend on the James River. Upon his arrival he received orders to immediately rejoin with Heintzelman now at Malvern Hill. The men marched off "in good order, full ranks, and determined spirit" and arrived in the midst of a "furious cannonade". Walker remembered that "soon after arriving on the hill a shell burst in my lines killing Serg. H. U. Cowing, and as I then supposed mortally wounding Charles F. Wood. The brigade was immediately ordered to entrench.[61]

---

[58] Ibid.
[59] Whitman, op. cit., p. 94.
[60] Ibid.
[61] Walker, op. cit., p. 27.

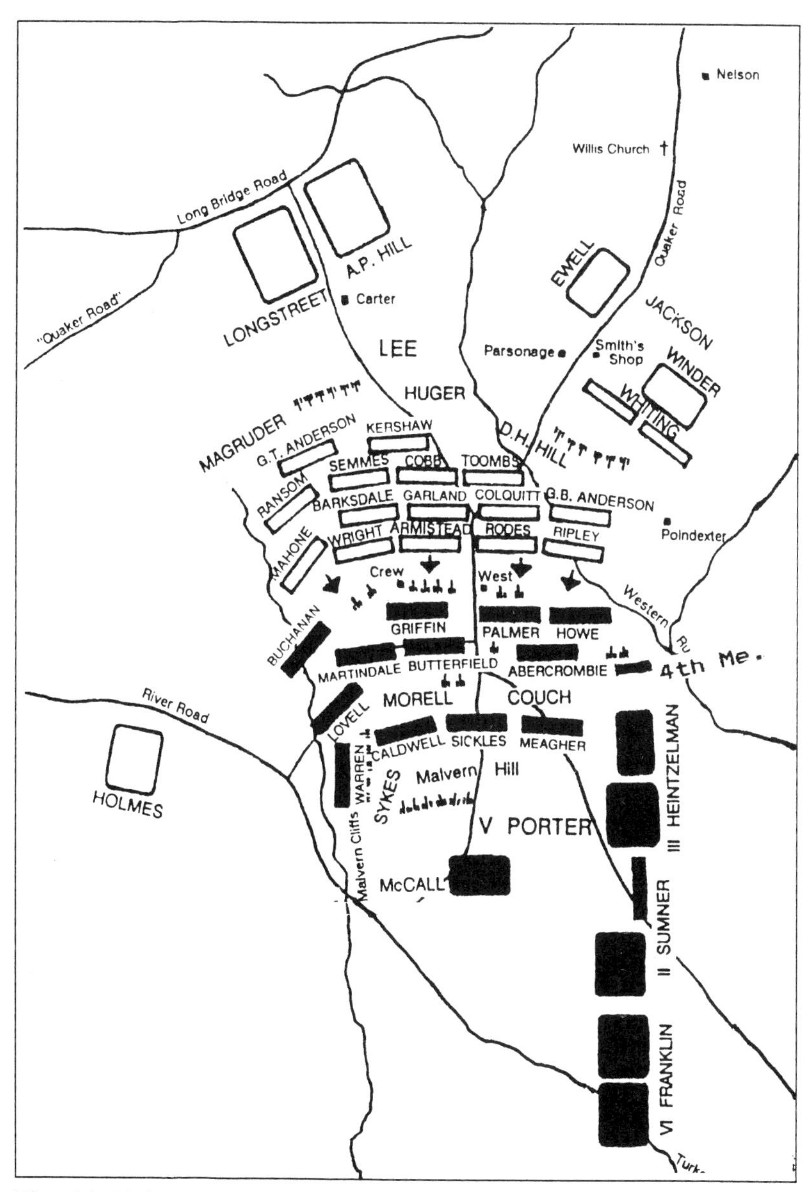

The 4th Maine provided battery support on the right of the line at the Battle of Malvern Hill.

About 3:30 the rebel attack began to close in on General Couch's center and Kearny's left. The 4th Maine and four companies belonging to the 3rd were sent to occupy a "wooded ravine in front of Kearny's line". When Couch was in danger of being overrun General Birney relates the story of an "unexpected and furious onslaught of the enemy, in which "that portion of my command gallantly aided him (Couch) in driving the enemy back".

As some of Jackson's men had advanced out of the bedimmed woods and swamps they ran into a small, but determined, band of skirmishers under the command of Elijah Walker. The scrappy Maine boys put up "one hell of a defence", enough so that even Stonewall Jackson, in the smoke and fading light, was overheard discouraging his men from carrying through with the attack. The rebs withdrew leaving behind, in that bloody, wooded ravine, the patriarchal heritage of many a Southern family.

In Heintzelman's report of the action of July 1st, he relates that only Maine skirmishers and division artillery were involved in the fight. He goes on to explain that "the Fourth Maine was particularly distinguished for its coolness in holding a ravine and repulsing the enemy's skirmishers." During the night Heintzelman withdrew his corps to "Harrison's Bar" on the James River.

The 4rth Maine Boys had fought, marched, fought and then marched again for two straight days. Walker later related that that he did not "believe that there was the amount of ten hard biscuits eaten by our 750 men" during the entire period. Hunger made the march from Malvern Hill to Harrison's Landing all the more difficult. "After a march of seven or eight miles through a drenching rain, we came upon some wagons loaded with pork and hard tack. I rode in advance of the men, procured an ax, and cutting the hoops from the pork barrels and smashing open the hard tack boxes, the men marched by, helping themselves. No feast of rich and rare viands was ever so thoroughly appreciated as was this hard and homely but welcome fare."[62]

McClellan withdrew his forces as soon as the fighting ended. In the two days of combat the Maine regiment lost but one killed, five wounded, and fourteen missing. Those who were absent were the wounded and sick they had been forced to leave behind due to the rapid

---

[62] Ibid.

movement of the army.[63] In the same period of time the Army of the Potomac lost about 4500 men, Lee lost more than 9000. In the Seven Days Battles the fighting claimed over 36,000 casualties. Though the Confederates had lost all but one battle, they had driven a numerically superior army from the doorsteps of Richmond. The cost of their success was enormous.[64]

On the day that the battle was being fought at Malvern Hill, Dr. Libby had been accompanying the regiment's sick and wounded to the James River. Once they were safe he had immediately attempted to return to the Maine regiment. That evening he had stopped at a residence to get some sleep. About 3 A.M. on the morning of July 2nd, the doctor was awakened by a cavalry man. "I turned out to find that the army had passed and that we were within rebel lines. I had for comfort my hospital steward, Chas. McCobb, the chaplain, Rev. Chase, & Dr. Hildreth, surgeon of the 3d Maine. Our horses were teathered to the fence with saddles and bridals off in charge of a man, who had fallen asleep. We hurredly harnessed our horses and hastened after the army which we soon overtook."[65]

Following the battle at Malvern Hill the Union Army dug in around Harrison's Landing. For the 4th Maine Infantry the remainder of July would pass quietly by. The men spent their time constructing defensive positions against an expected rebel attack that never materialized. Here they also tried to get reprovisioned with tents and other basic equipment by the Army of the Potomac. Unfortunately this effort was not totally successful.

In his journal entry of July 2nd, just prior to his resignation as regimental surgeon, Dr. Libby put things pretty much in perspective. "The rebels are in pursuit. We have reached the landing without much fighting. Here the gunboats are our protectors, and the salvation of this noble army, which, was ready and able too, to go to Richmond one short month ago, if they had had a fit general to lead them forward. This is the prevalent feeling among the men. They have lost confidence in McClellan: he is not as we fondly supposed, a great general."

On the day before the anniversary of this country's own independence, the doctor gives us one last glimpse into the condition of

---

[63] Whitnman, op. cit., p. 95.
[64] McPherson, op. cit., p. 471.
[65] Libby, op. cit., pp. 27-28.

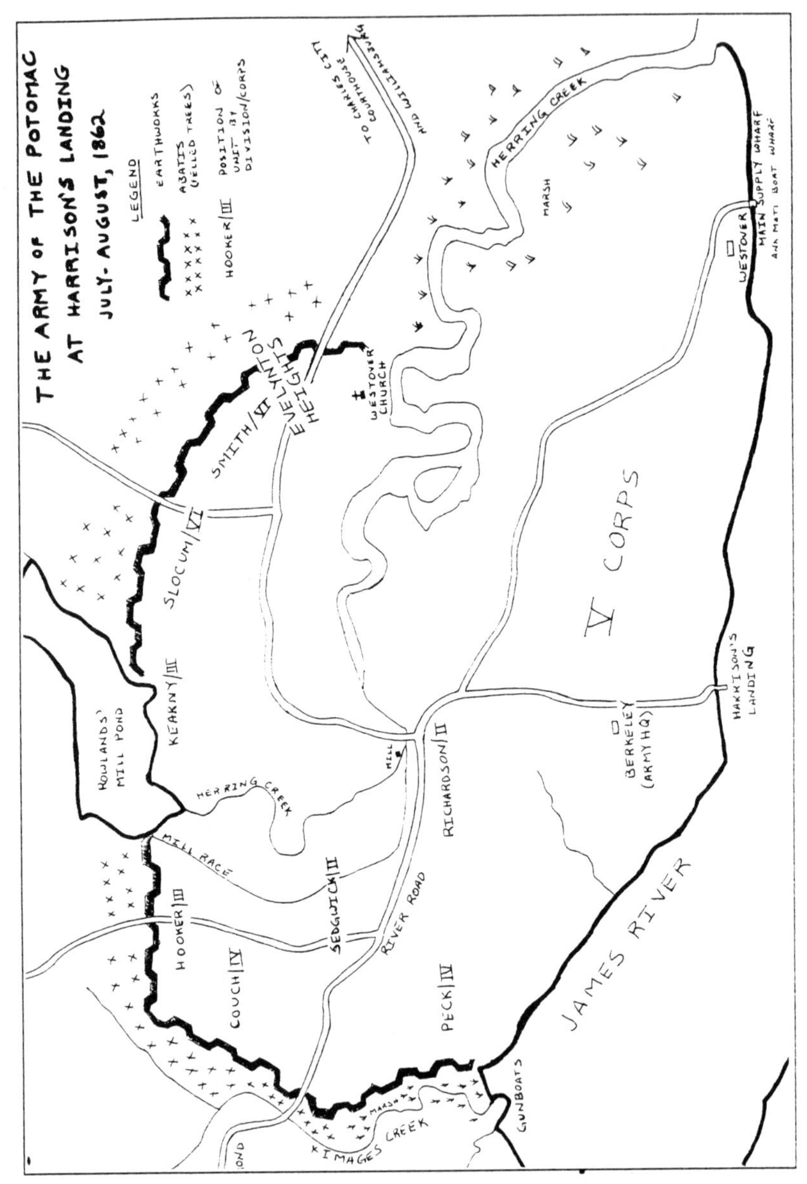

Map showing the position of the Army of the Potomac on the James at Harrison's Landing near Berkeley Plantation.

the 4th Maine. "Our regiment is encamped about a mile and a half from the river. I went to the landing this morning...The sick and wounded were lying on the ground in the mud. Poor fellows, I pitied them and that was all I could do for them. On the way a shell went wizzing over my head and burst in the mud a short distance ahead of me...The army is sick, disheartened, and despondent, for instead of driving the rebels, we have been driven. This is one phase of War, I suppose!"[66]

---

[66] Ibid., pp. 27-29.

Chapter 6

"You Must Never Be Afraid of Anything"

"Harrison's Landing was a fearful place." Elijah Walker later recollected that the men "were shelterless and without clothing, save that which we wore...Our water was obtained from bogs and was the poorest kind of bog water imaginable. Its debilitating effects, in conjunction with those of malaria, were such that I had serious fears of losing all my men by sickness."

As war and disease were wrecking havoc on the officers and enlisted men, so too were they having a decided impact on the regiment's surgical staff. Dr. Hunkins was, as has been previously related, captured at the first battle of Bull Run. The assistant surgeon, Daniel Weisell, was reported as missing at Williamsburg. His fate was never known to the surviving members of the regiment. Soon after their arrival at Harrison's Landing Dr. Libby was forced to resign. Dr. Libby had become "so depressed on account of the serious illness of his wife at home, that he was unfit for duty." As a result, Dr. George Martin was ordered to report from Maine for duty with the unit.

Under Dr. Martin's constant care "the general health of the command began to improve, and the sick list daily grew less formidable." Colonel Walker even issued an order restricting all of the sick to the hospital grounds. None were allowed to leave without written permission from regimental headquarters. This "proved to be a great benefit to the sick, for they were confined to hospital food."[1]

Meanwhile, John Pope had been designated to protect Washington while McClellan's Peninsula campaign was underway. As Lee became more and more pressed around Richmond, it was even thought that Pope would bring his army directly to Richmond to reinforce McClellan. It was also hoped that Pope's maneuvering might shut off vital supplies from the

---

[1] Walker, History of the 4th Maine, p. 29.

Shenandoah Valley by disrupting both food crops and the Virginia Central Railroad.

By the first week of July, Pope had advanced his Union Army of Virginia to occupy a line between Fredericksburg and the Blue Ridge Mountains. In order to accomplish this he had been forced to scatter his forces in a thin echelon across the Virginia landscape. Pope now realized that, with Lee no longer occupied by McClellan's legions, he must concentrate his army in order to keep it from being defeated piecemeal. By mid-July he pulled in his wings and gathered about him some 55,000 troops, with the promise that more would soon be on the way.[2]

4th Maine's Losses Due to Disease at Harrison's Landing

S. P. Boynton Co. C 7/15/62	*Samuel Fales Co. E, 7/31/62*
Josept Evans, Co. F, 8/22/62	*John Barlow, Co. F, 8/22/62*
E. B. Richards, Co. F, 8/11/62	*Silas B. Leathers Co. F, 8/12/62*
J. W. Frye, Co. G, 7/6/62	*William Wentworth, Co. H, 8/1/62*
Frank Pierson, Co I., 8/8/62	*George W. Pope, Co. I, 7/18/62*
Arthur D. Mathews, Co. I, 7/3/62	*Charles W. S. Gunn, Co. I, 8/15/62*

On July 12, Pope occupied Culpepper and seemed to settle himself in. Lee responded by sending Jackson and 14,000 Confederate troops to oppose him. He had been fearful to send any more away from Richmond on the chance that both Pope and McClellan had planned a simultaneous attack on the rebel capital. As evidence to the contrary began to mount, Lee finally dispatched A. P. Hill to join with Jackson on July 27, thus giving Jackson enough troops to think in offensive terms.[3]

Lee gave Jackson discretionary permission on August 7th to take whatever initiative he saw fit. Coincidentally, Jackson also learned on this same day that Pope had sent out a spearhead under the command of General Nathaniel Banks. Jackson immediately put his directive into action and began to advance on this small command in the hope that a victory against Banks would force Pope's command to back away from the Confederate capital.

[2] Hennessee, Return to Bull Run, pp. 8-23.
[3] Ibid.

The two small armies maneuvered toward each other until they made contact on August 10th, near Cedar Mountain. Banks lunged at Jackson as soon as he was within range. For the first two hours of the fight Union forces performed very well, despite the extreme heat and inferior numbers. Maine units, like the 1st Maine Cavalry and Hall's 2nd Maine Battery, an artillery unit also organized in the Rockland area, would receive their baptism of fire this day. At first Jackson was staggered. He struggled, reorganized his forces, and was finally able to drive Banks' men from the field of battle. Union forces would lose some twenty-four hundred men; Jackson about fourteen hundred.[4]

While Banks was burying his dead under a flag of truce at Cedar Mountain on August 11th, the 4th Maine began breaking camp down on the Peninsula. The men's knapsacks were taken to Harrison's Landing and put aboard barges to be transported north. The knapsacks were crammed with all of the recently replaced army issues and personal belongings, which had been lost when they had hurriedly abandoned their positions at White Oak Swamp. Shortly after their departure from the dock, the "worthless" canal boats promptly sank. Most of the clothing they had received on July 8th was lost. What was worse, there was no provision to replace that which had already been charged against their yearly clothing allotment.[5]

On Friday the fifteenth, the 4th Maine Regiment departed from Harrison's Landing, along with the rest of Heintzelman's corps, and began an arduous march of five days through intense heat to Yorktown. On Friday night they camped at James Bridge on the Chickahominy, Saturday at Diascond Bridge, Sunday at James City Court House, and Monday at Williamsburg. They arrived at Yorktown on Tuesday evening.[6]

On the twentieth the Maine boys embarked on the steamship Merrimac for Alexandria. Four other regiments were also loaded aboard. Conditions on shipboard were extremely uncomfortable. The men were assigned bunks that were closely stacked between the decks. There was no outside light and very little ventilation. Add to this the common smells and odors associated with men not used to sea voyages or regular bathing, and you had a very unhealthy situation. Still, the transit was made rather

---

[4] Ibid., p. 28.
[5] Walker, Historical Record from January 1st to November 1st, 1862, Maine State Archives, p. 15.
[6] Ibid.

quickly and they arrived at Alexandria on August 22nd, none too much the worse for the experience.[7]

As Heintzelman began his move from the Peninsula, Lee and Pope had begun a complicated waltz attempting to find the best defensive and offensive positions for their troops. As Pope's army was growing in size almost daily, Lee decided that he had to act quickly while he was still able. Lee divided his army in the face of a larger force and sent Jackson with 23,000 men on a march around the Union right flank. Longstreet would hold the line of the Rappahannock with his 32,000, hoping that, once outflanked, Pope would be forced into retreat. Longstreet's Corps would follow in Jackson's steps as quickly as possible. As Jackson departed on his mission on August 22nd, the strategy for the coming battle had been set.[8]

The 4th Maine made camp with its' brigade on Friday, the 22nd, about two miles outside of Alexandria. On Saturday evening they were loaded on a train and transported on the Orange and Alexandria Railroad to Warrenton Junction. From here they marched that same night another eight miles along the railroad to Bealeton Station and bivouacked for the night. The 4th was posted as advanced guard for the division and remained in this locale adjacent to the Rappahannock River.

On the 25th Walker received orders to send scouts three miles up and three miles down the river. Reports were to be made back to division headquarters at Bealeton Station every half hour. A small detachment of cavalry was dispatched to the Maine regiment to help with the assignment. There proved to be too few cavalrymen for the job at hand, however, and Walker was finally forced to request an additional company be assigned to him from the 1st Rhode Island Cavalry. This was finally done and the assignment was efficiently executed without loss of life.[9]

Colonel Walker relates the story of a Confederate cavalryman... "who had become tired of the service, came to the river, and asked to join my men. His proffered services were accepted and he brought in his horse and equipments. Gen. Birney with his staff arrived just as the prisoner was brought into me. He appropriated his horse and trappings, leaving the new comer to be escorted on foot to Bealton Station."

---

[7] Ibid., p. 16.
[8] Foote, The Civil War, Vol. 1, pp. 615-617.
[9] Walker, op. cit., p. 16.

Shortly after General Birney's arrival at the camp a section of artillery (two guns) and two companies of infantry appeared to help provide support to Walker's regiment. Their stay was short lived for when Walker's cavalry reported on the 26th that rebel infantry were crossing the Rappahannock in force just five miles upstream, the reinforcements, including cavalry, were immediately withdrawn the following morning.[10]

By the morning of the 27th Jackson had reached Manassas. Before him he found over a square mile of supplies of every description. After a brief skirmish, Jackson was able to drive off the few defenders who guarded the depot, capturing provisions desperately needed by his men. As quickly as he had arrived at Manassas, Jackson hastily departed in search of an easily defensible position.[11]

Shortly before midnight, the same day that Jackson reached Manassas Junction, the 4th Maine received orders to retreat and rejoin with their brigade. The night before Walker had sent out a detachment to procure bread and coffee for his men. When his men got there they were refused rations due to the fact that the division was all packed and ready to move. All the regiment had to eat, therefore, was the fresh mutton they had procured from the fields of a local farmer. And there was very little of that to go around.

The 4th Maine was now all alone, far in advance of their division. The hours from four a.m. until almost noon were extremely anxious ones. Rebel cavalry was everywhere. Every crack of a branch, the sudden movement of an animal, or unexpected motion of a fellow soldier, gave rise to fears of an impending attack. Fortunately for the Maine boys the enemy did not bother them.

About noon six Union cavalrymen and three aides materialized with orders to rejoin their division. Walker immediately called back his pickets and in a few short moments had his regiment hiking northeast toward Bealeton Station along the tracks of the Orange and Alexandria Railroad.

When the men arrived at Bealeton they were in high hopes that they would be greeted with bread and coffee. Instead, all there was to be found were "a few crumbs of hard tack, which had been left upon the ground." Most of the Union food supplies had been loaded on a hand car, and this had run off the tracks into a bog.[12]

---

[10] Walker, History of the 4th Maine, p. 31.
[11] Foote, op. cit., pp. 618-619.
[12] Walker, History of the 4th Maine, p. 31.

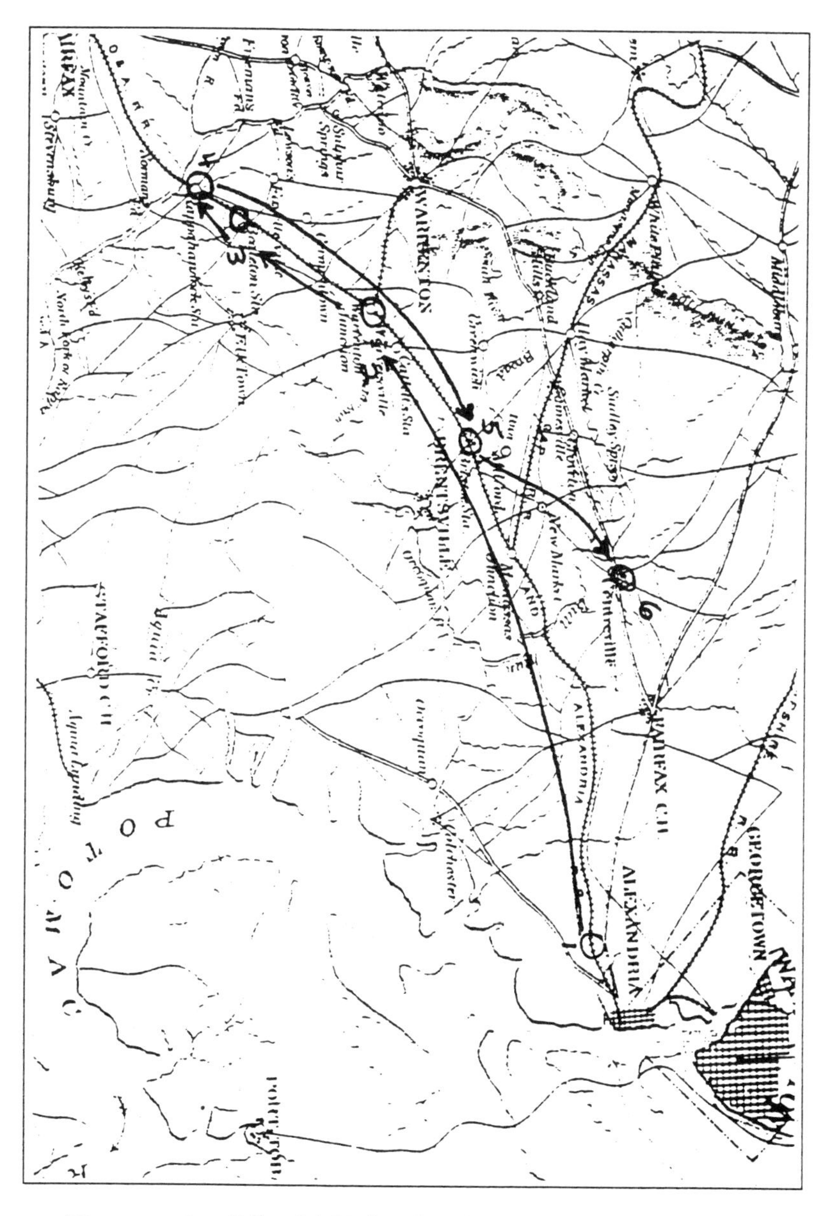

Movements of the 4th Maine leading up to 2nd Bull Run.

Walker later related that the men were... "hungry, and weakened by the fresh meat they had eaten without bread, we moved in the direction of Warrenton Junction, where we counted on finding our brigade, but again we were disappointed. They had not been there and we could not get any information of them. I sent the cavalry and aids in different directions for information, but without learning anything to guide me as to the direction in which to move. We kept upon and near the railroad, marching until 9 o'clock p.m. The day had been fearfully hot, the men were weak from the causes stated, and growing weaker. Everyone that broke down we were obliged to leave to the care of the enemy's cavalry which followed us, picking up and paroling all who left our ranks, and in some cases taking their outer clothing, leaving them only shirt and drawers."[13]

Sergeant Herman Burpee of Rockland was one of those poor unfortunates who collapsed from heat exhaustion. Unable to escape he was immediately picked up by rebel cavalry. He was stripped of his shoes and garments and sent along his way. Early on the morning of the 28th Burpee came stumbling along, half naked, into the camp of the 4th Maine. He was a welcome, but sorry sight to behold.

Colonel Walker had brought his troop to a halt at about nine P.M. As the column slowed the men dropped in their tracks from exhaustion. Sleep overcame them quickly. As Walker recalled, "my men slept until 3 o'clock, but I felt too anxious to close my eyes. Then we resumed our march on the railroad, but our advance was slow. As the morning was intensely dark I halted with the determination to wait until daylight. At a distance of a quarter of a mile I saw a light and on approaching it found an officer and two cavalrymen, who were acting for him as orderlies. Recognizing our uniform I made myself and my men's condition known. The officer said he was Major Taylor of Gen. Pope's staff; that Kearney's division was ordered to be at Bristoe Station at sunrise; that he wrote and sent the order by direction of Gen. Pope. He further informed me that we were only about five miles from Bristoe Station."[14]

The regiment continued its journey along the tracks. The regiment had moved on about a mile and just as dawn was breaking they "came to a fine residence, of which our mounted escort, that had been separated from us in trying to get information of the division, had taken possession, and were having a chicken breakfast prepared. I joined in the feast, for which

---

[13] Ibid.
[14] Ibid.

Some of the damage caused by the Confederates that would have been witnessed by the 4th Maine during the 2nd Bull Run Campaign. (Brady Photos)

we paid liberally. My men took what fowl were left about the barn, and the owner was obliged to charge their price to the government."[15]

After partaking of a hastily prepared meal, the Maine boys found themselves skipping along the railroad ties. It was about seven A.M. when the 4th Maine came marching into Bristoe Station. Their arrival was timed almost perfectly with the appearance of their division. The soldiers of the division were surprised to see the Maine regiment as they had all assumed they had fallen into rebel hands.

The 4th rejoined with its brigade and then pushed on with them past Kettle Run and on to Manassas Junction. From a high point of ground Walker observed the "ruins of the train of cars that had been burned the day before, the 27th, by Jackson's rebels...Here, on a high point of ground, I saw for the first and last time our commander, Gen. Pope, consulting with generals Heintzleman and Kearney. A major battle now seemed imminent"[16]

An interesting anecdote to Jackson's flanking movement around Pope's army involves Captain Charles A. Rollins of Company C. When the Maine regiment had arrived at Alexandria, Rollins had been detailed to remain behind to attend to some regimental business. With the venture completed, he headed south intending to join up with the regiment at Bristoe Station on the 27th. Bristoe Station was the point at which Jackson had chosen to attack the Orange and Alexandria Railroad. As a matter of fact Jackson had bivouacked here on the night of August 26th and 27th. When Captain Rollins arrived in town on the morning of the 27th, he was immediately taken prisoner. As fate would have it, the captain would have a chance to participate in the second battle of Bull Run, and Chantilly, but only as an observer.[17]

Meanwhile, after a short rest the division moved on to Centreville, arriving there on the evening of the 28th at about nine P.M. Here they camped for the night, dining on such luxuries as pork and hardtack, and knowing that, somewhere, just beyond the shadows, lurked Stonewall Jackson's corps.[18]

While Pope sent his divisions north to find the Confederate Army, Jackson concentrated at Groveton. Here Jackson set a trap that was

---

[15] Ibid., p. 32.
[16] Ibid.
[17] Hennessy, op. cit., pp. 187-188.
[18] Walker, Historical Record, op. cit., pp. 16-17.

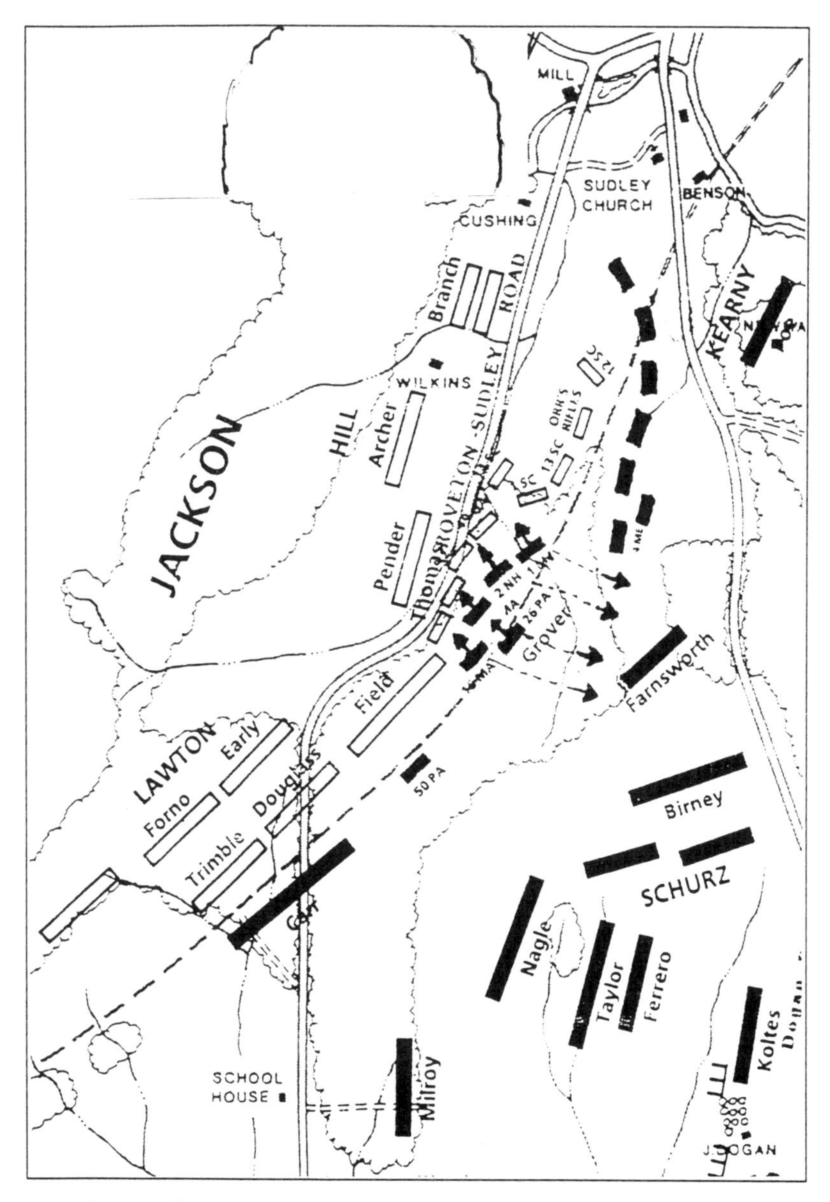

Morning action at 2nd Bull Run on August 29. The 4th Maine has taken up position on the right of the line.

happened upon by some Union forces very close to sunset on the 28th. At Groveton about 2,800 Union soldiers fought against twice their numbers and were able to hold their own for about two hours. Approximately one thousand men fell on each side. Jackson had tangled with a very feisty group of soldiers who would soon become known as the Iron Brigade. Before a year had passed they would fight themselves practically out of existence.[19]

Following the action at Groveton, Pope was convinced that Jackson was trying to escape. He sent Sigel, Reno and Heintzelman's corps, which included the 4th Maine, against him on the 29th. Jackson had chosen his ground well, settling himself in behind an unfinished railroad cut. Pope managed to get about 32,000 troops into action, and though Stonewall's position was in doubt several times that day, he managed to hold on.[20]

Heintzelman's men came closest to breaking through on Jackson's left. The 4th Maine's division commander, Philip Kearney, had been ordered to engage the rebel troops to their north along with Brigadier General Carl Schurz's division. Schurz moved his men up to the area near Sudley Church and engaged the Confederates there. Kearney moved his division up toward the front at about 10:30 A. M., but instead of attacking the enemy, he spent his time deploying his batteries.

As Kearny had moved his division northward he had led off with his 3rd Brigade under the command of Orlando Poe. Poe's advance toward Sudley Ford had threatened Jackson's supply train. This sudden move caused the Confederates to adjust their positions to protect the wagons. As a result Poe ran into artillery fire from Pelham's Confederate battery and the carbine fire of Major William Patrick's 1st Virginia Cavalry. Poe, observing a sizable enemy force next to the battery, decided to retreat back to the safe side of Bull Run.[21]

Kearny's other two brigades busied themselves as best they could. John Robinson's 1st Brigade supported Poe's crossing of Bull Run. Birney's 2nd Brigade, which consisted of seven regiments including the 3rd and 4th Maine, was broken up in order to accomplish several tasks. The 3rd Maine and a second regiment were sent to support the division's batteries located adjacent to the Mathew's House of first Bull Run fame. One regiment, the 1st New York, got a little too close to the fighting and

---

[19] Hennessy, op. cit., p. 219.
[20] Ibid., p. 219.
[21] Ibid., p. 220

was charged by a South Carolina regiment. The 38th New York became a reserve for the brigade. Birney's remaining three regiments, including the 4th Maine, moved out to support Poe.[22]

As Birney's three regiments neared the Newman House they came upon a large concentration of artillery, supported by infantry. Crenshaw's and Braxton's batteries laid in a heavy fire upon the men. As a result of this Birney redirected these regiments to the left in the direction of the heavy fighting which now seemed to be occupying Schurz. The regiments went crashing into the woods driving in the Confederate skirmishers and capturing several ambulances.

The tiny force was soon surrounded by rebel forces. General Birney, sensing the apparent hopelessness of the situation, quickly backed off and left the men to take care of themselves. The ambulances were retaken and the survivors were forced to fight their way out of the pocket.[23]

Walker never forgave Birney for the day's indiscretion. Later he would write that when his men had been ordered into the woods he believed General Birney to be "filled with morphine and whiskey. For this move, which had nearly destroyed the regiment, "Kearney gave Birney one of his blessings." Walker remembered that their attack drove back the enemy's skirmish line "capturing several ambulances and getting near their main line. Our leader, seeing the situation, left us to care for ourselves. We were now nearly surrounded and a large force was in our front. The ambulances with their rear guard were retaken and we escaped by hard and determined fighting."[24]

Shortly thereafter, the Maine boys moved over to Schurz's left and kept up a rather ineffective fire for about a half hour. The regiments were then ordered to return to their original positions where the fighting continued to rage all about them.[25] General Hooker's First Brigade's commander, Brigadier-General Cuvier Grover, had attacked the Confederate line on Kearny's left sometime before three P.M. Grover's attack was initially successful, but when Thomas's southern brigade was suddenly reinforced by William Pender's, the tide quickly shifted. Grover's men quickly routed rearward at about the same time that the 4th Maine

---

[22] Ibid., pp. 220-221.
[23] Walker, History of Fourth Maine, op. cit., p. 32.
[24] Hennessy, op. cit., 220.
[25] Ibid., p. 221.

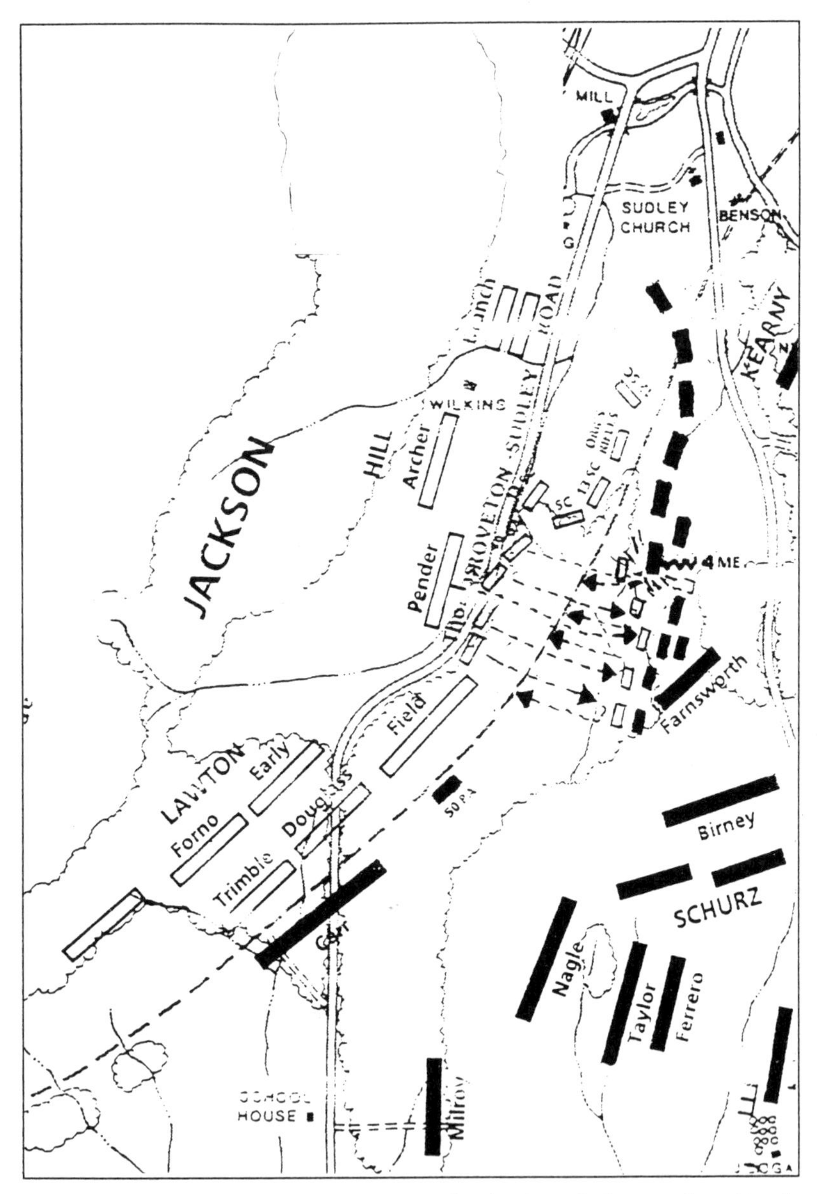

Robinson's 3 P.M. attack is repulsed. A rebel counterattack passes through the 4th Maine's position and scatters them.

was attempting to recover from its first round of fighting with the enemy.[26]

About three P.M. Kearny had ordered Robinson's brigade to attack the unfinished railroad. The 4th Maine and 1st New York regiments were ordered to support the charge in their front. The 1st New York took position behind Robinson's reserve regiment. The 4th Maine fell in to the left of Robinson's brigade. Before the Maine men had even set their line Pender's men came crashing into their regiment. The Maine boys attempted to contest the rebel movement by changing their front but it was too late. They were quickly outflanked.

Elijah Walker later recorded that "the General ordered me to the left of the brigade, where we were attacked on the flank by a large force, charging my front. We became hotly engaged and during our struggle the brigade withdrew, allowing the enemy to come in on our rear."[27]

John Hennessy, in his book Return to Bull Run, quotes a 4th Maine soldier as having said, "superior numbers enabled them to flank us on the left." The regiment became "hotly engaged, and during the struggle the brigade (Robinson's) withdrew, allowing the enemy to come in on our rear." Walker ordered the bugler to sound the retreat. "The order to fall back was executed with some confusion." It would take the regiment almost two hours to gather up its soldiers and recover from the encounter.[28]

Robinson's attack fitted in well with the other piecemeal attempts that were being made against Jackson. Robinson managed to get his line across the unfinished railroad cut in a diagonal fashion. As far as achieving his objective of breaking the Confederate line, the assault was a dismal failure. Still, the action that took place at three set the stage for the attack ordered by Pope a couple of hours later.

At five P.M. Kearny was ordered to attack Jackson near Sudley Church. Robinson's brigade was readied from its position across the unfinished railroad. Walker's 4th Maine still had not completely recovered from its scare at the hands of Pender's troops. At about the time the newly conceived attack was to take place the regiment found itself on the left of Robertson's men, half in woods and half in a field.

---

[26] Ibid., p. 256.

[27] Walker, History of the 4th Maine, op. cit., p. 32

[28] Ibid., p. 220.

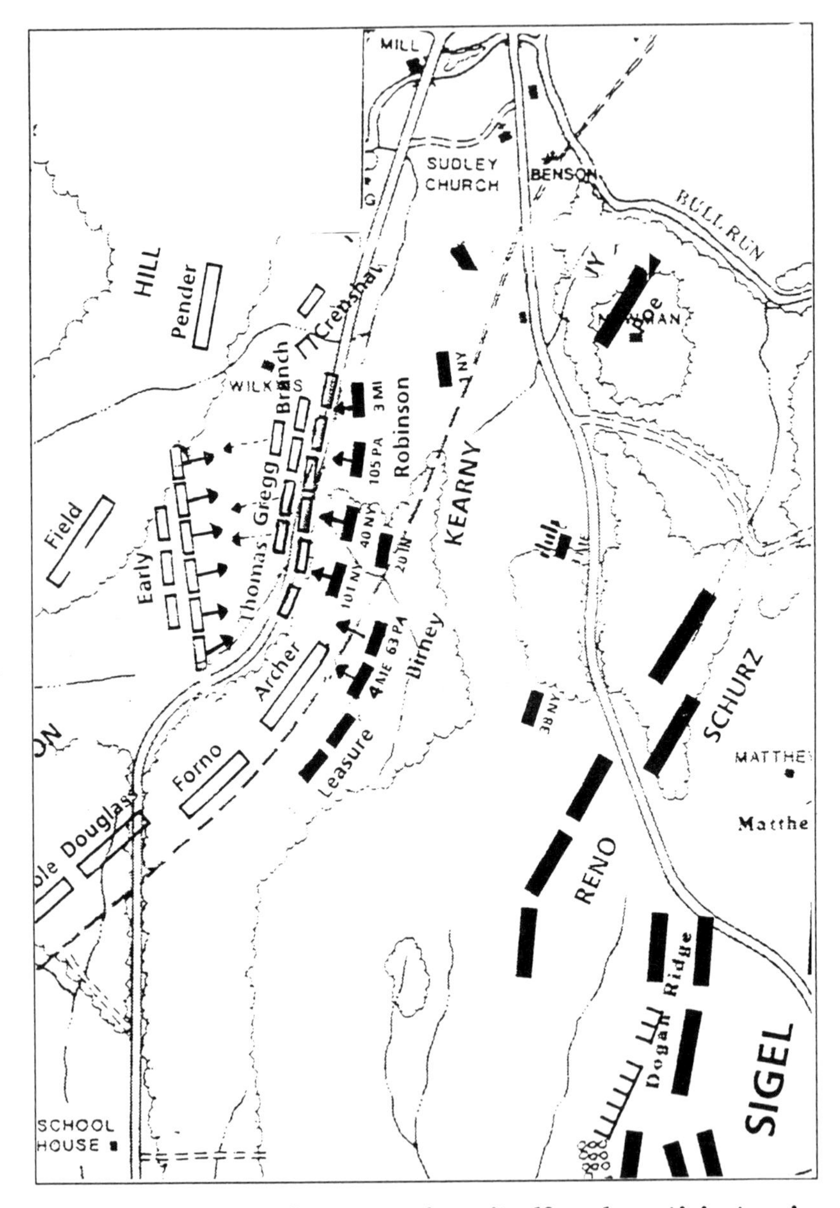

The 4th Maine finally reorganizes itself and participates in Kearny's attack at 5 P.M. The fight was close and desperate.

Suddenly the 3rd Maine, the 40th and 101st First New York Infantry, came sweeping through the field, carrying with them into the fray the remains of the Limerock Regiment. The Mainers let the New Yorkers pass and then joined in on their left. As they moved forward one member of the 101st New York observed, "The ground was literally covered with dead bodies, there being one every few feet and sometimes two or three together." Picking their way over the casualties they exchanged fire with the Confederates and drove them back. When the assault stalled, the men in blue fixed bayonet and pushed forward even further. The rebels routed back .[29]

The resulting combat was desperate, hand to hand, not only with bayonets, but with clubbed muskets and even sticks and stones. The defenders retreated, but in so doing they became concentrated by the impact of the encounter. The Confederate brigades of Brigadier Generals Edward Thomas and Maxcy Gregg found themselves almost completely surrounded. Some of Brigadier General Branch's rebel forces, presently in the process of extending their line, helped to take some of the sting out of Robinson's attack. It was Jubal Early, however, whose sudden appearance, once again, snatched victory from Pope's grasp. The net result for the northerners was the gain of about three hundred yards of ground, which was paid for dearly. According to Walker the regiment had joined with the 3rd Maine and 40th New York in their attack. The regiment then "turned and advanced, driving the enemy across the railroad cut, but they were reinforced and we were obliged to retire." With this sudden appearance of Confederate reinforcements Kearny's troops were forced to surrender even this most precious soil.[30]

During the fighting of the 29th, Company I and Company K were detached under the command of Lieutenant Colonel Carver to the support of Randolph's artillery battery. As a result of this decision only about two hundred Maine men had participated in the attack. Of this number seven were killed, thirty-three were wounded, and seven were reported as missing. Casualties amounted to almost twenty-five per cent of those committed.[31]

---

[29] Ibid.

[30] Walker, History of the 4th Maine, op. cit., p. 32.

[31] As a note of interest Colonel Walker's horse was also wounded in the days fight. He continued to ride him though. He remember that the horse later became disabled for a time and "ever after carried Confederate lead in his flesh."

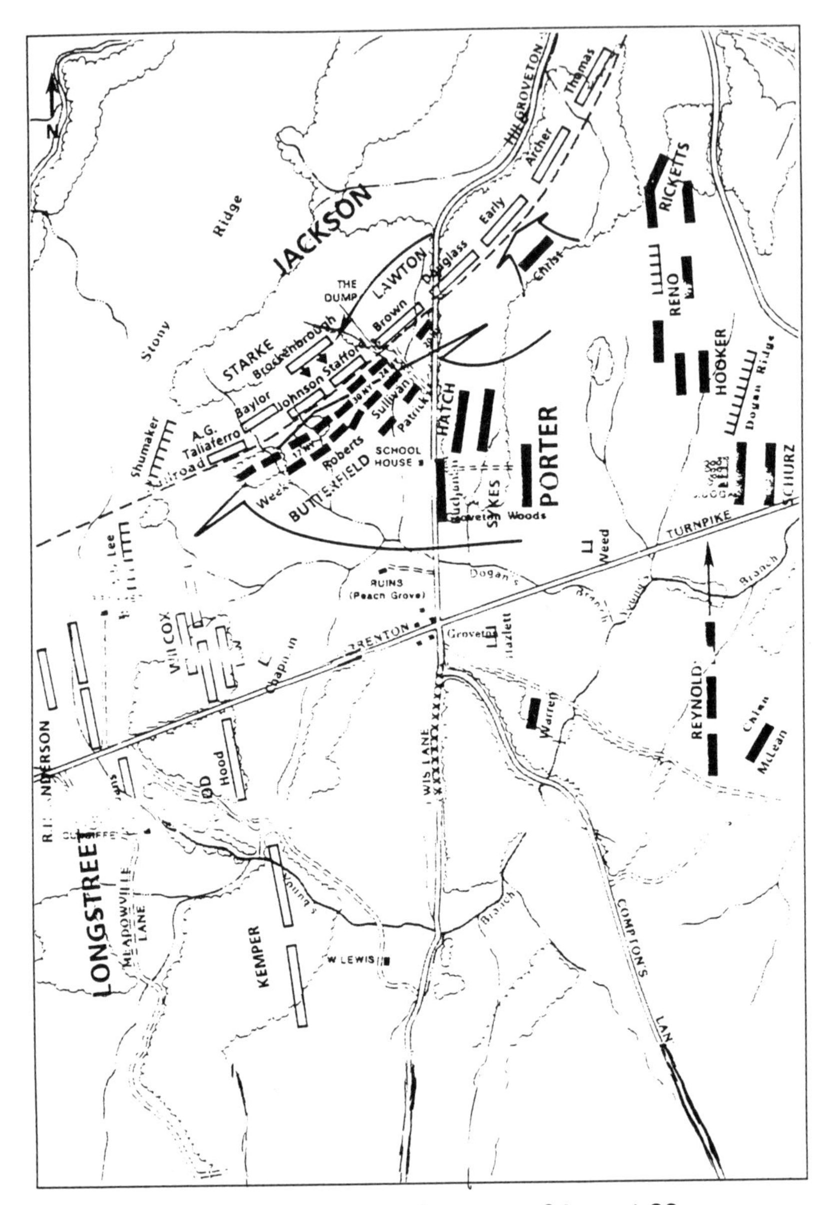

Porter's assault on the afternoon of August 30.

As the battle had progressed on the 29th, Longstreet had moved his men into a position forward, and at a right angle to Jackson's men. This was done without Pope's knowledge, or at the very least, without his understanding. All day long Longstreet had remained hidden, refusing to commit his troops to the battle until he felt the time was right. Jackson had been too proud to ask for his assistance. Most of the fighting ended shortly after dark.[32]

On the following afternoon, August 30th, the fighting was resumed. Interpreting the backward movement of some of Jackson's regiments as a retreat, Pope ordered an attack in force. In actuality Jackson was only attempting to rest some of his soldiers. Once again the rebel line nearly broke as the bluecoats surged forward. Jackson's troops fired volley after volley. As the men began to run out of ammunition many were forced to throw stones in their defense.

Jackson sent out a desperate call to Longstreet to commit his troops. At the point where the two commanders' lines met, Longstreet had hidden eighteen artillery pieces. The guns, commanding the field for two thousand yards to the east and northeast, were rolled out. As the guns began to fire, the Union troops were suddenly caught in enfillade. The cannon fire caught the troops by surprise, causing many of the Northerners to break and rout back. Longstreet took this moment to commit his five nearly fresh divisions to an attack on the weakened Union flank. Jackson's men joined in as well.

Pope's line bent back under the weight of the offensive, all the way back to the now famous Henry House Hill, which had been the scene of fighting during the first battle of Bull Run. Where a year before McDowell had sent his men to attack these heights, here now a final stand was made that brought the rebel offensive to a complete halt.

Walker remembered the day's activities, thusly:

"Kearney's division was on the right of our line, in reserve. At 3 o'clock p.m. there was hard fighting on our left and in front, by McDowell's corps. We could tell by the sound that our men were being beaten and were falling back. Our division was in a small field surrounded by thick bushes. An ox had been slaughtered and the meat was being issued to the men. General Kearney appeared in the nick of time, and in tones of thunder exclaimed, "Get out of here as quick as God will let you!"

---

[32] Hennessy, op. cit.,p. 286.

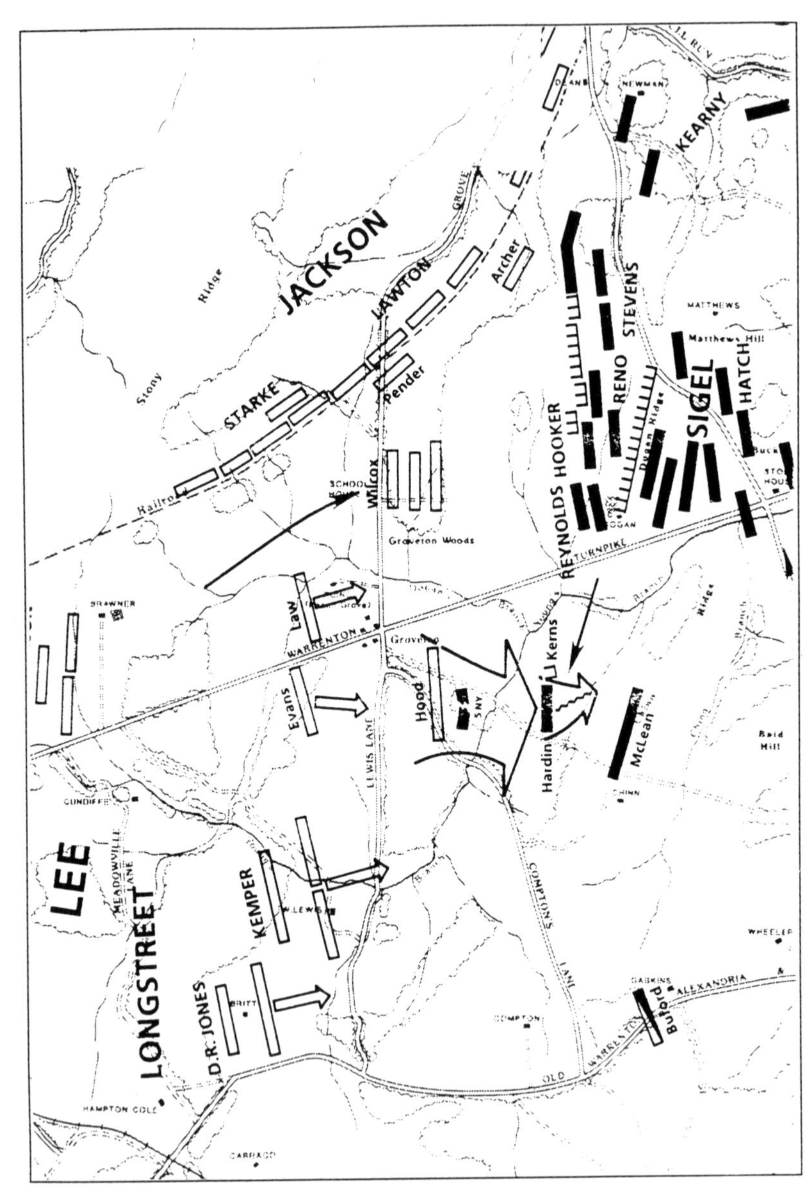

Longstreet's massive counterattack on August 30.

and get out we did, none too soon, for all were not clear of the field before it was occupied by the rebels. The picket line in our front had been surprised and captured, leaving us exposed without any warning. General Kearney soon had his command in line and moved between McDowell's troops and the enemy."[33]

During the fighting on the 30th, the 4th Maine, along with its division, were pulled back to the left and center. This new position soon became heavily pressed and nearly surrounded. Once again the true valor of the Maine men was put to the test. "The Fourth Maine and the Fortieth New York were the last regiments to leave the field, about 10 o'clock."

Colonel Walker was ordered "to leave my videttes to be sacrificed as a blind to the enemy." Those in the woods he called in. The men in the field, including Orlando Brown, George Dunbar, Ephraim Cross, and George Hall, "were, left to the tender mercies of the rebels." In the process of stumbling around in the dark these men came across a small party of mounted rebel soldiers. Fully realizing that the discharge of their muskets could bring large numbers of enemy troops down around them, the Mainers leveled their guns at the men and demanded their surrender. Fortunately for them, the rebels gave up without a fight. Among the captured was an assistant adjutant general, a cavalry lieutenant, an orderly, and two Negroes, including horses and equipment. All were turned over to General Birney who appropriated the horses and equipments but neglected to say a word in praise of the men who made the capture.[34]

Writing in 1893, Elijah Walker took the stand "that had our command possessed the authority, and dared to act, the enemy could have been defeated at the second Bull Run. Army commanders were so completely under the dictation of the authorities at Washington that they had no heart to do what they would have done had they been left to, and acted upon their own judgment...but a small part of the troops had been engaged. A few had had severe fighting, while the others had stood back and looked on. There was no confidence in General Pope, and less in Halleck and Stanton."[35]

By the morning of September 1st, it had become apparent that Jackson was once again attempting to flank Pope's army. Jackson had

---

[33] Walker, History of the 4th Maine, op. cit., p. 33.
[34] Ibid.
[35] Ibid.

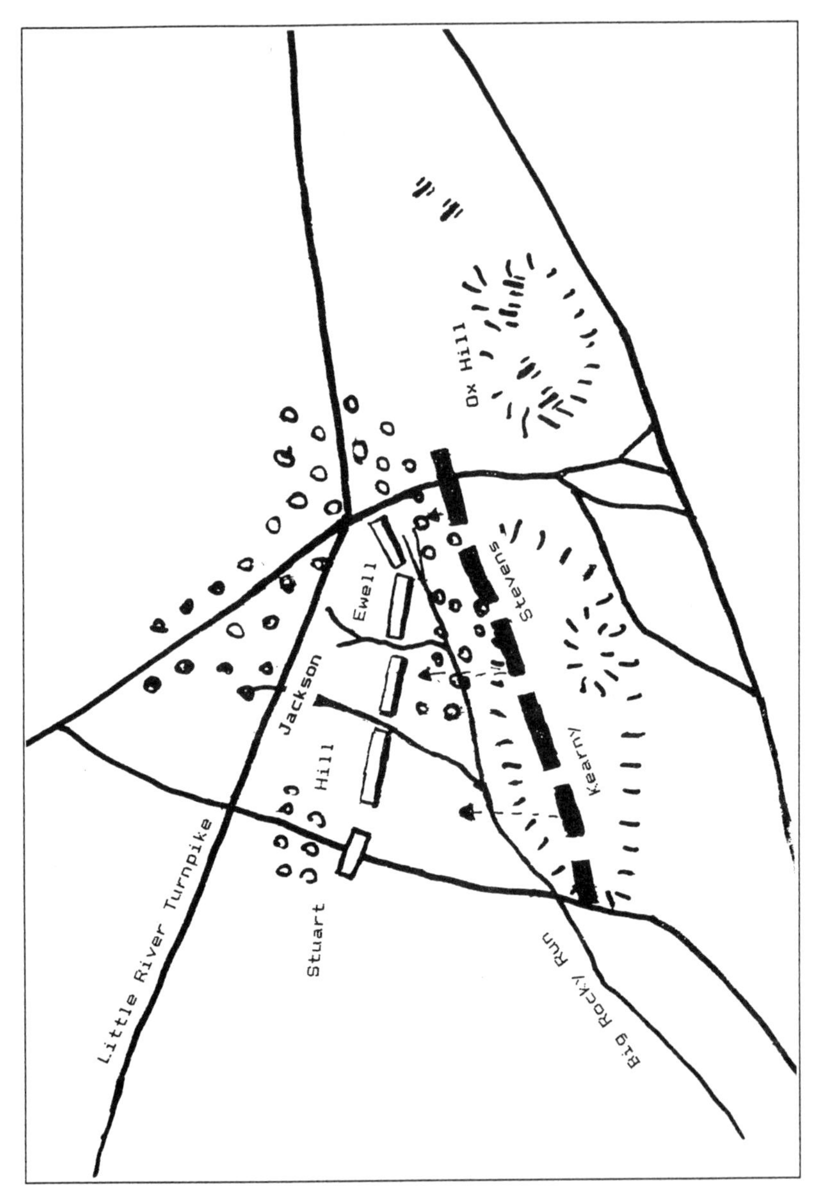

Author's conceptual map of the Battle at Chantilly.

crossed Bull Run at Sudley Spring and advanced to the Little River Turnpike. He followed this road southeast to Fairfax Court House, which was several miles in the Union rear. Here Jackson rested his men and awaited the Union reaction.[36]

Meanwhile, Pope sent one of Burnside's Divisions under the command of Brigadier General Isaac Stevens to intercept the Confederates. The two forces collided at about five P.M. at a mansion named Chantilly, during a particularly violent thunderstorm. Here began a desperate two hour clash of wills. The noise of the bise was so great that even the sounds of the cannon were drowned out. Still, in the midst of all of the confusion, the two opponents stubbornly contested their ground.[37]

Kearny's division, still not recovered from the mauling they had received at Jackson's hands a couple of days before, was ordered out of their muddy camp at Centreville. The division advanced along the road to Fairfax Court House. As they marched, with the approaching storm at their heels, the sounds of battle were heard near Chantilly. The Maine boys were ordered to pick up their pace, marching now at the double quick, and, upon their arrival, were thrown into the fray to relieve Stevens' heavily pressed troops.[38]

The 4th Maine advanced into the firefight with the other regiments of its brigade. They were immediately met by a punishing fire served up by a superior force. When it became obvious that they were being surrounded, the regiment was forced to retire, and in so doing found "a more advantageous position". From this post they kept up a continuous fire for more that one and a half hours. They discharged their guns until either their cartridges were exhausted or drenched by the continuous rain. Finally, left with only their bayonets as weapons, they were forced to retire. This they did grudgingly, and only when they were relieved.[39]

While the conflict had been raging all about them, General Kearny had been dashing about the field on horseback attempting to move his troops up to the fighting. His stated philosophy of combat was "that you must never be afraid of anything". In a fit of rage Kearny charged mistakenly up to a group of A. P. Hill's Confederates and shouted out an order. A flash of lighting illuminated him to the rebels. Realizing that they

---

[36] Foote, op. cit., p. 644.
[37] Ibid., pp. 644-645.
[38] Walker, Historical Record, p. 19.
[39] Ibid.

were being given commands by a Union general, Hill's men demanded his surrender. The general turned his horse about and attempted to flee his predicament. The rebel soldiers loosed a volley and poor Kearny was dead.[40]

The battle of Chantilly ended at nightfall. In addition to Kearny, General Stevens had also fallen during the fight. As for the 4th Maine, the regiment had eight killed, fifty-four wounded, and two were listed as missing. Two hundred and forty had entered the fight, and, once again, for the second time in less than a week, casualties had amounted to more than twenty-five percent of those involved. Looking at the 111 total casualties of the Bull Run campaign, including Lieutenant Crabtree, who was wounded once in each of the battles, total losses amounted to thirty-eight percent.[41]

The 4th Maine remained on guard duty at Chantilly during the night. The rain had thoroughly soaked the Mainers and, without the benefit of fires, the men spent a cold and miserable night. About 2:30 A.M. the regiment was withdrawn to the Centreville Turnpike and from there to Fairfax Court House, arriving in the vicinity about dawn. The flank had been defended, and even though it was Union troops who had retreated from the battlefield, they believed that the victory was theirs.[42]

The regiment continued their retreat and by September were located near Fort Lyon in Alexandria once more. On the tenth they were relocated to Alexandria Heights and on Friday the twelfth to Fort Barnard in Arlington, overlooking Four Mile Run. The men were placed within the works and assigned to temporary garrison duty. Here they had a roof over their heads for the first time in months. Their rest, however, would be but five short days.[43]

Lee was once again on the move, only this time he planned an invasion of the north. Though poorly timed, due primarily to his losses in the Bull Run campaign, he would bring his 40,000 men north seeking the victory that could bring recognition of the Confederate States by Europe, and, perhaps, even an end to the war. The 4th's numbers had been greatly depleted by the Peninsula Campaign, and Second Manassas. Their role at

---

[40] Hennessy, op. cit., p. 450.
[41] Walker, Historical Record, pp. 19-20.
[42] Ibid., p. 20.
[43] Ibid.

Antietam would, therefore, be limited. Still, the upcoming maneuvering of the regiment would help set the stage for the Fredericksburg campaign.

The Maine boys had played at this game of war for just over a year. During this time they had seen more than their share of fighting. Little did they know that there would be a full two more years of it. Fortunately for them they were becoming very proficient at this art called war. Maybe even a little bit cocky. In the upcoming clash they would once again be reminded of their own mortality. The regiment's most devastating moment was just ahead.

Chapter 7

"...Living on Pork and Hard Bread..."

The men of the 4th Maine received their pay on Friday, September 5th. It was the first time since they had left for the Peninsula. A week later they were given temporary residence in the defenses of Washington at Fort Barnard in Arlington, Virginia. The occasion brought with it genuine excitement among the men, for they knew that garrison duty might allow them to visit the city. With their newly acquired riches they would certainly be able to do up their visiting style. Having been in the field almost constantly since the first of April, and having suffered greatly in the line of duty, these soldiers desperately needed a rest.

Garrison duty for the Limerock Regiment, however, lasted just three short days. There is no evidence indicating whether or not anyone got to town. They were probably not allowed the extravagance. On Monday the fifteenth, at nine P.M., their brigade received orders to march to the Potomac River. Early the next morning they crossed over Aqueduct Bridge to Georgetown and moved on about fifteen miles to Rockville, Maryland. On the seventeenth, they marched eighteen miles to Poolesville. The next day they moved to the mouth of the Monocacy River and bivouacked for the night.[1]

Nathaniel Robbins, quartermaster sergeant and later 2nd lieutenant, gives his interpretation of the reason that the regiment had not moved north to Antietam with the rest of the army in a letter addressed to Maine's Adjutant General, Seldon Connor, on December 23, 1895. The except reads as follows:

"The only pitched battle of the Army of the Potomac which we did not share in was the battle of Antietam, and the reason for this was that after the great battle of 2nd Bull Run, in the little but severe battle of Chantilly we lost in killed and wounded, 121 men and our General Phil

---

[1] Walker, Report to the Adjutant General for 1862, p. 2.

Kearney : consequently our Regt. was left at Poolesville on the Monocacy to guard the fords of the Potomac."

By the time that the 4th Maine had arrived at Poolesville on the 17th, the fighting at Sharpsburg, just a day's march away, had already taken place. In the time it took for them to march eighteen miles 28,365 soldiers had fallen dead or wounded.[2] On the morning of the 18th, while soldiers both Union and Confederate, eyed each other across the no-man's land at Antietam Creek, the Maine men cautiously moved a couple of miles to the mouth of the Monocacy River. This was the very place where Lee had crossed the Potomac with his men on his way north. Luck had, once again, saved the regiment from possible disaster in some of the most savage fighting ever seen on this continent.

As General Lee was executing his retreat from Maryland, the regiments of the brigade were assigned guard duty at various fords along the Potomac. On Sunday the twenty-first of September they were sent to Point of Rocks, Maryland, and remained there until October 8th. The time they were there was spent primarily performing picket duty. On October 1st, however, the regiment sent a scouting party across the river about eight miles in the direction of Waterford, Virginia. While patrolling the area the Maine boys managed to capture a cavalry sergeant and three privates before their return to camp.[3]

On Wednesday, October 8th, they moved twelve miles down river to Conrads Ferry, and reunited with the rest of the brigade. On Saturday, the 11th, the 3rd and 4th Maine, both now under the command of Colonel Walker, received orders from General Stoneman to countermarch in the direction their previous day's position on the Monocacy. Walker was ordered to command the expedition. You can well imagine the grumbling these orders caused in the ranks. Still, the men did what they were told and were on station by nightfall.[4]

The reason for the return to the Monocacy had been inspired by a cavalry raid into Pennsylvania led by Jeb Stuart, and accompanied by 1800 of his best troopers. Stuart had crossed the Potomac above Martinsburg on October 10, with the intention of destroying the railroad bridge at Chambersburg. The act would deny one of two rail links providing supplies for McClellan's huge army. Unfortunately for the

---

[2] Foote, The Civil War, Vol. 2, p. 702.
[3] Walker, op. cit., p. 2.
[4] Ibid.

rebels, the bridge was found to be made of iron and proved impossible to destroy. Denied this objective, Stuart decided to take all the horses and supplies he could find, in addition to a few civilian hostages. The mission was more what "Dicken's Mr. Wemmick might characterize as an example of the Confederate fondness for 'portable property'".[5]

Halleck had, in fact, ordered McClellan to take whatever immediate steps necessary to destroy the Confederate force. McClellan in turn ordered General Alfred Pleasonton's cavalry, accompanied by a couple of artillery pieces, to intercept Stuart. He then proceeded to back this force up with whatever additional troops were close at hand. Enter onto the scene the 3rd and 4th Maine regiments.[6]

On the 11th Stuart moved out of Chambersburg in an easterly direction and into the town of Emmitsburg. Here they stopped, resting and feeding their animals, before continuing on. The rebels moved on without sleep and on the morning of the 12th they were approaching the mouth of the Monocacy, about three miles below the spot where the small Union force had been posted. McClellan had promised General Halleck, and the President, that the rebs would be intercepted and punished for the atrocities which they had committed on their raid. McClellan's future, in fact, rested squarely on the results of the drama that was about to unfold.[7]

The standard treatment of General Pleasonton's encounter with the rebel cavalry expounds upon the idea that the Northern hero had been in constant pursuit of the Confederates for over thirty-six hours when they joined up with the Maine men, early on the morning of October 12. Within minutes of their arrival, Stuart's cavalry did, indeed, make their appearance and immediately began to cross the Potomac. General Pleasonton, assuming command of the combined force of infantry, cavalry, and artillery, quickly marched his men to intercept. Pleasonton presently bumped into Stuart's rear guard. Stuart, having just a few moments to make preparations for his crossing, had placed his artillery on the near side of the river to provide cover for his troopers. Pleasonton deployed his men and began an immediate advance. While all of these preparations were going on, however, Stuart had continued to throw his men across the river. At the moment that the Union troops

[5] Walker, History of the 4th Maine, p. 34.
[6] Foote, op. cit., p. 749.
[7] Ibid., pp. 749-750.

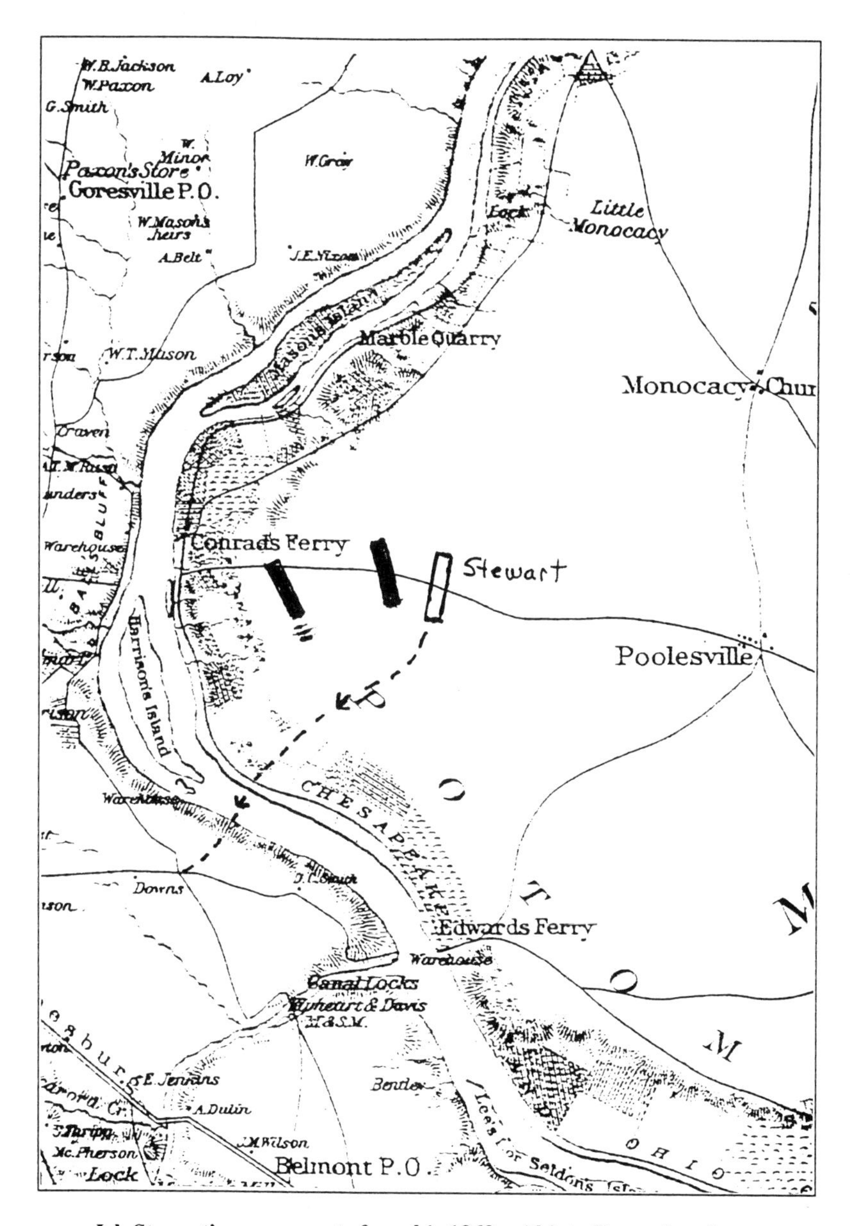

Jeb Stewart's escape route from his 1862 raid into Pennsylvania

were deploying, the Confederate artillery was already limbering up. When the attack began in earnest, the artillery was rolling across the Potomac into Virginia.

In Colonel Walker's yearly report to Maine's Adjutant General, dated November 1, 1862, he refers to the incident in the following manner:

"That the failure to intercept and capture the enemy's force on this occasion was the result of gross neglect and mismanagement in some quarters, there is no doubt; but no blame can be attached to our regiment or any of its officers, all of whom were ready and prompt in using their force to oppose the enemy, so far as they were allowed to do so by Gen. Pleasonton" [8]

The obvious implication here was that Walker believed that Pleasonton had not handled the affair very well. In the course of General Stuart's travels he had managed, right under the nose of McClellan and his 100,000 troops, to capture civilians, horses, and supplies, and cause over a quarter of a million dollars in damage. He had done as he pleased while in northern territory, and on top of all this had escaped untouched. The incident itself, in addition to the escape of Lee's army after Antietam, was embarrassing to everyone involved, especially to the Lincoln administration. No wonder Colonel Walker felt compelled to write an explanation.[9]

In his more detailed 1893 account of the incident, Elijah Walker recalled that anxiety over the movements of the rebel force had made it impossible for him to sleep on the night of the 11th. "General Ward arrived at twelve o'clock, direct from army headquarters, where he had been to get assigned to duty in his new rank, he having been commissioned a brigadier general. He said that at the headquarters they thought there was no danger of the raiding party attempting to cross in that vicinity, but it was believed they would return and try to cross beyond the right of our army." It was only then that Walker was able to rest.

About eight the next morning, just as Colonel Walker had decided that the rebels were not going to bother them, the quiet of the camp was disturbed by the arrival of one of General Pleasonton's advance scouts. The cavalryman proclaimed that Stuart and his band were close by.

---

[8] Walker, op. cit., p. 22.
[9] Foote, op. cit., p. 750.

When Walker asked him how many enemy there were, he reported that he had "laid secreted by the road last night, as they passed, and counted eighteen hundred."[10]

Walker immediately sent Major Pitcher with one hundred and fifty men to extend and strengthen his line on the Poolesville road as well as fifty men "to secret themselves near the ford, so that in case the enemy should pass us they could be shot while slowly wading the river." Walker was now left with about three hundred and fifty men with whom he had decided to attack the rebels. Colonel Walker remembered that:

"Our cavalry were arriving, a thousand strong, with the two battery guns, and I now heard firing by my pickets on the Poolesville road. My men had divested themselves of all superfluities and were eager for the fray. We were already advancing when Gen. Pleasonton approached me and inquired who was in command."

"I am sir."

"How many men have you?"

"Who are you?"

"Don't you know me? I am Gen. Pleasonton," opening his outer garment and showing his star. "Fighting has commenced and I assume command."

"Have you any artillery?" he inquired; to which I answered in the negative.

"Then," said he, "I want two hundred and fifty men to support my battery."

"I was confounded, but it was orders and I obeyed. My pickets had been driven in and the major had been dismounted by having his horse shot by the enemy. Pleasonton and the rebels opened an artillery duel, at a distance of more than half a mile, which was kept up for more than half an hour without doing any injury to either party. The shots from Pleasonton's guns did not reach the enemy's position by twenty rods. During the cannonading I went to Gen. Pleasonton and explained the condition of things. I told him the enemy were crossing the road and would go to White's Ford and cross without opposition, as I knew the ninety-ninth Pennsylvania, with only three hundred and fifty men would run without attempting to oppose them; that the shots were falling far short of the mark and amongst my men, and if he would let me have my

---

[10] Walker, History of the Fourth Maine, p. 34.

men I would stop some of the enemy. His reply was: "I am in command and will manage this fight without your advice."

"Not withstanding his hauteur, I approached him the second time, and urged him to send a force from his fifteen hundred cavalry to Whites Ford, to prevent some of the confederates from crossing; and after a few minutes parley he called one of his officers and told him he might take a force and go to the ford. The officer formed about three hundred of his men and left. They did not appear to be in as much of a hurry as my father used to be when sending his boys into the field to hoe potatoes. They reported they arrived in time to see the last one cross. Fifty good men placed on the island they were obliged to pass, could have prevented any number from crossing, as the horses had to wade more than half a mile in water from one to three feet deep, and to pass within one hundred feet of the head of the island, which was in the center of the river. The battery firing had been going on for about thirty minutes when I collected a few of my men and advanced, and the enemy, seeing us, left in a hurry. Most of them had crossed the road and were making tracks across the field, in the direction of the river. Three or four of their rear guard had their horses shot and fell into our hands."

As soon as the firing had commenced the Fourth Maine Boys that had spent the night at Poolesville began to march to the sound of guns. As soon as Pleasonton spotted them he immediately ordered up his guns. Walker was forced to send one of his officers out to prove to Pleasonton that they were his own men. "When Pleasonton learned that they were our men, and that there was no further danger, he was the bravest of the brave. Ordering an advance and assuming all the authority of a royal duke, he went to the ford where all the rebels had crossed, and fired a few shots across the river."[11]

Walker always considered the Stuart affair a fiasco and even issued an official complaint to General Stoneman. Stoneman stated that there would undoubtedly be an investigation and asked that the Colonel be prepared to back up his report. No inquiry ever resulted and the whole matter was hushed up by the Army of the Potomac. Walker later expressed the opinion that "this was one of the most disgraceful affairs that came under my observation while in the service. Had Kearney, Sheridan, Barlow or Berry been in command there, or any on of others whom I might name; or had I been left to act according to my judgment,

---

[11] Ibid. pp. 34-35.

there would not have been so many rebels re-enter Virginia that morning."[12]

The 4th Maine marched to Poolesville on the same day that the Stuart affair took place. Here they joined with the rest of their brigade, which was now under the command of General Ward. General Birney had been reassigned to another post, acting as division commander. Captain Glover of Company D resigned his commission and returned to Maine in the company of Colonel Walker, who was returning to Rockland for the purpose of recruiting soldiers for his regiment.

On Tuesday October 28th, along with the rest of its division, now under the direction of General Stoneman, the Maine boys traversed the Potomac into Virginia. The men crossed at White's Ford and camped just a few miles beyond. They remained there until October 31st when they moved to Leesburg and bivouacked.

On the morning of November 1st, 1862, the regiment did its annual survey of the state of the regiment. Following are the results:

Commissioned Officers

Present for duty	24
On detached service	5
Absent with leave	3
Absent without leave	1
Absent Sick	1

Total	34

Enlisted Men

Present	377
On detached service	92
Absent with leave	12
Absent without leave	32
Absent sick	223
Total	736

[12] Ibid., pp. 35-36.

Encampment of 4th Maine near Fort Lyons in Virginia.
(Photo U. S. Army Military History Institute, Washington, D. C.)

On November 1, there were 770 officers and enlisted men remaining in the regiment out of the original 1000 that had left Rockland just seventeen months before. Thirty per cent of the soldiers were sick and in various hospitals. Five percent had deserted or were missing in action. Only 401 men could be counted on for service on this day, which was actually pretty much on par. Historically, the average strength of a Union regiment during the Civil War was about 400 soldiers.

The 4th Maine's division, during the month of November, was in a constant state of motion. Slowly, yet deliberately, it crept along, crisscrossing the Virginia countryside. The regiment visited places like Middleburg, Salem, and Waterloo. On November 10th they were detailed, once more, to support General Pleasonton's cavalry when it crossed the north fork of the Rappahannock River. The detail lasted just three days, including one day's picket duty after they re-crossed the stream. They then continued on to Warrenton, Bealeton, Morrisville, and finally to Stafford Court House. It was here that Colonel Walker rejoined the regiment following his recruiting trip back home.[13]

When Colonel Walker returned to his unit on November 28, the regiment was in a sad state of affairs. A great many of the men were very poorly clothed. Most were without overcoats, and a legion of them did not even have shoes. Many of these essential items were in short supply due to their loss when the canal boat had overturned the previous summer. The Mainers had stoically suffered through the cold and blustery weather of late fall, however. For the record, it was not until the evening of December 2 that new, replacement clothing arrived for the soldiers.[14]

Meanwhile, the rebels discovered that the new Federal commander, General Ambrose Burnside, had ordered General Sumner's Grand Division, consisting of two army corps and over 30,000 troops, to make their way to Falmouth, a village on the north side of the Rappahannock River opposite Fredericksburg. This was one of the few times during the war that Robert E. Lee had not been able to foresee the intention of his opponent. Burnside had stolen a march on him. The design was for Sumner to cross the Rappahannock, before the rebels could send forces against him. Lee, always quick to react, sent

[13] Walker, Report to Adjutant General on the Battle of Fredericksburg, January 1, 1863, p. 1.
[14] Walker Adjutant General Report 1862, p. 23.

Longstreet's Corps on a forced march to the town, arriving on the opposite bank of the river at about 3 P.M. on November 21.[15]

By this time General Sumner had already positioned his troops and artillery on Stafford Heights overlooking Fredericksburg. The same day that Longstreet arrived, Sumner sent an ultimatum to the town's mayor stating that he must surrender the city by 5 P.M. If he did not Sumner would allow sixteen hours for the women and children to be removed and then shell the town. Feeling more secure with the presence of Confederate troops about him, the mayor, at Longstreet's urging, let the demand expire. Sumner did not shell the town, however. By the end of the day, though, Burnside would have over 110,000 troops along the banks of the Rappahannock at Falmouth.[16]

Burnside had ordered pontoon bridges a week before the beginning of the campaign. For some unexplainable reason, though, the boats did not arrive until November 24. By this time 35,000 rebel soldiers had already begun to entrench on the heights west of town. Jackson had been ordered from the valley on November 26. When he reached Fredericksburg he was dispatched to guard against a Federal crossing farther downstream.[17]

On the morning of December 3 Colonel Walker was ordered to report to General Woodbury's engineer brigade. The 4th Maine was to prepare four days rations for what was known as "fatigue duty". As Burnside had not decided where he would cross the river to attack Lee, the 4th Maine, in company with the 128th New York, was ordered to move down river about seven miles and cut timber for the construction of corduroy roads and bridging. Being from Maine it was naturally assumed that the men were lumberjacks as well. Though the vast majority of them were actually farmers, it soon became obvious that most could handle an ax.[18] In the space of four days they cut enough logs, twelve feet long and six inches in diameter, "to fill three hundred teams."[19]

On the morning of December 9 the 4th Maine, numbering three hundred and seventy-five men, along with the 128th New York, nearly eight hundred men strong, and the 300 teams, were instructed to haul

---

[15] Longstreet, Battles and Leaders, p. 70.

[16] Ibid.

[17] Luvas and Nelson, U. S. Army War College Guide to the Battles of Chancellorsville and Fredericksburg, pp. 3-4.

[18] Walker, Fredericksburg, p. 1.

[19] Walker, History of 4th Maine, p. 37.

The man standing on the boxes between the gas generators was later identified by his wife as John Kellock, a private in company B. See arrow. (Brady Photo)

the timber ten miles downstream to a place on the Rappahannock called Skinker's Neck. A crossing of the river at this point was now being more seriously considered as a way of getting around Lee's flank. Their instructions were to build a corduroy road twenty-four feet wide and eleven hundred feet long across a swamp. They were also to grade a two-hundred-foot section as an approach to this wet area. One of General Woodbury's staff accompanied the men to the area in order to make sure the instructions were carried out correctly.

Burnside, with his huge army and massive assemblage of artillery, at least to all appearances, had waited patiently on the opposite bank for Lee to assemble his army. Early on December 9, the army commanders met to determine the strategy for the crossing of the river. It was decided that the corps would cross directly in front of Fredericksburg. To keep the Confederate Army off balance, and to keep Jackson's men scattered and south of the town, it was decided that the Maine and New York men would be sent to build the road at Skinker's Neck anyway. The noise of the axes and the camp fires would serve as a diversion, but would not actually be used. Pontoons would be put across the river in the early morning of December 11.[20]

The unit arrived within a half mile of their assigned work area at about 3:30 P.M. It was then decided to wait for the cover of darkness before taking up their position. At 4 P.M. Colonel Walker received orders to park the teams and to provide enough food for the men and the teams for three days. The road over which they had traveled "had not been traversed by large bodies of troops, and the fields were well stocked with corn and fodder from which the teams were well supplied." Walker immediately sent for rations, as well as blankets and tents. Unfortunately, the supplies did not arrive until the next morning. As a result the men spent a very cold and miserable night along the banks of the river. "All that the men could do was to build fires of fence rails, which were in abundance, stand as near as possible to the blaze, and by changing front thirty times a minute keep themselves as comfortable as possible."[21]

After the supplies arrived early the next morning, the soldiers spent the day preparing their quarters. "The weather had moderated during the day and all were expecting a night's rest; but in the army the

[20] Foote, The Civil War, Vol. II, p. 26.
[21] Walker, History of 4th Maine, op. cit., p. 37.

best laid plans and most confident hopes are liable to summary disruption."[22] About 4:30 in the afternoon the unit was ordered to unburden the wagons and complete their assigned labors. Walker's "heavy weight", Lieutenant Colonel Lorenzo Carver, was put in charge of the construction project. "A ship carpenter by trade he had no superior in such duty." By 9:00 P.M. all the wagons had been unloaded and the corduroy road was well underway.[23]

The activity on the north shore of the Rappahannock had not gone unnoticed. Major Pitcher, who was in charge of the pickets, had taken note of the arrival of Confederate troops on the opposite bank, all within two hundred and fifty yards of the work party. Marksmen were dispatched to the river bank to protect the men. Not a single shot was fired by either side, however, throughout the night.

More than eighteen hundred feet of corduroy road had been completed by 4 A.M., making a good approach to a crossing by the army on a narrow stretch of the river. In the mean time they were commanded to rejoin their brigade as soon as possible. The soldiers were allowed to rest for two hours and then put on the march. The roads were muddy and the trek was slow for men who had had little rest for two days. It took more than six hours to cover the ten miles, arriving back at their old camp about noon.[24]

As soon as Colonel Walker returned to the encampment he went immediately to see the quartermaster. As all of the men were exhausted from having worked around the clock unloading wagons and building roads, he instructed them to get some rest. The quartermaster, however, had received orders for the regiment to rejoin the brigade and prepare to move out immediately. The colonel was so incensed that he started for brigade headquarters on his own to plead for rest for his men. On the way, though, he bumped into one of the General Burnside's aids who had special orders for him to rejoin the brigade without delay. Colonel Walker stated that the order, "was the first since being in the service I was tempted to disobey". The colonel did his duty, however, and by 3:30 all but seventy-five of his men, who were too exhausted to march and had been excused for duty by the regimental surgeon, attempted to

[22] Ibid.
[23] Ibid.
[24] Walker, Fredericksburg, p. 2.

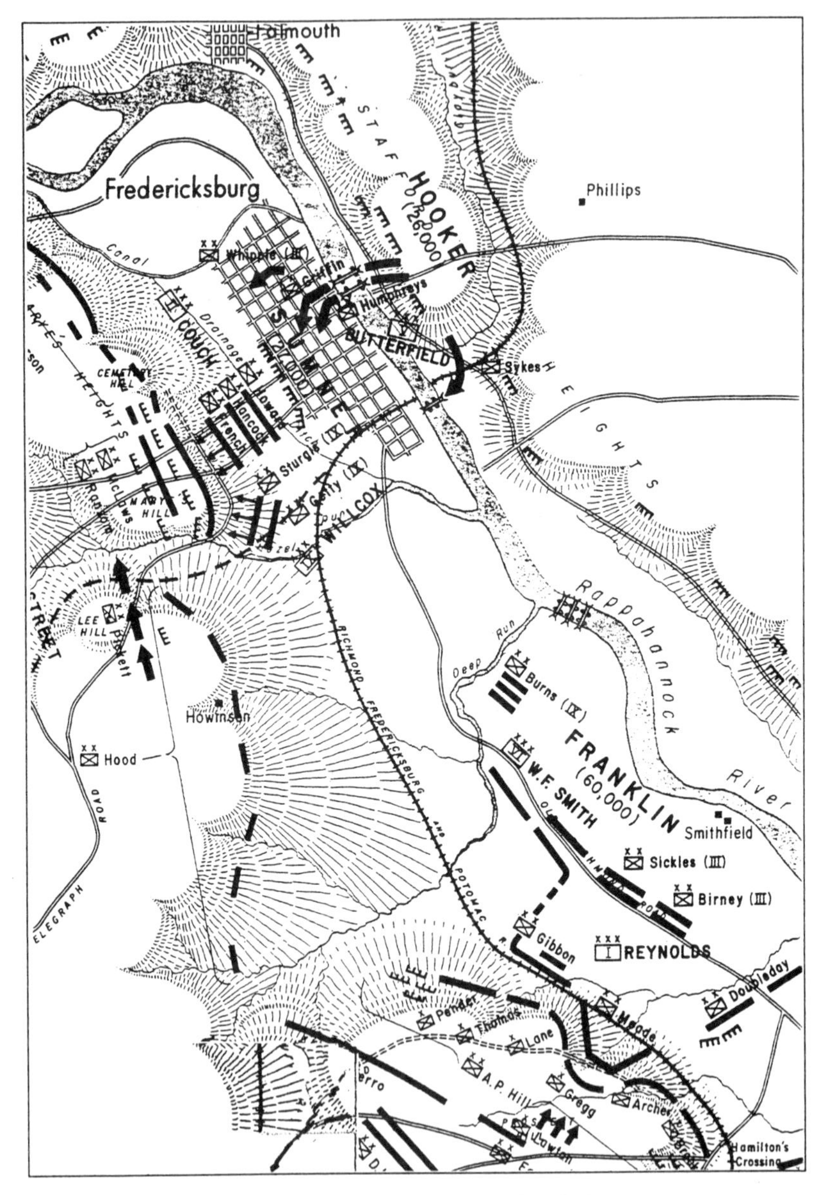

Map showing troop positions at Fredericksburg

join with the rest of their brigade. Unable to locate them, the regiment spent another cold, miserable night without shelter or fires.

Much of Burnside's army had already crossed the river by dawn on the 12th. Ward's brigade, however, did not make its move to the river until 4:30 in the afternoon, and did not actually make the crossing until the following morning. To further complicate matters, one officer and thirty of their men were detached from the 4th Maine to assist Professor Thadeus Lowe's Balloon Corps. Though a unique and vital assignment in 19th century warfare, it was one that would serve only to further weaken the regiment at a time when numbers were vital.[25]

The men of the 4th who were assigned to the Balloon Corps probably only added their muscles to Lowe's work at Fredericksburg. Professor Lowe's title was purely complimentary, for his official designation was "Chief of Aeronautics, Army of the Potomac". In any case Burnside had ordered that the two, rather sizable yellow balloons, be raised over Stafford Heights. One can only imagine the men, high in their cold and lofty observation posts, peering through the fog to the shrouded landscape beneath them, attempting to glean whatever last minute information they could which might prove decisive in the fight. Perhaps they would even witness the drama that was about to overtake the rest of these "fighting tigers" from mid-coast Maine.[26]

As the battle was about to begin, it is important to get a picture of the overall disposition of troops on the field. General Sumner's Right Grand Division, consisting of two corps and 25,000 men, had positioned themselves in the town of Fredericksburg in front of a soon to be famous hill known as Mayre's Heights. On the 13th these Union soldiers would be thrown against this almost impregnable bastion in wave after wave of suicidal attacks. The men attacking here would be cannon fodder to Longstreet's 35,000 defenders.

To the south Franklin had crossed the river with about 60,000 soldiers, two large corps, including cavalry and artillery. These men had been located in front of Prospect Hill, and though it would not be as well remembered as the promontory just to the north, it would leave a lasting impression on all who gazed upon it. Here a small portion of these numbers would be led in a deadly assault on Stonewall Jackson's corps of 34,000 waiting warriors.

---

[25] Ibid.

[26] Foote, op. cit., p. 33.

The Center Grand Division, under Fighting Joe Hooker, numbered 26,000 souls. Hooker's two corps were to be split up. Major General Daniel Butterfield's Fifth Army Corps was sent across the upper pontoon bridges and would provide support to Sumner. The Third Army Corps, led by Brigadier General George Stoneman, would cross over the lower bridges and provide support to Franklin. The 4th Maine was a part of Ward's Second Brigade, of Brigadier General Birney's, 1st Division. If the men were to see action it would be with Franklin, against the now legendary Stonewall Jackson.

The fighting at Fredericksburg began on the Union left flank. Reynold's I Corps, consisting of three divisions, and 18,000 men, began their advance through the rapidly thinning fog. The attack would begin here in hopes of breaking through Jackson's lines and getting behind Longstreet. This would cut the rebel's of retreat on Mayre's Heights. As soon as this attack was in motion General Sumner would advance his lines, catching Lee in the middle.[27]

As the blue line drove forward they immediately began to take rebel artillery fire. Major John Pelham of Alabama moved two of his guns into an exposed position without infantry support. From here he could fire lengthwise down the flank of the Federal troops as they advanced. Pelham maintained his fire incessantly, and was able to stall the assault. Union artillery then began an intense barrage upon the Confederate guns until they finally knocked one of them out of commission. Eventually, Pelham was forced to retreat. He had performed a remarkable deed of daring and courage for which history would not forget him, even after his death.

The Union guns turned on the ridge next which was the objective of the attack. When Stoneman felt that the rebel positions were sufficiently softened up he ordered the advance to continue. Abner Doubleday's Division moved out on the left. Shortly after their departure his brigades were forced to oblique to the left in order to protect the corps' flank. Doubleday held his force here astride the Old Richmond Road for the greater part of the day.

Once the rise to his front had been riddled by artillery, General George Gordon Meade charged forward with his 4,500 Pennsylvanians. The troops drove straight for the railroad and into an unprotected gap in the Confederate line. General A. P. Hill had purposely left this spot

[27] Ibid.

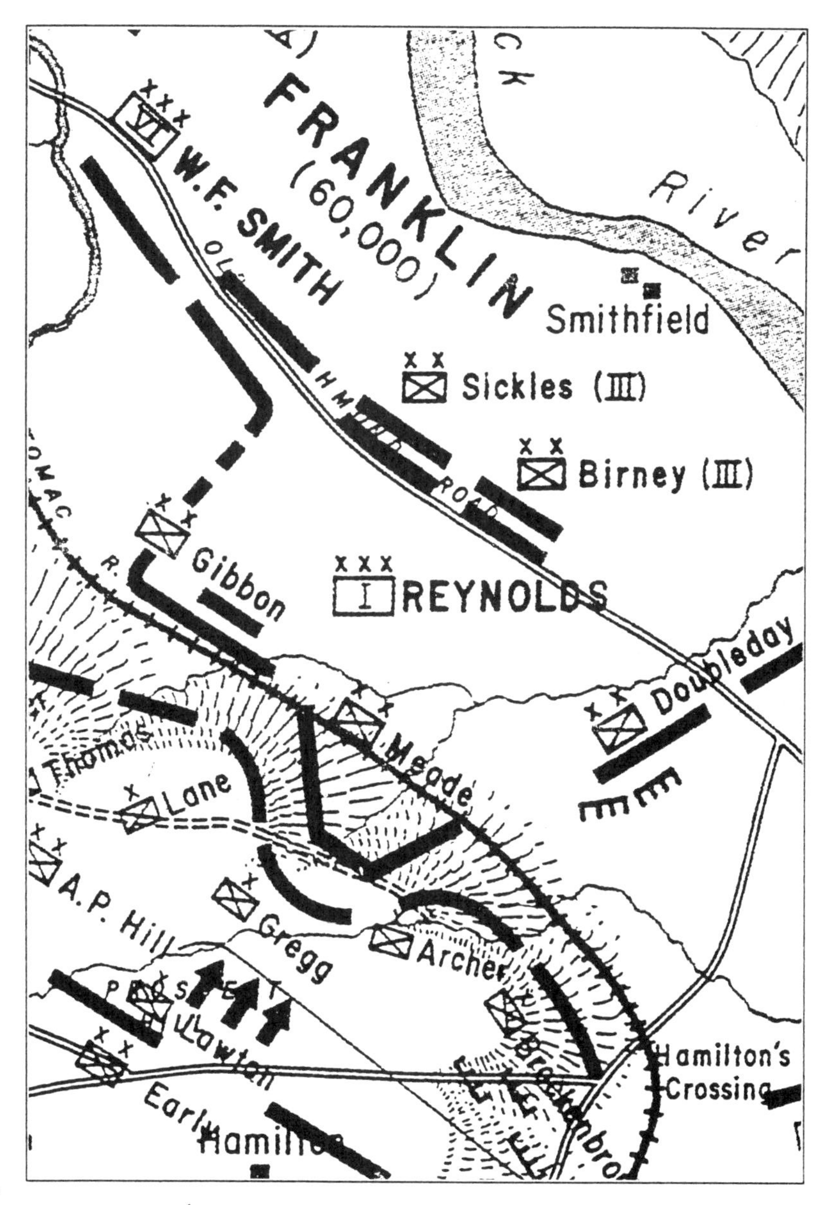

Meade's attack created a huge buldge in the Confederate line.

undefended, thinking that the bog that was located in this area was impassable. Meade quickly proved him wrong. His attack continued forward, bumping into a second line of defenders. These too they passed, moving all the way to the military road at the top of the hill and into the clearing beyond. Two battle flags and over two hundred prisoners were taken.[28]

Brigadier General John Gibbon's Division had also moved out with Meade but got only as far as the railroad before the advance was halted by heavy enemy infantry and cannon fire. Hill's regiments held their ground tenaciously. The rebels fired down on the Union troops from their elevated position, and as a result they took a heavy toll of Federal troops. Gibbon was wounded in the battle and had to be carried from the field. Meade and Gibbon had now reached their high water mark.

Meade's troops were in a very dangerous predicament. In moving so far forward and having left all of their flank support far behind them, they were very nearly surrounded. The enemy was firing at them from all sides. Jubal Early, sensing the importance of sealing up the breach immediately, charged Meade's division and began to drive it back through the bog and into the fields beyond.[29]

As Meade began to be forced back he immediately sent a message to General David Birney to lend his support without delay. Birney sent the 99th Pennsylvania, the 55th New York, and the 3rd Maine to support Meade's batteries. These guns were without ammunition, in soft ground, and nearly crippled. Birney then sent the 38th and 40th New York forward to help rally the retreating forces by a rapid advance. The 4th Maine was also ordered to join in the charge, and did so, following about two hundred yards behind the others. It was soon found that the Pennsylvania boys were unstoppable in retreat and when Gibbon's men saw what was happening they too joined in the withdrawal.[30]

Previously, about 9:30 A.M. the 4th Maine Infantry had crossed the Rappahannock on the lower pontoon bridges and passed about two miles to their south. This brought them into a position between Gibbon and Meade. Hamilton's Crossing was to their front and slightly to the left. Here they awaited for their call to arms. Shot and shell were falling

---

[28] Ibid., p. 37

[29] Luvas, op. cit., p. 49.

[30] Official Records, Ward's Report.

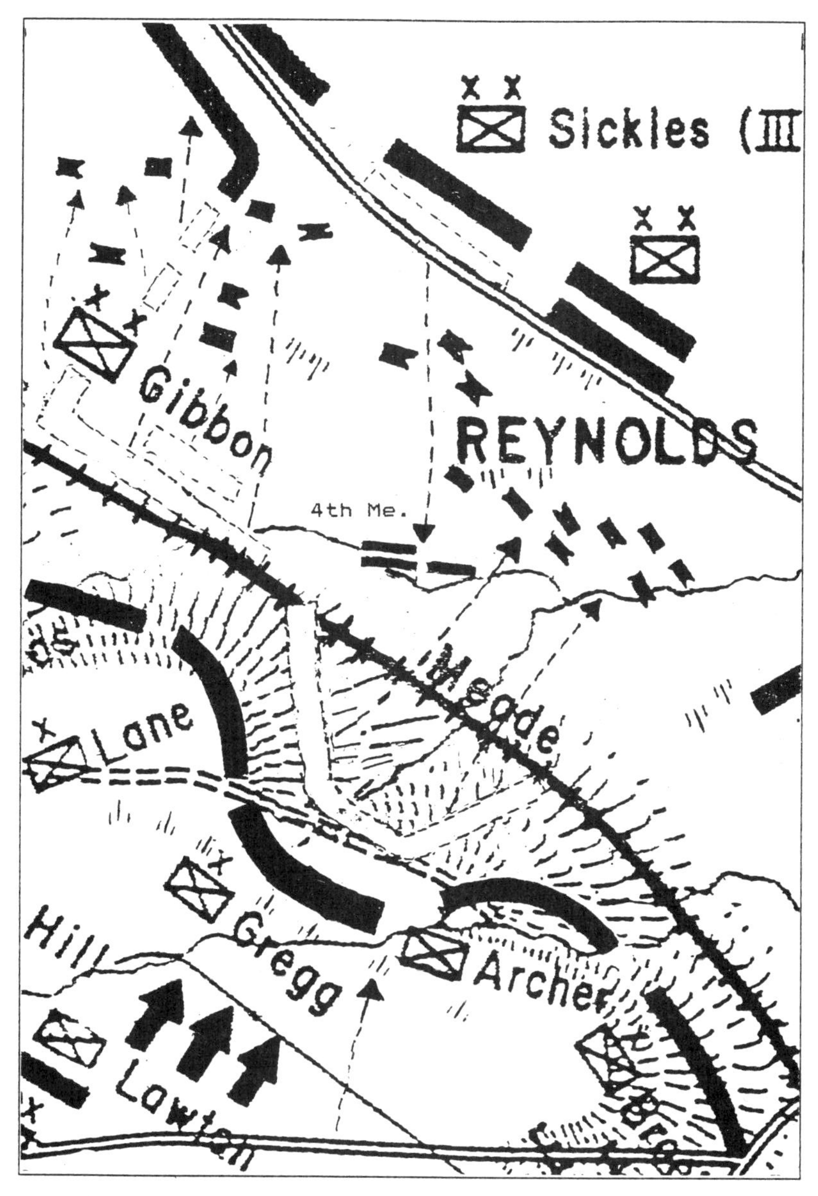

The 4th Maine Infantry, along with the 38th and 40th New York, charges into the same gap that Meade's troops were now being driven from.

all about them, bursting in the air above them, and exploding in the ground beneath their feet. Standing and waiting, amid all the clamor of war was, without doubt, the most difficult thing a soldier had to do. He was totally helpless, not knowing if the next artillery projectile was earmarked for him. The whole situation was totally unnerving.

The Limerock Regiment now consisted of just twenty-one officers and one hundred and ninety enlisted men. As stated earlier, thirty-six had stayed behind due to fatigue. Thirty had been siphoned off to assist the balloonists. Thirteen were assigned as brigade guard, and an additional ten had to be left behind as pioneers to guard knapsacks and personal belongings. The rest of this now tiny command, charged across the open field and into the woods with the New York boys.[31]

Colonel Walker recalled much later in life that General Ward's brigade "was the first of the division to make an advance. We went in where Gen Meade's division had been driven out. The Fortieth New York, on the left, was the first to advance, then the Thirty-Eighth New York, Fourth and Third Maine and Fifty-Seventh Pennsylvania, each regiment one hundred yards in rear of the one at its left. The Fortieth and Thirty-Eighth were in the open field, driving the enemy's skirmish line and advancing to the railroad embankment, where they received a murderous fire."[32]

As the Mainers neared the woods in their line of battle they worked themselves abreast and to the right of the other regiments. Colonel Walker joined the members of his unit on their right side. At this point the line was joined to the other regiments by what Walker called "an acute angle of 25 degrees". The New Yorkers, having arrived at the railroad, were the first to observe the position of the rebel infantry. In the midst of all the commotion the two regiments became so unnerved by the sight that they panicked and routed back upon themselves, leaving the 4th alone to their fate.[33]

Walker remembered that his "men struck a point of woods which was filled with the enemy's advanced line, which retired before us to the railroad, where we met them at close quarters. Officers used their pistols and the men their steel. The Third Maine and the Fifty-Seventh Pennsylvania, realizing the futility of the attack, did not advance as far

---

[31] Walker, Fredericksburg, p. 3.
[32] Walker, History of 4th Maine, op. cit. p. 38.
[33] Walker, Fredericksburg, op. cit. p. 3.

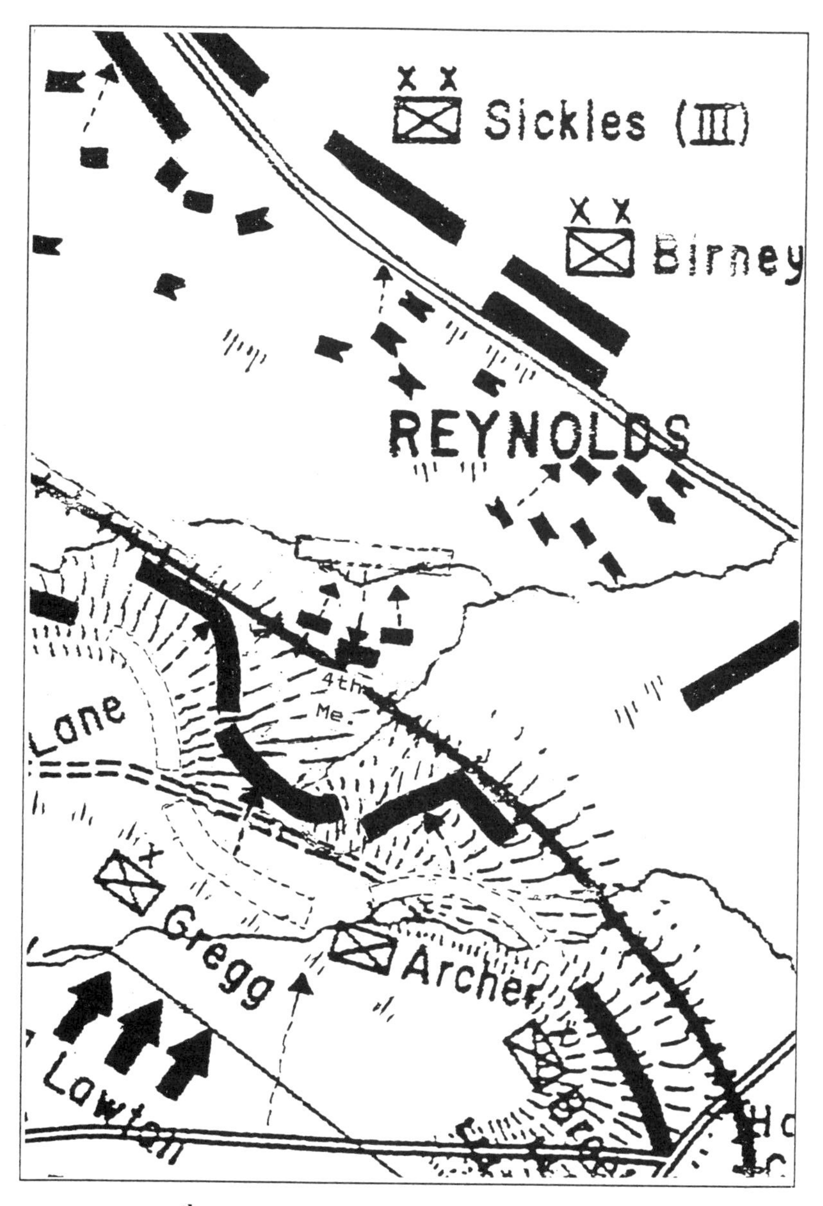

The 4th Maine advances alone beyond the railroad.

as we did, and the Thirty-Eighth and Fortieth New York having withdrawn, my right and left flanks were exposed. It might have been a saving of a life at that time to have surrendered, but I could not see it."[34]

Shot, shell, canister, and projectiles of every description were falling heavily among Walker's force. Major Pitcher was killed instantly as he urged his men to stand their ground. Adjutant Libby was seriously wounded by two bullets, one in the shoulder and the other in the thigh. Lieutenant Colonel Carver's clothing was riddled with bullet holes and yet none of these found their mark. Of the four Captains on the field, three were bloodied. Five of the six first Lieutenants, and five of the eight second Lieutenants were either killed or wounded, leaving the combatants with little or no command structure. Still the line held.[35]

Colonel Walker now attempted to bring his regiment "off by the left flank". In this way he hoped to hold the line that had been vacated by the New Yorkers. This standard military maneuver was begun on the left, but the right part of the line never responded to the command. They were, at this point, occupied in driving back the Confederates in their front. The effect of the order was to separate the two wings of the unit by some thirty to forty yards. Walker saw what was happening and immediately halted his men, forcing them to hold their ground against the huge force that had routed the other two regiments.

The right wing was now stalled at the railroad. The tiny force was outflanked and nearly surrounded. The left now had to hold until the right rejoined them or they would most certainly be lost. The men resisted the hail of lead as they continued their tedious task of loading and firing, loading and firing. In the one or two minutes that it probably took for the two wings to rejoin, dozens of men fell, struck not just once, but repeatedly. The 4th Maine was rapidly disappearing before their colonel's eyes.

Reunited at last, the regiment began to fall back. It is important to realize that even in the midst of their own destruction they stopped to pick up their wounded. In small, scattered groups, the men emerged from the woods and out onto the open field, most dragging a friend or comrade with them. Even the wounded helped the more seriously wounded. Sixty-three men were dragged to safety. Occasionally a soldier would stop, load, and fire a shot to his rear in a vain attempt to

---

[34] Walker, History of 4th Maine, op. cit. p. 38.

[35] Walker, Fredericksburg, op. cit., 3.

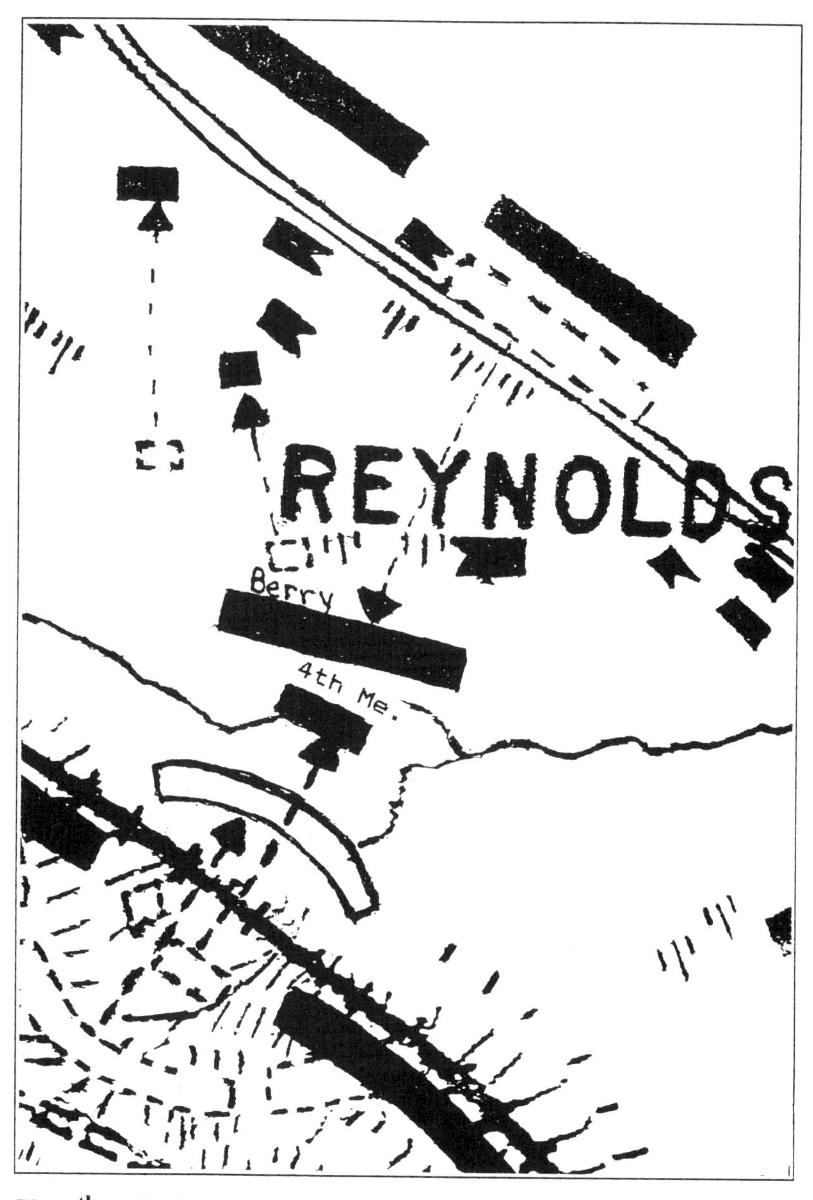

The 4th is finally forced to retreat. Hiram Berry, seeing the 4th Maine's situation, moves his men out to aid in their rescue.

retard the advance of the enemy. All the while the Confederates were nipping at their heels in a countercharge intended to capture or destroy what was left of this small body of soldiers. General Lee, looking down upon his troops as they filled in the gap caused by the federal attack told General Longstreet, " It is well that war is so terrible - we should grow too fond of it."

When General Berry, now commanding the 3rd Brigade of Brigadier General David Birney's division, saw his old regiment come stumbling out of the thickets and across the field, his concern for them turned to action. Berry quickly charged his regiments across the open ground. His brigade fired round after round into the rebel troops that were threatening to cut off the 4th's retreat. The enemy hesitated momentarily and quickly fell back to the relative safety of the trees, now leaving their own dead and wounded behind.[36]

While the officers, always more visible and tempting as targets, were dropping, so too were the privates, corporals and sergeants. Fifty-six percent (56%) of the regiment's soldiers in the field were either killed, wounded, or captured. The day after the battle Company C had all but disappeared. Of the eighteen who entered the fight, only Corporal Warren Austin of Thomaston, and Private Austin Cunningham, of Warren, were able to report for duty. Many of the other companies were in similar shape, though none were quite as devastated.

Many, like 1st Sergeant James Sholler of Company D, had multiple injuries, wounded once in the left hand and once in the left leg. Sholler was fortunate and only had to have a finger amputated. Private William B. Tibbets of Company E, was shot in the right lung, the right foot, as well as the left arm. He would eventually expire from his injuries, four days after Christmas. Private D. M. Allen was wounded severely in the head, his right arm, and his right side. The list of injuries is frightening, especially considering the poor quality of medical care that was available. The names of the participants and the severity of their impairment can be seen in the list in the appendix, as submitted by Colonel Walker to Maine's Adjutant General early in 1863.

As the regiment continued in their sad retreat, they fell back to their original position. Here they took cover from rebel artillery fire as best they could. Fred Lowe, Eben Sanborn, Alfred Cunningham, and Mark Cunningham, all musicians, were immediately dispatched by Colonel

---

[36] Ibid.

Second Lieutenant George Abbott was wounded at Fredericksburg and was later transferred to the Invalid Corp. (Photo Maine State Archives)

Walker to help out at the hospital. Later it was assumed that they had crossed the river with the wounded on the 15th. Dr. Martin later stated that they had not, and so at the time that the list of casualties was being composed it was assumed that they had been taken as prisoners. The men would later return to their regiment and once again assume their duties as musicians.[37]

While the 4th was throwing itself against the Confederates in their front, Sumner and Hooker were sending suicidal assaults against Longstreet's entrenched troops along the stone wall in front of Marye's Heights. Repeatedly, these men charged, and repeatedly they were met with round after round of canister. The Federals dropped to the ground, like leaves from a tree in a fall breeze. For those still unbroken, the Georgians and North Carolinians would stand up from behind the wall and let loose successive volleys. More troops would melt away, eight thousand and more by day's end, mounded one upon the other on a narrow stretch of ground between the canal and the stone battlement.

A Confederate artilleryman, William Owen, said of the fighting at Mayre's Heights: "...volley after volley is poured into the enemies ranks. Great gaps appear. We give them canister again and again. A few leave the ranks. More follow. The lines halt for an instant; and, turning, are seen running in great disorder towards the town... The field before us is dotted with patches of blue... the dead and wounded of the Federal Infantry."[38]

The 4th Maine, along with the rest of the army, spent a cold and sleepless night on the battlefield. The cries of the wounded who had been left behind filled the air. Some of the men were forced to take overcoats from the lifeless bodies strewed upon the ground in order to survive the cold and wind. The night sky, despite the absence of warming camp fires, was aglow with the northern lights. Each thought that this, certainly, was his last night on earth, and for many it was.

With the coming of the sun's first light, Colonel Walker dispatched thirty of his men to work Randolph's 1st Rhode Island Battery. The few who remained were sent to relieve the brigade guard. Elijah Walker was placed in charge of the III Corps skirmish line. Walker remembered that "in front of our line all was quiet. The opposing pickets were in open field, not more than two hundred yards

---

[37] Ibid.

[38] Wheeler, Lee's Terrible Swift Sword, p. 285.

apart. They had agreed not to fire at one another unless ordered to advance, and then to fire the first shot high. This agreement was strictly carried out, and not a shot was fired on the Third Corps picket line, while on our right and left they were popping away continuously. I rode along the line as unconcerned as though we were friends, and the officer in command of the Confederate line did the same."[39]

The fighting on this day involved only the pickets. Occasionally, these Maine men would have to take cover from a stray artillery round, but nothing more than that. The 4th Maine had fought itself out. The regiment knew that their comrades had been sacrificed by generals who had senselessly sent them on fruitless and entirely uncoordinated attacks upon the enemy. Their morale was now the lowest it would ever reach.

At dark on the evening of December 15, the 4th was ordered to retreat along with the rest of its brigade back across the Rappahannock River. Colonel Walker, who was acting as division officer of the day, was forced to remain behind in charge of the pickets who were guarding the retreat. "Of all the places to try my nerves, the worst was to be in command of the last troops to leave when the army was retreating from the victorious enemy...It was the longest seven hours I ever experienced, while waiting for the order to withdraw the pickets. My only companions were two cavalry orderlies, whom I kept busy replenishing the fires so as to deceive the enemy. I had nearly given up when Captain Bristow, topographical engineer of the corps, came with the order. Leaving my horse with the orderlies, I walked the entire length of the line, giving orders to fall back to the road and assemble at the right...I found the pickets assembled as ordered, and we followed our guide. Capt. Bristow, to the pontoon bridge."

Walker stated that, though it was done without accident it was an unpleasant task. Walker goes on to relate that he "remained to see the rear of my command on the bridge. Our picket line had been composed of two small regiments, one of two hundred, the other of four hundred men, who had all followed us from that fated ridge. To my dismay the smaller regiment had not arrived. This was the most trying time of all. All the pickets, except Gen. Doubleday's, had arrived, and the general in command said he would wait but a few minutes for the missing men. The horrors of a rebel prison stared me in the face, but I resolved to find the lost troops or go to Richmond with them. I found them huddled

---

[39] Walker. History of 4th Maine, op. cit., p. 38.

together about half a mile away, and forced them to the bridge, which was reached not an instant too soon. I was the last man to cross the bridge, and when safely over daylight was rapidly strengthening."[40]

Once across Walker rejoined his command. He continues; "On the morning of the 16th we arrived at our present encampment, the same we had left on the morning of Dec. 3rd, having been exposed seven days and nights without shelter, and living on pork and hard bread...I can but speak in the highest terms of praise of my men and officers during this fearful engagement. Several of those slightly wounded returned to duty as soon as their wounds were dressed."[41]

One of the regiment's casualties was Major Pitcher. The major's body had been discovered, in addition to two other officers and twenty of the enlisted men, during the armistice on the afternoon of the 15th. "Lieutenant Goodale and the men were robed in blankets and laid side by side in one grave. Major Pitcher's body was carried across the river by the boys, embalmed, and sent to Bangor, where rests one of the noblest of Maine's sons."[42]

In praise of Major Pitcher, the division commander, General Birney, said that he "died as one of our own division dies, with breast to the foe, doing his whole duty." Colonel Walker called him "a good and brave officer and Christian. He was beloved and respected by all the Regt." Birney, in fact, carried his show of respect a step further by naming the divisional camp, Camp Pitcher. The 4th Maine, breaking their own tradition of using the name Camp Knox, did the same.[43]

The 4th Maine was devastated at Fredericksburg. Fortunately for them though, they had tucked eighty-nine soldiers away in detached service prior to battle. With more targets on the field there certainly would have been even more carnage. Exactly 100 men had crossed back to the heights at Falmouth, and eleven of these were walking wounded. On Christmas Day the regiment could count only 189 men for active duty.

Christmas left the men little to be thankful for. Their term of duty was now about half up. Their confidence in their commander, General Burnside, had totally vanished. They were alone, amidst the many thousands, in their trenches of despair. There had been much pain and

---

40 Ibid., p. 39.

41 Whitman, Maine in the War, p. 100.

42 Walker, History of the 4th Maine, op. cit., p. 39.

43 Ibid.

sacrifice and very little gain. Eighteen months of death and dying and they were no closer to Richmond than when they had started. It was the day of the celebration of the birth of Christ, and all there was to eat was salt pork and hardtack. It was difficult to think of anything, except their neglected stomachs. This was the army's revenge for a job well done. It was Christmas dinner, served up cold.

Chapter 8

"We Can Go to Richmond as Prisoners... or Charge them Breastworks."

The army had bivouacked at Falmouth following the battle of Fredericksburg. The men were cold and hungry. Timber in the region had previously been stripped and there was little available for shelter or for warmth. Their larder consisted, almost totally, of a starvation diet of salt pork and hardtack. This was due, almost entirely, to the dishonesty of Union commissary officers. Morale was dismally low and there had been almost constant talk of a winter offensive. Desertion was rampant in the ranks. Everyone was unhappy and miserable. It was their winter of discontent, the so-called "Valley Forge of the Union Army."[1]

The Union Army had lost 12,653 soldiers at Fredericksburg. This amounted to almost thirty men a minute. Both sides needed time to recover. Burnside, however, had different feelings on the matter. He had petitioned Halleck and the President almost immediately to resume the offensive. The government had been slow to respond, especially after so recent an embarrassment. Still by mid-December Burnside had prepared an acceptable plan to flank Lee on his right, thereby cutting him off from Richmond and trapping him against the Rappahannock.

Before beginning his campaign Burnside allowed women to visit the men in camp. On January 13th they began to arrive. General Birney, the 4th's Maine's Division Commander, traveled to Washington to meet a group of "ladies, sisters, or relatives of officers of his staff". This caused a great deal of justifiable excitement in the ranks of the regiments. The presence of the women, the sound of their voices in the camp, did more for morale in three days than any other course of action General Burnside could of taken. A subordinate writes of the visit; "They arrived at headquarters on the 13th, where everything was ready to receive them, and for three days there was nothing but gaiety, rides on

---

[1] Furgurson, Chancellorsville, p. 11.

horseback and drives in carriages, collations, reviews, music, and improvised dances by moonlight".[2]

All good things must come to an end, however, especially for an army in the field. When the orders came to prepare to march, the ladies were immediately escorted to the Aquia Creek Railroad, "like a flock of frightened grasshoppers", for their return to Washington. As the soldiers began to strike their tents there was disappointment on their faces but signs of animation in their movements. They were ready for a fight.[3]

Burnside, in early January, had begun to make feints in every possible direction. In actuality he had decided to cross his men at U. S. Ford, but due to delays caused by the weather, decided to use Banks' Ford instead which was much closer. At dawn on January 21st, the engineers were to put a pontoon bridge across the river and two of his Grand Divisions were to cross. Another Grand Division would traverse at Fredericksburg and pin down Lee's forces.[4]

As the camps began to stir to life, wagons loaded with pontoon boats, rations, ammunition, and supplies, began to lumber along the frozen roads. Artillery began to be pushed up to Banks' Ford to guard the crossing. As this army of men and equipment began to move along the river bank, the cold morning fog intensified and became even more penetrating. During the afternoon the fog became a light sprinkle, and by evening, transformed itself into an incessant deluge.

As the rains fell the roads began to soften. The clay laden soils caused the roads to begin to give way to the heavy loads dragged upon them. The pontoon wagons began to cut deep ruts into the paths. With each succeeding conveyance the ruts became even deeper until everything began to grind to a halt. The wagons were double teamed, but to no avail. Groups of one hundred and fifty or more men tugged along with the horses and still nothing moved. The effort was quickly becoming hopeless.[5]

Burnside insisted that the operation continue. He ordered up extra food, and the soldier's rations of whiskey, which only made the situation worse. Artillery sank so deep that only the muzzles showed their

---

[2] Wheeler, Lee's Terrible Swift Sword, p. 332.

[3] Ibid., p. 334.

[4] Furgurson, op. cit., p. 29.

[5] Ibid.

location. Wagons and equipment littered the landscape. The soldier's "morale sank with the wagons and the animals."[6]

The elements were finally victorious. While Burnside fought the mud, Lee had moved his men to meet the expected assault at Banks ford. The Confederates began to taunt the hapless Northerners by hanging signs on the trees with false directions on how to get to Richmond. By this time, however, the emphasis of the campaign had radically changed. It was not whether Burnside could continue the offensive, but whether he could keep the army from disappearing in the mire. With great effort, the Army of the Potomac wheeled and retreated to its camps at Falmouth. The 4th Maine, which had actually reached Banks' Ford, was forced to retreat with the rest.[7]

On their return to Camp Pitcher, the 4th busied itself with regimental drill and routine duty assignments. General Burnside, embarrassed once again in his efforts to gain a decisive victory for the north, was dismissed by President Lincoln and replaced by General Joseph Hooker. Hooker was a new and mysterious ingredient, and nobody knew quite what to expect from their new leader. The survival of the war effort, however, now rested squarely in his hands.

When Hooker took command he had 256,545 troops. A full 85,000 of this number were absent without leave. The men were deserting at the rate of nearly two hundred a day. On January 30th there were 147,184 ready for duty, including 30,000 that would be mustered out in May at the end of their nine month terms of enlistment. Change was desperately needed before the army self-destructed.[8]

In the lull between the mud fiasco and the spring offensive, Hooker reorganized the army by ridding it of the Grand Divisions and returning to the corps system. Each of the corps were then given distinctive badges so that they might better identify with their units and thus develop more pride in their successes. He also instituted a furlough system for the troops, based solely on their soldierly performance. Being able to see family and friends back home helped to improve the outlook of the enlisted men and raised morale significantly.[9]

---

[6] Ibid., pp. 15-16.
[7] Whitman, Mine in the War, p. 100.
[8] Furgurson, op. cit., p. 29.
[9] Ibid., p. 31.

The army had suffered greatly under Burnside in the area of nutrition. Therefore, Hooker next undertook the task of improving the soldiers' diet. He ordered that the men receive fresh bread four times a week and fresh vegetables twice. If the regiments did not receive this food allotment then the commissary officers were required to submit proof that it was not available. Finally there was accountability in the chain of supply.[10]

In early April President Lincoln paid a visit to Hooker at Falmouth. After reviewing the troops, the two men sat down to discuss plans for the impending offensive. Hooker told Lincoln, "My plans are perfect, and when I start to carry them out, may God have mercy on General Lee". The president, believing that his lieutenant was overconfident, retorted with this now famous line. "The hen is the wisest of all the animal creation because she never cackles until the egg is laid."[11]

Hooker had planned a large cavalry raid under the command of General George Stoneman in Lee's rear along the railroad, effectively cutting him off from Richmond. The infantry would then begin a secret flanking movement to their right and cross the upperRappahannock. The army would then assemble at Chancellorsville and immediately begin to press upon Lee's rear. While all this was transpiring several divisions would cross in front of Fredericksburg and threaten Lee's front. Lee would then be cut off and surrounded, with no avenue of retreat.[12]

Once again rains played havoc with the Union's battle plans. While the cavalry raid was delayed, Hooker's infantry began their march on schedule. The V, XI, and XII Corps were to cross the river at Kelley's Ford. Major General Darius Couch was to send two Divisions to Banks' and U. S. Fords while keeping another on display at Fredericksburg. Reynolds and Sedgwick were to cross at Fredericksburg. Sickles III Corps was to remain on the ready at Falmouth to move in whatever direction proved necessary.[13]

With Longstreet's two divisions on detached duty, Lee had barely 60,000 men. Joe Hooker had actually stolen a march on him and when Lee finally realized that the game was afoot, the Federals were already coming up quickly on his rear. To counter the threat, which at this point

[10] Ibid., p. 33.
[11] Wheeler, op. cit., p. 63.
[12] Furgurson, op cit., p. 63.
[13] Ibid., p. 67.

he could only guess at, Lee sent Anderson's lone division in the direction of Chancellorsville. When the Fredericksburg front remained inactive, he ordered Early and Barksdale's Brigade's, along with the reserve artillery, to defend Mayre's Heights. At midnight McLaw's Division was sent to join Anderson. In the early dawn of May 1st Stonewall Jackson and his men were also dispatched to the rear.[14] Lee, at this point, had a corps and a half to Hooker's seven. Lee had six divisions to the Union's twenty-one. This thin gray line was all that stood between success and disaster.[15]

Meanwhile, by the evening of April 30, the Union corps had begun to assemble around Chancellorsville. By two P.M., 50,000 soldiers had gathered. When Meade and Slocum met at the Chancellor's House both were ecstatic. Meade said to Slocum, "Hurrah for Old Joe! We're on Lee's flank. and he doesn't know it." Meade then attempted to get Slocum to choose his route to Fredericksburg, which was now only a half days march away. Meade was not aware, however, that Hooker had already ordered the troops to hold their positions for the night. This decision would prove to be fatal.[16]

Joe Hooker now issued General Order #47 to his command.

It is with heartfelt satisfaction the commanding general announces that the operations of the last three days have determined that our enemy must either ingloriously fly or come out from behind his defenses and give us battle on our own ground, where certain destruction awaits him. The operations of the Fifth, Eleventh, and Twelfth Corps have been a succession of splendid achievements.[17]

Meanwhile, on the 28th the 4th Maine had been ordered to break camp about four in the afternoon. They then marched five miles below Fredericksburg and acted as support for the troops crossing the river. This accomplished the unit then moved two miles upriver and bivouacked for the night. They were now directly across the river from the point at which they had gone into battle in December. Many a depressing memory were, doubtlessly, brought to mind.[18]

---

[14] Wheeler, op. cit., pp. 340-350.
[15] Furgurson, op. cit., p. 88.
[16] Ibid., p. 110.
[17] Ibid., p. 111.
[18] Whitman, op. cit., p. 100.

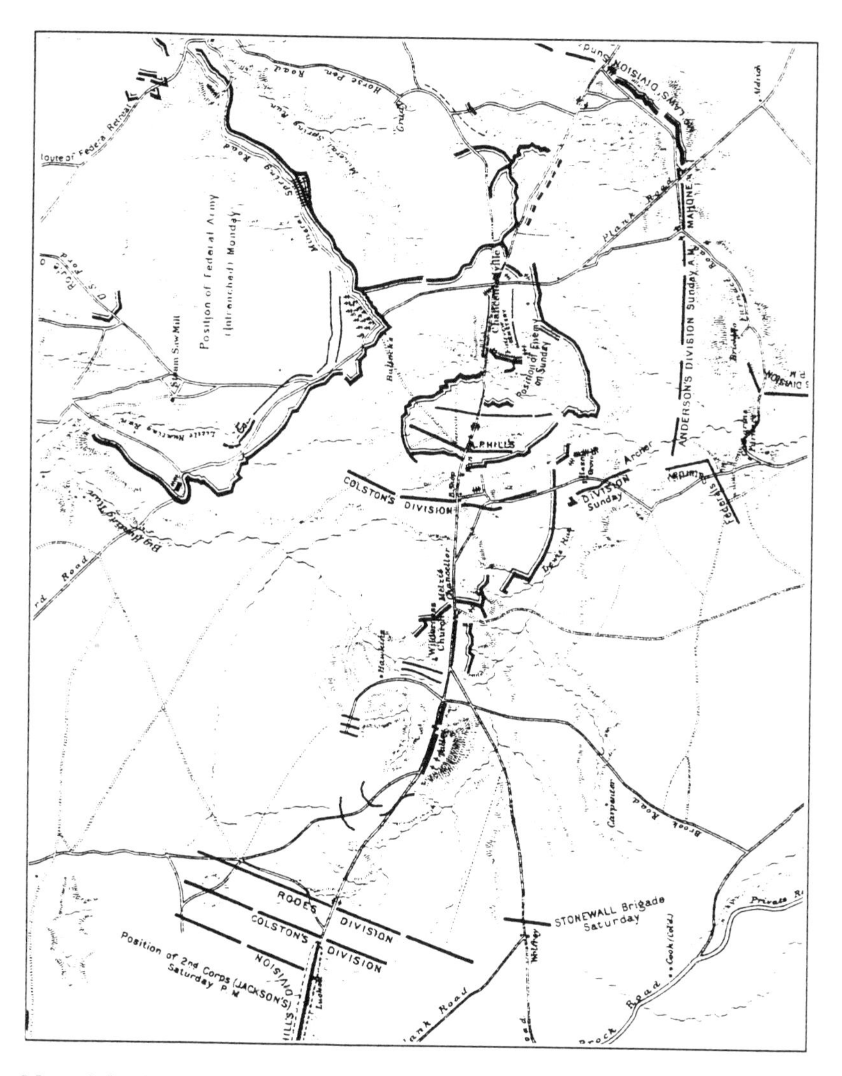

Map of the Chancellorsville battlefield. Jackson's troops are shown in position for their famous flank attack.

After ordering the Union right wing to hold he then ordered Sedgwick to move on the rebels at Fredericksburg to make sure they were still in place. Shortly after making this decision he sent another order revoking it. He then ordered General Sickles' Corps to march to Chancellorsville by way of U. S. Ford. Sickles responded quickly to the request and by midnight was about half way there. Early on the morning of May 1, they proceeded to Chancellorsville and bivouacked in a grove of oak trees near the front lines.[19]

When Jackson arrived at the front it soon became obvious to him that he had massed some 40,000 of his own troops along a easily defended position. Jackson, true to his nature, determined that now was the time to go on the offensive. Jackson moved his force along the Plank Road and met the Yanks head on. The Confederates turned Hooker's men back all along the line. Fearful that he could not hold them back in such an exposed position, he issued orders for Sykes to retire to his position of the previous night. Here he entrenched and fortified his position.[20]

On the night of May 1, Lee and Jackson met to determine their course of action. It was decided that Jackson would attempt to turn the Federal right with a wide flanking move through the Wilderness. Jackson would march directly across the Union front with his command of 28,000 men and into a position perpendicular to Oliver Otis Howard's XI Corps on the Union's right flank. Lee, left with but 14,000 men, would face Hooker's 65,000. He would then demonstrate against Hooker's lines in order to cover the movement. Of course any Union counterattack which might occur during Jackson's march could prove to be the end of Lee's Army.[21]

As Jackson's column was passing by Catherine's Furnace it was spotted by Birney's Division from Hazel Grove. Birney held the portion of the line between Slocum's and Howard's Corps. The other two divisions of Sickle's Corps, which included the 4th Maine, were being held in reserve just to the rear of Birney's. When Sickles observed for himself the troop movements which Birney had reported, he immediately asked General Hooker for permission to attack. Hooker,

---

[19] Ibid., p. 101.
[20] Furgurson, op. cit., pp. 124-126.
[21] Ibid., p. 142.

interpreting the information he was receiving as a Confederate withdrawal, promptly gave Sickles permission.[22]

Sickles sent Birney's three brigades immediately south to attack the rebel troops at Catherine's Furnace. As the brigades pushed forward they ran into the 23rd Georgia, which was Jackson's rear guard. Some sharp fighting, which did not include the 4th Maine or its' division, took place around the Furnace. The Georgians were quickly overwhelmed by the weight of Birney's attack and nearly surrounded. The division quickly captured some 350 rebels, including several officers. Sickles' other divisions were brought up to support the attack, which stalled when Union troops ran up against several twelve pound Napoleons about a half mile south of the Furnace. As a result of this move, a large gap was created between Howard and the rest of the army. The action on Jackson's rear would in no way affect his plan of attack.[23]

Jackson pulled up on the flank of Howard's XI Corps, pretty much undetected, at about four P. M. He formed his line of battle three deep and extended it for a mile on both sides of the Turnpike. By doing this he made the attack deep enough so that the disrupted Union regiments would not fall back on his flanks as he charged into his tightly compacted enemy. He also put two cannon from Stuart's Horse Artillery on the Turnpike, with two guns in support. these would move, and then fire, by turns. By five P. M. all was in readiness.[24]

Oliver Otis Howard, of Leeds, Maine, had paid no attention to the warnings he had received throughout the day with regard to an imminent attack on his flank. At five P.M. his men had stacked their arms and were preparing the evening meal. The first indication they had that something was amiss occurred when startled deer, and various small animals, began to bound through their camps. Just as suddenly as this had begun a rebel yell was heard, accompanied by the sound of bugles, and the thrashing of troops as they bounded out of the trees and on to the flank of Howard's Corps. It was 5:15 P.M.[25]

Howard's men abandoned their positions, completely routed. With the gray line nipping at their heels they left behind their weapons, ammunition, and supplies, thinking only of their survival. At this

---

[22] Ibid., p. 150.
[23] Ibid.
[24] Ibid.
[25] Ibid., pp. 365-366.

moment there was almost nothing between Jackson and the rear of the Federal line except a division of the XI Corps under General Schurz, which was attempting, against all odds, to form a line of defense. In the gathering twilight all was noise, smoke, and chaos.

"After marching all day and struggling through the thickets...they attacked as wildly as any fresh troops in the whole war." The southerners pushed on through terrain so densely populated by trees and scrub that it was impossible to maintain any unit cohesion. Regiments became jumbled and the soldiers fought, not as units or bodies of men, but as individuals. It was not encroaching darkness that began to slow their progress on the field, but rather the very success of their attack.[26]

As the Union troops were being thrown back, General Oliver Otis Howard tried to rally his men. Howard rode to his only remaining division, under the command of General Schurz, and turned its two brigades to face the enemy's advance. As he rode back and forth he stuck the broken staff of the flag of the United States under his arm stump, and began to yell at the soldiers to stop and join him. Several of the routing men were shot by their officers as an example to the other men of what happened to "skeedadlers." Despite his efforts, few of the men were stopped.[27]

The portion of Sickle's command which had moved on the rear of Jackson's line of march was now moving back to Hazel Grove. Sickles' had left General Hiram Berry's division around Chancellorsville as a reserve. Hooker, realizing now that the gap in his line had to be repaired quickly, ordered General Berry to take up a defensive position on the right side of the turnpike. Hooker told Berry, "General, throw your men into the breech! Receive the enemy on your bayonets." Berry obeyed orders, and urged his men into the immediate path of the charging rebels.[28]

At about the same time, Pleasonton's 8th Pennsylvania Cavalry, were directed to report to General Howard. As they advanced out of Hazel Grove they ran directly into the advancing Confederate Infantry. The regiment, under Major Pennock Huey, was left with little choice but to attack. The Major ordered his men to "draw sabers and charge." According to many of the rebel veterans, it was this charge that caused

---

[26] Ibid., p. 178.
[27] Ibid.
[28] Ibid.

General Jackson to be fatally wounded by his own men. By all official records Jackson was wounded at about 9:30 P.M. The 8th Pennsylvania's attack occurred between 7 and 8. It is, therefore, highly unlikely that Huey's attack was the cause of Jackson's injury. Immediately following this event, however, rebel forces began to pull back to reorganize. General Pleasonton, of course, took immediate credit for repulsing the enemy.[29]

The rest of Sickles' divisions, which included the 4th Maine, responded to the sounds of fighting in their rear by retreating back in the direction of Hazel Grove. Here they formed around the artillery batteries on the heights. Williams' division, which had also moved south with Sickles during the morning, soon found itself retracing its steps to the din of combat. Williams formed his men up opposite Berry's division on the left side of the turnpike. Here both commanders had their men dig in, in preparation for a continued attack.[30]

Jackson's men were extremely disorganized by their success. J. E. B. Stuart, being the ranking general on this flank, took over command of Jackson's Army following his wounding. Stuart ordered the cessation of fighting and immediately began to reorganize his forces for a continuation of the attack in the morning. The stage was now set for the 4th Maine Regiment to play out its part in the battle ofChancellorsville.

Sickles had become uncomfortable in his position at Hazel Grove. Feeling that his left flank was unsupported and in the air, he requested permission from General Hooker to attempt to regain the fortified trenches they had occupied that morning. Additionally, he would try to recapture some abandoned cannon that had been taken by the 4th Georgia during the rebel assault. He also requested that General Williams' and Berry be allowed to support his attack. In the end not only were they not asked to provide support, they were not even made aware that an assault was about to take place.[31]

About 9:00 P.M., the men of Ward's Brigade were told to take off their knapsacks. Instead of preparing for rest, however, the order was given to prepare for action. The moon was full and bright in the night sky giving everything an eerie, shadow-like appearance. Thoughts of things that go bump in the night filled everyone's mind. Nobody could

---

[29] Ibid., p. 188.
[30] Ibid., p. 137.
[31] Ibid., pp. 208-209.

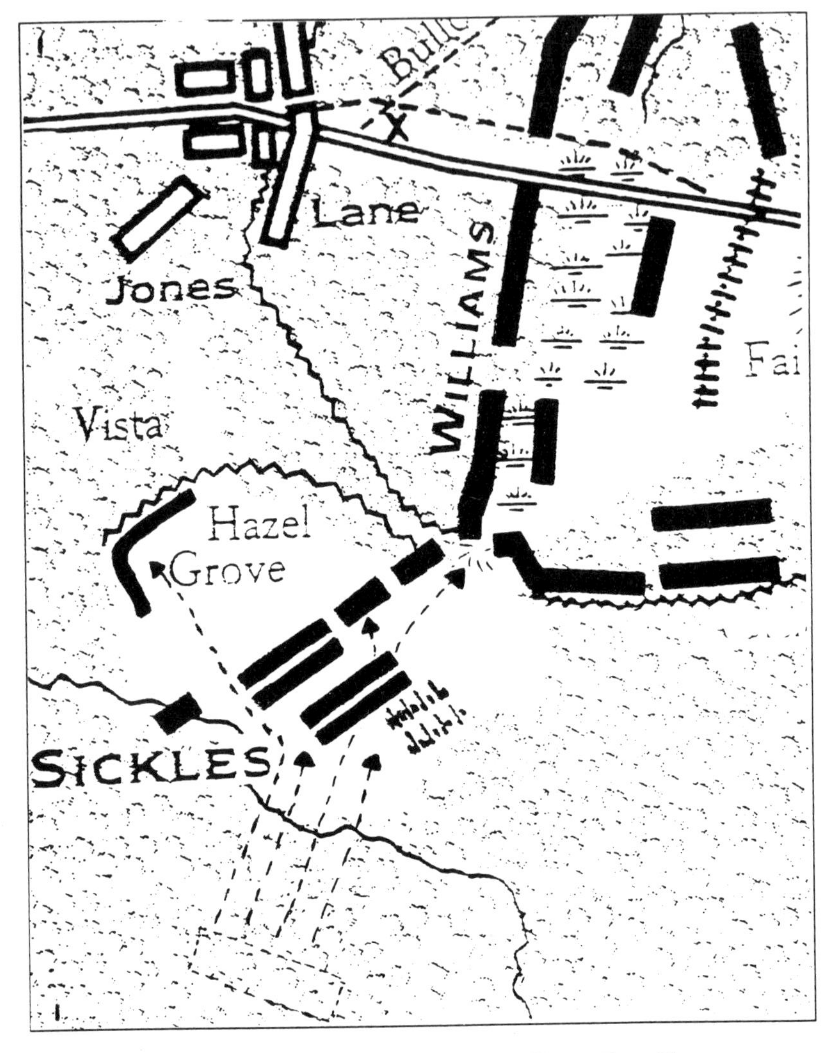

Sickles's famous "Midnight Charge" at Chancellorsville.

remember when a night attack had ever been called for, and this one, as it so happened, was to take place at the witching hour. The 20th Indiana had not yet returned from the front. The 17th Maine, from the 3rd Brigade, and the 63rd Pennsylvania, from the 1st, had been assigned to Ward. The men of the 3rd and 4th Maine, the 99th Pennsylvania, and the 38th and 40th New York began to write notes to their loved ones. Many pinned them to their jackets. The situation, they were told, was desperate.[32]

A member of the 3rd Michigan later recalled that their general had explained the situation to each of the regiments thusly; "We were cut off from the main body of our army, that the breastworks we had built and left in charge of the 11th Corps were now in possession of the rebels and there were two things for us to do - either, go to Richmond as prisoners or charge them breastworks, drive the rebels back and join our army. We all said charge..."[33]

By 11:30 Ward had formed his re-enforced brigade into a line of battle. The remainder of Birney's Division was formed a hundred yards to the rear to act as support. They were told that this was to be a bayonet charge and the clank of these weapons being fixed to their guns echoed through the night. Next the men were ordered to load their guns but not to cap them until they reached the earthworks. Nothing but the sounds of the men crashing through the woods of the Wilderness would announce their intentions to the enemy. Charging with guns that could not fire would insure a rapid march.[34]

Here the men waited, with dreaded anticipation, their order to advance. Just about midnight Ward's Brigade was instructed to move forward in the direction of the woods which they believed concealed Confederate troops. All of the men yelled and screamed as they ran toward the spot where they hoped the breastworks were located. The front line reached the woods and then beyond. Only a few yards into the thickets the regiments received a thunderous volley of musketry fire. The charging troops capped their rifles, returning the favor, and then continued their advance on the enemy works.[35]

---

[32] Whitman, op. cit., p. 101.
[33] Furgurson, op. cit., p. 209.
[34] Whitman, op. cit., p. 101.
[35] Official Records, Series I, Vol XXV, p. 429.

Birney had guided his approach along the Vista Road. The 40th New York, 17th Maine and 63rd Pennsylvania had advanced on the left of this landmark. About five hundred yards south of the Plank Road they had received the first devastating volley from the rebs. The 40th New York, which was the leading regiment, returned fire. The firing of the enemy, even in the dark, was devastating. The New Yorkers routed back into the 17th Maine and 63rd Pennsylvania, causing the collapse of this portion of the attack. Still, in spite the confusion, they were able to recapture two of their own artillery pieces as well as several caissons.[36]

On the right of the line the 3rd Maine led the attack. As these Maine boys moved toward their old earthworks they bumped into a regiment of Tarheals, the 18th North Carolina. It was like two boxcars full of gunpowder had bumped into each other in the dark. The impact was deafening and devastating. The Third was quickly overwhelmed. In the moonlit landscape the Mainer's were forced back to the right and front. Numerous prisoners were taken and regiment's colors were captured.

The units participating in the attack, including the 4th Maine, were now located squarely between the Union and Confederate lines. As the 3rd Maine obliqued right, followed by the rest of the regiments, the troops came crashing in on a second line of troops. Now these soldiers, under the direction of Union General Alpheus Williams, let loose a tremendous volley into Ward's men. Artillery joined in as well. Williams had never been notified of the attack planned by Sickle's and immediately assumed that it was rebel troops continuing the assault begun earlier. Caught in the open, the soldiers bravely charged on, passing over a set of breastworks and into a battery of artillery. Only now was it discovered that they had inadvertently strayed into the lines of their own 12th Corps.[37]

The 4th Maine, acting in a support roll, had actually come undera crossfire from both armies. In the darkness and confusion of the fighting, the men capped their rifles and began to fire back, blindly. Soldiers of the various units became hopelessly mixed. Though some of the men reached their objective of the Plank Road, it was soon found to be an untenable position and all were forced to fall back, or be captured.

In later years Sickles' attack was commonly referred to as "one of the most comical episodes in the history of the Army of the Potomac."

---

[36] Furgurson, op. cit., p. 210

[37] Ibid.

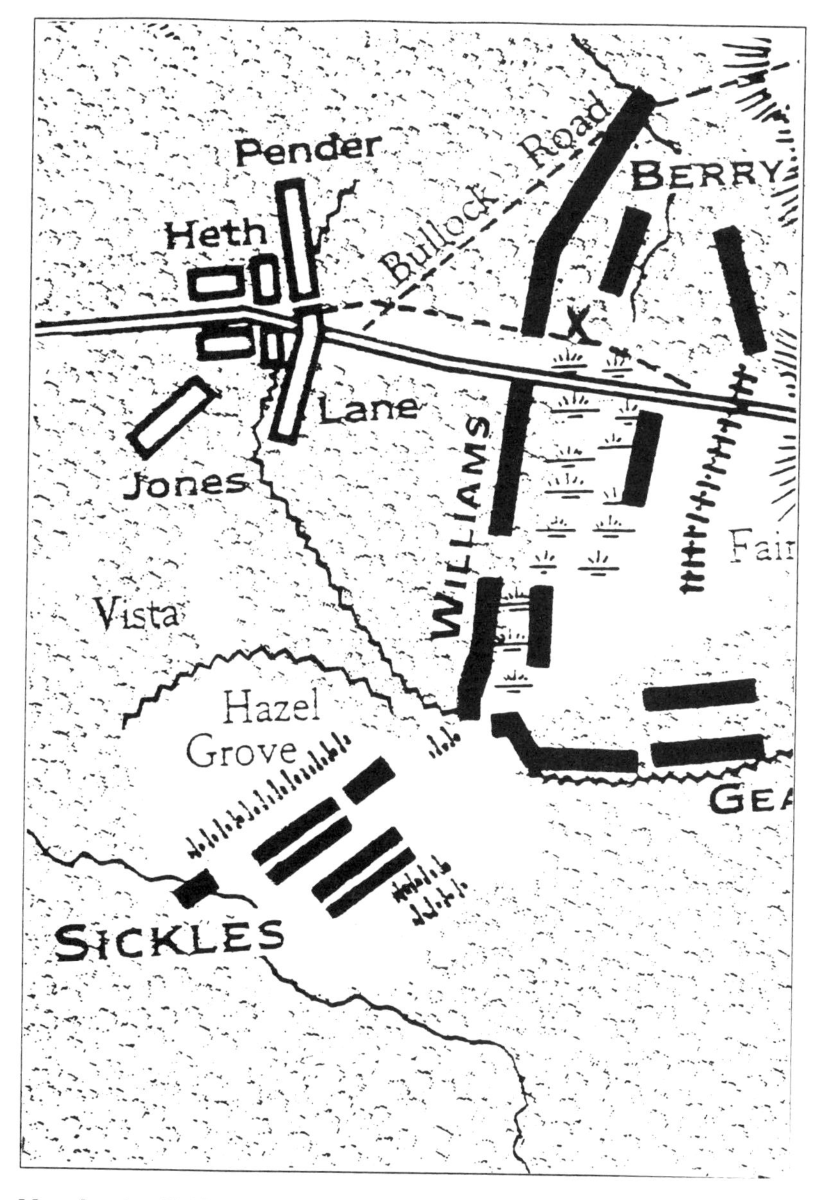

Map showing Sickle position as well as that of General Berry's. The X marks the approximate spot of Berry's fatal wounding.

To those that were involved in the tragedy, however, it was anything but funny. Even though General Sickle's reported that the operation was a success, and to a great extent it was, any gains made were at great expense. He did, after all, connect the right of his line to the rest of the Union Army. The high ground at Hazel Grove, whose artillery commanded the battlefield, was still in Union hands. In addition, the confusion created in the Confederate lines caused a reconsideration of any plans they might have had for a night attack of their own. As a result both sides decided to settle in for the night.[38]

As dawn neared on the morning of May 3rd, the 4th Maine, as part of Sickles' Corps, still found its line bulging way off to the southwest, its left flank hanging. Sickles command consisted of two of his own divisions, an additional brigade of infantry, a collection of five batteries of artillery, as well as some cavalry. As the Third Corps commander began to realize how valuable their position at Hazel grove was, he dispatched a courier to General Hooker requesting that it be included in the army's main defensive line. Hooker, as it turned out, was sleeping and the message did not get through to him in time to make a difference.[39]

When Hooker awoke he responded to the communication by visiting Sickles in person. He perceived the Third Corps' present location as being extremely vulnerable to attack. He decided that he needed to make their position more compact. An order was given on the spot for the divisions to retreat back to Chancellorsville. Sickles obeyed, ordering his men to abandon their defenses and to march northeast. The best artillery position available on the field of battle was thus abandoned without a fight. The gift of Hazel Grove to the Confederates would prove to be decisive.[40]

As the regiments began to fall back rebel units under Lane, Archer, and McGowan slammed into their rear guard. Some of General Berry's batteries began to provide cover for Sickles' as they moved northward. The 4th's division crossed the Plank Road and took position to support some of the guns near the brick house at Chancellorsville. Soon, artillery shells begin to fall in on them from their old post at Hazel Grove. Union counter-battery fire was totally ineffective. Williams' and Berry's

---

[38] Ibid., pp. 218-219.
[39] Ibid., p. p. 21.
[40] Whitman, op. cit., p. 102.

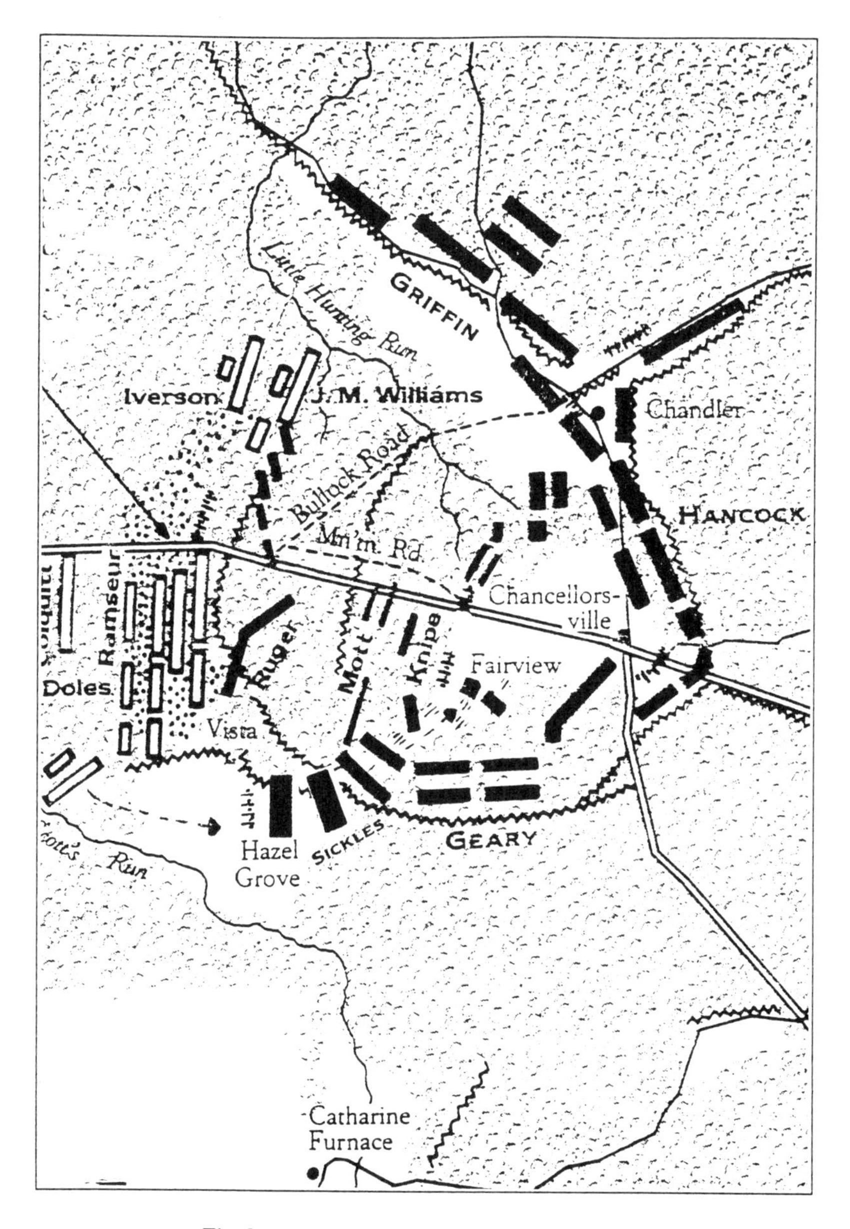

Final troop positions at Chancellorsville.

divisions were repeatedly attacked from the west. The Union position was deteriorating by the minute.[41]

About nine A.M. General Hooker was leaning on a pillar of the mansion which was serving both as his headquarters, and a hospital. An artillery shell came arching in from the grove and struck one of the other columns, sending a fragment into Hooker and knocking him senseless. A short time later Hooker turned command of the army over to General Couch, but not before ordering him to withdraw the army to a new defensive position one third of a mile up the road fromChancellorsville. The move aided Lee in rejoining his divided army. Though Lee's finest hour, it could not have been achieved without Hooker's cooperation.[42]

By the end of the day the fighting for the northern wing of Hooker's army was pretty much over. Sedgwick's men had broken through and taken Fredericksburg that very morning and were rapidly approaching Lee's rear. Lee, once again, divided his army in order to deal with the threat. This was successfully done, and eventually all of Hooker's army would return to their pre-invasion positions. The manner in which General Lee had dealt with Hooker's overwhelming numbers, and the relative ease with which he handled his forces, would be one of the most embarrassing moments for the Army of the Potomac. Even Lincoln did not know how to deal with the disastrous news.

The 4th Maine returned to their old bivouac at Potomac Creek near Fredericksburg. Casualties for the "Tigers" were, in comparison to previous engagements, fairly light. Throughout the eight days of the Chancellorsville Campaign the 4th Maine was actually directly engaged only once, that occurring during the moonlight attack of May 2nd and 3rd. Total casualties for the campaign amounted to one officer killed and three wounded. One enlisted man was killed, eighteen wounded and nine were taken prisoner. A casualty list is provided in the appendix.[43]

Following this campaign, it is a small wonder that General Lee began to look upon his men as being invincible. They had performed one of the most remarkable feats in the annals of military history. This battle would be studied in the years to come by all the great military leaders of the world as a model of what an outnumbered army could achieve while it maintained the advantage of interior lines. A participant in this fight at

---

[41] Ibid.
[42] Furgurson, op. cit., p. 224
[43] Maine Adjutant General's Report, p. 312.

Chancellorsville, General George Meade, would make use of its lessons within sixty days in a peaceful Pennsylvania town. For the 4th Maine Infantry, Meade's rendezvous at the crossroads, however, would be anything but peaceful.

Chapter 9

General Berry Comes Home

"At the time the movement on Chancellorsville had commenced, General Berry received his orders to march, with gloomy foreboding. About 9 o'clock at night he sent for his chief quartermaster (now Brevet Brigadier-General) James F. Rusling, told him of the impending battle and of the presentiment that he would not survive it. He committed to Captain Rustling's care certain papers and valuables, and got his pledge that, should he fall, the captain would use every endeavor to recover his body and send it home to Maine. Captain Rustling tried to dissipate the foreboding from Berry's mind but without success."

"Captain James D. Earle, Berry's commissary of subsistence, on his arrival at headquarters that night, found the General greatly depressed. He seemed anxious to hear once more from his wife and daughter, and Earle volunteered to return to Stoneman's Switch, a ride of eighteen miles, and bring him the mail. At first Berry refused to permit the young officer to take the journey, but as he persisted, asking only for a fresh horse, Berry consented and gave him one of his own horses for the trip. As Earle galloped into camp at 2 o'clock the next morning the General came out to meet him, eagerly seizing the package of letters which was handed to him, and hastened to the camp-fire to devour their contents. After caring for his horse, Earle returned to the camp-fire, where Berry was still reading the letters, and on his approach the General thanked him warmly for his kindness, showed him photographs of his daughter which the mail had brought and read extracts from the letters. 'Now,' said Berry, 'I will try to get some sleep, as I look for warm work in the morning.'"[1]

General Berry, like so many of his other comrades, seems to have had a premonition that his life was near its end. There are many, many recorded instances in which soldiers seemed to know that death was at hand. There are many cases of soldiers clipping notes to their clothing

---

[1] Gould. Major General Hiram G. Berry,

just before battle proclaiming their identity, or writing letters to loved ones announcing their final devotion. Such was General Berry's state of mind on Saturday, May 2nd, as he sat in reserve with his division near the Chancellor House, listening intently to the sounds of battle all about him.

Abruptly, the sounds of heavy fighting were heard on Berry's right. Almost as suddenly, the woods were alive with "the rapid flight of panic-stricken fugitives and the close pursuit of Jackson's victorious fugitives was bourne to the ears of his men, first in faint, indistinct murmurs, constantly increasing in volume until it seemed as though pandemonium had broken loose. Then came the fugitives, frantic and terror stricken, blindly pushing their way through the steady ranks of Berry's division."[2]

In the midst of all the confusion General Hooker appeared abruptly. "General," he shouted, "throw your men into the breach - receive the enemy on your bayonets - don't fire a shot - they can't see you!"

General Berry seized the moment, as he had a habit of doing, and charged forward with his first and second brigades. Orders were to form a line perpendicular to the Plank Road. The Excelsior Brigade was placed in the first line, and the bulk of Car's brigade in the second about 150 yards to the rear. General Berry was in a critical position and the fate of the Army of the Potomac rested squarely in his hands. He personally attended to the disposition of his troops and as A. P. Hill formed his men for an attack Berry "faced the danger calmly and with a confident manner, inspiring his men by his presence and reassuring his anxious subordinates by a few quietly spoken sentences."[3]

About 9:30 P.M. Hill mounted his first assault on General Berry's Division. The combination of accurate artillery fire and the stubborn resistance of his infantry not only held the rebels in check, but finally forced the enemy to retrace their steps in retreat. It was a night filled with constant fighting and turmoil. There was little sleep to be had.

Colonel Robert McAllister of the 11th New Jersey Infantry remembered that as he filed his regiment into line that General Berry rode up to him and yelled: " 'Now, Colonel, do your very best.' 'Yes, General, I shall,' was my reply. I knew I had the boys who would fight,

---

[2] Ibid., p. 258.
[3] Ibid ., p. 262.

and felt confident that we would make a good one. That noble and brave man rode along the lines that night wherever there were points of danger, and words of comfort and encouragement fell from his lips. He knew well the responsibility resting upon him, and like Leonidas with his brave band, was ready to do or die. These scenes I shall never forget. The night was beautiful and clear, the moon shone brightly, but the heavy forest shade above cast a gloom around us. All would be still and calm one moment, then crack! would go a gun, followed by many others, telling us we were again attacked and our pickets engaged soon followed by a tremendous roar of musketry. The enemy marched in front of us and were determined to break our lines."[4]

About six A.M. the Confederate line began their advance on the enemy. Berry's men waited behind the log works which they had erected. To their front they had cleared an opening of about fifty to one hundred yards in width. The rebels could advance, concealed and unmolested, up to that point, through the black-jack and vines of the Wilderness. The crossing of this opening could be accomplished in a matter of a few seconds. The delay in their advance would come at the Union abatis. Here, too, Berry's men would have something to say about their continued progression.

It was about this time when General Berry noticed two of his regiments, the 1st Massachusetts and the 74th New York, retreating from the front without orders. When he stopped some of the men to find out what had happened, he was told that an officer had ordered them to withdraw. Berry was beside himself with anger and immediately requested that the officer be brought to him. When the man arrived he reached out to strip him of his rank and accidentally ripped open his coat. Only then did he discover that the officer was wearing a rebel uniform underneath. He was immediately taken as a prisoner of war.[5]

General Berry's brigades quickly became hard pressed by the rebel advance. As confusion continued to develop on the left of the line, the situation was hastily taken advantage of by Pender's infantry as they fell upon Berry's exposed left flank. As the Confederates began to cross the Plank road Hiram Berry began to have second thoughts about the security of their present position. It was now about 7:30, and,

---

[4] Gould, op. cit, p. 262.
[5] Furgurson, Chancellorsville 1863, p. 224.

perhaps doubting for the first time the ability of his men to hold on under the mounting pressure, he decided to send his adjutant, Captain Greenhalgh, to General Hooker to see if he should try to hold his present line or fall back to a new one.[6]

One member of the before mentioned 1st Massachusetts watched as the rebel troops "come up close in column, close to our entrenchments...and our whole line poured the shot into them. You could see them drop all around but as soon as one man fell another stepped into his place. They fight like the devil there is no rubbing that out. But our line stood firm." This they did until their flanks were totally compromised.[7]

Shortly after Captain Greenhalgh's departure General Berry dismounted from his horse and moved to cross the Plank Road in order to confer with General Mott, who was senior division officer. "His officer's remonstrated and offered to go in his stead, pointing out that the enemy's sharpshooters were posted in the trees and sweeping the Plank road with their unerring rifles. The General replied that he preferred to give the order in person, and started on his way." The general crossed the road and gave Mott his orders, and then attempted to traverse the road again to rejoin his staff. General Berry had nearly reached this group of officers, "when, from the trees in which the North Carolina sharpshooters were posted, came a wreath of smoke, followed by the sharp crack of a rifle.[8] A "Minie rifle ball struck him in the arm close to the shoulder, passed downward through his vitals, and lodged in his hip." His staff moved quickly to his side. Lieutenant Freeman began attending to him, and heard Berry say, "I am dying, carry me to the rear." The Lieutenant asked if he had anything else he felt compelled to say. The general shook his head, and a few moments later, died.[9]

General Berry's body was taken immediately to the Chancellor house. When General Hooker saw the body it is reported that he broke into tears. "Kneeling down he kissed the cold forehead, and then exclaimed, 'My God Berry, why was this to happen? Why was the man on whom I relied so much, to be taken away in this manner?'"

---

[6] Captain Greenhalgh had been one of the original members of the 4th Maine and had been adjutant since Berry's promotion to Brigadier General in the spring of 1862.

[7] Fergurson, op. cit. p. 224.

[8] Bigelow, Chancellorsville, pp. 349 - 351.

[9] Gould, op. cit., pp. 266-267.

When the Confederates threatened the Chancellor House, Berry was once again moved, this time farther to the rear. As this was being done, it is reported that the entourage bumped into a squad of men from the 4th Maine. When the men learned that the body was that of their old commander they asked that they be allowed to pay their last respects. They, as Hooker had done before, knelt down and kissed Berry's forehead, then "silently and tearfully took their places in the ranks."[10]

Writing under the date of July 20, 1895, Miss Anna Ethridge, who had distinguished herself repeatedly under fire as proven by her receipt of the Kearny Cross, and who served in a Michigan regiment in Berry's brigade, addressed her friendship and respect for the man. "I remember better then anything else, all that is associated with General Berry, because I was so deeply attached to him, in common with all the soldiers - for we all worshipped him for his bravery, and for all that goes in the highest degree to make an ideal soldier and perfect gentleman...I do not recall any incidents, except those usually connected with marches and the routine of army life, prior to the awful battle of Chancellorsville where General Berry lost his life. I recall it was May 3d, my birthday. I was always with headquarters, marching with it. The night before, I had filled my canteens with hot coffee and started down the Chancellorsville road in company with the surgeon of the regiment. I knew that General Berry was stationed on the right. When we were seen coming we were met by an artillery officer, who told the surgeon that we were on the line of battle within the rebel lines, and he must take me back. I knew General Berry was on the right and I said he must take me to him - I must see him! The officer wheeled his horse, rode back and reported. General Berry said: 'It is Annie; bring her here, I would risk my life for her!" This the officer told me after he was gone. When I reached the General, who was on the line of battle, he drank the coffee and said: ' We are going to have a midnight charge,' at the same time pointing to a white house in the distance. 'Go there, where you can attend to the wounded, and if I get killed I want you to go home with my body.' He was killed as near as I can learn, the morning of the midnight charge, and before I knew it his body was carried off the field and sent away. I remember the bitter

---

[10] Maine Adjutan General's Report, p. 312.

tears I shed that day, for I felt at the time that if he had been my own father, my grief could have not been deeper."[11]

President Lincoln and General Halleck requested that General Berry's interment services be held in Washington. The family, however, insisted that it should be held in Rockland. The funeral, itself, was probably one of the largest ever held in the town. It was attended by Vice-President Hamlin, Governor Fessenden, Senator Fessenden, and hundreds of other distinguished guests. The buildings were draped in mourning and all of the flags were flown at half staff. The body laid in state at his home for several days until he was finally interred with full military and Masonic honors. Three volleys were fired over his grave. Quite a fitting end for this carpenter from Rockland, Maine.[12]

The Rockland Gazette
May 9, 1863

DEATH OF GENERAL BERRY

Before the news on the splendid achievements of General Hooker's army which occurred on Saturday and Sunday had reached us, our community was thrown into deep gloom and sadness, by the receipt of a telegraphic dispatch, on Tuesday morning, containing the mournful intelligence that our beloved and gallant **General Berry** was no more! Then came the news of the fighting on Saturday and Sunday, telling us of the impetuous attack of the enemy on our right flank, on Saturday evening, of the disgraceful flight of Deven's division, and of the glorious bayonet charge of General Berry's division, as they swept into the deadly breach, forced back the rebels to the breastworks which Deven's division had abandoned, and saved our forces from imminent disaster; and of the desperate contest of Sunday morning, in which General Berry's division, on the right, gallantly engaged the enemy "and if it were possible for them to add more laurels to their fame, then they did it thrice over again." In this

[11] Gould, op. cit., pp.
[12] Maine Archives Regimental Files.

fight of Sunday morning, our gallant townsman fell, at the head of his brave division, shot through the heart. So he died gloriously, fighting for freedom. His death is a loss to the army, a loss to the nation, a cause of mourning to his native State, a deep affliction to his family and friends, and a grief to his fellow-citizens. But though he is dead, he lives, and will live forever, in history, as a patriot who gave himself to the cause of the nation, and died in valiant defense of that legacy of freedom which will be trebly prized by posterity for its re-baptism in blood today. He has fallen before the great contest in which he has rendered signal service is finished, but he has won an undying share in his country's fame. Williamsburg, Fair Oaks, and Chancellorsville pronounce his noble eulogy, and will perpetuate his name through future generations. His family and friends will weep their loss, but they share the sympathies of a nation in their affliction.

The body of General Berry was taken from the field, with no other mutilation than that of the fatal bullet, and was immediately sent to Washington and embalmed. It was received in New York on Wednesday, and will arrive in Portland today, (Friday) and be forwarded here tomorrow on the Harvest Moon. A deputation of our citizens have gone forward today, to receive the remains in Portland. We understand that flags will be displayed at half mast throughout the city to-morrow morning, and the city rooms will be draped in mourning. At twelve o'clock stores and places of business will be closed, and on the appearance of the steamer minute guns will be fired and the bells of the churches will commence to toll. The arrangements are not yet so far advanced as to render it possible to state precisely when the funeral will take place, but it will probably occur on Wednesday or Thursday. The remains will probably lie in state at one of our public halls for a suitable time before the burial. We have heard that the Bangor Fusileers have been ordered by the Adjutant General to attend the obsequies, and that the Tenth Regiment will also probably be sent, but we have not been advised that the military arrangements are yet completed.

The Rockland Gazette
May 16, 1863

Home of Major-General Hiram G. Berry in Rockland. The home no longer exists. (Photo from the book Major General Hiram G. Berry)

The Remains of General Berry in Rockland

The remains of General Berry were received in this city last Saturday, amidst general demonstrations of sorrow by our citizens. At an early hour on that day flags were displayed at half-mast throughout the city, and on the shipping in the harbor, and nearly all the blocks and stores on our principal street were decked in mourning, as well as many of the houses of our citizens. The body was to be received at Atlantic Wharf, in the vicinity of which a vast throng of people had gathered, while upon the wharf a procession of citizens headed by the committee designated by the City Council, were in waiting. The steamer arrived at about a quarter to one o'clock, and when she appeared, minute guns were fired and the bells of the churches began to toll. The body of General Berry was brought in charge of the committee who had been delegated to receive the remains in Portland, and was attended by a detachment of Company F of the 7th regiment under command of Captain Warren, as a guard of honor. The remains were also accompanied by the widow and daughter of Gen. Berry, his brother, John T, Berry, Esq., of this city, and Capt. Greenhalgh, late of his staff.

On being conveyed from the steamer, the body of the honored dead was delivered by Joseph Farwell, Esq., chairman of the committee delegated to receive it in Portland, to the committee in waiting to take charge of it as the representatives of the city. Mr. Farwell performed this duty in a brief address, which was fittingly responded to by Hon. S. C. Fessenden, in behalf of the committee. A hearse had been prepared, appropriately draped with national flags, in which the coffin was then placed, and attended by the guard of honor marching with reversed arms, escorted by the committee and a large procession of citizens, and followed by the family of the deceased and a long train of citizens in carriages, the body of Gen. Berry was conveyed to his late residence.

The body of the General was placed in the parlor, where it lay in state until Thursday, and was visited by hundreds, who came to look upon the honored dead. The body was enclosed in one of Weaver's patent burial cases, which was richly lined with white satin, and stuffed and covered outside with black broadcloth. The lid of the case

Mrs. Hiram Berry. (Photo from the book Major General Hiram G. Berry)

was removed, but there remained an inner lid of glass, exposing to view the whole form of the General, clothed in full dress of his rank. A bouquet lay at his feet, and another upon the body, while across the breast was the beautiful wreath which was the offering of the President. Upon his breast also appeared the Kearney Badge, presented by Major DeLacey of the 37th New York Volunteers. The countenance was much swollen, and few of his fellow citizen's would have recognized it in the face they knew so well. The outer lid of the burial case bore this inscription:

MAJ. GEN. HIRAM G. BERRY
KILLED AT CHANCELLORSVILLE, VIRGINIA,
MAY 3, 1863
AGED 38 YEARS, 8 MONTHS, 6 DAYS

All the surroundings were in keeping with this solemn repose of the gallant dead. The entrance to the house had been hung with two large national flags, draped with crape, and parting like the curtains of a tent. Directly opposite, in a small field across the street, but a few rods distant, were the tents of the guard of honor, while two of their number paced their solemn sentry-beat in front of the house, and two more guarded the remains within the parlor. On a small table at the head of the coffin lay excellent photographs of the general, and upon the same table the sword which he used in battle, and the more elegant one which was presented him by the officers of the Fourth Maine Regiment. In a corner of the room stood the tattered and bullet pierced colors of the gallant Fourth Regiment, which had been presented to them in New York, and received by General Berry, then their Colonel.

ORDER OF PROCESSION

Maj. Gen, Wm. H. Titcomb, Marshall of the Day
Aids, Maj. Charles A. Miller, Maj. E. W. Stetson,
Maj. G. W. Kimball, Jr. and
Lt. Col. John S. Case

Bangor Cornet Band and Drum Corps
Masonic Fraternity
Military Escort
Rockland Band
Maj. Gen. Butler and Staff
Adj. Gen. Hodsdon, Col Harding and Lt. Col.
Osgood of the Governor's Staff
Guard of Honor
Bearers
Pall Bearers Funeral Car Pall Bearers
The General's War Horses
Family and Relatives in Carriages
General's Military Staff
Vice President of the United States
and Governor of Maine
Ex-Governor and Members of Congress
Justices of Supreme Court
Members of Legislature
Officiating Clergymen
Disabled Soldiers
Invited Guests
Mayor and City Council of Rockland
Committee of Arrangements
Citizens and Strangers

The Vice President of the United States...is a member of the Bangor Company, and performed duty as a private in its ranks during the day. We have heard that this course of Mr. Hamlin was unfavorably remarked upon by some, who thought he should have appeared in his official character as Vice President, on this occasion; but those who know the regard in which the Vice President held Gen. Berry, the great estimation which he set upon his services, and the depth and sincerity of the sorrow with which he mourned him, will be furthest from criticizing the manner in which he paid the tribute of honor to his memory. Mr. Hamlin felt that his mere appearance at the obsequies as Vice President of the United States would be a representation of the official character which might be borne by any man upon whom that position might have devolved, but would fail to express the deep feeling with which he mourned, and desired to honor the memory of, General Berry; that he could not speak to the mourning widow any words of formal consolation that would mitigate her grief or express his own. He desired to render the highest honor in his power to the memory of General Berry, and he felt that he could best do this by serving in his place in the ranks of his company, in performing the last sad duties with which the soldier pays his last farewell tribute to a fallen commander. To perform this duty, the Vice President would have marched leagues, with gun and knapsack, if necessary, and those who saw him, standing unmarked in the ranks of his company, and paying the tribute of his tears at the obsequies of the man he loved and honored, must have felt that in no other way could he have more deeply honored the fallen brave.

CEREMONIES AT THE GRAVE

When the procession arrived at the burial place the cemetery was lined with a large throng of people, who pressed as near as they were allowed to approach. The Masonic ceremonies at the grave were impressively performed by Past Grand Master Hiram Chase, of Belfast. The sacred scroll and the lamb-skin were deposited in the grave, with the usual ceremonies, and the brethren sadly and silently dropped upon the hero's coffin the evergreen emblems of immortality. The flag which had been wrapped about the burial case, was also deposited upon it. The Masonic ceremonies being concluded, the State Guards were ordered forward, and in three divisions fired separate volleys over the grave, and the last sad duties of love and respect to the honored dead were concluded.

The procession then reformed, and returned to the city, and the several bodies composing the escort proceeded to their places of refreshment. Thus the sad ceremonies of the day were concluded - thus the people of our city and State laid to their last rest the earthly remains of one who has reflected lasting honor upon both, and whose memory shall be green in our hearts as long as the grass is green over his grave.

In Memoriam
Headquarters 2d Div., 3d Army Corps,
May 9, 1863

Whereas, It has pleased God in his divine dispensation to take from us our beloved commander, Major General Hiram G. Berry, U. S. Volunteers, commanding the 2d Division, 3d Army Corps-

We the member of his Staff, desire to give expression to the deep sorrow that saddens us, and casts a gloom over the army.

While we recognize God's hand in the stroke, and bow humbly to the decree, we mourn the loss of a nobler soldier, a true patriot, a firm and generous friend, a good man, whose memory it will be ours to cherish through life.

While his absence oppresses us, our sympathy turns to his stricken wife and daughter, and we seek consolation in the reflection that our sorrow is but the shadow of that now agonizing their hearts. With them we mourn, with them we weep - with them we condole.

In remembrance of him, whom we all so loved, we wear the badge of grief.

That his family may remember our laments are mingling with theirs, we send them this token with the prayer that God will comfort them and be to them from this time forth forevermore, husband and father.

(Signed)

Major Charles Hamlin, Assistant Adjutant General.

Captain J. S. Papland, Chief of Staff, and Assistant Inspector General.

Captain LeGrand Benedict, Acting.

Captain James D. Earle, Chief Commissary of Subsistence.

Captain James A. Cross, Provost Marshall.

Capt. Charles W. Squier, Engineer Officer.

Capt. William H. Chester, Judge advocate.

Capt. Thomas W. Osborne, Chief of Artillery.

Capt. Benj. W. Hoxsey, Ordinance Officer.

Major J. Theodore Calhoun, Medical Director.

Capt. James F. Rushing, Chief Quartermaster.

Lifelike statue of Hiram Berry.

Lieut. Seth Cushman, Commissary of Musters.
Lieut. William J. Rushing, Chief of Ambulance Coops.
Capt. Jabez B. Greenholgh, Senior Aid.
Lieut. George W. Freeman, Aide.
Lieut. J. Henry Washburn, Aide.

Chapter 10

"By the Right Oblique, Charge!"

Shortly after the Southern victory at Chancellorsville Jefferson Davis and Robert E. Lee began to consult on what their next move be. Lee was in favor of another invasion of the North, and it was his opinion which finally prevailed. On June 3rd, the Army of Northern Virginia began to move out of its positions near Fredericksburg and began its trek into Pennsylvania. The rebels had decided to offer up Richmond for Washington.

On June 11th, Hooker began to respond to Lee's activity. The commander of the Army of Potomac was aware of Lee's movement but had no idea where his opponent was going. It had been decided to keep the Northern Army between Lee and Washington. It was further hoped that a suitable defensive site could be located where the Confederates might be enticed to attacked. In the meantime both armies were in a constant state of motion, both on a collision course with destiny.

With temperatures and apprehensions rising, the Union Army took Sunday, June 28th, as a day of rest. For the 318 men of the 4th Maine and the 94,974 in the Army of the Potomac, it was more than a day of relaxation, it was a fateful moment of change. It was on this day that General Hooker was replaced by George Meade. Meade, the man the army called a "damned old snapping turtle", would have just two days before he would fight the greatest battle ever fought on the American Continent. What is truly remarkable about this last minute change in command is not just the fact that it was attempted but that it succeeded beyond anyone's' wildest expectations.[1]

The Fourth Maine had broken camp on June 11th along with the rest of the Third Corps and began its march north. The unit arrived at Catlett's Station on the 13th. From here they moved on through Manassas Junction, a place they were now intimately familiar with,

---

[1] Foote, The Civil War, Vol. II, pp. 454-455.

and on to Centreville and Gum Springs. The regiment then crossed the Potomac River into Maryland arriving at Frederick on June 28th and received their well deserved day of rest.[2]

On June 29th and 30th the Union regiments once again resumed their northerly trek in search of Lee's Confederate army. Meanwhile, on this very day Heth's Division, a part of Hill's Corps, had gone into camp at Cashtown. The following morning, in response to a rumor of a cache of shoes that were stored in the town of Gettysburg, Heth sent a brigade of troops toward the town to see if the rumor were true. The commander of the detachment was Johnston Pettigrew. When his troops bumped into a number of Union Cavalry on the outskirts of the community he immediately obeyed orders and withdrew. Petigrew reported the incident to Hill and it was decided that Heth would take his whole division to Gettysburg first thing in the morning. Thus was set into motion the events that would commence the great Battle of Gettysburg.

Meanwhile, on July 1st, Sickles' had continued marching his men north, arriving at Emmitsburg, Maryland about three P.M. As the Maine regiment began to make camp news arrived of a battle that was at that very moment taking place in the small town of Gettysburg, just ten miles to the north. The Third Corps was ordered to come immediately to their aid. The men fell back into march column along the Emmitsburg Turnpike and was force marched, through the heat and humidity, toward the sound of the guns.[3]

To the North at Gettysburg Heth's, Division had collided with Buford's cavalry. The Union cavalry were armed with seven shot Spencer's carbines. The troopers were able to fire over twenty rounds a minute and were able to hold out much longer than they would have otherwise. Reynolds' Corps, which was only six miles away, had joined into the fight as the day had progressed, along with troops from Howard's hard luck 11th Corps. The Confederates had continued to strengthen their line all day, and as a result Union forces had been pushed through the town to the high ground to the south. Losses for both sides had been rather substantial.[4]

---

[2] Whitman. Maine in the War, p. 103.
[3] Foote, op. cit., p. 465.
[4] Ibid.

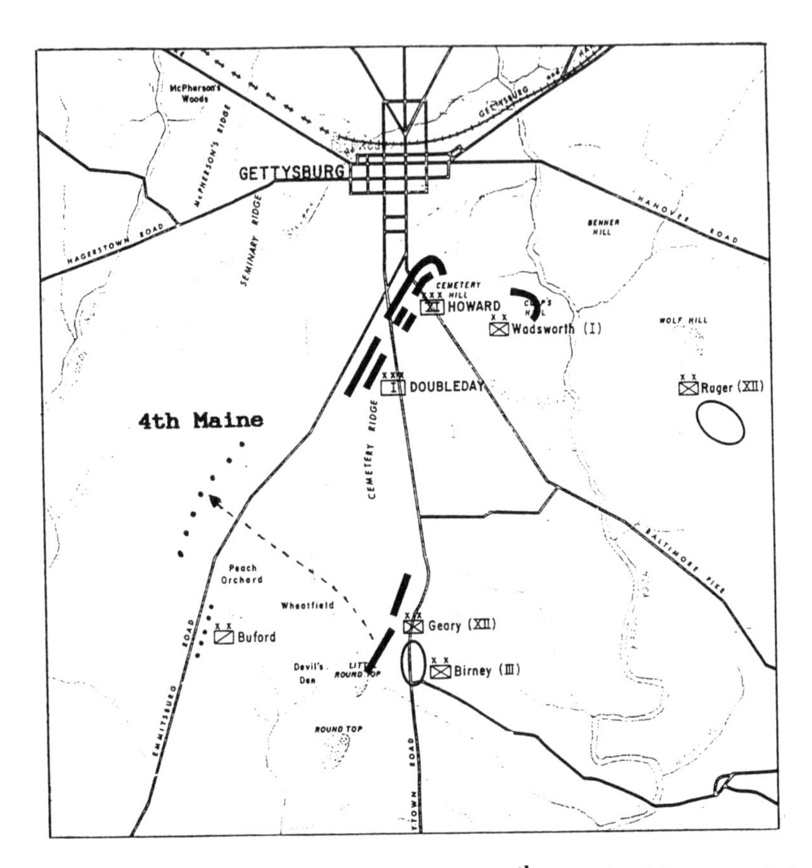

Dots indicate the approximate position that the 4th Maine's pickets occupied during the night of July 1st. The regiment was pulled back the following day and placed on the extreme left of the Union line in the Devil's Den.

Birney's first and second brigades, under Graham and Ward, had arrived at Gettysburg during the late afternoon and evening of July 1st. By this time the fighting had mostly died away. Both brigades had been moved off the right side of the Emmitsburg Road onto the Wheatfield Road, or Trostles Lane. Here they made camp in front of Cemetery Ridge for the night. Graham's men stacked their arms in the woods south of the Weckert House. Ward's Brigade, including the 4th Maine and their divisional batteries, bivouacked nearby.[5]

During the night of July 1st and 2nd, General Meade's army had assumed a defensive posture along Cemetery Ridge and the ridges to the north. The line formed was in the shape of a fish hook. Early in the day General Sickles had pointed out to Meade that there was a stronger defensive position farther to the West which he wished to occupy. Meade ordered General Henry Hunt, chief of artillery, to go with Sickles to examine his proposed line. They proceeded to the area of the Peach Orchard. Hunt agreed that Sickles' proposal to occupy the ridges in this area was a good one. The move would, however, cause a dangerous salient to be formed which would greatly lengthen the line. It would also make it more difficult to maintain contact with the Second Corps on their right. In any case Sickles could not hope to hold the line without support from the Fifth Corps. Hunt, reporting back to General Meade, recommended against the change.[6]

About 2:30 in the afternoon Sickles ordered his Corps, consisting of about ten thousand men, to move forward. The divisions moved out in full line of battle with their drums pounding and their bugles sounding the advance. General Gibbon of the 2nd Corps observed the sudden movement and wondered if he had perhaps missed an order for a general advance. Hancock, who was standing beside Gibbons, observed the spectacle. Turning to Gibbon, Hancock said, " Wait a moment, you'll see them tumbling back." They soon did.[7]

The Third Corps had now moved out into the salient which extended from the Peach Orchard, south and east, to the Devil's Den at the base of Little Round Top. The new line was a half mile to the west of their old one. The movement had created a half mile gap between the Second Corps' left and the Third Corps right. Sickles

[5] Phantz, Gettysburg, the Second Day, p. 86.
[6] Ed., Maine at Gettysburg, p. 180.
[7] Hunt, Battles and Leaders, pp. 301-302.

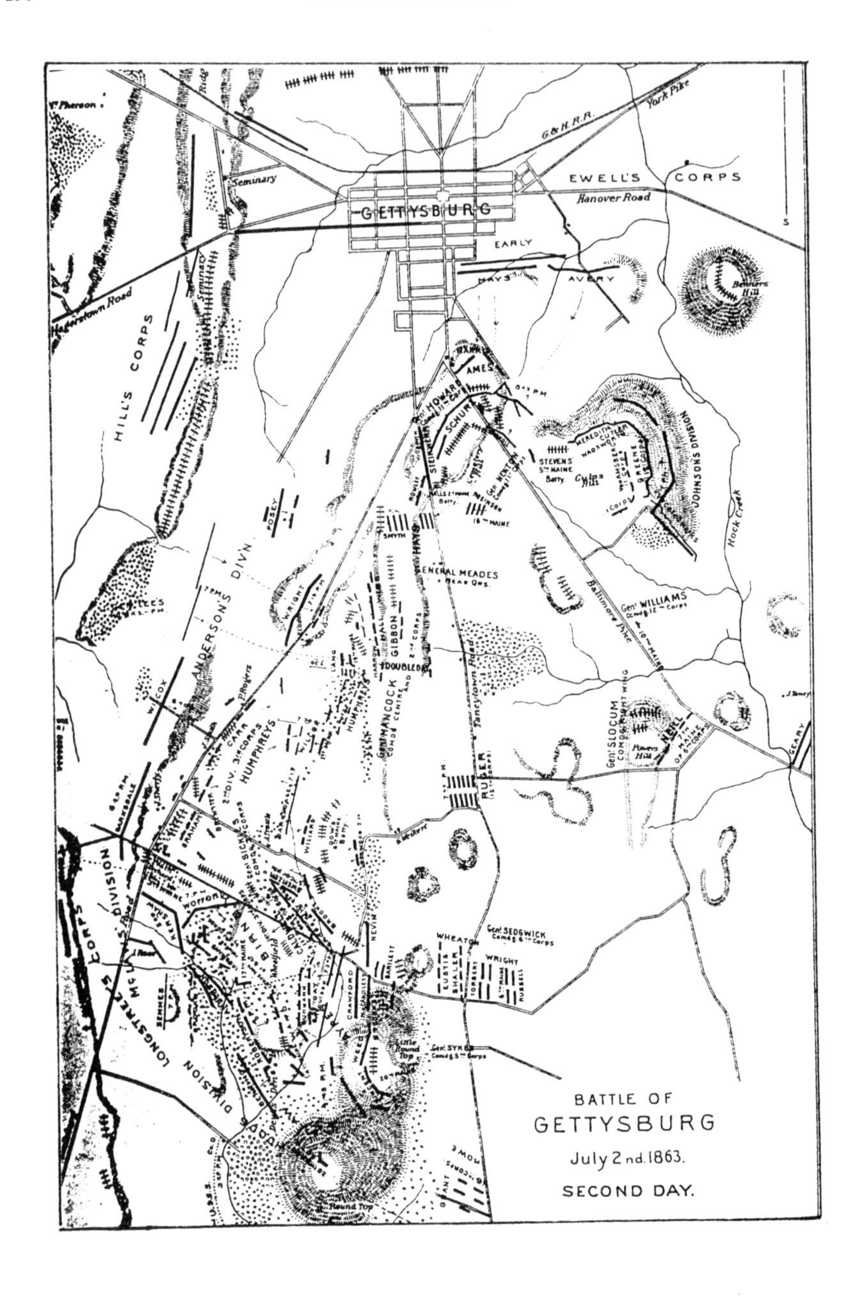
GETTYSBURG
EWELL'S CORPS
Hanover Road
York Pike
Seminary
Hagerstown Road
HILL'S CORPS
ANDERSON'S DIVN.
JOHNSONS DIVISION
Baltimore Pike
Taneytown Road
GENERAL MEADES HEAD QRS.
Little Round Top
Round Top
Rock Creek
LONGSTREETS CORPS
BATTLE OF
GETTYSBURG
July 2nd. 1863.
SECOND DAY.

right flank was now hanging and totally vulnerable to enfilade. His line was fully twice as long, now, as it had been while they were on Cemetery Ridge.[8]

As the regiments of the various brigades were assigned their defensive positions, many of the troops began to discover that they had very little cover. For most this was the case. For the 4th Maine, though, the opposite was true. The Fourth was assigned a position on the far left flank in a place that was known as the Devil's Den by the locals. The regiment was joined on their right flank by the tiny 124th New York. On the high ground immediately in their front was posted Smith's 4th New York Battery. The Mainers quickly kindled some fires and began to make coffee. There being a supply of beef cattle in the valley between the Den and Little Round Top, a couple of men even slaughtered a couple of the cows and began to cook the meat to satisfy their hunger. Most had not had anything to eat in almost three days.[9]

The feast was never completed. About 3:45 the rebs were observed coming out of the woods about a half mile distant. They brought forward with them their artillery and quickly began to saturate the Union position with their fire. The Third Corps batteries soon returned the favor. Only Smith's battery remained mysteriously silent. General Hunt now rode to the Devil's Den to see what the problem was. As he arrived the men were just finishing the placement of four of his ten pound Parrotts to the top of the hill above the Den. The guns were in plain sight of the enemy, posted on the east side of a triangular stone wall. The other two guns of the battery were placed in Plum Run Valley one hundred and fifty yards to the rear. From here they would be able to cover the approach to Little Round Top.[10]

As the fighting began to heat up along the Union left General Meade began to take notice of all the noise and commotion. Presently, he rode to confer with General Sickles. Meade was appalled at the way his Third Corps commander had placed his men. On meeting with him, Meade said, "...General, I am afraid you are too far out." Sickles said he would be able to hold if he could be

---

[8] Foote, op. cit., p. p. 496.
[9] Ibid.
[10] Op. cit., Maine at Gettysburg, p. 180.

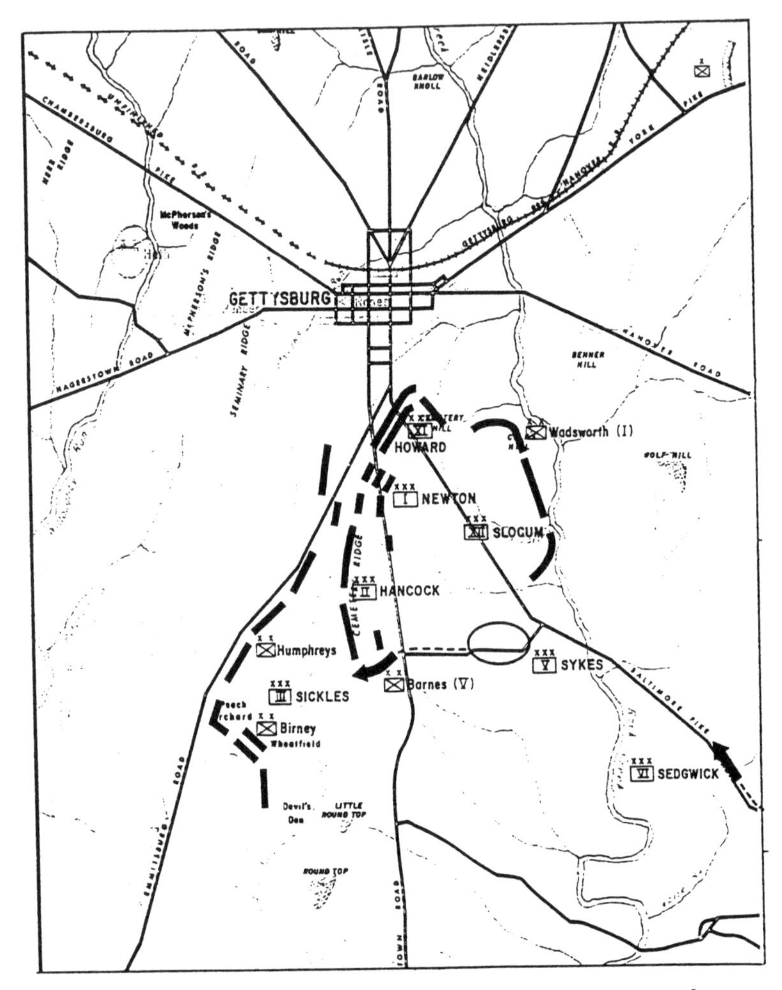

Approximate positions of Union troops at 3:45 P.M. on July 3rd. The 4th Maine in the Devils's Den has just begun to prepare coffee and to cook a recently slaughtered beef critter when a line of enemy troops are seen advancing out of the woods to the west. This is Hood's division.

supported. If not, he would withdraw if so ordered. Meade simply stated, "I think it is too late, the enemy will not allow you."[11]

Meanwhile, back at the Devil's Den, General Hunt had sensed the vulnerability of Smith's Battery. As soon as Smith began to fire, Reilly's and Latham's Confederate Batteries retaliated. Hunt informed Smith that he believed that he would not be able to hold his station. Smith then asked General Ward if he would dispatch the 4th Maine from the ridge on his left to the woods in his rear at the foot of Little Round Top. Ward, instead, ordered the Maine regiment into Plum Run Valley, confronting the Devil's Den.[12]

Colonel Elijah Walker was not happy about his new assignment. Having made the move, Walker sent a group of skirmishers under the command of Captain Edwin Libby into the trees in his front at the base of Little Round Top's slopes.[13] He also sent a party of some seventy skirmishers directly into the Devil's Den. Along with these men he sent four officers, including Captain George Davis, J. B. Litchfield, and 1st Lieutenant Solomon Stearns, both of Company F.

It is also interesting to note that 2nd Lieutenant Nathaniel Robbins, Company H., of Union, Maine, was also recruited for the task. It might also be mentioned here, just as a point of interest, that Mr. Robbins had been a student at Bowdoin College in the mid-1850's. As a matter of fact one of his professors, Joshua Chamberlain, was presently in command of the 20th Maine Infantry. Soon, Chamberlain would place his command on the slopes of Little Round Top on the left flank of the 4th Maine. From there he would teach the Confederate Army a lesson in military tactics that it, and the world, would not soon forget.[14]

Smith, and the Rebel artillery, participated in counterbattery fire for about half an hour. The New York gunners fired both shell and case, depending on the cover that the Confederate troops were attempting to take advantage of. Smith paid careful attention to his guns and gave instruction to them in ..."distinct tones that could be heard above the tumult by the men of the 124th." Since it was at

---

[11] Ibid., p. 181.
[12] Ibid.
[13] Foote, op. cit., p. p. 496.
[14] Pfantz, op. cit., p. 178.

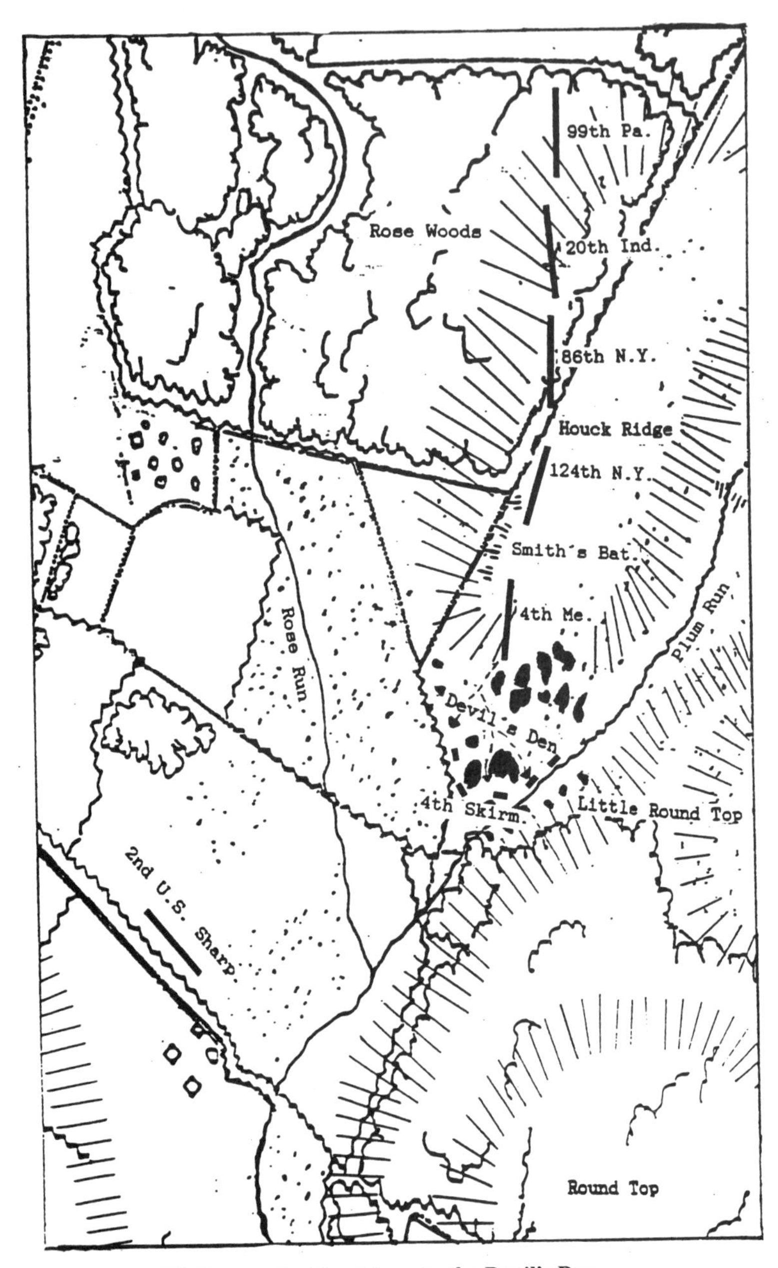

Walker sends skirmishers to the Devil's Den

about this time that General Hood was wounded by shell fire, it might even be supposed that this battery was responsible for the injury.[15]

Hood's regiments had by now crossed Slyder's lane and were beginning to press toward Smith's Battery and the 124th New York Infantry. General Ward noted at this point that the rebels were advancing in double line "in columns en masse." The 1st Texas and the 3rd Arkansas regiments had advanced to, and crossed, the West Branch of Plum Run. From here, in whole or in part, they had taken advantage of the cover offered by Rose's Woods as they advanced uphill to Ward's line. As the Confederates advanced, running and yelling at the top of their lungs, the Northern regiments did not open fire until they reached a range of about two hundred yards, a distance which had been prescribed by General Ward. The fight for the stone wall which was held by Smith and the 124th New York would begin now and continue for more than an hour and a half.[16]

About this time the 44th and 48th Alabama regiments began their advance toward the Devil's Den from the trees to the south. The 44th had formed a line in the scrub brush near the fork of Plum Run. This unit would now split, and advance its left toward Smith's Battery along the stone wall, while its right would advance through the boulders of the Devil's Den toward Plum Run gorge. This second detachment would provide the major challenge to the 4th Maine's skirmishers attempting to hold the Den.[17]

When the 44th Alabama moved to the attack, the 48th moved as well. The 48th had formed into line of battle at the same time as had the 44th. This they accomplished in the woods on Little Round Tops slope. Both regiments advanced slowly, due primarily to the large number of obstacles in their path. The 48th's objective was to secure the valley in preparation for an attack on Little Round Top.

When the right wing of the 44th Alabama got within fifty yards of the Devil's Den, the 4th Maine's seventy skirmishers, along with a small contingent of sharpshooters, opened fire. Several shots were fired somewhat prematurely, followed by a single volley. Many, as a result, were able to take cover but the volley still caused extensive

---

[15] Robbins, 1895 Service Report,

[16] Op Cit. Maine at Gettysburg, p. 181

[17] Pfantz, op cit., p. 178.

casualties. The 44th was forced to halt and return the musket fire. For now at least, the tiny band of skirmishers were safe.[18]

As the men in the Devil's Den released their first volley, the remainder of the regiment, still posted along Plum Run, took note that a brigade of Union infantry was taking up position on the east slope of Little Round Top. This was Vincent's Brigade of the Fifth Corps. The lead regiment of this advance was the twentieth Maine, and they, too, were given the duty of holding the extreme left flank of the army. Upon seeing this Colonel Walker ordered his own skirmishers, under the command of Captain Libby, back from the slopes of Little Round Top.

Shortly after Captain Libby's return a squad of men from the 2nd U. S. Sharpshooters dashed up to Colonel Walker with news that a large number of Rebel Infantry were close on their heals. Their obvious intent was to flank and destroy the 4th Maine. A few moments later Vincent's brigade began to receive rifle fire from the Confederates below. At the same moment a force of southern infantry appeared on the regiments left, about fifty yards distant. The Limerock Regiment fired six or more volleys into them before their shots were returned. In the noise and confusion the advancing rebels did not realize that the 4th was taking advantage of flank fire down the length of their line.

Finally the enemy returned the fire, concentrating on the 4th's left and center. Walker remembered that "when he did open fire upon us we soon found, to our sorrow, that we had no mean foe to contend with." It was here that Maine the regiment suffered their greatest loss. The unit received "a biting musketry fire." The men they were firing at were those of the 48th Alabama who had unwittingly exposed themselves in the rocky open area on the East side of Plum Run. This valley was now beginning to earn its reputation as the "slaughter pen." The pressure was so great that the 4th Maine was forced to fall back a short distance and reform their line.[19]

Colonel Sheffield remembered his contact with the 4th Maine as having taken place at "a range of twenty paces." He reported that the concentrated fire from the Maine men forced the left of his line to fall back. Though the 48th's right held, it was not until "the Fourth Maine

---

[18] Ibid., p. 179.

[19] Harrison, Gettysburg Magazine, 7/89, p. pp. 5-57.

fell back a short way and formed another line" that the intense pressure was taken off Sheffield's men.[20]

Up above the 124th New York Infantry, the so-called Orange Blossoms, staffed with a mere 238 officers and enlisted men, were attempting to hold against the onslaught of some four Confederate regiments. This was Hood's support line, and it threatened to disrupt the balance which now existed. From the floor of Plum Run valley the Maine men were well aware that if the 124th, along with Smith's Guns, could not hold on, then their own position would soon be untenable. Fire from the high ground above the Devil's Den would cut their meager numbers to pieces and force their retreat.[21]

The 124th now attempted to charge down off the hill in order to relieve the mounting threat, both to themselves and the battery. Though they crashed through a several lines of enemy troops, they were, inevitably, forced to withdraw with great loss. Smith's artillerymen had withdrawn from their guns while the charge was in progress, being unable to fire without injuring their own men. As the men returned to their guns one of the pieces was struck and disabled by rebel cannon fire. This piece was immediately sent to the rear.[22]

Smith's position was now even more uncertain than before. The 124th's line was so depleted that now it did not even reach the guns. Smith pleaded with the men of the 124th to come to his aid but they either could not or would not. He pleaded with them saying, "For God's sake, men, don't let them take my guns from me." Realizing that there was no help to be had here he returned to his guns and ordered his men to stay with them as long as they could. When they were finally forced to withdraw he told them to take all of the implements they could with them. Without these items the guns would be totally unserviceable to the Confederates.[23]

Meanwhile, the 44th and 48th Alabama regiments were continuing to put pressure on the 4th Maine. Colonel Perry of the 44th, with his right wing, had had his attack stalled by the seventy 4th Maine skirmishers stationed in the Devil's Den. Totally frustrated by his lack of progress he finally ordered his men to charge the den. The

---

[20] Phantz, op. cit., p. 183-184.
[21] Ibid.
[22] Official Records, XXXIX, p. 510.
[23] Pfantz, op. cit., p. 184.

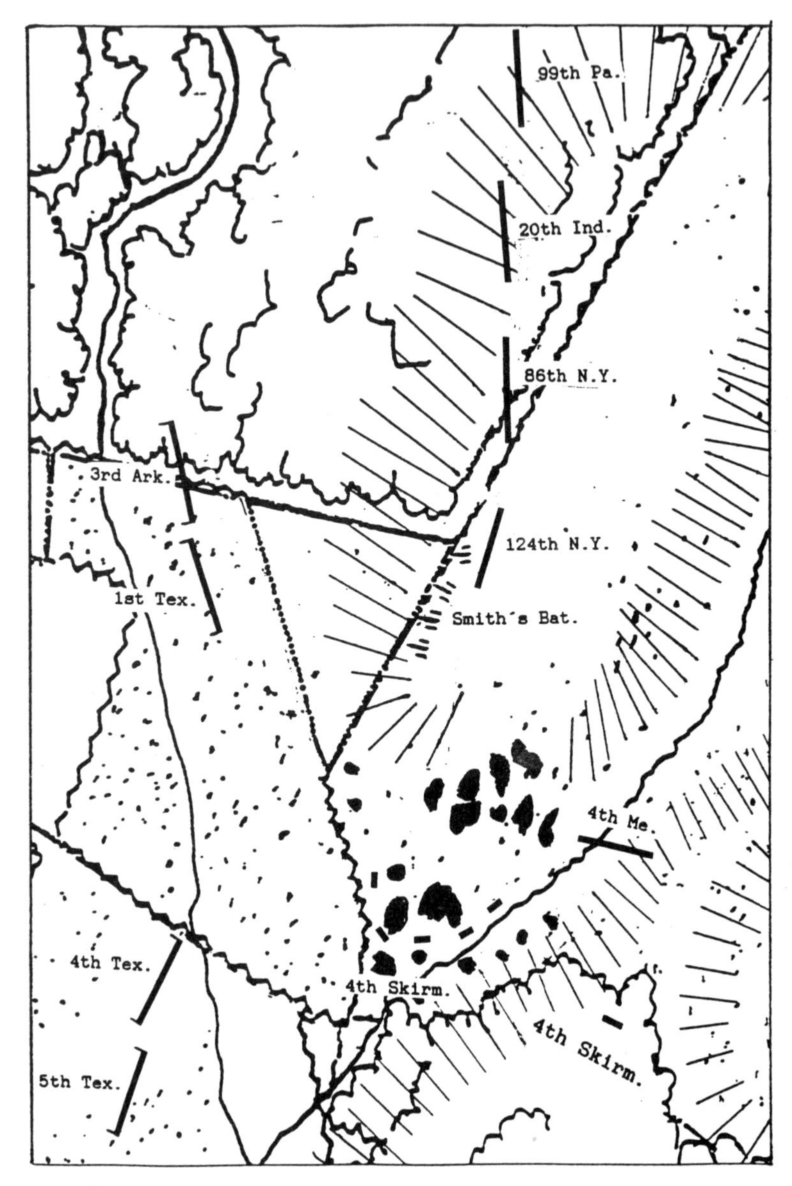

The 3rd Arkansas and 1st Texas begin advance on Houck's Ridge. The 4th Maine moves to Plum Run Valley. Skirmishers are sent to trees in their front.

Second Lieutenant Nathaniel Robbins of Union was among those men that were captured in the Devil's Den. (Photo Maine State Archives)

rebels jumped up from their prone positions and swarmed into the boulders. According to Colonel Perry, two of the men of the 4th Maine surrendered to him personally. Some thirty-eight others were captured by his Alabamans as they combed through the rocks.[24]

One of the loose ends in the history of this regiment is the identity of the skirmish detachment posted at the Devil's Den. It is obvious from the existing records that all of the men of 4th Maine hidden in the rocks were not apprehended. The regiment, itself, had but seventy-one men captured. Colonel Perry claims that he took forty prisoners. Probably some of them were members of the sharpshooter regiment previously reported on station here. In the book, Gettysburg, the Second Day, it is noted that the men occupying the Den were probably the men of Company F. Even Lieutenant. Charles Sawyer's report in the official records mentions "one company (F) being left on the brow of the hill." On July 2nd, this company was reported as having only thirty-seven members, however, including officers. Of this number only eleven were reported captured. Nathaniel Robbins of Co. H., by his own record, was one of the officers taken prisoner here. Company H. had but forty-one members on the field that day and only five of these became guests of the Confederate prison system. Probably we will never know the identity of the men posted here, or what company they came from. In all likelihood it was an assortment of men from each of the companies.[25]

Sometime prior to this loss both Colonel Walker and Major Walker were wounded. According to records on file at the National Archives, a bullet had passed through Walker's left leg, about four inches above the ankle. This bullet "partially severed the Tendo Achillis" and then, continuing on, entered his horse, causing the horse to go down.[26] Lieutenant Charles Sawyer reported that the Colonel's wound had occurred "in the first of the engagement." He also stated that the wound was extremely painful to him. Based upon the descriptions of the injury there is little doubt that the Colonel was

---

[24] Ibid., p. 185.
[25] Ibid., p. 190.
[26] Ibid., p. 191.

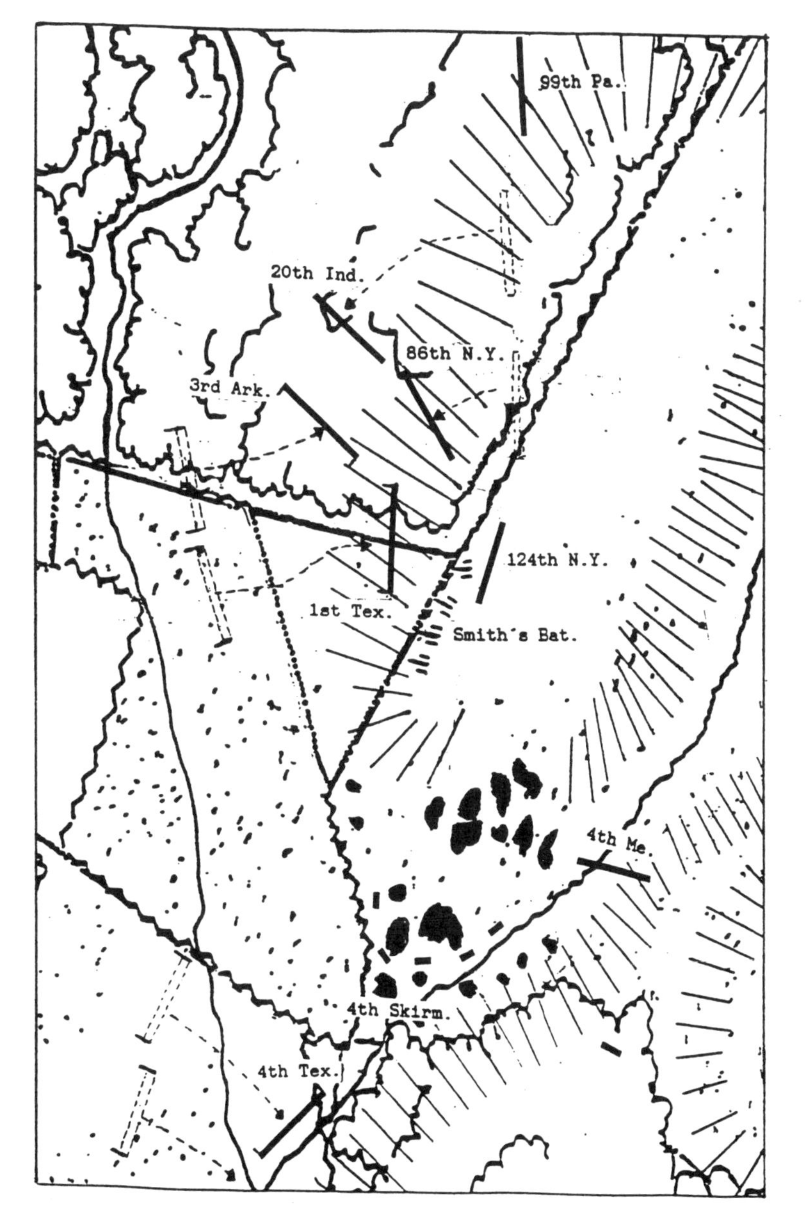

The Confederate regiments continue their advance. Union forces adjust their positions to their best advantage

now pretty much hobbled. In light of this, the events which were now about to unfold are all the more remarkable.[27]

With the capture of the 4th Maine's skirmishers, there was now nothing between the 44th Alabama and Smith's Guns on the summit of the Devil's Den. Realizing that Confederate occupation of these heights would, undoubtedly, cause the collapse of Ward's entire line, Colonel Walker decided that he must take the location himself. He now pulled his men back away from the 48th on his left and the 44th in his front. Next Walker reformed his line and then ordered his Maine men to fix bayonets. Later Walker wrote, " I shall never forget the 'click' that was made by the fixing of bayonets, it was as one." Then the next fateful order rang out. "By the right oblique, charge!"[28]

The 4th Maine now came surging up out of the "Valley of Death" up the steep incline to the heights above the Devil's Den. They swarmed around Smith's now abandoned Guns. Smith would, later in his official report, dispute this. He stated that the "fighting became so close that I ordered my men to cease firing, as many of the Fourth Maine had already advanced in front of the guns. I then went to the rear, and opened that section of guns, firing obliquely through the gully, doing good execution."[29]

The one thing in Smith's description of the fight at the Devil's Den that was particularly accurate was the closeness of the fighting. In addition to a part of the 44th Georgia putting pressure on Walker, Benning had ordered his four regiments into the fight. Now men from the 1st Texas, the 15th, the 20th, 17th, and even the 2nd Georgia began to add their weight to the fighting on the crest. Without direct and immediate support, the Fourth Maine's situation was quite hopeless.

The Maine regiment had been involved in the melee on the top of the hill for about five minutes when Ward pulled the 99th Pennsylvania off the right of his line in Rose's Woods and sent them to Walker's assistance. Major John Moore of the 99th got his men into a crude line of battle and shouted, "Up and Charge." These men were then heard to shout "Pennsylvania and our Homes!"[30] The attack

---

[27] Ibid., p. 193.
[28] O. R., op. cit., p. 509.
[29] Service Records, Elijah Walker, National Archives.
[30] O. R., op. cit., p. 510.

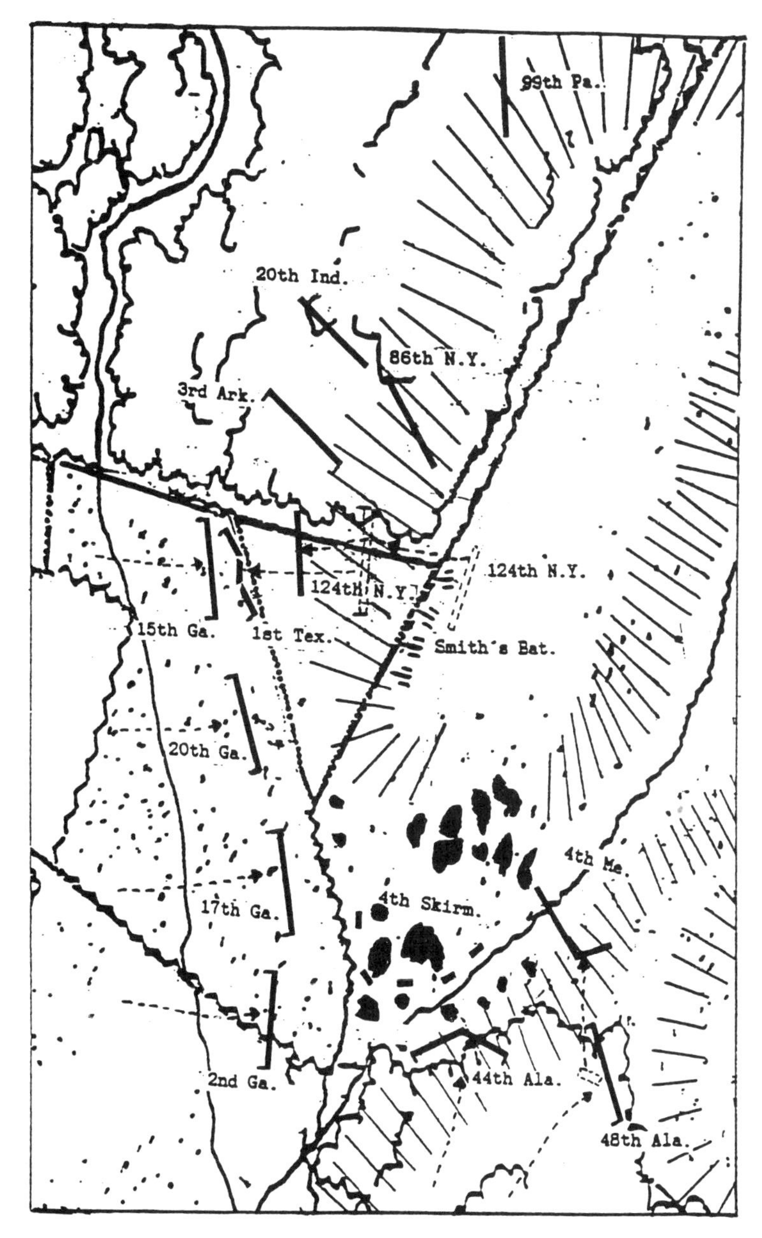

The 1st Texas assaults the 124th New York and is counterattacked by them. Devil's Den shirmishers halt 44th Alabama. The 4th attacks the 48th Alabama.

Sergeant Henry O. Ripley of Rockland distinguished himself once again at the Battle of Gettysburg by bearing the regimental flag throughout the fight. The flag received 31 bullet holes while Henry was uninjured. (Photo Maine State Archives)

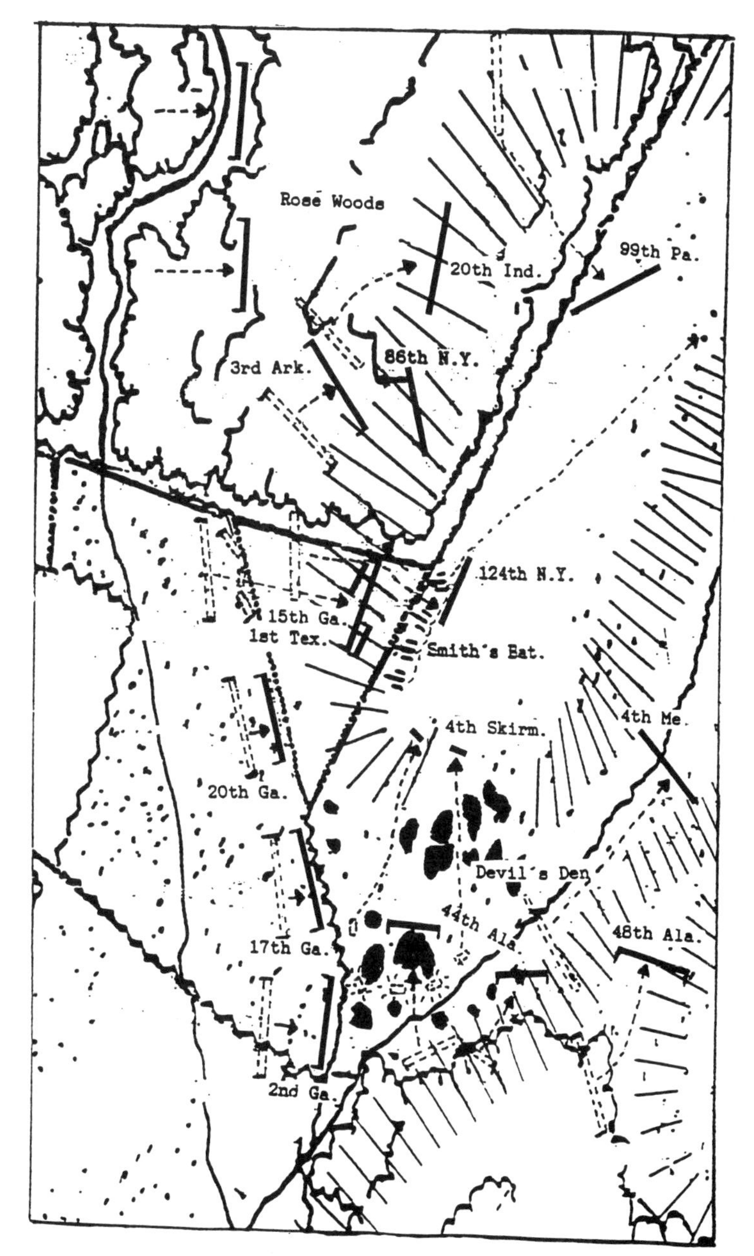

Benning's Brigade is added to the attack on the ridge. The 44th Alabama captures the 4th skirmishers in the Devil's Den while the regiment retreats.

actually helped prevent the 4th from becoming totally cut off and surrounded. The confederates were, for now at least, driven from the ridge, taking cover in the rocks of the Devil's Den. An officer of the 4th Maine later recalled, "the whole line was alive with burning powder."[31]

The attack of the 99th Pennsylvania was now reinforced with the arrival of the 6th New Jersey and the 40th New York. Captain Smith reported, "These regiments marched down the gully, fighting like tigers, exposed to a terrific fire of musketry, and when within 100 yards of the rebel line, the 4th Maine, which still held the hill, were forced to retreat. Very soon afterward the Fortieth New York and Six New Jersey were compelled to follow."[32]

When Anderson brought his brigade into the fight on the right, the 1st Texas and the 15th Georgia were suddenly relieved. No longer pinned down by the flank fire that had been troubling them for the past hour or so they moved to the crest and brought the struggle for the guns to an end. The 4th Maîne, now intermingled with remnants of several other regiments, could no longer hold out against the overwhelming numbers of Confederates. Colonel Walker, finding it more an more difficult to move, had his sword taken from his hands by a rebel soldier and then, he himself, fell into enemy hands. Walker remembered that it now about sunset.[33]

The order to retreat had already been given. Both the 99th Pennsylvania and the 4th Maine were now falling back. Both regiments had lost more than a third of their numbers. In spite the orders, however, there was some immediate business which had to be attended to. Sergeant Mowry of Company B and Corporal Freeman Roberts of Company F both refused to leave without their Colonel. The two men, displaying a total lack of concern for their own safety, "wrestled him from the foe" and then carried Walker back to safety. Even the Colonel's sword was retaken.[34]

In the course of the fight the 4th's regimental colors had its staff sheared off by a shell fragment and then was itself pierced by two more fragments and thirty-two more bullets. The color bearer of the

---

[31] Pfantz, op. cit., p. 193.
[32] O. R., op. cit., p. 589.
[33] Pfantz, op. cit., p. 193.
[34] Harrison, op. cit., p. 59.

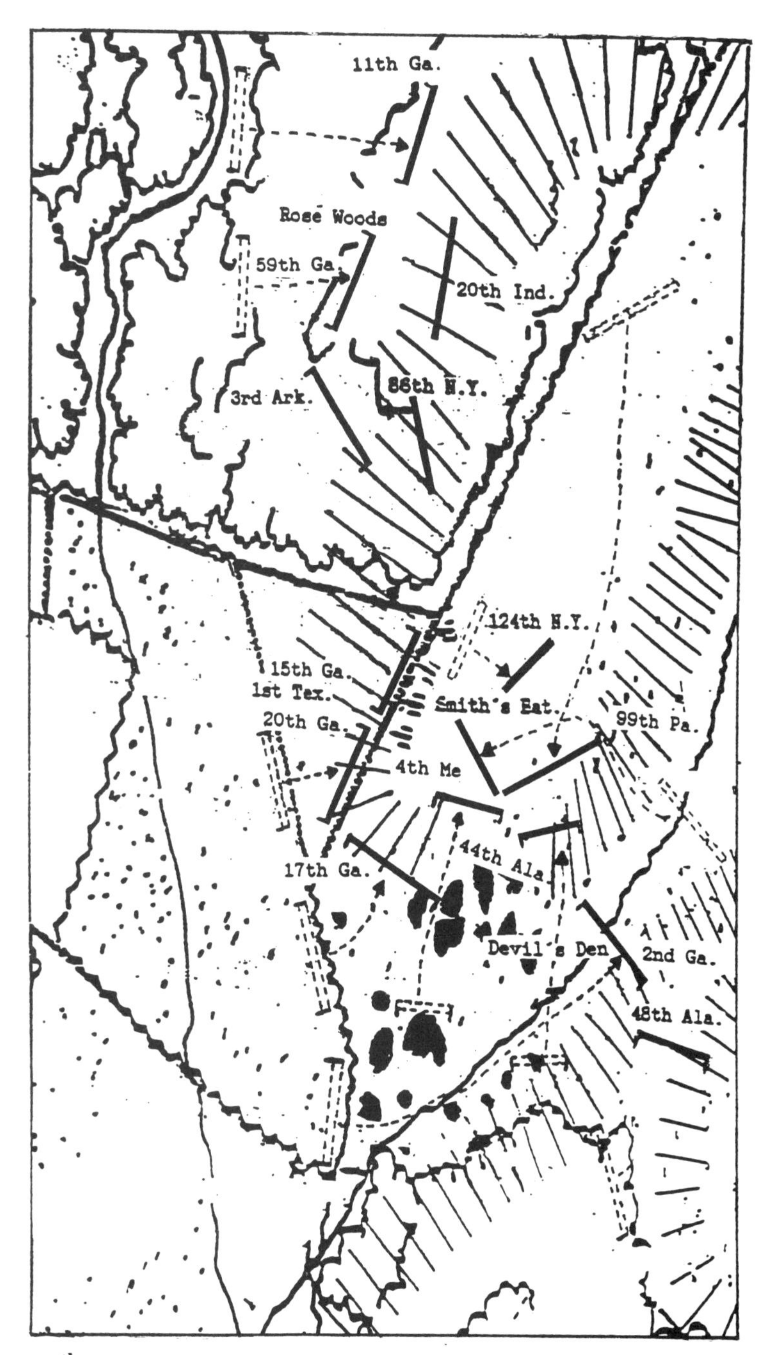

The 4th Maine charges up Houck's Ridge retaking Smith's Guns. Joined by the 99th Pennsylvania they hold for a brief time and then are forced to retreat.

regiment this day was Sergeant Henry O. Ripley, of Rockland, already a recipient of the Kearney Cross. Throughout the fight, in the face of fierce enemy fire, Ripley had proudly carried the regimental flag. Despite having the staff shattered in his hands by a projectile, and having the rest of the color guard fall around him, he never once let the colors hit the ground. An officer that was a witness to Ripley's repeated acts of valor stated; "That color bearer ought to be made a Major General." Though never a general he was later promoted to 1st Lieutenant as a result of the courage shown this day. Captain Edwin Libby would later report Sergeant Ripley's actions, thusly:

"I would also bring to your notice for gallant and meritorious conduct Sergt. Henry O. Ripley, the color bearer of the regiment, whose daring and gallantry won for him the admiration of all - thirty-one bullet holes being put through the flag and the staff being shot off from his hands. His color guard all being killed or wounded, he waved his flag defiantly in the face of the enemy."[35]

As the 4th Maine fell back from the Devil's Den, Colonel Walker was finally forced to relinquish his command. General Ward had come up to Walker and inquired if he were wounded. He replied that he was only slightly so and if he could be helped in remounting a horse he would be all right. The General said; You are hurt more than you think and had better go to the rear."[36] Being the senior officer Captain Edwin Libby assumed command of the regiment. Once the men had fallen back through the cover and protection of the trees, Libby immediately began to reassemble his men. This, he later reported, was done quite quickly as there were very few stragglers. The regiment then, with equal promptness, rejoined the brigade.[37]

Captain Smith of the 4th New York Battery would show a great deal of bitterness toward the men of the Fourth Maine. As the Maine boys retreated from the Devils Den three of Smith's Guns fell into the hands of the Confederates. During the entire battle the Army of the Potomac had lost only six. Due to the rather light number of the casualties to the battery, Smith was subjected, naturally, to a great deal of criticism. At the time he had abandoned the guns he said he expected that the 4th would hold on to the ground. He also stated that

[35] Pfantz. op. cit., p. 194.
[36] Walker, History of the 4th Maine, p. 52.
[37] Ibid.

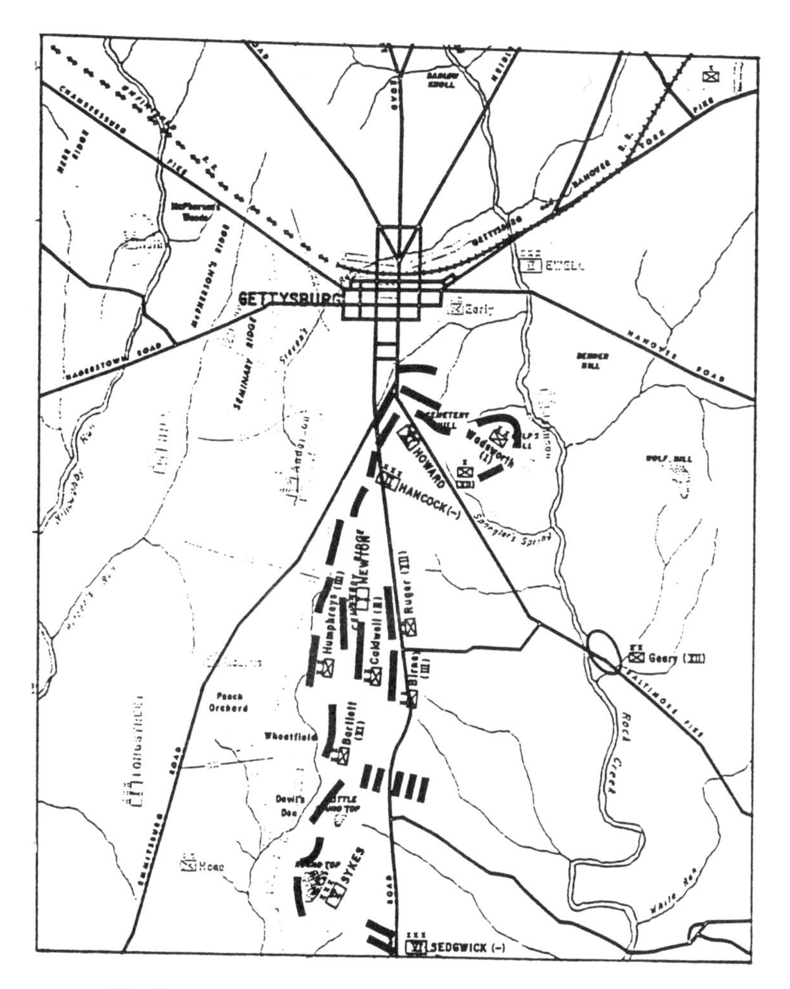

Final positions of Union troops on the night of July 2nd.

he expected the Maine regiment would take the guns with them if forced to retreat. Since the 4th had abandoned the position Smith felt the blame for their loss rested, not with him, but with the 4th Maine. Captain Smith stated in his official report, I trust no blame will be attached to me for the loss of my guns. I did that which in my judgment I thought best."[38]

In Brigadier-General J. H. Hobart Ward's official report, who at the time was in command of the division due to General Sickle's wounding, he speaks repeatedly of the gallantry of the 4th Maine and its Brigade. Ward reported that for nearly two hours the brigade had opposed nearly ten thousand of the enemy. The brigade, itself, had numbered just fifteen hundred, of which eight hundred had become casualties. Eight of the fourteen field officers were also lost. Ward further states that the "veterans of this brigade, to their world-wide reputation have added new laurels, and, if possible, excelled themselves."[39]

The 4th Maine entered the battle on July 2nd with three hundred enlisted men and eighteen officers. Of these officers, three were killed, two wounded, and four were be captured. Three were be taken in the Devil's Den alone. Lieutenants Charles McCobb and Orpheus Roberts were killed outright. Lieutenant George Bragg was seriously wounded and died July 5th. Major Whitcomb would cling to life until October 5th of that same year. Of the enlisted men, ten would be killed, fifty-five wounded, and seventy one were taken prisoner. Losses represented a full forty-four percent of the soldiers present for duty.[40]

As the Fourth was falling back to regroup, the 20th Maine was, just a few yards away, performing their miracle on Little Round Top. Here, too, Maine men would fix bayonet and charge upon the

---

[38] Pfantz, op. cit., p. 195.

[39] O. R., op. cit., p. 589.

[40] Eight of the 4th Maine's sergeants were captured at Gettysburg.They are:

Co. A. Marcian McManus	Unity	Age 25
Co. A. Thomas Gurney	Waldo	Age 22
Co. A. Tolford Durham	Waldo	Age 19
Co. C. Rufus O. Fales	Thomaston	Age 22
Co. E. Zuinglas Gowan	Nobleboro	Age 24
Co. F. Henry Leach	Knox	Age 36
Co. I. Ivory Baird	Camden	Age 25

advancing rebel lines in what they certainly thought to be a futile effort. Showing the remarkable courage that would set the Maine men apart from all the other states in this war, this small regiment succeeded in their task in a manner far beyond even Joshua Chamberlain's desperate expectations. As darkness closed in upon the battlefield at Gettysburg on this the second day, the outcome of the fight was still anything but certain.

Following the day's fighting, the entire line of the army was pulled back from the salient created by General Sickles. The lines were, once again, intact from the town along Cemetery Ridge, all the way to the Round Tops. Both the right and left flanks of the Union Army had been severely pressed, and yet had held out gallantly. Meade's men had fought well. The question in the minds of all the men was who would be asked to make the next move. The 4th Maine would spend a hot and restless night in nervous anticipation of what the Confederates would attempt next.

The Fourth spent the early morning hours of July 3rd improving their defensive positions in anticipation of a rebel attack. About two P.M. the regiment was ordered to arms and sent to support the 2nd Corps. Lee had put into motion one of the great artillery barrages of the entire war in preparation for a grand assault on Cemetery Hill. Pickett's famous charge was underway and the Fourth Maine, all that remained of it that is, was moved into a position to serve as support for an artillery battery. The gray wave swept forward to their high water mark and then went stumbling back in defeat. Though the Limerock Regiment viewed the entire spectacle of the suicidal Confederate charge, not a single one of their numbers were killed or injured.[41]

On the morning of July 4th the two armies stood facing each other across a no-mans land littered with dead and wounded. Into this intervale the Fourth Maine was sent, on this the Fourth of July, to act as skirmishers, and to probe out the enemy positions to try to ascertain their intentions. In their exposed positions they would observe the birth of their nation and would even offer up two of its numbers as wounded in its defense. Corporal James Gall was wounded in the hip and Private Dennis Sweeney was wounded in the

---

[41] Pfantz, op. cit., p. 195.

Private John F. Shuman, Company K, of Belfast. He died from his wounds at Gettysburg on July 15, 1863 at the ripe old age of 20. (Family Photo)

4th MAINE
INFANTRY

hand. Several times shots were exchanged between the two lines, and several times the Maine men would wonder if this were the beginning of yet another Confederate offensive. When darkness, once again, enveloped the battlefield the Fourth Maine was allowed to return to the battery they supported the previous day. The Battle of Gettysburg had ended.[42]

John Shuman's final resting place at Gettysburg's National Cemetary.

[42] Ibid., p. 196.

Chapter 11

No Conscript or Bounty Jumper

Colonel Walker in his later years, in reflecting upon the events at Gettysburg, expressed the opinion that "there was no battle fought during my term of service, in which our men were so obviously determined to beat the foe. Every soldier did his whole duty. So it can be said in all truth, that the humblest private who fought in it is deserving of as much honor as they who served in the more responsible positions. Another member of the 4th that fought by Walker's side authored the following thoughts on the fighting at Gettysburg:

"It is worthy to note, too, in the light of the subsequent history of the war, that this battle was fought entirely by troops who had voluntarily enlisted for the defense of their country. No conscript or bounty jumper aimed here his unwilling musket at his country's foes. The cohorts of the lame, the halt, the deaf, the blind and the aged, with their gray hair dyed to the semblance of youth, who from the following fall to the close of the war filled our ambulances and hospitals and obstructed the prosecution of the war, had not made their appearance. The rapacious and unscrupulous recruiting officer had not then sent forward his levies from the slums of the cities and the jails of the counties. None of these can claim any share in the glorious victory. It was won by men who had a personal interest in the issue, who knew what that interest was, and were willing to risk their lives for the success of the cause for which they fought."[1]

On the afternoon of July 4th, General Lee began to withdraw his defeated army from its positions around Gettysburg. Lee headed his Confederates off in the direction of Williamsport in the midst of a huge rain storm. Williamsport had been the spot at which the rebels had crossed the Potomac on their way north. A long pontoon bridge had been specially constructed for the crossing. As the lead elements of the Confederate army began to arrive there the very next day they

[1] Walker, History of the 4th Maine, p. 56.

found that the bridge had been destroyed and the river was too high from recent rains to be forded. The Confederate army was in serious danger of becoming trapped.

In desperation Lee laid out a defensive line of almost six miles long. The entrenchments began to the south at Falling Waters, and ran in an arc to the North, terminating at Conococheaque Creek. Ewell's Corps was given the left flank, Hill's the center, and Longstreet the right. Low on ammunition and vital supplies, however, Lee nervously awaited the arrival of Meade's army.[2]

Meade wasted two days in beginning his pursuit. Four of his Corps had been quite badly mauled in the three days of fighting. Still by July 9th the Union army had arrived at Middletown. Meade immediately began to probe out the enemy lines in order to determine the best spot for an attack. Several assaults were planned but each of them were canceled for various reasons. When the attack was finally made on July 14th there were no Confederate troops to receive it as Lee had slipped across the river the night before on an improvised pontoon bridge. The single best opportunity to end the war had just slipped through Meade's hands.[3]

The 4th Maine, now under the command of Captain Edward Libby, began its move south on July 7, passing through Middletown and Frederick, Maryland, and bivouacking for the night in one of the many mountain passes. The evening of the 9th they camped at South Mountain Pass and on the 10th stopped at a place called Mill Point. On the 12th they formed into line of battle near Antietam in preparation for an attack on Lee's trapped army. The 4th was a part of the assault that took place on the 14th and proceeded to assist in both carrying and occupying the vacated Confederate works.[4]

As Lee's army made good their escape they took with them, among their many prisoners, sixty-eight enlisted men and four officers belonging to the 4th Maine. For these men the war would now take on a new dimension, that of survival in Southern prisons. Writing thirty years after the war, Nathaniel Robbins reflected back on his confinement. Following their long trek back to the rebel capital with Lee's retreating army, Robbins' states that they were "held in Libby

[2] Ed., Maine at Gettysburg, p. 182.

[3] Ibid.

[4] Ibid.

Prison until May of 1864 when we were taken to Danville, Va. thence to Macon, Ga. then to Charleston and Columbia, S. C..." The movement of the prisoners farther south coincided, of course, with the beginning of Grant's Wilderness Campaign.

Many of the captured soldiers would die in prison from their wounds or from disease. Lieutenant Robbins would spend his career attempting to escape from the bonds of detention. Robbins actually made two unsuccessful attempts, before actually winning his freedom on the third try. Speaking to the subject he explains that he "made two escapes and recaptured each time, the second time in Nov. 1864 below Hamburg and within sound of Sherman's artillery then moving to the sea via Branchville, Ga. The third and final escape was from Charlotte, N. C. and ended on the U. S. Gunboat "Lenape" on the Cape Fear River."[5]

On July 15, the Maine boys crossed Antietam by the bridge south of that named after Burnside. On the 16th they marched to, and bivouacked at, Maryland Heights. The next evening the regiment crossed the Potomac at Harper's Ferry, then continued south passing near Hillsborough and through Snicker's Gap. On the 20th, the 4th arrived at Upperville. On the 22nd they marched with the army once more, arriving at a place near Manassas Gap on July 23rd.

At 4 A.M. the regiment moved to support the 4th Maine Battery, remaining for about two hours near a place called Wapping Heights. Here a force of Confederates had entrenched themselves on the summit of a hill faced by a steep incline. General Ward assigned the task of clearing the hill to the 3rd and 4th Maine Infantry. While the two Maine regiments crept up the promontory, Union sharpshooters kept up a brisk and accurate fire on the rebels above. As soon as the Maine men reach the crest, they stood, and at once and fired a deadly volley which both surprised and routed the enemy. Many of the Confederates were captured, but many more fell dead or wounded from the deadly musket fire. Those that survived were routed and pursued at a brisk pace by the Maine boys for more than a mile and a half. The 4th lost just one man to wounds, out of the thirteen officers, and one hundred and sixty-nine sergeants, corporals, and privates participating in the engagement.[6]

---

[5] Official Records, XXXIX, p. 510.

[6] Ibid., p. 494.

Following Lee in his escape across the Potomac, Meade himself crossed the river at Harper's Ferry. Though there would be several fights with the rebels during the ensuing days and weeks, and none of them would bode well for the Confederates. Lee would be defeated at a minor engagement on October 14th at Bristoe Station, and, once again, at Kelly's Ford during the first part of November. The two armies would then dance back and forth with each other between Manassas and Mine Run. For the most part, there would be very little fighting for the Army of the Potomac, and a whole lot of maneuvering.

Due to seriousness of Elijah Walker's leg wound, he was sent home to Rockland for the purpose of recuperation. Walker recounted that "the bullet had severed the heel cord, so that I had no more control of my foot than if it had been attached by a string. At first the outlook was discouraging, but after sixty-five days I was able to move my toes, and this convinced me at some future day I should again be able to walk."

By October 5, Colonel Walker was prepared to leave home and return to his regiment. Walker proceded to Washington, reporting to the "surgeon-general of the army, who pronounced me unfit to go to the front for active service and offered to furnish me quarters and put me under surgical treatment. Supposing the army to be lying quietly in camp, I expressed myself as prefering to rejoin my regiment, to which the surgeon-general assented, saying I would be as well off there if I could remain quiet." The trek to Freeman's Ford and his reunion with the 4th Maine on the 12th, proved to be a joyful, yet painful experience, for by 11 P.M. that very evening the regiment was placed in motion in the direction of Bristoe Station.[7]

Though 4th Maine missed the fighting at Bristoe Station, it was involved in the battle at Kelly's Ford. On November 7th the Union army made its' approach on the rebel army in two columns. The right section advanced on General Early's wing, which had established a bridgehead on the near side of the Rappahannock River. The left wing consisted of the 1st, 2nd and 3rd Corps and was under the direction of General French. French had brought up artillery and shelled the enemy positions. The rebs were routed back and 350 prisoners taken. A pontoon bridge was thrown across the river and the 1st and 2nd

---

[7] Walker, op. cit., pp. 58-59.

divisions of the 3rd Corps were sent across the river to establish their own bridgehead.[8]

To the north Union troops had attacked Early during the night and drove him back across the river. This attack made Lee's defensive position totally untenable, and necessitated a forced withdrawal during the night. At dawn the Third division, along with two brigades of the Second, were sent in pursuit of Lee's army. About noon the unit bumped into a well posted force of cavalry and infantry. Immediately the men were formed and called upon to charge the rebel position. This they did, and with their typical courage and determination, drove the enemy line back along the railroad to Brandy Station.

Colonel Walker was at the time of the fight serving as a brigade commander. He recalled that the "enemy had seen the advance of our skirmish line and had increased their pickets to the number of six or seven hundred, who, when they saw us advance in force, took to their rifle pits. Our general had, unobserved, placed some brass cannon in the woods above and below the Ford. There was a bend in the river, so the guns could rake the rear of the rifle pits with grape and canister. As we advanced the artillery fired a few shots and the enemy, seeing their chances of escape imperiled, dropped their rifles and met us in the stream. About 550 surrendered. The enemy's forces came up, and DeTrobriand's brigade and a part of the one I commanded had some sharp skirmishing. A bridge of boats was made and the balance of the army crossed without getting wet. I sent the Fourth Maine as a support to Randolph's battery, and they crossed in the evening, on the bridge."[9]

In the fighting that took place here a very unusual incident occurred. In the fighting that took place on the right of the line a vigorous and highly successful charge took place upon the enemy. Several guns and two regimental flags were captured, in addition to many prisoners. The 5th and 6th Maine were a vital element in the success of the attack. Among the captured booty a sword was taken from a rebel officer by a member of the 5th Maine Infantry which bore the inscription "G. W. Bourne, 4th Maine". As was mentioned before, Lieutenant Bourne had fallen at Fredericksburg and his body had been left behind on the battlefield. Colonel Walker remembered

---

[8] Ibid., p. 510.

[9] Walker, op. cit., p. 60

that the sword was brought to him by Colonel Edwards. Walker later forwarded the prized possession to the lieutenant's family in Bangor.

The 4th Maine now set up camp at Brandy Station and remained there until November 26th. Colonel Walker, having partially recovered from the leg wound he had received at Gettysburg, returned to command of the regiment on the evening of the 25th. His reinstatement coincided almost perfectly with the commencement of active campaigning by the Army of the Potomac. On the very same day Meade sent a directive to his corps commanders to prepare their troops for a march on the enemy positions the following morning, Thanksgiving Day. The men were told to carry eight days worth of rations with them such that they would not be forced to drag large numbers of supply wagons behind them. Most of Meade's army would cross the Rapidan River at Ely's and Germanna Ford. The Third Corps would cross at Jacob's Ford, and due to their resulting proximity to Lee's Army, would give them the lead in the coming campaign.[10]

General William French had been given command of the 3rd Corps following Sickle's wounding at Gettysburg. His ascendancy to the conduct of the corps would, over the next few days, serve only to tarnish its excellent reputation. On the morning of the 26th, French was late in getting his men moving. In addition, when his troops reached the river crossing he found the opposite bank too steep for his artillery to ascend, and, consequently, sent them to Germanna Ford to cross. The addition of these units to those already trying to keep up with the pace of the march, served to slow even further the crossing there. As a result it was dark before French had gotten his whole force across the river. He immediately set the men to making camp. The speed which was so desperately needed in maintaining the initiative in this campaign was rapidly being lost.

The following morning French got his troops up and moving once again. The Third Corps immediately got lost and it was almost noon before the issue was finally straightened out. As his lead 1st division, which included the 4th Maine, finally began their advance on Lee's flank they immediately ran into a strongly posted line of skirmishers. Before French realized what was going on he had become involved in

---

[10] Official Records, op. cit., p. 510.

a full scale battle. The deadly fight lasted until dark, and cost each side about five hundred casualties.[11]

After dark, Lee pulled his troops back to the entrenchments which had been carefully constructed on the far side of Mine Run. The fortifications were very much like those which they had built at Fredericksburg. Never the less, Meade brought his troops up the following morning in a heavy rain and put them in positions opposite the enemy. French's troops were given the center of the line, with Warren's Fifth Corps on the left and Sedgwick on the right. All was in readiness for the expected assault on the impregnable rebel works. The prospects for a slaughter seemed good.

As the two armies faced off against each other, Lee sat outnumbered in almost seven miles of entrenchments. On November 30th, the Union forces began to bombard the rebels in preparation for the grand assault. The men of the 4th Maine once again wrote their names on pieces of paper and pinned them to their clothing. As the sounds of the cannonade grew louder, all of the men waited anxiously for the command to attack. At the last moment, though, Meade found the inner courage to call off the offensive. On the night of December 1st, Meade pulled his army back, narrowly missing a planned attack by Lee the following morning.[12]

In the maneuvering in front of Mine Run the 4th Maine had escaped with only minor casualties. Only one officer and five enlisted men were wounded, while five men were taken prisoner. Considering the severity of the brief skirmish fought on November 27th, this was clearly quite remarkable. If the regiment had only been as fortunate last July at the Devils Den the prospects for the regiment would be much improved.

On December 14th the 4th Maine began to construct winter quarters. They dug holes in the earth, boarded up the walls with chinked logs and spread shelter halves over their tops for roofs. Many of the men constructed crude chimneys that they might build fires for warmth. All things considered, the unrefined structures were quite comfortable, though they were notorious for harboring bugs and undesirable creatures of every description.

---

[11] Foote, The Civil War, Vol. II, p. 585.
[12] Ibid.

The weather turned very cold as Christmas approached. The ground froze and the winds blew strong. On the 23rd there was a light snow in the morning and a review of the troops was ordered for the afternoon. "General Meade arrived 2 o'clock, the division line was formed and he reviewed it." Colonel Walker "received the general's compliments for the appearance of and correct moves made by the brigade in my charge."[13]

Walker remembered that January 1, 1864, dawned "clear, and late in the afternoon very cold." The men of the 4th Maine were on the move, not toward the front and battle, but back towards home on temporary furloughs. Men like Captain Arthur Libby, Lieutenant Joseph Conant, and even Chaplain Chase departed for Rockland on fifteen day furloughs. The going and the comingwas almost constant. For many this was to be their final journey home to visit with friends and loved ones.

On January 14, fourteen fresh recruits arrived from Maine. "Some of these were good men, others had better been left at home." With them came the long awaited commissions from the governor. Captain Davis was promoted to lieutenant colonel, Captain Gray to Major, Lieutenant Abbott to Captain of Company I, and SergeantRankin to first lieutenant.[14]

Walker had been on excellent terms with GovernorWashburn and with Governor Cony. Problems had materialized between he and Governor Coburn during his recuperative stay in Maine, however. Walker had observed that Coburn had "yielded to the influence of political demagogues at home, and commissioned men who were the reverse of worthy and desirable. GovernorCoburn could commission whomsoever he chose, but at this time there was a board to examine those making application to be mustered, whenever the regimental desired to have such examinations made." Walker had questioned one of the governors appointments and the applicant had been dismissed. Governor Coburn had been embarrassed by the episode and punished Walker by neglecting to make any additional appointments when he was notified of vacancies. The fact that the new commissions had

[13] Walker, op. cit., p. 62.

[14] Ibid., p. 64.

arrived hinted that those ill feelings might have been put to rest, at least for now.[15]

In terms of his own promotion, Elijah Walker stated quite unequivocally that he had no personal desire for promotion. Yet in the spring of 1864 several Walker's friends had other ideas. He was told that the "honorable who had last vacated the executive chair had charitably remarked, when asked if he would recommend my promotion: 'If Col. Walker was hungry he might starve before I would give him a piece of bread.' But this eminent humanitarian was now out of office and his place was filled by a man of honor and ability. Generals and regimental commanders advised me to accept a promotion, if offered, and as I thought my chances almost sure I consented that my friends at home should make an effort in my behalf."

Meanwhile, back home Governor Cony wrote a recommendation in support of Walker's promotion to brigadier general. "Every state senator and a large number of representatives - all who were asked, - signed a petition; Gens Birney, Ward, French and Sedgwick gave letters, and a petition was signed by every brigade and regimental commander in our division. Our representative of the Fifth district had agreed to present these papers and favor my cause. The documents were placed in his hands March 8th, but were never presented. The honorable F. A. Pike recommended another man, a fine worthy and brave officer, who was promoted. At the expiration of the three years' service I returned to my home and family. The man for whom advancement was secured was carried home a dead brigadier general. And now, after nearly thirty years, I feel thankful that I am yet living and able to tell the story."[16]

As the dust began to settle over Colonel Walker's narrow escape from promotion, the regiment continued its adjustment into its springtime routine. As the Ides of March approached General Birney returned form his leave of absence and Walker was finally able to return to his regimental duties. Coinciding with his return, an inspector arrived in the 4th Maine's camp in accordance with General Order No. 74. At the time Walker attempted to get the government to supply the unit with Spencer rifles. Though he argued valiantly, his efforts were

---

[15] Ibid., p. 58.

[16] Ibid, p. 66.

in vain. The men were supplied with the Springfield rifle. Only the 1st and 2nd Sharpshooters received the weapon.

During Walker's absence several disciplinary situations had arisen in the unit. Private James Butler, for example, had been brought up on charges of straggling and for absence without leave. Aso called "field officer's court" was held and Private Butler was tried and found guilty of the charges. His sentence was the forfeit of onemonths pay. The fine was approved by the brigade commander and an official reprimand was placed in private Butler's military record.

Another problem had arisen when General Birney assigned some of his staff officers to inspect the regiments of his division. A Captain McMichael had been assigned to the Fourth Maine. A previous incident had caused Walker and McMichael to cross paths, late in 1863, when Walker had been left in command of the division. The Captain had requested a leave of absence for himself and had pressed his claim in earnest. Walker refused to grant the favor, whereby McMichael had expressed some very unsoldierly remarks. Walker placed the man under arrest, but later released him when he promised he would, henceforth, conduct himself in an honorable manner.

Captain McMichael had, however, held a grudge with regard to the incident. On the occasion of his inspection, he reported to General Birney that the regiment was in "reprehensible condition". In point of fact, the only thing he found in satisfactory condition was thesutler's tent and quarters." The general sent Walker a report expressing his surprise at the condition of the regiment. Colonel Walker then retaliated by replying to General Birney in the following manner:

"No one could be more surprised than myself at the report of Captain McMichael with regard to the condition of the Fourth Maine regiment. You have, for the past two years, often visited us, and have several times spoken such words of praise that myself, the officers and men have always been pleased to have you inspect us. I had supposed we stood fair among volunteers, but I did not imagine we were up to the standard of the regular army. Our books are reported to be in bad condition, they are so kept that we are able, and ever have been, to account for all our men at the shortest notice. I do not flatter myself that they conform strictly to the requirements of the regular army, from which the inspector received his rank and title. In fact, I am as surprised as you say you are, that everything about our regiment should be found in such lamentable condition, when inspected by a regular army officer. The only thing he found in good condition was the sutler's department, where judging from his appearance at the time he left, we think he was well treated."

Elijah Walker was summoned immediately into the presence of General Birney upon his receipt of the letter. Walker remembered him as "the maddest man I ever met." After being verbally assaulted and reprimanded General Ward and his staff were then sent to the 4th Maine to conduct their own inspection. General Ward "reviewed the men; the ranks were opened, knapsacks unslung and their contents displayed; the general walked down the line and said he never saw men have things in more perfect condition. He then examined our quarters and books and visited the sutler's tent, but without finding anything of absorbing interest, as there had been no fresh arrivals since the captain made his visit of inspection."[17]

When General Ward reported the results of his inspection back to division headquarters, General Birney became even more enraged. This altercation forever after altered the general's attitude toward the 4th Maine and its commanders. Birney "ever after used every means in his power to injure us." Strangely enough though when on March 13th, the occasion arose for the christening of David Birney's son, Philip Kearney Birney, Chaplain Chase was the man selected to perform the honor.

For most, this would be the final time they would spend the winter exposed to the elements. For most this was to be the last six months of their enlistment's. For many, though, it would be the last six months of their lives.

[17] Ibid. p. 68.

Chapter 12

Out of the Wilderness

The Fourth Maine spent its winter near Stevensburg, Virginia. On March 31, 1864, however, the men were forced out of their rustic shebangs. General Ulysses Grant had taken charge of the army. The event occasioned the breakup of the 2nd Corps and the assignment of their division to the 2nd. The command of the Corps was in the hands of Major General Winfield Hancock. General Birney had risen to lead the Third Division while General Ward had received command of the First Brigade. Included within its ranks was the "Iron Fourth", a name which the Maine regiment had picked up after the fight at Gettysburg and had become rather fond of. [1]

With the dissolution of the III Corps in March, Birney's men became the II Corps' 3rd division. The 3rd and 4th Maine were split up for the first time in the war. The 3rd stayed in Hobart Ward's brigade while the 4th was assigned to Brigadier General Alexander Hay's. Hay's was one of Hancock's, and U. S. Grant's, favorite commanders. He was also one of the more capable leaders in the army. In battle he had a habit of leading his troops from the front, exemplifying the bravery and courage he expected of his men in a fight.

The departure of General Ward was a traumatic experience for the men from Maine. On March 31, 1864, Colonel Walker, and the officers of the 4th addressed the following letter to the general. It is hard to believe from the wording of this letter that Ward would, in less that sixty days, be dismissed from the army for cowardice and drunkenness.

HEADQUARTERS, 4TH MAINE VOLS.,
March 31st, 1864.

---

[1] Whitman, Maine in the War, p. 106.

GENERAL J. H. H. WARD:--*Dear Sir--The undersigned, Officers of the Fourth Regiment of Maine Volunteers, wish to express their regret at the changes which have occurred in the reorganization of our army. Not alone because they have resulted in breaking up of the Third Corps, but in addition removed this regiment from your Command.*

Be assured General we should have been most happy in remaining under you with and under whom we have served from the first formation of the 8th Brigade, in August, 1861.

With this Brigade, known as the 2d, since the organization of the Division, we have been through several campaigns and participated in many hard fought battles, and never has our late commander failed to be present to direct and encourage, in the midst of danger. Many of our brave companions have been left, struck down on the battle fields of our several engagements, or carried away by disease arising from toil and exposure in the swamps of Virginia.

This has served but to strengthen and render more endearing the ties and associations among those who remain, and it is with the utmost sorrow,--even could we feel that it was for the interest of the service,--that we find ourselves separated from the handful left from the original organization.

Better feeling, we think, never existed in the command. Each regiment had the full confidence of the rest, and all the most perfect satisfaction in their brigade commander, which we are was fully reciprocated by him. With the hope that your present Command may prove all you desire; may learn to regard you with the esteem and respect which we feel; that we may find as pleasant associations, and as worthy a commander as we have lost--we are very respectfully,

Your obt, servt.
ELIJAH WALKER, Col. 4th Me. Vols.
and all OFFICERS OF THE REGT. present.[2]

The following letter was quickly penned and returned to the regiment:

HEADQUARTERS, 1st BRIG. BIRNEY'S DIV. A. C.
April 17, 1864

[2] Rockland Gazette, April 4, 1864.

COL. WALKER AND OFFICERS OF THE 4TH MAINE VOLUNTEERS:-- *Gentlemen--Your communication expressing regret at the separation of your regiment from my command was duly received. I can assure you that the regret is mutual. On account of the long and pleasant intercourse which has existed between us, your exemplary conduct in camp as well as in the field, and your undoubted valor, witnessed on many a tried occasion. I was somewhat dismayed when the official intelligence was conveyed to me that my command was to be deprived of your honored regiment. I trust that in the organization to which you have been transferred, you will continue to pursue the same characteristics of officers and gentlemen, that marked your career in my command. Your new commander is in every way entitled to your respect, esteem and confidence.*

A true and gallant soldier, he is worthy of such men and you are worthy of such a commander. Please accept my sincere thanks for the kind and flattering manner in which you have conveyed the expression of regret at parting with my command. I fully appreciate such evidence of esteem and respect, when coming from such an organization as the 4th Maine.

I am, gents, your obt. servt.,
(Signed) *J. H. Hobart Ward*
Brigadier General[3]

On April 12th, 1864, General Order 17 was issued to the troops. It asked that personal property, all sutlers, and citizens without passes be sent to the rear. The 4th, naturally, obeyed orders. In addition, the Maine men were permanently moved from their winter quarters and issued tents. It was becoming increasingly obvious that the long anticipated spring offensive was about to begin.

Many of the Maine boys viewed the renewal of fighting with great apprehension. For many of the soldiers their terms of service were about to expire. For those that had suffered so much and survived the fighting of the previous three years, many just wanted only to go home to their families. The closer they got to the end of their enlistment's the more anxious and fearful they became. The Army of

---

[3] Ibid., May 1, 1864.

the Potomac, aware that many of their original three year men were due to return home soon, had begun to offer various inducements to entice them to stay. Among these were thirty day furloughs and additional bounties. In the end over half of those eligible for honorable discharges chose to stay on. In the Fourth Maine forty-three of the troops re-enlisted. Twelve of these would come from Company H alone.[4]

On May 3rd the 25,000 men of the II Corps, with Gregg's cavalry division leading, began their march south into harms way. Their objective was a crossing of the Rapidan at Ely's Ford. The temperature this day was particularly mild. Still, many of the new recruits in the 4th Maine chose to throw away their overcoats and blankets to lighten their loads. By eleven P. M. that night the Maine men had arrived at the newly laid canvas pontoon bridge which had been thrown across the river by army engineers. Crossing the river, they at once continued their march, not stopping until they arrived at Chancellorsville about nine A. M. the next morning.[5]

The 4th set up camp on the sight of the great battle that had occurred there almost a year ago to the day. The ground upon which they camped was strewn with human skeletal parts. Many of the dead had been only hastily buried and many a human skull was seen peeking above the leaves. As the soldiers walked about, it was difficult to tell if what was breaking beneath their feet were twigs or corpses. Most of the men were sickened by what they saw and reminded of what their own fate might be at the hands of Lee's Army. Most believed that being situated here, upon this hallowed ground, could not be a good thing.

Earlier that morning, as Warren's 5th Corps had begun to move out to the West they immediately ran into the Confederates that were moving in on him. Lee, feeling that Grant had placed himself in the same position that Hooker had the previous spring, decided to go immediately on the offensive. The fighting which took place as the 2nd Corps was retracing their steps in the direction of the front was particularly severe. Casualties on both sides had been heavy. The fight which Grant had hoped to elude by moving rapidly through the Wilderness was now unavoidable. The plans of the Army of the Potomac were quickly modified.

---

[4] Trudeau, Bloody Roads South, p. 13.

[5] Official Records, XLVII, pg. 318.

Sometime around four A. M. Hancock's men were awakened by their officers. One of the members of the 2nd Corps wrote that they ... "turned out stiff and sore this morning ... drenched to the skin with dew." By five A. M., on the morning of May 5th, the 2nd Corps had hastily broken camp and moving out in the direction Shady Grove Church. The men marched at a "moderate gate ... with occasional halts." They had advanced about two miles beyond Todd's Tavern when Hancock received a message from General Meade instructing him to hold the ground near the tavern. The men stacked their arms and began to make coffee. As the soldiers awaited orders, they listened anxiously to the sounds of battle off to their West.[6]

Shortly after eleven A. M. General Hancock was instructed to move to the intersection of the Brock and Orange Plank Road. The troops fell into line once again, only this time their march was at a more rapid pace. Getty's 2nd Division was already in possession of this strategic intersection when Hancock arrived at about two P.M. Birney's Division, which was at the head of the 2nd Corps' column, was instructed to make a line on Getty's left. When Mott's and Gibbon's divisions arrived, they were sent to Birney's left.[7]

Sometime before three P.M., Hancock received a dispatch from Meade ordering him to attack the rebels in conjunction with Getty. What Meade did not know was that most of Hancock's Corps still had not arrived. Hancock sent a message to Meade to let him know his situation. In the meantime, at four P. M., General Getty attacked his division in double and triple line both north and south of the Orange Turnpike. The men had charged out only about two hundred yards when they ran into a mass of Confederate infantry hiding in the woods. The concentrated musket fire of Heth's Confederate troops, though deployed in single line, quickly brought the federal attack to a halt less than fifty yards from the rebel line.[8]

With Getty bogged down, Hancock now received instructions to put a division on Getty's right and left and then come immediately to his support. Hay's Brigade, which included the 4th Maine, was presently situated on the immediate left of Colonel Lewis Grant's all Vermont Brigade. General Birney was instructed to send his two

---

[6] Trudeau, op. cit., p. 43.

[7] Lowry, No Turning Back, p. 79.

[8] O. R., op. cit., pp. 319-320.

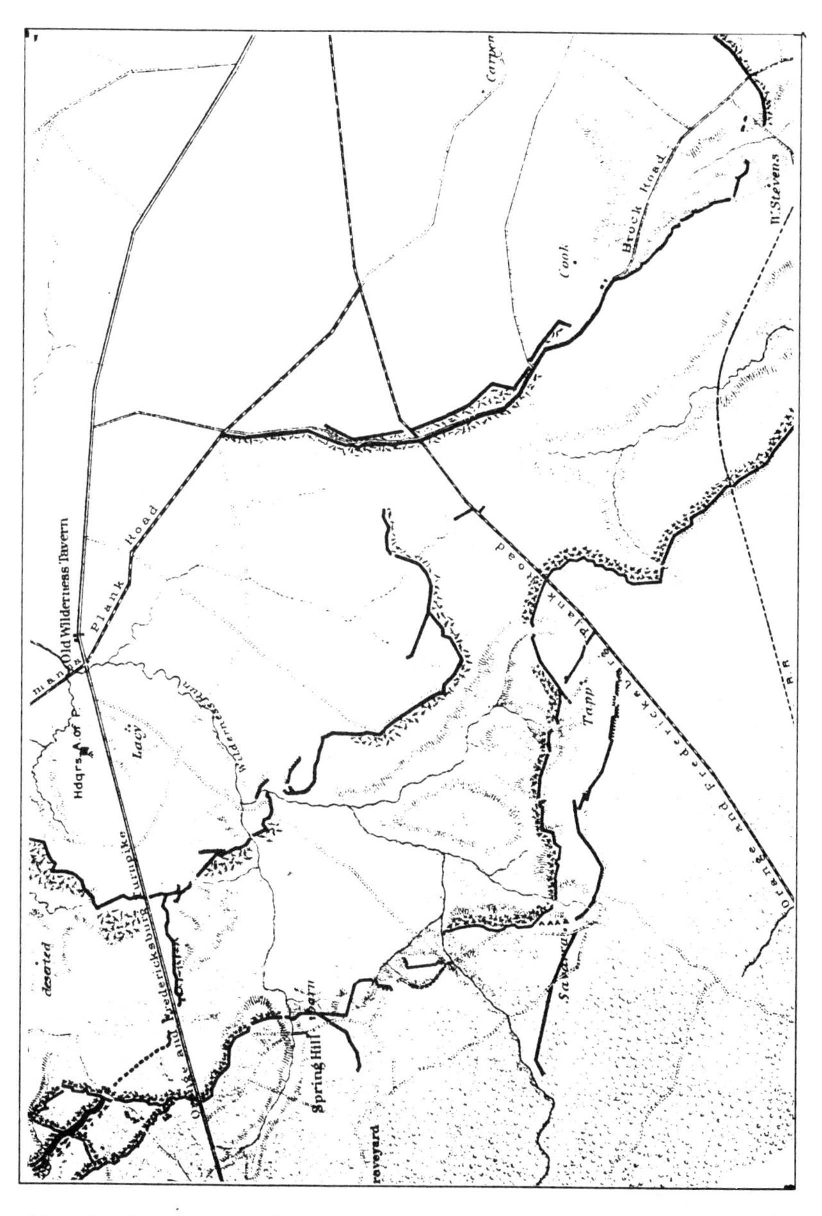

Map showing the troop placements on the Wilderness Battlefield on May 5th

brigade division around behind Getty and come up on his right. Mott's division would fill the gap created by Birney's departure. As Birney began to move out, the Confederates discovered that Getty's right flank, which was occupied by Brigadier General Henry Eustis's Brigade, was totally exposed. The rebels launched an immediate counterattack, causing the Union right to cave in. Eustis immediately sent for help.[9]

By the time Hays had arrived on Getty's right, Eustis' Brigade was already retreating. General Birney now divided his command. He sent Hay's men to the far right and General Ward's brigade to help Grant's Vermonters. Hay's brigade, which included the 4th and 17th Maine as well as some seven other regiments, came charging in over the rapidly deteriorating Federal line and crashed into the remnants of Brigadier General Joseph Davis' Brigade. The 2nd, 11th, and 42nd Mississippi infantry regiments were now providing most of the defensive power for the brigade. The collision, it might be mentioned, bought the Confederate attack to an immediate halt.[10]

Colonel Walker speaks of the fighting as a "battle raging fearfully." The combat was nothing short of slaughter. The two opponents, staring at each others gun barrels, would wait for an incoming volley. One side or the other would then make use of the pause to rally themselves into a charge of their adversaries' position. One would charge, only to be driven back by the others counterattack. Captain Edwin Libby was struck by a rebel bullet and died instantly. For all of the death and suffering neither side could achieve anything more than a bloody stalemate. The 4th Maine suffered most severely.[11]

A member of the 17th Maine, Private John Haley, recalled that the fighting was "a continuous roar of musketry, rising and swelling like the sound of surf pounding on the shore." In the midst of all the commotion and chaos, General Hayes tried one last time to rally his men to charge the enemy. He had paused briefly near the 63rd Pennsylvania, and while in the midst of a rallying cry, an enemy bullet tore through his skull. The sound was distinctly heard above the deafening tumult. Death for the respected commander was

---

[9] Lowry, op. cit., p. 182.

[10] Trudeau, op. cit., pp 68-69.

[11] Ibid.

instantaneous. By morning, command of the brigade would devolve upon a 4th Maine boy, Colonel Elijah Walker.[12]

General Hancock, in his official report of the fighting, stated that "the battle raged with great severity and obstinacy until about 8 p.m. without decided advantage to either party." After sustaining the better part of fifty casualties, the 4th Maine was withdrawn from their position leaving their dead and dying behind in the burning woods. The regiment now joined with the rest of their division. And as all of this was transpiring, Hancock was even now receiving orders from Grant to renew the attack by 4:30 A. M. the next morning.[13]

During the night General Wadsworth's division of the 5th Corps, and two divisions from the 9th Corps were ordered to support Hancock's right flank. General Wheaton, with Getty's wounding, took over the 6th Corps' 2nd Division. These men still remained under General Hancock's overall direction, however. In all Hancock had nearly 25,000 men under his dictate. The man who stood in his way, General A. P. Hill, could count only 14,000.

Early the next morning, just prior to the planned attack by the Federals, news was received that Longstreet's forces were approaching Hancock's left flank along the Catharpin Road. At the last moment, he ordered that Barlow's Division, along with the artillery, be placed in such a manner as to cover the path leading from the Catharpin Road to the Brock Road. This movement would effectively refuse the flank in the face of the attacking divisions. It would also diminish the effectiveness of the coming offensive, however.[14]

At 5 A. M. the order was given to charge. The Union troops ran directly into a hail of rebel gunfire. The men of the 4th Maine found the assault much less frightening than the anticipation of it, though. As the Maine men charged the rebel line, a whole brigade routed before them. The regiment reached, and then passed through, the rebel works. The whole Confederate army seemed to be running. The enemy was driven back almost a mile and a half. Hancock was so excited by what was happening he sent an ecstatic message to the Union Commander. "Tell Meade we are driving them most beautifully, sir. Birney has gone in and he is clearing them out be-au-ti-fully."[15]

---

[12] Haley, The Rebel Yell and the Yankee Hurrah, p. 145.
[13] O.R., op. cit., p. 320.
[14] Ibid.
[15] Lowry, op. cit., p. 203.

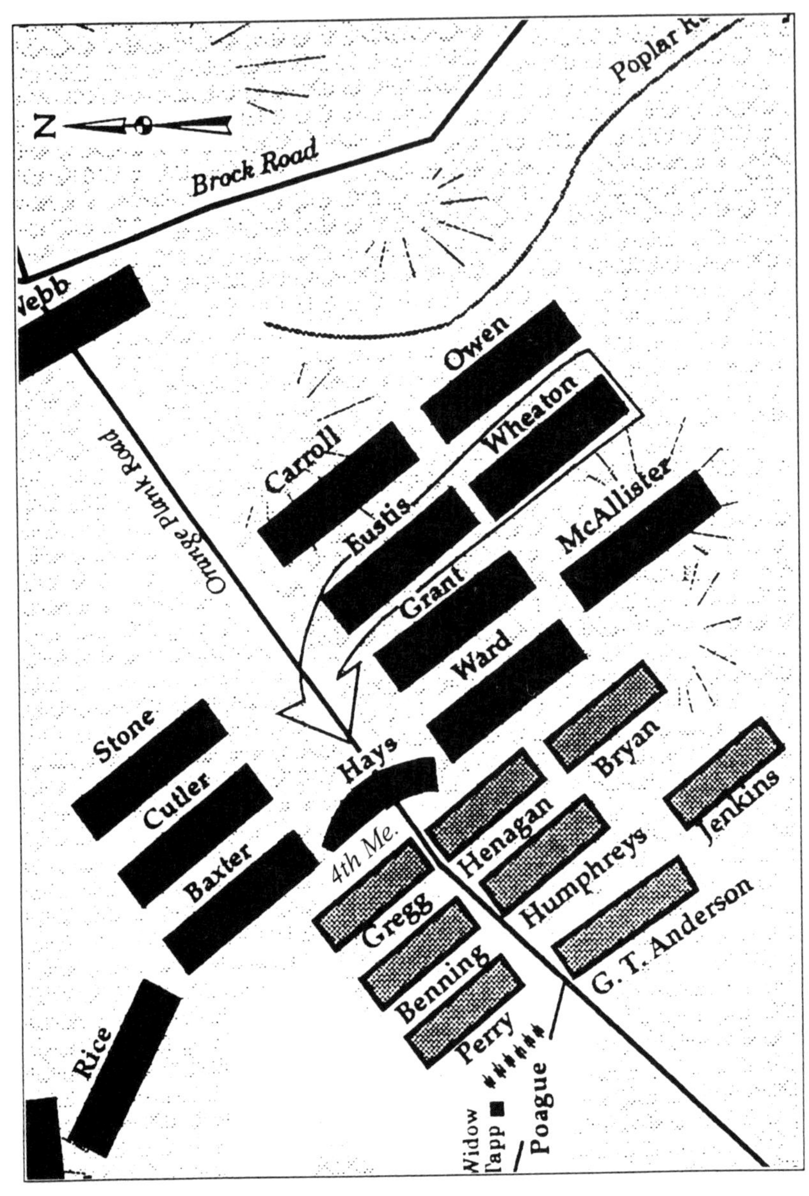

Position of the 4th Maine in the line of attack. With Hay's having been killed on the previous day Colonel Walker was now in charge of the brigade.

Hays' brigade, now under Walker's leadership, had begun its assault along the Orange Plank Road. The 4th and 17th Maine had formed the lead in the attack, accompanied by the sharpshooters who were out in front of them acting a skirmishers. As the Maine boys pushed on, they punched ahead of the main Federal body, and as they did so, immediately came up against Kershaw's brigade of Southerners. The rebels in their front were, once again, quickly routed by their advance. Suddenly, though, the Maine boys broke from the forest into daylight. Wadsworth's men were still far to their rear. To their front was the Widow Tapp farm and to the left of that a thin line of artillery. Victory seemed within their grasp.[16]

The deepness of the underbrush and the overwhelming presence of smoke and haze caused a great deal of confusion. While the 4th Maine's line had remained intact, other units had become intermingled with those of other regiments. The further Hancock's men advanced the more acutely disorganized the situation became. As the blue jackets began to appear along the edge of the field only Poague's artillery stood between Hancock and complete victory. Hill immediately ordered Poague to fire obliquely across the Orange Plank Road. The rebel commander was slow to respond primarily because Confederate troops were mixed with the rapidly advancing Union troops. Poague opened a slow fire with short range shells. "Flames spit from the rebel guns. Smoke filled the air, and projectiles whined into the approaching federals doing 'great execution'."[17]

Slowed by the shower of shot and shell, the Maine boys hesitated. Orders were passed to push on, but the movement became one of encirclement as the troops attempted to close in and around the menacing artillery. Poague's stand in the field was later judged to be one of the bravest and most critical of the entire war. "The gunners worked with almost superhuman energy, the muzzles belched their withering blast."[18]

Despite Poague's gallant efforts, his guns were quickly becoming surrounded. Just when things looked bleakest for the rebs thought, Longstreet's long awaited troops finally arrived. Longstreet's Corps was being led by Gregg's Texas Brigade and as they began to

---

[16] Rhea, The Battle of the Wilderness, p. 293.
[17] Ibid., p. 294.
[18] Ibid., pp. 294-295.

funnel into the area of the Tapp Farm Lee sent them straight into the center of the fight. Eight hundred Texans, accompanied by General Lee himself, headed straight for Walker's command. Though Lee was ultimately forced to return to the rear by his own men, it is entirely possible that some of the Maine boys might have gotten a glimpse of the old man himself.

As Gregg's troops advanced, Walker's 1st U. S. Sharpshooters leveled their guns and began to fire into the advancing foe. The Texas boys pushed on and quickly brushed the sharpshooters aside. A veritable explosion was heard as the two enemies collided. The carnage was horrible. The troops engaged were by now very unfamiliar with each other. For the soldiers of the 4th Maine it was a rematch. Here, once again as at Gettysburg, the two old adversaries found themselves slugging it out. Eight hundred men from the 1st, 4th, and 5th Texas, as well as the 3rd Arkansas, went rolling in. Twenty-five minutes later two hundred and fifty came tumbling back. It was as if Gettysburg had been avenged.[19]

As the Texan's came tumbling back, Benning's Brigade, which included the 2nd, 15th, 17th, and 20th Georgia, rumbled in to take their place. Law's Alabama Brigade came on in behind them.[20] For the Maine men, it seemed like a Devil's Den reunion. Once again the old adversaries collided, and once again the explosion was deafening. Both sides were rocked by the impact, but this time the lines held solid against each other.

About seven A. M., Hancock called up his reserves under the command of General Alexander Webb. The 2nd Division's 1st Brigade, was sent immediately forward to rejuvenate Birney's attack. Shortly after giving this order, he also instructed Gibbon, who had been left behind to hold their left flank against an attack by Longstreet, to move against the rebel line as well. Gibbon ignored the order. When instructed to attack a second time, Gibbon continued to stall but did contribute at least one brigade to the effort. Hancock would later express his disappointment in Gibbon in the official records by stating that, "had my left advanced as directed by me in several orders, I believe the overthrow of the enemy would have been assured."[21]

[19] Ibid., p. 301.
[20] Law's brigade included the 4th, 15th, 44th, 47th, and 48th Alabama.
[21] O. R., op. cit., p. 321.

At about eight A. M. Stevenson's division from the 9th Corps and Wadsworth's division from the 5th Corps reported to Hancock. Wadsworth had almost 5,000 men in his command. He moved into the underbrush and moved up on Birney's right flank. Once completed Hancock ordered that the offensive be renewed along the Orange Plank Road at about 8:40. Birney and the men of the 4th Maine moved forward but were unable to make any further gains. The accretion of Longstreet Corps to the rebel line, in addition to the delay caused by the reorganization of Union troops, brought the whole offensive to a halt.[22]

At about the time that the federals had renewed the attack on the Confederates, General Longstreet had sent Major General Smith to check out a report that a railroad cut existed which extended beyond the left flank of the Union army. Smith found that it did indeed exist and was perfect for the movement of troops. By eleven A. M., with the fighting raging in his front, Longstreet ordered General G. Moxley Sorrel to guide three brigades, G. T. Anderson's, W. T. Woffard's, and William Mahone's, along the railroad cut and to conduct an attack on the Union flank. As soon as Longstreet heard the firing, he also planned to launch an offensive of his own, causing Union forces to be attacked on two sides.[23]

At 11:45 General Sorrel began his attack on Frank's brigade of Barlow's division. This brigade had used nearly all of its ammunition, and as a result, the Confederates met little opposition and passed right through. Mott's division was impacted next, and it too was routed. Each Union unit that was contacted gave way in succession and before long nearly 20,000 soldiers were caught up in the retreat. The Federal Army was now facing the prospect of complete defeat.[24]

As the Union left flank began to collapse General Birney decided to withdraw his men to the pre-constructed breastworks along the Brock Road. The project was particularly difficult owing, once again, to the density of the forest growth and the nature of the terrain. Still, the officers of the brigades, and the regiments, persisted, and before long General Birney's troops were formed behind the abatis in double line of battle. Mott's division and Ward's brigade of Birney's

---

[22] Ibid.
[23] Lowry, op. cit., p. p. 213.
[24] Trudeau, op. cit., pp. 100-102.

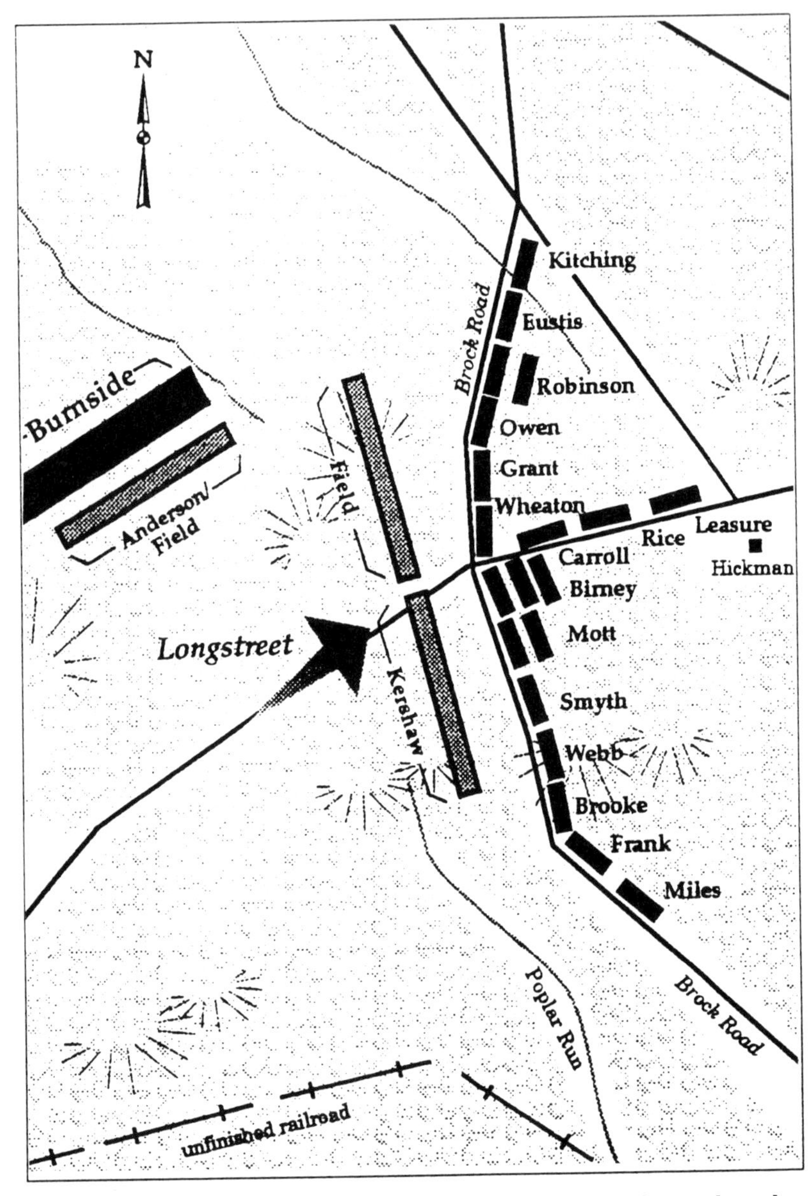

Longstreet's counterattack forces union troops back to the defences along the Brock Road. Here Union troops held in spite of the ferosity of the attack.

division, were now the front line. The rebels were as disorganized by their success as the Federal forces were by their defeat. Confederate units were intermingled and had to, themselves, be regrouped in order to continue their attack. Still, the rebels managed to push within a "hundred paces" of Birney's troops. Orders to press forward were not received due to a crisis in leadership which developed when General Longstreet was himself shot. The irony of the situation was that Longstreet, as had Jackson while on a similar flank attack the year before, was accidentally shot by his own men.[25]

The Limerock Regiment was now a part of the thin blue line. Earlier that morning they had charged out in the direction of the Widow Tapp Farm. They had moved on command, hard and fast, only to be met by deadly artillery fire. When the Union left flank caved in, the Maine men were withdrawn, all the while covering the retreat of Hancock's troops. They were then put into a defensive posture inside the breastworks, their tired eyes, smarting form the smoke of burning scrub brush and gunpowder, scrutinized the no man's land between the warring armies.

At 4:15 P. M., General Lee threw every available man, nearly thirteen brigades, up against the entrenched Union forces. "Though firing was very heavy, little execution was done among our troops... After fighting for a half hour, Ward's Brigade of Birney's Division in the first line retired in disorder toward Chancellorsville." The Fourth Maine, in Hay's old brigade, was forced into service. Though the officers rallied the Maine boys, it was the intervention of the Dow's Sixth Maine Battery that sealed the breach. As for Ward's veterans, many did return though "a portion of them could not be collected until the action was over."[26]

It is difficult to believe that Ward's battle hardened veterans were so easily frightened into retreat. The first thought is since most of the regiments were so near to mustering out, the men might have lost their stomach for fighting. In point of fact, however, the retirement had been caused, not by enemy musket fire or hand to hand combat, but by an inferno of smoke and flame. General Hancock explains that "the breastworks on this portion of my line were constructed entirely of logs, and at the critical moment of the enemy's advance were a mass of

[25] O. R., op. cit., p. 323.
[26] Ibid., p. 324.

Above : John Henry Hobart Ward, was the 4th Maine's Brigade commander. Ward performed brillantly at Gettysburg but was later accused of being drunk at the Wilderness, and relieved of command, without a court-marshall, at Spotsylvania, for the same reason. Ward spent the rest of his life trying to clear his name. He was struck and killed by a train in 1903. [Who Was Who in the Civil War, pp. 690-691.]

flames which it was at that time impossible to subdue...The intense heat and smoke, which was driven by the wind directly into the faces of the men, prevented them on portions of the line from firing over the parapet, and at some points compelled them to abandon the line." In many cases the fire had gotten so close that the soldiers own cartridges had ignited in their pouches.[27]

General Birney then ordered Carroll's brigade into the impending breach. The Confederates had already begun to post their battle flags upon the burning breastworks as Carroll rushed forward in an attempt to repair the damage. The brigade moved by the left flank and at double quick. The two forces met in the smoke filled works, a position neither could hold for long. Unable to push men quickly enough into the void, the whole rebel line wavered and then slowly began to fall back. Meade's army had been saved.[28]

The two days of fighting in the Wilderness were now sputtering to an end. Losses for the Union army were 17,666. The Fourth Maine had sent 311 men into the fight. Of this number two officers were killed and six were wounded. Thirty enlisted men were killed, 130 were wounded, and three were captured.[29] In less that thirty hours fully fifty-eight per cent of the regiment's numbers had become casualties. As Colonel Walker stated following the battle, "The old Fourth has made a gallant record in these battles and nobly sustained its well-earned reputation." This they had done despite the fact that they were just forty days away from their discharge.[30]

Included in the list of casualties were several recognizable and distinguished names. Colonel Walker himself was wounded, though not seriously enough for him to relinquish command. Major Robert H. Gray of Searsport was also mortally injured. Mr. Gray should be remembered from an earlier chapter in which he narrowly escaped from the hands of the rebels at First Bull Run. Though he survived his first encounter, ironically, he did so only to die in a Union hospital at Fredericksburg on May 9th. Captain Edwin Libby, who had at times commanded the regiment in Colonel Walker's absence, was himself felled by a rebel bullet. Captain's Arthur Libby and Jason Carlisle received insignificant wounds and remained on duty. "Captain Amos

---

[27] Ibid.
[28] Ibid.
[29] Ibid., p. 122.
[30] Rockland Gazette, May 22, 1864.

B. Wooster fell on the evening of the 5th, while leading his men in the charge to re-establish the line that had been broken at the left of the Plank Road. He died instantly, the bullet passing through his heart."[31]

There was one other significant casualty of the combat in the Wilderness. It involved an individual who was not actually a member of the regiment at all. It was the Fourth's old brigade commander, Brigadier General John H. Hobart Ward, who fell victim to the demon whiskey. Apparently during the course of the fight he had became totally intoxicated. In the book, Who was Who in the Civil War, it is stated that Ward, "Fought at the Wilderness but was drunk and apparently ran away." This is very much unlike the Ward of Gettysburg fame. But it seemingly happened, none the less. Such are the fortunes of war.

---

[31] Walker, History of the 4th Maine, p. 69.

Chapter 13

"I Think You Will Find Work Over There."

On May 7th, Meade's army began to shift by their left flank. The object of the move was Spotsylvania Court House, through which passed the Richmond Road. The Richmond Road was a direct route around the Confederate flank and into the Confederate capital. Though Lee believed that the Union move was a retreat, he also realized the importance of making sure that Spotsylvania was in Confederate hands. .

As the two armies were, quite unknownst to each other, both racing towards Spotsylvania Court House, there was still a great deal of uncertainty as to the actual disposition of the two forces. About eleven A.M. the 4th's brigade was sent on a reconaissance to determine if the rebels were still in force in their front. The men moved out from their trenches along the Brock Road toward the line that the Confederate army had held the day before. Lee's men were gone, however, leaving behind only their dead and wounded. The scene was ghastly, sickening even to hardened veterans such as these. Gathering up what wounded they could find, the Maine boys returned to the Brock Road defenses. Here they spent a nervous night listening to the sounds of the forest all about them and expecting any moment to see the advance of the enemy.[1]

Always the pragmatist, Elijah Walker realized that his men marched and fought on their stomachs. With the almost constant fighting his men had by this point either eaten or lost all of their rations. Colonel Walker remembered that when salvation arrived it did so when "quartermaster, K. C. Rankin, made his appearance with hard bread, meat, coffee, etc., of whose sustaining quality we all stood in need. His duties were not so dangerous as those of the men who met the enemy face to face, but no man could have performed them more satisfactorily nor with greater promptness."

---

[1] Whitman. op. cit.. p.106.

Shortly following the morning banquet, the brigade was given orders to march to Torbet's Tavern. Here the men occupied the ground which had previously been held by Gibbon's division. Though there were already existing rifle pits, the Maine men immediately began to strengthen them for a stronger defensive position. Over the past few days the value of works had become firmly established. From now on, no matter where the regiment would go, the digging of trenches would become a protective reflex. They were to become very skilled at the art.

On May 9th the Maine men, once again, continued their march toward Spotsylvania. Colonel Walker later recalled that during the battle their "only drinking water had been that obtained from holes dug in the clay soil, and I was suffering for a fluid that would quench my thirst. After a march of two miles we came to a spring of crystal purity, and there, by the roadside, stood our foresighted hospital attendant, loaded down with brimming canteens. I would not have exchanged that draught for a 'full blushing goblet' of the 'nectar that Jupiter sips.'"

Though fighting had raged here on the 8th, it was relatively quiet now. Birney's division was ordered to move in on the far right of Meade's army. Late in the afternoon, sensing an opportunity to get behind Lee's flank, Grant ordered Hancock to put his divisions across the Po River.[2] It was about 1 P.M. when the 4th Maine was ordered to advance with the rest of it's brigade. Leading the procession the regiment "marched about three miles, crossed the Po river at 7 o'clock and bivouacked a mile and a half from the place of crossing. It was thought by our general officers that the rebels were retreating toward Richmond."[3]

Early on the morning of the tenth, Grant ordered Hancock to pull his divisions back across the Po in order to support an attack expected to be made by Warren's 5th Corps. The 4th Maine, in company with "a part of the Seventeenth Maine and a few men who had been detailed for picket duty", had moved out early that morning on a reconnaissance mission. Their orders were to drive back the enemy's skirmishers and ascertain if the rebs were in force in their front.

---

[2] Ibid.

[3] Walker, op. cit., p. 70.

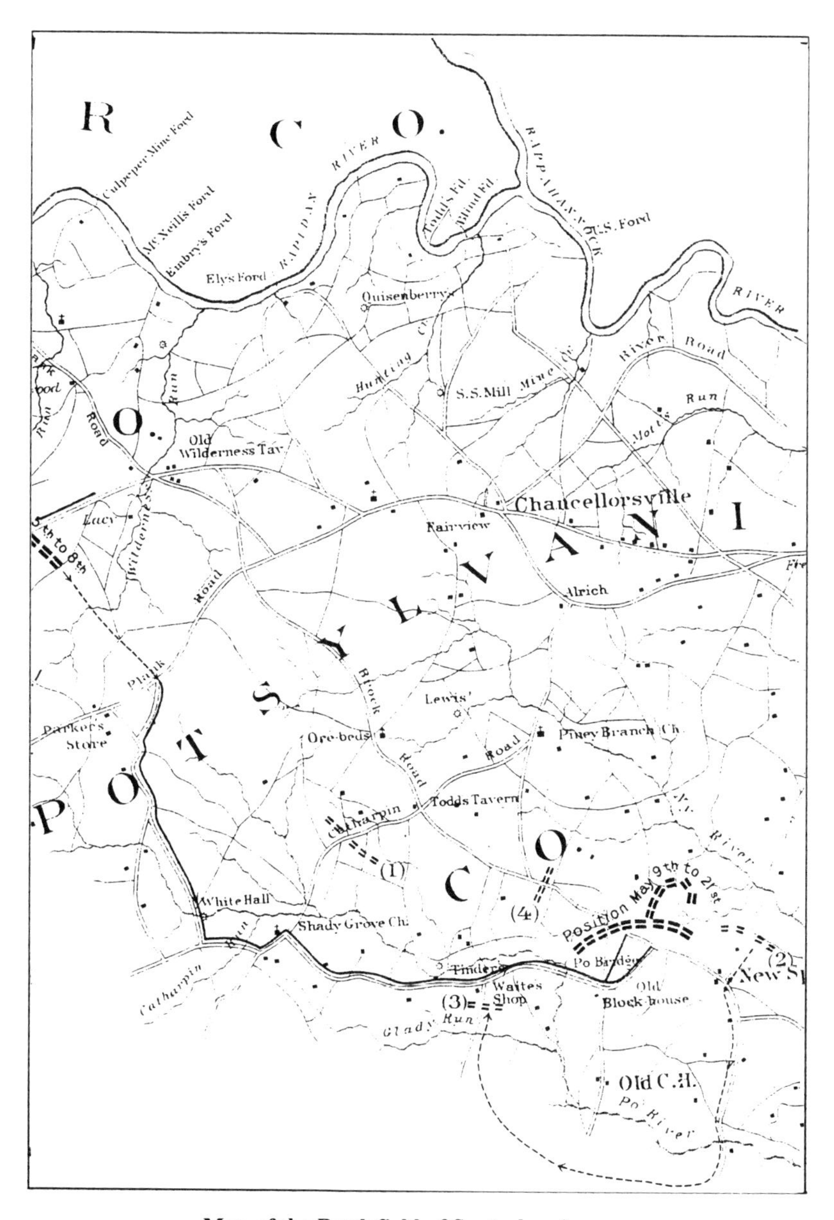

Map of the Battlefield of Spotsylvania.

Walker was suffering painfully from the wound he had received a couple of days before as he attempted to keep himself upright in his saddle. Walker led his small force across Glady Run, a tributary of the Po River. The 17th Maine detachment was under the guidance of Major Briscoe of General Birney's staff. According to Walker the "river was a small stream, which, at this season, could be crossed at the ford by carefully stepping from stone to stone, without wetting the feet. Above the crossing the stream was swampy; the stream was some ten or twelve feet wide and from four to six feet deep. With Capt. Bristow, topographical engineer of the division, I crossed the stream in advance and reconnoitered. We decided to have the Seventeenth Maine and the picket detail advance on the road nearest the river, under guidance of the engineer. I led the Fourth Maine by a road further from the river, but running parallel with it, as we supposed the roads converged at a point not far distant." [4]

John Haley of the 17th, questioned in his diary the wisdom of such a movement. "The farther we advanced, the wider grew the gap, our lines being at right angles to each other. If this arrangement was in accordance with Briscoe's original intentions, he is a stupid, drunken cuss, for he was dividing his forces in the face of the enemy and making a breach between them, which in the case of attack invited disasters irreparable." As the 17th moved on they came upon a clearing which showed a small run. The sounds of rifle shots soon filled the air. "We immediately put ourselves in position to engage them. It didn't take long for us to find our that we were working at a decided disadvantage, both as to position and number."

Bristoe attempted to get his men to charge the enemy, but despite his incessant cussing the men refused to respond. As he continued in his fruitless efforts a sudden volley of fire nipped at Major Bristoe's horse, striking it in several places. "Briscoe wheeled about and put the spurs to what was left of the animal. With surprising agility and brilliancy of execution he made tracks for the rear, yelling as he departed, "You must all now look out for yourselves and, if anyone gets out, he might have a chance to make coffee. The boys of the 17th flew in pursuit of their retreating commander. "The rebs pursued us with all the spead attainable, but we, having much more at stake, almost flew. Also we had the promise

[4] Ibid.

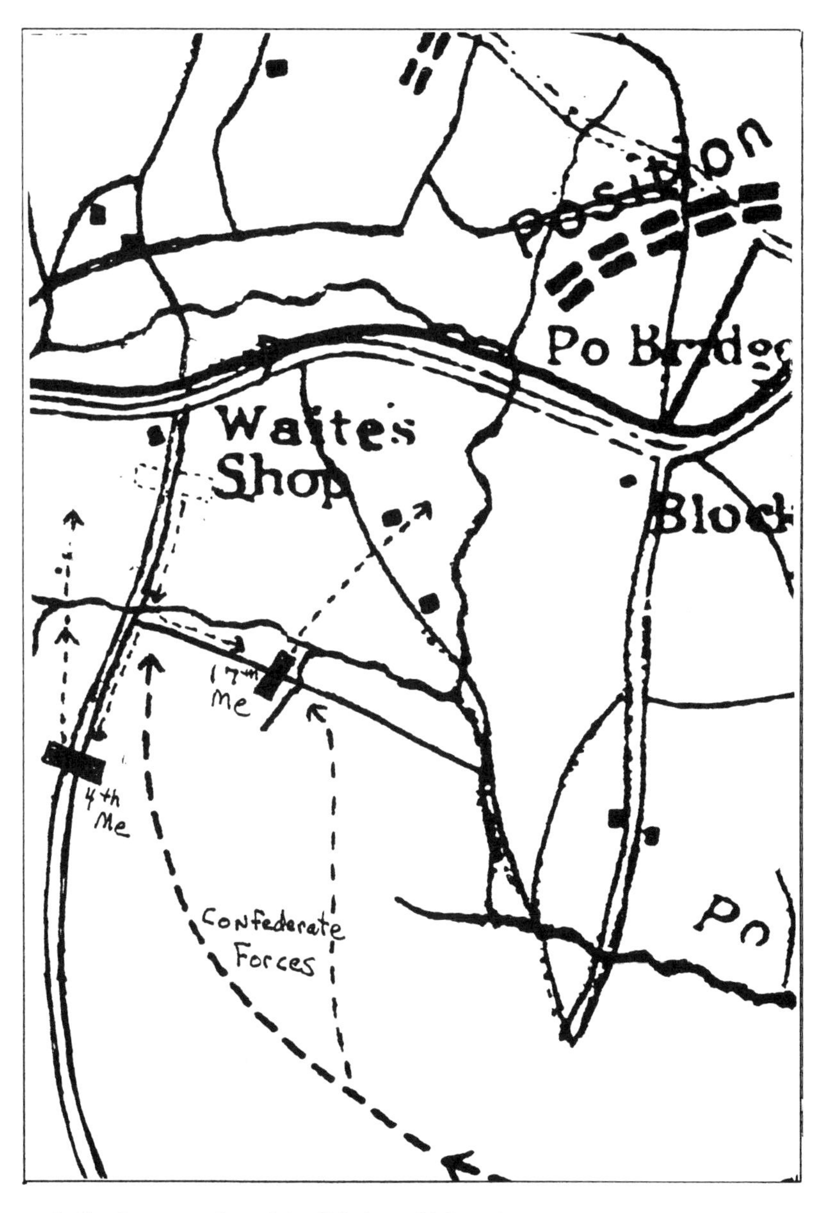

Author's conception of the fighting which took place along the Po River.

of Bristoe's coffee to spur us on." The men ran on until they reached the Po River and, seeing it as no obstacle, quickly jumped in and swam to safety.[5]

Meanwhile, the rebels had exploited the gap between the two units. Suddenly Walker spotted enemy pickets in his front. As the 4th advanced the enemy retreated. Walker remembered that he made " an advance of about two miles, wounding two men, whom we captured with their horses. While reconnoitering some distance in advance of my men, I came within 150 yards of a gray-apparelled line of battle, which I had been prevented from sooner discovering by reason of many scrub pines, whose low-growing branches obscured my view. I lost no time in returning to the road where Bristoe, with the detail, had made his advance and was skirmishing with the 'graybacks'. I wanted to call him and cross the stream, for I knew the enemy would be after us in large numbers; but I received an order from our division commander, brought by his aide-de-camp to go in and assist Bristow's force and drive the enemy's pickets back. I protested, but could not disobey the order."

Elijah Walker sent his "color guard, with prisoners and colors, across the river, and leaving Lieut. Henry O. Ripley, with a squad of men to guard the road", and then attempted to carry out his orders. "Captain Bristow was then a mile away. I had advanced about half a mile when I received an order to join the division on the other side of the river. I sent Capt. Arthur Libby with a few men to see if we could return by the road over which we had come, but he soon returned, exclaiming: 'My God, colonel, the woods are full of them!' This was one of the situations that test a man's nerves. We were in open ground, while the enemy near us were in the woods. I ordered my line formed under the brow of a hill, and while I was calling Bristow and his men from their perilous position, with orders for them to retreat across the river, my boys were bravely holding the enemy in check. We then dashed through the swamp and into the river, where the water and mud were up to our arm-pits; this was our only chance of retreat, as the enemy had gained the river on our right and left."

When Colonel Walker arrived at the stream he was afraid that his horse would have to be abandoned. To his surprise, his horse followed his men into the water. "I feared he would have to be

---

[5] Haley, op. cit., pp. 150 - 151.

abandoned; but two of our gallant boys, George W. Taylor and John Sanborn of Co. K, who had crawled from the water and were standing on the opposite side, seized the animal by the bridal. I leaped over his head and in a moment both horse and rider were on terra firma."[6]

Looking to his left, Walker noticed his men carrying someone in a blanket. As he approached the men with their burden he discovered, much to his horror, that Lieutenant Henry O. Ripley was the occupant. He immediately dismounted and helped carry his old friend to safety. Ripley, "on the enemy's approach had rallied his men to check their advance, and the next instant a bullet had passed through his neck, inflicting a fatal wound. His men retreated across the river at the road crossing."

First Lieutenant Henry O. Ripley of Rockland had been a recipient of the Kearney Cross, and was famous for his exploits as a color bearer at both Fredericksburg and Gettysburg. Due to seriousness of his injury, Lieutenant Ripley was removed to a Washington hospital. In spite of all the attempts made to spare him, though, Ripley died of his wound on June 7th. His mother had arrived in Washington that very day from Maine, and missed his passing by just hours. She would bring his body back to Rockland where his funeral would be marked by a significant amount of ceremony. Ironically, after three years of fighting, against both the enemy and disease, he had expired just one week before his discharge became effective. Knowing Henry, I am sure he would remained at the front as a part of the 19th Maine.[7]

Death Notice, June 1, 1864

Death of Lieut. Henry O. Ripley. *Lieut. Henry O. Ripley, of the 4th Maine Regiment, who was wounded through the right lung in the late battles, died in the hospital at Washington on Tuesday of last week, and his body was received here last Saturday morning. His mother, who started for Washington, on learning his dangerous condition, arrived there only in season to accompany his lifeless remains to this city, he having died the day before she reached Washington.*

---

[6] Walker, op. cit., p 70.
[7] Ibid.

Lieut. Ripley was a young man of good habits and estimable character, and of distinguished gallantry and ardor as a soldier. He was born in Appleton, but for some years past had been a resident of this city, and before his enlistment had worked as a compositor in the office of the Free Press. He was one of the first to volunteer in Company B, of the Fourth Maine, and was in every battle in which the regiment participated up to the time of his death, and displayed marked bravery on several occasions. As the color-bearer of the regiment he distinguished himself at Fredericksburg, and again at Gettysburg. In the last named battle, while bearing the colors, in advance of the regiment, the color staff was shot off above his head, when he caught the falling flag and raised it again upon the shattered staff, continued to bear it, with great coolness and daring, under the enemies heavy fire. For his marked bravery, he was subsequently promoted to the position of Second Lieutenant, and was acting First Lieutenant at the time of his death, although he had not yet received his commission for the higher rank.

His funeral took place on Sunday forenoon, at the residence of his mother, and was attended by the State Guards, the City Council, and a large concourse of citizens. A prayer was offered by Rev. Jos. Kalloch, who also made an appropriate address. The funeral procession was then formed, the State Guards marching first, with reverse arms, followed by the City Council, and then came the hearse and mourners, followed by a number of citizen's carriages. Among those following the body as mourners, we noticed M. L. D. Carver, late Lieut. Colonel of the 4th Regiment, Adjutant Sawyer, of the New York Ira Harris Cavalry, and several wounded soldiers now at home, companions in arms of the deceased. The interment took place at the Jameson Point Cemetery, where the usual military honors were performed by the State Guards.

The casualties for the 4th Maine would have been very minor if it was not for the fact their numbers had already been so drastically reduced by the fighting of the previous week. In this case just three of the enlisted men were wounded. Nine were overrun in the Confederate assault and captured. Patrick Crowley was wounded and died of his wounds on May 29th. Josiah Spear of Co. B was wounded by a shell. First Lieutenant Christopher Gray of Stockton received a more serious injury. Gray was carried from the field by his comrades but died before he could receive adequate medical attention. Casualties for the campaign, thus far, looked fairly serious.[8] (See Appendix for this chapter.)

On their return to their brigade on the morning of the eleventh, the regiment could count only 114 enlisted men who were fit to carry rifles. Despite their dwindling numbers, by three P.M. that afternoon the Limerock Regiment received new marching orders. The regiment was detailed to march directly to Piney Branch Church, and, in company with the 120th New York, and the 82nd and 111th Pennsylvania regiments, instructed to guard the 2nd Corps' wagon train. Colonel Walker was placed in charge of the detachment.[9]

Walker later recalled that they left "corps headquarters at 5 o'clock. They found, and bivouacked near, the train at 9 P.M., having marched about ten miles in a Virginia rain and thunder shower of about three hours' duration. The train moved at 6 o'clock the next morning. I thought it was going to Fredericksburg, but after proceeding five miles it was parked about six miles from the supposed place of destination."[10] Ironically, it would be the movement of this supply train which would cause Lee to decide to pull his artillery out of line in the Salient, or Mule Shoe, and help assure success for Hancock in his attack on May 12th. No better service could have been done for the corps, for it probably saved hundreds of lives.[11]

Late on the night of May 11th, Hancock's Corps began to assemble for a planned assault on the left of the Sixth Corps. Barlow placed his troops in the front line of the planned attack. The men were lined up one regiment wide and thirty or so deep. Birney's men were placed on the right, while Gibbon and Mott's troops were placed in back of these. The soldiers were then given orders to attack at 4 A.M. They were ordered to move forward silently and not to fire their weapons until they reached the rebel lines.[12]

---

[8] Whitman, op. cit., p. 106.
[9] Catton, A Stillness ar Appomatox, p. 108.
[10] Walker, op. cit., p
[11] Catton, A Stillness at Appomatox, p. 108.
[12] Ibid., p. 120

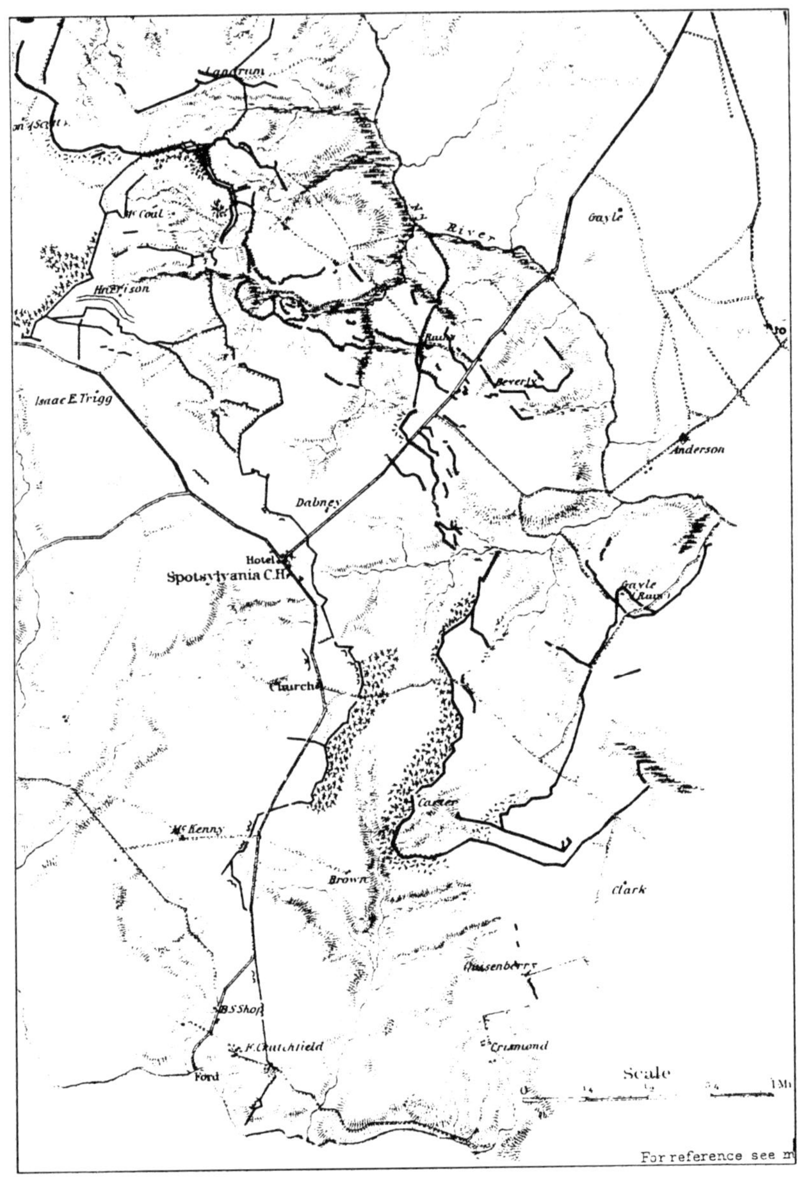

Troop placements around Spotsylvania, May 14th to 16th.

The attack actually took place at 4:35 A.M. The men moved up the slope, quietly, "about half way to the enemy's line, when the men broke into a tremendous cheer, and spontaneously taking the double quick they rolled like an irresistible wave into the enemy's works, tearing away what abatis there was in front of the entrenchments with their hands and carrying the line at all points in a few moments, although it was desperately defended." The attack was fiercely resisted by the Confederates. Nearly 4,000 prisoners, twenty pieces of artillery, and hundreds of muskets were captured.[13]

As Hancock's men had breached the center of the Confederate line the survival of Lee's army hung in the balance. Lee was forced to hold back the charging Federals while his reserve forces built a new defensive line. "Each side was making a charge and repelling a charge at the same moment and with the same troops."[14] "Never before on earth had so many muskets been fired on so narrow a front and at such close range. About all that kept the two armies from completely annihilating each other was the fact that most men were firing too rapidly to aim."[15] The result of the days' fighting was several thousand casualties for both sides and the gain of a few yards of bloody turf for the Army of the Potomac. It was darkest moment in the War of the Rebellion.

The 4th Maine missed most of the action, spending its time, instead, countermarching from its stint at guard duty with the wagon train. The 4th's brigade, however, was in the thick of the fight. Private Haley of the 17th Maine remembered that "every Confederate realized the desperate situation and every Union Soldier knew what was involved. For a time, every soldier was a *fiend.* The attack was fierce - the resistance fanatical. We captured one of their strongest entrenchments, but it was done in a tempest of iron and lead, in a rain of fire."

Ward had attempted to lead his brigade into battle along with the rest of the Second Corps. Once again demon whiskey got the best of him. In the midst of the fight at the Mule Shoe he was relieved of command and placed under arrest. Further, Ward was mustered out of service on July 18, 1864, without a court marshall. Many of his close

---

[13] O. R., op. cit., p. 335.
[14] Catton, op. cit., p. 122.
[15] Ibid., p. 125.

friends would spend the next several years attempting to clear his name. Ward, himself, would spend the remainder of his productive years as a court clerk. The tragedy of his life did not end at the Mule Shoe, for in the eightieth year of his life he was struck by a train and killed. Many of his close friends believed he had committed suicide.[16]

Meanwhile, back at the wagon train, Walker recalled that it was about the time that the "sun was crossing the meridian" that he was "arroused by an orderly, who handed me a paper. It was an order from army headquarters for me to report with my train guard of four regiments with all possible dispatch. Mounting my horse, I soon had the men in line and on the move, but not without a good deal of grumbling, the only thing soldiers have to fall back upon when inconvenienced or disappointed. We had gone but a short distance when we met general Johnson and the greater part of his division, guarded by our soldiers as prisoners of war. I reported as ordered, and each regiment was sent to its division."

"Meeting our division commander about half a mile from and in full view of where his men were fiercely engaged, he pointed and said : 'I think you will find work over there.' I moved to the scene of action and was glad to find that the hardest part of the contest was over. The enemy had made their last charge to drive our men from the works, and were repulsed. Skirmishing continued until late in the evening."[17]

"While looking about, taking in the condition of affairs, Capt. Arthur Libby came to me and said : ' Colonel, walk with me a few yards. I saw the Fair Oaks and Gettysburg battlefields after the battles, but I have never seen anything like this.' I went with him a short distance, to where the dead and wounded, the blue and the gray, filled the trench three deep. I saw a man taken out alive after three dead men were removed from him. Much has been said about an oak tree at this place, which was literally cut down by musket balls. I was within 200 yards of the tree when it fell. Our commanders, desirous of preventing the enemy from stealing in during the night and recovering their six cannon, had a force of about 2500 men keep up a constant musketry fire over them all night. The tree was between the guns and the troops that were protecting them, which explains this

[16] Sifakis. op. cit., p. 691.
[17] Walker' op. cit., p. 71.

remarkable occurrence. A part of the broken piece, which is about seventeen inches in diameter, is preserved in the Smithsonian Institute at Washington."[18]

In the official records, Hancock speaks of the bravery and gallantry of the men of General Birney's and Barlow's divisions. He states, "the magnificent charge made by their divisions, side by side, at Spotsylvania, on the 12th of May, stands unsurpassed for its daring, courage, and brilliant success."[19]

Following the combat of May 12th, the 4th Maine spent the next five days under almost constant fire from the rebels, channeling out entrenchments. The men were constantly shifting positions in order to keep their opponents off balance. The constant activity, coupled with the heat and humidity of the South, was wearing the regiment thin. Fortunately, it was having an equal effect on their opponents.[20]

During the night of the 17th, portions of the Sixth and Second Corps were moved into position for an attack. Many of the men quickly recognized their surroundings. It was the now familiar Mule Shoe. Walker, now in brigade command, was ordered to provide support to the Second Division as its units charged out of the woods. The troops moved with the resolution of individuals marching to certain death. The attack never had a chance of success, and they knew it from the beginning.

The line which the Federal forces attacked "was screened by a heavy abatis and bristled with twenty-nine artillery pieces." Though the enemy's skirmishers were easily driven in, the attack was itself halted at the abatis. According to one of the combatants, "The artillery cut our men down in heaps." The men held on in what little cover could be found for about five hours. About ten A.M. General Meade finally called the whole thing off.[21]

Though losses for the two corps were quite heavy in the morning's combat, casualties for the 4th were very light. Serving in a reserve capacity, only ten of the enlisted men were wounded, and most of the injuries were very minor. As the men retreated from the

---

[18] Ibid., pp. 71 - 72.
[19] O. R., op. cit., p. 340.
[20] Whitman, op. cit. p. 106.
[21] Trudeau, op. cit., p. 195.

field, through the heaps of dead and wounded, most found it difficult to hide their feelings of antipathy. How long would it take for Meade and Grant to realize that heavily defended works could not be taken by direct assault, no matter how much courage the soldiers exibited. Certainly the carnage all about them now should serve as an adequate example of that.[23]

The 4th Maine spent the rest of the day and all of the 19th strengthening their own works in anticipation of an attack by Ewell. At first cockcrow on the 20th Colonel Walker led his brigade forward toward the Harris farm at Spotsylvania. The operation was a combined effort of both Birney's and Tyler's divisions. Walker's men had been among the lead elements, and soon discovered that the Confederate forces had abandoned their entrenchments. All that were to be found were a couple of hundred "stragglers many of them still asleep." The rebels were quickly rounded up by the brigade. Following is the report issued by Colonel Walker later that day.[24]

No. 70
Report of Col. Elijah Walker, Fourth Maine Infantry,
commanding Second Brigade, of operations, May 19-20

Hdqrs. Second Brigade, Third Division, Second Corps,
May 20, 1864

Major : I have the honor to report that during the operations of last night, 19th instant, and this a. m. 246 prisoners were taken by my command, but by some authority, either valid or otherwise, the guard who conducted them to the rear for the purpose of turning them over to the division provost-martial were ordered to turn 102 over to the First Brigade, commanded by Col. T. W. Egan, Fortieth New York Volunteers; also 11 were turned over to the 1st Massachusetts Heavy Artillery. These commands are accredited with them, although the Second Brigade captured them.

Very respectfully, your obedient servant,
ELIJAH WALKER,

---

[22] Whitman, op. cit., p. 106.
[23] Lowry, op. cit., p. 411.

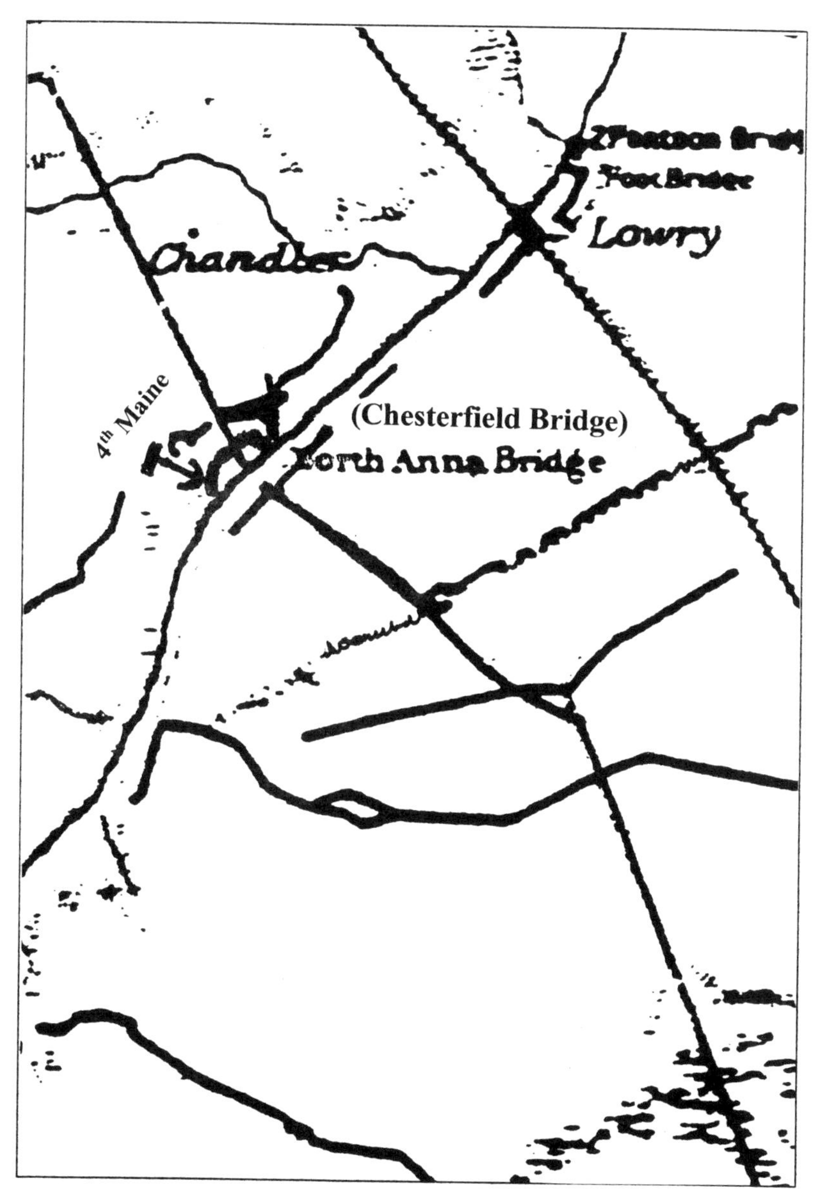

Author's conception of the attack on Chesterfield Bridge, led by Colonel Walker and the 4th Maine Infantry. This was to be their last major fight.

Colonel, Commanding Brigade.[24]

About eleven P. M. that night Hancock began to move his troops south once again. The 4th Maine marched to Massoponax Church, only to discover that the cavalry that were to screen their movements were not yet ready to move. The soldiers were allowed a short repose which lasted until about 1:30 A.M. The Maine boys then fell back into march column, advancing a distance of about twenty-five miles to Milford Station. Here they crossed the Mattapony River and were immediately advanced to the front. Without the benefit of any rest, they were once again, put to work building breastworks.[25]

The Maine regiment remained on post here until six A.M. on the morning of May 23rd. "Coffee, pork and hard bread were the materials of the matutinal meal."[26] The men were then gathered into march column and once again stepped off, this time in the direction of Hanover Junction. Grant had begun to slide his army to the left, trying to pass around Lee's flank. By late afternoon they had arrived at a spot on the North side of the North Anna River, adjacent to the rebel held Chesterfield Bridge. The Confederates had established a bridgehead here, which consisted of a small fort held by some South Carolinians under the command of Colonel John Henagan, and some artillery hidden on the opposite bank.[27]

About 7:15 P.M., in the midst of a heavy downpour, Hancock ordered General Birney to send two brigades to attack the bridgehead. The first and second brigade, no longer under Colonel Walker, but under the more permanent direction of Colonel Pierce of the Third Michigan, were detailed for the assault. The men were formed into line on the edge of the woods. Walker remembered the anxious moments as he and his men lay in the woods anticipating the signal shot that would kick off the attack. "The work before us might justly have been termed a 'forlorn hope.' The division general had disappeared, taking his pet colonel, so our brigade had no commander. Regimental commanders desired me to take command. I

---

[24] O. R., op. cit., p. 479.
[25] Whitman, op. cit., p. 107.
[26] Walker, op. cit., p. 73.
[27] Lowry, op. cit., pp. 421-423.

First Sergeant of Company K, James E. Doak of Belfast.
(Family Photo)

walked the entire length of the brigade line, trying to encourage the men and advising the advance be made upon the run, without firing a shot until we met the enemy face to face.[28]

The Iron 4th, its proud colors unfurled, weak in numbers but never in courage and determination, charged, on command, into the rebel ranks. "The men sprang forward on the run, as I had suggested, the flag of the Fourth Maine borne in advance by Sergt. Preston J. Carter of Co. K." The air was full of minnie balls and canister, and the concussions of artillery shells. "The shot and shell from the opposite bank of the river plowed up the ground under our feet, and it was at this time that the five Fourth Maine men were killed. The infantry line in our front was swept away, the men being captured, killed or forced to take their chances in the water."

"Our brigade advanced to the edge of the stream where the levee afforded a partial protection from the hail of bullets and projectiles. But from a bend in the river a few of the enemy, who had esconced themselves behind rocks and the piers of the bridge, were firing into our rear and flank, which were unprotected. Seeing the condition of affairs, I called for volunteers to dislodge the concealed rebels, and 150 men responded. It was a desperate undertaking, but successful, the extemporized guerillas being either driven across the river or incapacitated from further mischief. Several of my volunteers were disabled, among them the First Sergeant, James E. Doak of Co. K, Fourth Maine, who was badly wounded...Our ammunition being nearly expended, the brigade was relieved from the front line by troops from the Fourth Division."[29]

In the Official Records, Hancock, who was a witness to the sally, describes the action thusly. "The enemy were found to be in force in rifle-pits on the north bank of the North Anna on the tongue of land between the river and Long Creek. General Birney, having reconnoitered the position, was of the opinion that it could be taken, and was instructed to make the attempt to carry it...Egan's and Pierce's brigades, led gallantly by their commanders, charged from four different points over an open field several hundred yards in breadth, which ascended sharply toward the enemy's position, carrying the entrenchments and driving the enemy pell-mell across

[28] Walker, op. cit., p. 73.
[29] Ibid., p. 74.

the stream with considerable loss to them... The enemy made several attempts to burn the bridge, but were frustrated by the vigilance and good conduct of our troops."[30]

General Grant was a witness to the attack at Chesterfield bridge as well. Grant recollected the attack by stating, "the bridge was carried quickly, the enemy retreating over it so hastily that many were shoved into the river, and some of them were drowned." Horace Porter recalled that the attack was carried off "hansomely, some of the enemy being captured, and the rest being driven over the bridge, followed closely by our men."[31]

The praise for the attackers was quick in coming from all levels of command. Though the job was accomplished quickly and efficiently by the veterans, it was not done without bloodshed. The two brigades lost about a hundred and fifty men.[32] With just a little over three weeks left on their enlistments, and their numbers already seriously depleted, the tiny Maine regiment had five of their numbers killed and eighteen wounded.[33]

4th Maine Casualties at Chesterfield Bridge

Killed. Serg. T. K. Chapman; Corp W. B. Perkins and Edward Palmer, Co. E. Serg. E. S. Bisbee, Co. G.; private Michael Rooney, Co. K.
Wounded. Col. E. Walker, slight; Ajt. C. F. Sawyer, slight.
Co. A. - Ira P. Allen, severe; Richard Allen, slight.
Co. B. - Albert Goodwin and Geo. Taylor, severe.
Co. D. - Edward Joy, slight; Geo. Perkins, severe.
Co. E. - A. C. Trott, severe.
Co. F. - Serg. H. G. York, moderate; Joel Mixer, severe; Frank McCarrick, severe.
Co. G. - Wm. Nutter, slight.
Co. H. - Joel Jackson, severe; Sam'l Kenniston, severe; Geo. Cox, slight; Wm. Heal, severe.
Co. I. - Serg. A. Merrithew, serious; Joseph Boardway, slight.

[30] O. R., op. cit., p. 340.
[31] Trudeau, op. cit., p. 227.
[32] O, R., op cit., p. 340.
[33] Whitman, op. cit., p. 107.

Co. K. - Lieut. J. E. Doak, severe.[34]

At Sunrise the following morning the rebels began a cannonade of shot and shell, "but little damage was done, however, as we were protected by the 'bowers of spades' we had prepared during the night. At 7 A.M. our brigade, preceded by sharpshooters, advanced across the bridge..., and after a severe skirmishing the enemy retired to a strong position nearly a mile from the river.". As the troops advanced they discovered that Lee had withdrawn from the river during the night and set himself up in new entrenchments in the shape of a V. Facing this new Confederate entrenchment the 4th busied itself building rifle pits. Their location in the line was somewhat exposed and their efforts were frustrated all day by the constant fire of skirmishers and sharpshooters. During the course of the day the regiment had one of its' men, Jaun Millano of Co. K, killed by a solid shot. "It had nearly spent its force but rebounded. striking Millano in the breast and causing instant death. He was one of the best of soldiers and had not been absent a single day from the time the regiment was mustered. He was truely loved and sincerely mourned by all his comrades." Two additional men were wounded.[35]

A full scale attack by Lee's army would, in all likelihood, have destroyed Hancock's Corps, isolated as it was on the south side of the North Anna. Lee, however, was very ill and was in no shape to be putting the Southern Army on the offensive. The opportunity to achieve a stunning blow to the North was missed. On the following day, May 26th, Hancock's divisions were allowed to slip back across the river. The movement took place after dark, under the cover of a noisy thunderstorm. The Confederates did not realize that the move had taken place until dawn of the next day.[36]

As the army slipped to the left, once again, the 4th helped to serve as a rear guard for the army. The regiment marched to a point about five miles from the Pamunkey and bivouacked for the night. About 5:30 A.M. the next morning, May 28, the men broke camp and marched to a newly established crossing point on the North Anna River, near Hanovertown. The crossing was effected a little after

---

[34] Rockland Gazette, June 1, 1864.
[35] Ibid.
[36] Trudeau, op. cit., p. 245.

noon. Hancock's troops were then pushed forward to Haw's Church where they dug in for the night.[37]

Midday on the 29th, Barlow's division was ordered to make a reconnaissance in their front. When they ran into a force of entrenched rebels they immediately engaged the enemy. Hancock's two other divisions were immediately brought up as reinforcements. At daybreak the next morning the whole of Hancock's Corps moved forward, and with very little loss to themselves, took the Confederate works. Several prisoners were taken. Though involved in the operation, the 4th Maine provided support to a battery of artillery and suffered no casualties.[38]

Duty assignments for those regiments whose terms of service were about to end soon became a very controversial subject among the men. Division and Corps commanders were used to turning to their most experienced veterans when the task before them seemed difficult. Old habits were hard to break and when times got tough they were very apt to call upon these men, as they always had, to take the lead in an assault. The subject is brought up by Elijah Walker in his recollections when "early on the morning of the 30th there was brisk skirmishing. Captain William H. Briggs of the Third Maine and Capt. George A. McIntyre of the same regiment wounded. Their term of service was to expire on June 3d and they should have been relieved and on their way to Maine; but so far from showing any mercy for the men of the Third and Fourth Maine, our division commander did all he could to have them assigned to the most dangerous positions and duties."[39]

About eleven A.M. on May 31st, General Hancock ordered Birney to advance his division across Swift Run. This they did, carrying the rebel line which was on the right side of the Richmond Road. Hancock's two other divisions were thrown into the fight but together could not accomplish anything more. Walker recalled that "our regiment was in the third line, as support to the battery which was shelling the enemy. The battery retired at dark and we joined the brigade."[40] The Corps was now hard up against the defenses of

[37] O. R., op. cit., p. 343.
[38] Ibid.
[39] Walker, op. cit., p. 75.
[40] Ibid.

Richmond. This is as close as the Maine men would get to the city. The following morning the Corps was pulled back across Swift Run.[41]

There was now just two weeks left to the term of service. All of the men of the 4th Maine regiment were well aware of their remaining time, and each resented, more and more, being asked to risk his life. As the skirmishing rattled along the front on this first day of June the men were even more careful to keep their heads low to the ground and not expose themselves, carelessly, to the fire of rebel skirmishers and sharpshooters. When the command came that evening to shuffle off to "Coal" (Cold) Harbor, the orders were obeyed, albeit reluctantly, for each man knew that a major offensive was about to take place there. Everyone knew that the attack would be against entrenchments, and each knew that their chances of being killed would be very good.

Walker recalled that the Sixth Corps, which had been on their right, was withdrawn during the night. On the morning of June 1, Walker found his right flank was completely exposed. "Our General was sleeping, without providing any protection for the flank of the lines. Expecting an attack, I had Capt. Libby keep his men well in hand for any emergency. At 11 o'clock a line of the enemy's skirmishers advanced to within 100 yards of the right of our lines and some shots were fired into the rear of our second line. Men who had gone 100 yards from our lines, for water, were shot. Captain Libby and his men went to the rescue, and a few of the Third and Fifth Michigan boys, from the rear line joined him. Some of our sharpshooters were soon on hand and the "grays" were put to flight. Six of them were captured and brought in; some were no doubt left on the field."

On June 2nd, Hancock moved his men to the far left of the Union line. A great deal of straggling had taken place due to the intense heat and the attack planned for this day had to be rescheduled. Birney's troops, with the tiny 4th Maine tagging along, did not arrive in position until almost two P.M., having been assigned to assist Smith's Corps with some skirmishing that had taken place near the Woody House. As the rest Hancock's Corps waited, they began to dig rifle pits. This they did all day and all night, awaiting the order to

---

[41] Lowry, op. cit., p. 439.

attack. Three full Corps, including Wright's and Smith's, anticipated the dictate. Darkness fell and the troops held their breath, hoping against all hope, that their leaders had reconsidered.[42]

By dawn of the next day Gibbon's division had been deployed near the Mechanicsville Road with Wrights Corps on his right. General Barlow's Division was on his left. General Birney's Division would act as support. As it turned out, this assignment would keep the 4th Maine out of the fight. It would mean that the regiment would suffer no casualties on this most bloody morning.

A single cannon was fired to mark the beginning of the attack. Hancock's two divisions drove in on the heavily entrenched line. Barlow located the Confederates in a sunken road. These troops were driven in, and into the works in their rear. The Union soldiers, all the while under severe musket and artillery fire, followed them, capturing about three hundred prisoners, a stand of colors, and three artillery pieces. Barlow's support troops, however, failed in their attempt to follow up on the success of the first wave. The first line, seeing that their attack had failed and fearing that retreat might cause even greater disaster, took advantage of a slight knoll and began to scoop out a line of rifle pits with their bare hands. They were only thirty to seventy yards from the rebel lines.[43]

Gibbon's attack, on the right, had even worse results. A few hundred yards out the division ran into a swamp which had not been previously detected. The attackers split and tried to go around both sides. Though one of his brigades was briefly able to breach the Confederate defenses, the heavy cross fire and constant sniping from the swamp took such a toll that the men were forced to withdraw. In less than twenty minutes the attack was over. Like Barlow, Gibbon simply took advantage of the terrain and began to dig rifle pits in their exposed position.[44]

Some accounts state that the attack lasted but fifteen minutes, others, a half hour. The shooting, however, did not end here, but lasted all day. Hancock listed his casualties for the day as 3,024. The brunt of the losses was born by Barlow's (1,279) and Gibbon's (1,507) divisions. Birney's Third Division, who was only lightly involved and

---

[42] O. R., op. cit., p. 345.
[43] Ibid., pp. 345-346.
[44] Catton, op. cit., p. 161.

lost but 336 men. Hancock, in reflecting on his losses at Cold Harbor, stated that the fighting was a "blow to the Corps from which it did not soon recover."[45] Bruce Catton states; "In all the war, no attack had ever been broken up as quickly or as easily as this, nor had men ever been killed so rapidly. The half hour's work had cost the Union army 7,000 men."[46]

Shortly after the fighting ended Birney's division was sent to support Warren's 5th Corps. The soldiers stayed here until June 5th, and then rejoined their Corps. In the period between the fifth and the eleventh of June the Army of the Potomac began to conduct siege operations. Mortars were used to get at rebel troops in their trenches. Hancock's men extended their line to the Chicahominy River on their left, while continually pressing their trenches ever closer to the enemy. A mine under the Confederate works was attempted and quickly abandoned. The 4th Maine spent this time, once again, digging trenches, supporting troops and artillery, and skirmishing with the enemy. The shooting was at times heavy and there were some minor losses in the Corps. The 4th had a single man wounded on the tenth. He would be the regiment's final battle casualty. His identity and fate are unknown.[47]

On night of June 12th, the entire Union Army pulled back from their exposed positions to a new set of trenches that had been constructed in the rear. At 11 P.M. this very night Hancock's three divisions moved from these trenches and marched for Long Bridge. The advanced pickets, which included the Limerock Regiment, were drawn in at 3 A.M. on the thirteenth, and ordered to follow immediately on the heels of their division. Grant was now quietly shifting his forces across the James river for a surprise attack on the fragile defenses at Petersburg.[48]

The Maine boys now had but three days left on their enlistments. The Corps, however, seemed to be conducting a race to get to the next battle before their terms expired. On the morning of the thirteenth the regiment crossed the Chickahominy at Long Bridge, and then were forced marched to Charles City Court House, arriving

---

[45] O. R., op. cit., pp. 345-346.
[46] Catton, op. cit., p. 161.
[47] Whitman, op. cit., p. 107.
[48] O. R., op. cit., p. 346.

there about 7 P.M. The regiment camped that night on President Tyler's Plantation, and though they were told that it would not be necessary to dig rifle pits, the men did so anyway. With the end of their term of service just hours away, nobody wanted it to end in tragedy.[49]

Though the Union army had built a half mile long bridge across the James River for the crossing of its' troops, the 4th crossed the river that morning on a steamer. Quickly disembarked, they were rapidly put in march column and advanced a distance of about "two miles to the front and taking position in line of battle." With sporadic firing going on all about them, the Mainer's, once again set up camp, and then dug themselves in. For the first time ever they were now on the South side of the James.[50]

Throughout the night, the rest of Hancock's brigades continued to arrive. Everyone was preparing for the planned early morning offensive on Petersburg. At dawn Birney's regiments moved out, save one, for it was on this day, June 15, 1864, a day which would see an opportunity to quickly end the war, pass very quickly through Grant's hands, that the 4th Maine finally received its orders to muster out. Two hundred and seventy-seven men, those who had enlisted late or had reenlisted, were transferred on this day to the 19th Maine to finish their terms. The remaining tiny band of Maine natives, one hundred and forty five in number, would take their leave from the army. For these men, they had done their whole duty, "with their faces to the foe".

---

[49] Whitman, op. cit., p. 107.
[50] Ibid.

Monument to the 4th Main Infantry located in Rockland at the site of their original encampment.

Chapter 14

The Limerock Regiment Returns

From the time that this research began, some two and a half years ago, I had pondered how this chronicle would read. I wondered if the regiment I had chosen to research would perform their duties nobly. I conjectured, whether at the end of my quest, I would say that they were the bravest, or the coolest under fire. Would I have to build them up beyond that which they were in life, or would the images which they had left behind speak for themselves. I also wondered if the passage of nearly a hundred and thirty years would cloud, or even diminished, the significance of their passing, and make the writing of this history impossible. In this respect, only you the reader can decide.

Still, on June 25th, 1864, the remnant of that thousand man force did, indeed, return to Rockland. The return route was quiet, like that of so many veterans of war, there had been no cheering crowds to greet them in the fashion they had enjoyed when they had left the state. There was to be no reception in New York, or in Boston. The only celebration of their return which they encountered was that in Rockland, itself. Here the flags were flown from every building, and across every street. A band was present, playing songs like "Sweet Home", and "When Johnny Comes Marching Home." A parade ensued in which the veterans were joined with their families and the widows of their friends.[1]

When the procession had arrived at the square the regiment was officially received by the City of Rockland. A brief speech was given by the Honorable N. A. Farwell, the substance of which follows:

"Co. Walker: I am instructed by the City Council to welcome you and your brave regiment back to the city, where, three years hence, you went at the call of your country. It is not the time nor the

---

[1] Rockland Gazette, July 2, 1864.

Some of the regiment's members taken in front of the Gen. Berry Fire House.

Hurricane Granite Company was the source of the stone for the Gettysburg memorial. Photo taken in the late 1800's (Photos Shore Village Museum)

place to rehearse the history of your noble deeds; it would be tedious to the men who have made that history, and unnecessary to the people here assembled, who have watched with so much pride every movement of your most cherished regiment. It is sufficient to say that wherever the noble army of the Potomac have met the enemy in battle, there, in the thickest of the fray, have been yourself and your command, and no friend of the regiment has ever had reason to blush for your conduct. And again permit me to express the thanks of the City Council and of the citizens, to each and all of you, and to invite you to partake of the hospitalities provided for you."[2]

A tremendous feast was prepared for them at Atlantic Hall. Here they dined as guests of honor, in a fashion they could only have imagined just a few weeks before. Then, as quickly as they had entered upon the stage of history, these "Fighting Tigers" slipped quietly away from the banquet tables, and the continuing saga of the war. Back they went to their families, their farms, and their businesses. The soldiers received a furlough which would pardon them until July 19th, at which time they would be officially mustered out. All back pay due them was paid, and a one hundred dollar bounty was awarded each man by the Paymaster, Major Elias Merrill.[3]

Thirteen officers and one hundred and thirty-two enlisted men was all that remained of the one thousand and two that had left on that June day in 1861 to fight a war that all believed would last but thirty days. As the weeks and months became years, new three year recruits were added to the regiment. In time the names ten additional officers and five hundred and thirteen soldiers were added to the rolls. Gross enrollment in the 4th's ranks would eventually total 1,525.

What happened to all of these men, these so called recruits? Well, fourteen of the officers and one hundred and fifty-six of the enlisted men were mortally wounded, or killed on the field of battle. One hundred and fourteen expired due to disease. Two officers and thirty-seven privates were, at the time the regiment was mustered out of service, listed as prisoners of war. The book, Maine in the War, lists three hundred and sixty-six men as having been discharged for

---

[2] Whitman, Maine in the War, p. 108.
[3] Ibid.

Faded photo showing the dedication ceremony of the 4th Maine monument At Gettysburg. Elijah Walker, with his white beard, stands in foreground.

disability. These were the soldiers so traumatized by their wounds that they were unable to return to their regiment. If you count the total number that were wounded in battle, the aggregate far exceeds this sum. What it tells us is that these men, though injured, would rather return to their regiment than seek the sanguine asylum of the hospital system.

Desertion, though lower than the average for the Army of the Potomac, was still fairly common in the 4th Maine. In the three years of their military life one hundred and thirty-one enlisted men deserted. Only some are listed as having been punished for the act, none were executed by firing squad which was the standard penalty for the act.

None of the officers are listed as having deserted. Of course if an officer became tired of the war he did not have to skedaddle, he could just resign from his position. Five officers were discharged, probably for injury. Forty-one others, however, simply resigned their commissions.

Four hundred and thirty five men, in the course of the regiment's history, were transferred to other commands. Several were shifted to river gunboat service in 1862. Two hundred and seventy-seven additional men were transferred to the Nineteenth Maine when the regiment was disbanded, many of whom were recruits whose three year term of service had not yet been completed. Of this number, some forty-three of the original volunteers in the 4th opted to reenlist, volunteers to the bitter end.[4]

Fates of Soldiers Who Re-enlisted

Company A
James Colley Wounded May 5th before transfer to 19th Me
Stephen Daggett 19th Maine and then to 1st Maine Heavy Art
George Fairweather Not known
Llewwllyn Lincoln Wounded August 17, transfer to 1st Me. Hvy
Manuel Sidelinger Prisoner June 22, transfer 1st Me, Hvy
Sanford Sylvester 19th Maine and then to 1st Me. Hvy.

Company B

[4] Ibid., p. 109.

Modern picture of the 4th Maine monument located in the Valley of Death at Gettysburg. Foreground stone shows where the right of the line was located. Little Round Top is in the background

Otis Spear Not known
Charles Hopkins Promoted Sergeant in 19th, wounded, disc.
Daniel Norris 19th Maine, and then to 1st Me. Hvy.
George Taylor Wounded and transferred to Veteran Reserve

Company C
Rufus Fales Not known
George Mega " "

Company D
Samuel Meservy Transferred to Veteran Reserve Corps.
Jacob Cunningham 19th Maine, and then to 1st Me. Hvy.
Simon Taylor " " " " " " " "

Company E
Thomas Campbell Discharged on November 22, as a 2nd Lieu.
John S, Chapman Not known.
William Hathorn 19th Maine, and then to 1st Me. Hvy.
Thomas Perkins Promoted Corp. 19th Maine, trans. 1st Hvy.

Company F
Charles Thompson Not known
Freeman Jones Missing June 22.
Warren Overlock 19th Maine, and then to 1st Me. Hvy.
Charles Wood Missing June 22, transfer to 1st Me. Hvy.

Company G
Timothy Call 19th Maine, then to 1st Me. Hvy.

Company H
Joseph Babson Promoted 2nd Lieut. in 19th Me.
Enoch Lurvey Not known
George Wood Promoted to 1st Lieut. in 19th Me.
William Tripp Promoted to 2nd Lieut. in 19th Me.
Jared Reed 19th Maine, then to 1st Me. Hvy.
Charles Allen " " " " " " "
Abram Furbish " " " " " " "
Daniel McMahan Died of disease on September 27.

The second 4th Maine monument is located a few yards behind the Copse of Trees that Pickett had targeted during his famous charge on July 3rd.

Edwin Mink 19th Maine, then to 1st Me. Hvy.
Charles Moore " " " " " " "
Morrison Young Deserted April 2nd, 1865.

Company I
Abiather Merrithew Not known
William Knowles " "
Leverett Boynton Missing and transferred to 1st Me. Hvy.
Franks Forbes Not known
Lemuel Jefferson 19th Maine, then to 1st Me. Hvy.
Benjamin Knowles Wounded, then transferred to 1st Me. Hvy.

Company K
George Burgess Not known

For those of the 4th who transferred to the 19th Maine Infantry, and for those that ended their term of service with it, life would not be boring. These men would fight at battles, the names of which would seldom be repeated, or long remembered. Countless assaults on Petersburg, including one made on June 18th, in which Joshua Chamberlain himself would be seriously wounded while leading the attack. Names like Jerusalem Plank Road, Deep Bottom, Strawberry Plains, Reams Station, Peeble's Farm, Hatcher's Run, Farmville, and High Bridge. Fighting occurred almost every day. The war was a now a struggle to wear down the enemy until they no longer had the means, or the will, to continue. It was a fight which seemed to have no end.

For those members of the 4th whose enlistment's would last beyond October 1, 1865, these men were transferred to one of the most famous Maine fighting units, the 1st Maine Heavy Artillery. For those that would muster out with this regiment, they would not return to Augusta until June 2nd, 1865.

Of the two hundred and seventy-seven soldiers that were transferred to the 19th, thirty-six were wounded in action. Twenty-three were captured, nine of whom would expire while in prison. Three would desert, four would die of disease, and thirteen would be killed in action. All told, almost one in three of these soldiers, would, in one way or another, become casualties of the war.

U-31 KEARNEY CROSS

Though the 4th Maine had been officially disbanded, the spirit of the regiment and its tradition of courage and sacrifice would carry on. Preston Carter would die at Jerusalem Plank Road in the thick of the fight. Carter was acting as flag bearer, and though he would be mortally wounded in the skirmish, he would die with the regimental colors clutched in his hands. The flag would never be allowed to drag on the ground, not even in death. That was the type of bravado that characterized these "Fighting Tigers".[5]

The Fourth Maine, though never having a member that received the Congressional Medal of Honor, had several members who certainly deserved one. Soldiers like Henry Ripley, Robert Grant, and James Gall, though deserving, would have to settle for the prestigious Kearny Medal, however. This decoration, which was a bronze Maltese Cross, had been the brainchild of General Birney, and was introduced to the army shortly after the Battle of Chancellorsville. It was intended as a means of recognizing courage and valor on the part of enlisted men in combat. A total of twenty-five men in the Fourth would receive the honor. Though many of these warriors would continue distinguishing themselves in battle, many would perish trying uphold the tradition.

Fourth Maine Infantry Recipients of the Kearny Cross

Company A : Private James Gall
Private Horace Speed
Company B : Sgt. Henry O. Ripley
Private Robert Grant
Company C : Corp. George Gardiner
Corp. Warren Austin
Company D : Sgt. James McLaughlin
Corp. Henry O. Davis
Private Henry Marshall
Company E : Corp. William Barstow
Private Nathaniel Waters
Private F. K. Chapman
Company F : Sgt. A. H. Rose
Private Henry Leach

[5] Smith, The History of the 19th Regt. Maine Vol., pp. 300 - 356.

4th Maine Infantry and 2nd Maine Battery Reunion photo. Elijah Walker is located in the front row, center. The beard is a dead give away. (Photo Shore Village Museum)

Photo of 4th Maine Re-enactment group located in "Germany".

Private J. S. Hill
Company G : Private Bradford Blinn
Private Daniel O. Howard
Company H : Sgt. Horace Jellison
Corp. George P. Wood
Company I : Corp. C. W. Gray
Private John Donahue
Private Juan Melano
Company K. Sgt. John Toothaker
Private Robert Whitehead
Private P. J. Carter
Adjutant Gen. Report.[6]

For those who chronicled the activities of the 4th Maine Regiment, there are constantly repeated references to the selfless sacrifice of its' members. From the first losses at Bull Run to the final deadly charge at Chesterfield Bridge, there are constant allusions that these mortal forfeitures would never be forgotten. Certainly future generations would always remember the names of those who had died, that the Union might be saved.

That their appellations would not be forgotten, the soldiers names were carved in stone. Their epitaphs proclaimed their patriotism and devotion to their country on tombstone after tombstone, in cemeteries, large and small, situated throughout the state. Cast iron G.A.R. markers grace the cemetery plots. Each Memorial Day these decorations cry out for attention as they are embellished with American Flags. Every town history lists it's roll of honor for the war, and nearly every community has a monument within its borders devoted to the remembrance of these soldiers. Civil War re-enactors honor these men's names nearly every weekend. We are surrounded, almost suffocated with manifestations of the war, and yet we cannot find a high school student that has heard of Hiram Berry, Adelbert Ames, Oliver Otis Howard, or Elijah Walker. Most believe that the State of Maine had but a single regiment, the 20th, and a single general, Joshua Chamberlain. But for Little Round Top, Maine's participation in this most costly of all wars is all but forgotten.

[6] Ibid.

Photo of the Edwin Libby Post GAR in Rockland.
(Photo Shore Village Museum)

Interior of the Edwin Libby Post.
(Photo Shore Village Museum)

The soldier's of the 4th Maine endured hardships, which by modern day standards, would be completely insufferable. These brave men suffered from sicknesses, which were not only untreatable by their own medical technology, but were often mistreated by cures more fatal than the disease. Wounds were often left unattended for days. Operations were conducted in which limbs were amputated and bullets removed without anesthetics of any kind. The soldiers often existed for days on end without food. Most of the time, while on campaign or in battle, they slept without blankets or tents, totally unprotected and exposed to the elements. Cold, extreme heat, insects, rodents, snakes, rain, wind, and storms of all kinds, battered, and at the same time, hardened the men, and made veterans of those who survived.

While many perished due to these forces, while many survived in spite of them. For those whose lives expired on the battle field, in Confederate prisons, or Union hospitals, many, if not most of the bodies, were never returned home. Still, the families dutifully erected tombstones and carefully carved out the histories of their loved ones earthly existence. Notice was almost always given to the regiment in which they had fought and the rank to which they had risen. Painfully, these memories were laid to rest in the boneyards of Maine. Only these monuments would serve as lasting notice of the sacrificial devotion to duty of their kin.

For those that survived the war, injured or not, each would carry back home the scars of their experiences. Most would never fully recover from the adventure. The return to farm life on the coast of Maine was, many times, almost impossible for them to adjust to. Many of the men moved away, some ran away, several even committed suicide in their attempt to readjust to the quiet life. The disfigurement caused by the war ran too deep to be forgotten. The return to rural farm life was difficult to endure.

If the return home was arduous for the veteran, it must have been even more difficult for their families. Three or more years of absence had forced them to become more dependent on their own energy and resources. The return of a disabled veteran could mean even more work. Many times this would stress family bonds to the breaking point. Life had never been easy. The war did not make it any less so.

More of those who found eternal rest at Gettysburg.

The fact remains that the history of the 4th Maine Regiment of Infantry has, over the course of one hundred and thirty years plus, been allowed to sift through the cracks. Though the records still exist, they are rapidly disappearing. With this relentless destruction, the proud heritage of the descendants, not only of this regiment, but of all of the Maine regiments, save maybe one or two, is rapidly being forgotten. It is our responsibility, not only as historians, but as participants in the human experience, to make sure that not one soldier, be it a private or a general, is forsaken. Understanding, ourselves, the precious and fragile character of life, we must try to understand how truly courageous it is to risk and sacrifice all, for an ideal.

Were the men of the "Limerock Regiment" courageous? Did they live up to, or exceed the standards of bravery or grit of the average Civil War Soldier? Though difficult to prove, it is my belief that they did. Granted, I am necessarily prejudiced by the amount, and the depth of the materials I have had to sift through in order to reach this point in my writing. Still, their record of service and sacrifice should serve as ample evidence of their bravado.

The men of the 4th Maine, by and large, did as they were ordered, even when to do so meant almost certain death. It was a rare combination of courage, idealism, and patriotic zeal which brought these men together and formed them into the unique fighting unit that they were. Perhaps it was best summed up by Stephen Chapman, who only hours before his own death at the First Battle of Bull Run wrote; "How can one better or more gloriously die than for his country?...Trust us dear friends, if we die, it will be 'With our Faces to the Foe'." It was by the light of this ideal that Stephen Chapman and the courageous men of the 4th Maine lived. It was also the way that they died.

Peter Dalton

Confederate trenches at Chesterfield Bridge on the North Anna River, site of the 4th Maine's last battle. (Battles and Leaders)

Appendix Chapter 3

4th Maine Casualties at Bull Run

COMPANY A

None are reported killed, but the following are missing : G. W. Syvester, S. B. Sylvester, E. W. Ellis.

Wounded - Wm. Kendrick, A. Buker.

COMPANY B

Killed. - A. Towns, B. W. Fetcher, C. O. Fernald.

Missing. - S. B. Lamb.

Wounded. - C. F Sawyer

COMPANY C

Killed. - P. H. Tillson, J. B. Grant, Dennis Canning.

Missing. - S. Hewett, S. B. Pease, N. B. Going, M. L. Woodcock.

COMPANY D

Killed. - Thomas Harden, J. A. Sparhawk, G. E. Starbird, W. B. Foss, J. Bailey.

Missing. - Lieut. T. B. Glover, Corporal G. W. Chatts, J. S. Gray, I. J. Milay, C. F. Merrill, Chandler Perry, I. V. Eaton, H. Haskell, H. P. Story.

Wounded. - J. A. Simmonds, J. Norton, Jr.

Company E.

Killed. - A. O. Hall, Fred. Stetson, Enos Clark.

Missing. - A. Robinson Ordery Sergeant, Freeman Hall 2d Sergeant, Geo. Osgood, Wm. Packard.

Wounded. - E. Hilton.

COMPANY F

Killed. - Lieut. C. H. Burd, H. A. Colagin, E. J. Barlow.

Missing - J. Mulherrin, R. G. Bickford, C. H. Rowell, G. B Getchell, H. A. Delano.

Wounded. - Capt. Bean, Lieut. J. S. Huxford.

COMPANY G

Killed. - Lieut. W. H. Clark, Joseph Wright.

Missing. - Freeman Shaw, J. E. Boynton, S,. P. Dickinson, J. Marston, C. R. Brookings.

Wounded. - Geo. Bragdon, J. Clark, Wm. Seavey, Fred. Barter, Acting Lieut. E. B. Carr, Ed. Jones.

COMPANY H

Killed. - W. W. Cooper, J. Trim. Geo. W. Cunningham, Geo. Anderson.

Missing. J. Knights, M. Jackson, H. Washburn.

Wounded. - Wm. Fountain, S. L. Young.

COMPANY I

Missing. - R. H. Gray, 2d Sergeant, G. W. Dwelly, A. D. Mathews, R. Trevett, F. Forbes, E. O. Maddocks.

Wounded. - Levi Temple, J. Melano, C. C. Gray, J. Trimble, F. W. Porter, J. E. Harriman.

COMPANY K

Missing. - G. F. Walker, Z. Berry.

Wounded. - L. B. Bisbee, E. D. Redmen.

Total. - Killed, 24 - missing, 42 - Wounded, 24.

Appendix Chapter 4

Life in Libby
By
C. O. Fernald,
Fourth Maine Infantry.

While engaged in the first battle of Bull Run, on the twenty-first day of July, 1861, my fighting was stopped by a cannon ball, which took the clothes clear to my breast, taking it all off but a little skin; then passing through the rear rank it struck a man by the name of Fletcher, just the same as it struck me. After I was hit I got up, looked at my arm and then started for the rear, when I was soon overtaken by two comrades, George Spalding and Fred Conley, who corded my arm and stopped the flow of blood, after which I walked for nearly half a mile when I again fell from loss of blood, the cord on my arm having become loose. I had not lain more than twenty minutes, when one of our ambulances came along with Fletcher in it and took me up, carrying us back to an old house just across the stone bridge. We were laid under some apple trees, the house already being full of wounded.

After taking us out, they tightened the cord on my arm and then went back on the field after more wounded. While waiting for the surgeon to dress my wound I cut the skin that held the arm on and buried it by means of an old bayonet, under the tree.

Just before dark the rebs passed us in pursuit of our troops which had passed a few minutes before. They did not stop even to place a guard around us then, but kept on in pursuit of our retreating forces. As it was growing dusk our regimental surgeon, Doctor Seth C. Hutchins, came to me, and they laid me on a temporary table, ready to take off my arm, when who should appear on the ground but a squad of Johnnies, who at once placed a guard around us. An officer rode up to our surgeon, who with his assistant was dressing my arm, and placing a revolver close to his head, ordered him to leave me and attend to their wounded; but he refused, saying if they shot him he could do nothing for them, but if they let him finish dressing my arm he would go with them.

When they found that they could not move him they stayed by until he got done with me, and then he went with them. This was the last that I saw of the surgeon. He had dressed Fletcher's arm just before mine, so when my arm was dressed they laid me beside him under the apple tree, where I lay for some days and nights with nothing to eat but a small piece of raw beef and one cake of hard bread. The agony of that first night will never be forgotten, for we were all suffering with thirst and our tongues were swelling out of our mouths. It was enough to touch a heart of stone to hear the poor fellows begging for water; but it was not enough to touch the hearts of our captors, for although there was plenty of water only a few rods away they would not leave their work of pillaging the dead and wounded to bring us any, neither would they allow those that could crawl around to pass the guard for water.

But God had not forsaken us. About half-past ten that night it commenced to rain, and it never rained harder, so that all that we had to do was to open our mouths and they were filled. All who were out of doors had plenty to drink that night, but it was different with the poor fellows in the house, whom we could hear begging for water all through the night, amid the groans of the wounded and dying.

On the eleventh day after the battle, we were carted to Manassas Junction, loaded in cattle cars and started for Richmond, which took one day and night. During the ride the rebs would reverse the engine every few miles, which piled us up in the cars, one on top of the other, causing us intense suffering. We had nothing to eat or drink on the road, being treated by the citizens on the way like so many beasts of prey that they would like to kill. After arriving in Richmond we were escorted to "Hotel de Libby", with the name of Libby & Son over the door. When we arrived the building was nearly empty, containing only a few political prisoners and a few officers and men who had preceded us. They recorded twenty-seven hundred of us in the building, which in addition to what was already there, filled it to the brim.

About six hours after arriving they issued to us some soft bakers bread and water from the James River. We began to think that we should not fare so very bad after all; but how soon that delusion was dispelled you will see. I was placed in the second story, and the boards on which I lay were by the second rear window, with a tobacco press for a pillow. I was without blanket, shirt or blouse, having lost my blanket in the fight and having my shirt and blouse taken nearly off by the shot that took my arm.

Just before dark one of the Fourteenth Brooklin boys approached the window by which I was lying, the windows all being protected with iron bars. When he got within about two feet of the window the report of a gun was heard, and he fell dead, with only a groan, for he had been shot through the left breast. The blood from his body spurted in my face. The news spread through the building and the boys kept back from the windows. After dark the officers came into the building to inspect us and to take our names and regiments. We complained to them of the shooting and they told us to keep four feet from the windows and we would not be shot. We then asked for some supper, and were told that we would probably get something the next day; which we did, about ten o'clock.

Our wounds were not dressed nor cared for (only what our own boys could do, those who were not so badly wounded as the rest of us) until we had been in Libby twelve days, and then Dr. Stewart of the Second Minnesota got permission to come in and see us, he being a Free Mason. He spent the day with us and amputated my arm again, which had become maggoty on the field and had sloughed open. I had got the maggots about all out with a bottle of hartshorn which I had picked up on the field. After that everything went on as usual in the building, our rations in the meantime consisting of one cake of hardbread and one pint of James river water per day to a man - unless we could buy some or steal some from the guards, which we frequently did.

On the fifteenth of August three rebel surgeons entered the room I was in and came to a man whose name and regiment I do not know. He had a flesh wound in the calf of the leg and the gangrene had got into it. The leg could have been saved with proper care, but they cut it off square without any flap just "for an experiment." The man lingered and died in about fifteen days.

We found out about the first of August that the basement or cellar of Libby was filled with tobacco, so we contrived to get into it, and then we began to live a little better, for we could trade tobacco with the guards and darkeys for something to eat. The Johnnies did not find out our reserve store until about the middle of September, and then finding they could not keep us out of it they hauled the tobacco away.

In the mean time our death rate had been from six to ten per day in our room, from wounds and lack of food. At times some poor fellow would get homesick and then his days were numbered. I never knew a man in

Libby to live more than fifteen days after he became homesick. After this our death rate increased, often towards the last numbering as many as twenty per day.

I had got so that I could walk around the building. One day while down stairs watching the guard and trying to get a breath of fresh air, I discovered that he had a loaf of corn bread and a big piece of liver which he was eating. He had not eaten much when an officer came along and the guard had to lay the food down behind him to salute the officer. That was my chance, and grabbing the bread and liver I went up stairs, and didn't I have a treat!

The last of September our boys began to tunnel out from the cellar where the rebs had taken out the tobacco. A large number got away through the tunnel. How many escaped or how many were recaptured I do not know, for not one that went through the tunnel was brought back into the building while I was there. This escape so enraged the rebs that they cut our scant rations off for five days, which finished many a poor fellow who was nearly dead before. The fifth day an officer came into our room with a fine fat blood hound. When the dog was near me I petted him and managed to detain him there until the officer went up stairs. I spoke to a Fourteenth Brooklyn boy who had a knife. I took the dog by the top of his head and yanked it up while the Fourteenth boy cut his throat. When the officer came down the dog was eaten up and there was not so much as a blood spot to show what had become of him. The boys had caught the blood in their cups and drank it as fast as it flowed. The officer raved a while but soon left without bidding us good-bye.

Matters continued thus until the tenth of October, as I recall it, when looking from the window, standing at the proper distance, I thought I saw a man I used to go to school with when a boy but who had been in the south for some years. I called to him from the window to attract his attention. He looked up, recognized me, called me by name and at the same time drew his revolver and fired six shots at me through the window, two of which cut the hair on my head, which convinced me that he was not shooting for a sham, but to hit.

I think it was the twenty-seventh of October, a day never to be forgotten by me, when in the afternoon an officer came into the building, called the names of fifty of us, whom they did not think would live, and told us to pick up our traps and be ready to go down the James River by 4 P.M. as we were to be paroled. I was the tenth on the list. At three they formed us and marched us to the office outside, where we signed the parole as best we could and then were carried to the boat that was waiting for us. There were only a few of us who could walk that distance. Before leaving the building we divided our effects with the boys who were left. And so we bade good-bye to old Libby Prison forever.

Maine Bugle

Appendix Chapter 6

Casualties of the 4th Maine at Second Bull Run, August 29 and 30, 1862.

Killed

Co. C., 1st Sergt, Franklin Achorn Co. D.,

Charles Clark

Co. E., Corp. James Hatch Co. F.,

G. W. Robinson

Co. H., Moses A. Debeck Co. K.,

Charles Brown

Co. K., William J. King

Wounded

Sergeant Major C. F. Sawyer

Company A

M. McManners

Anson Trussel

Company B

1st Lieutenant Julius B. Litchfield

Patrick Black

Daniel C. Norris

Edmund Cowing

Herbert J. Dow

Company C

1st Lieutenant G. F. Crabtree Corp.

Eben L. Higgins

Samuel N. Cain

Charles A. Libby II

T. E. Snowdeal

Charles H. Miller

Philander Procter

Company D

Joseph Clark

Corp. James Rhodes

Company E

Sergt. Zuinglas C. Gowan

Company F

1st Sergt. George M. Bragg Sergt.
Henry Leach

Corp. William H. Clark

Warren A. Dollif

Charles H. Elwell John
S. Shephard

Company G

Corp Hiram Hackett John
Carleton

Samuel Seavey

Albion Lowell

Company H

George Cox

Company I

Moses H. Witham 1st
Sergt. Frank P. Eames

Rufus Sidelinger

Company K

William R. Fowler

Missing

Sergt. Riley Greer, Co. A; Ellis Bigdall, Co.
B; Henry O. Davis, Co D; H. H. B. Hogan, Co. E;
Nicolas Butler, Co. E; Ephriah D. Tasker, Co. F;
John Malcome, Co. H; Thomas Doyle,
Co. I.

Appendix Chapter 7

4th Maine's Casualties at Fredericksburg

Rank & Name REMARKS
Lt. Col. Carver ok
Major Wm. L. Pitcher Killed
Serg. G.W. Martin OK
Adj. E. Libby Wounded in shoulder and thigh severely

Capt. J.B. Litchfield Wounded slightly in left side, retd. to duty after having wound dressed.
" Geo. G. Davis Wounded severely in left thigh & left arm.
" Wm. Clark OK
" Eben Whitcomb Wounded slightly in head-now on duty.
1st Lieut O.C. McGray Wounded in right arm-Taken prisoner & paroled.
" " Wm. Shields Wounded severely in right lung.
" " John Auld Wounded severely in right thigh & right wrist.
" " S. Stearns OK
" " Ezra Carr Wounded slightly in right side.
" " G. Bourne Wounded severely in side & arm-taken prisoner.
2nd Lieut A.J. Gray OK
" " E. Harding Wounded slightly in right shoulder-remained on duty.
" " C.H. Conant Wounded slightly in finger-Retd to duty after having wound dressed.
" " G. Abbott Wounded in both legs.
" " Wm. Barker Wounded slightly in right shoulder-Retd. to duty after wound dressed.
" " W.S. Goodale Killed
" " S.F. Miller OK

1st Sgt. Fred Aldus Wounded severely in left shoulder
Sgt. M.W.McManus OK
Corp. H.W. Ladd Wounded slightly in breast-now on duty
" T. Durham OK
" M. Dorcey Wounded severely in both arms
" J. Denning OK
Prvt. S.O. Curtis Missing
" E. Cross Wounded severely in lung and thigh
" Wm. Cullnan Finger Amputated
" G.S. Daniels OK
" G FairweatherOK
" James Gall OK
" Wm Kendrick Wounded in left shoulder severely-finger amputated.
" L. Lincoln Wounded in thigh and shoulder
" Wm. Moores Missing
" T. Mither Wounded in right thigh
" M.A. Nichols Missing
" A. Piper OK
" Geo. Russ OK
" E.W. Stinson Wounded in thigh
" H. Speed OK
" G. Sylvester Missing
" A. Trussell Missing

COMPANY B
Sgt. H. Pease OK
" H.O. Ripley OK
" E.L. Mowry OK
Corp. H. Mitchell OK
" C.W. Hopkins Missing
" F.M. Tower Wounded severely on right side
" J.B. Lougy Missing
" R. Christy Wounded severely in left side
" W.W. Ulmer OK
Prvt. A. Boynton Wounded in thigh and leg
" E. Bigdoll OK
" Robt. Grant Wounded in head

" D. Norris Missing
" J. Quimby Killed
" C. Turner Missing
" E. Carver Wounded in neck
" J. Spear OK

COMPANY C
1st Sgt J. Conant Wounded and missing
Sgt. O Blackinton Wounded severely in leg-flesh wound
Corp. G. Gardner Wounded in right thigh
" C. Miller Wounded in left thigh
" R. Fales Wounded
" J. Kellar Killed
" A. Candage Killed
" W. Austin OK
Prvt. H. Liscomb Wounded in right side
" C. Ramsey Wounded in head and left hand
" J. Devine Killed
" J. Bragg Killed
" P. Proctor Killed
" A. Pottle Missing
" R. Walters Missing
" T. Kellar Missing
" G. Sheldon Missing
" A Cunningham OK

COMPANY D
1st Sgt. J.S. Sholler Wounded in left hand & left leg-finger amputated
Sgt. I. Barnard Wounded in right leg
Corp. S. Young Wounded severely in abdomin
" J. Witham Ok
" L. Terry Ok
Prvt. M. Bartlett Killed
Prvt. J. Clark OK
" E. Hall OK
" A. Millay OK
" J.S. Gray OK

" L. Richards OK
" H. Story Wounded and taken prisoner
" A. Savage Missing
" U. Reynolds OK
" S.A. Wood Killed

COMPANY E
1st Sgt S.W. Place Wounded severely in left thigh
Sgt. T. Campbell OK
Corp. W. Perkins OK
" W. Barstow OK
" F.K. Chapman OK
Prvt. C.K. Chapman OK
" O.C. Gove OK
" J.S. Kinney OK
" J. Skinner OK
" J. Thompson OK
" J.K. Corey OK
" O. Pinkham Wounded slightly in left arm
" S. Jones OK
" Wm. Tibbetts Wounded right lung, right foot left arm -Died Dec 29th
" C. Clements Wounded severely in right lung
" M. Fuller Wounded in right arm
" F. Morang OK
" L. Hall Wounded slightly in arm

COMPANY F
1st Sgt Moses Ford Killed
Sgt. H. Leach OK
" F. Rich Killed
" A. Rose OK
Corp. F. Hill OK
" H. York Wounded slightly leg-Remained on duty
" J. Hilt OK
" R. Bickford OK
Prvt. L. Mitchell Killed
" C.F. Chapman Killed

" P. Getchell Wounded severely in arm
" D. Nickerson Wounded severely in right arm
" J.W. Clark Wounded severely in head (Skull Fractured)
" J. Poland Wounded slightly in right leg
" J. Shepard Wounded severely in right arm
" D. Higgins Missing
" A. Patterson OK
" G.R. Hall OK
" J. Bickford OK
" Wm. Rowe OK
" A. Condon OK
" F. Roberts OK
" S. Danforth OK
" F.E. Mellen OK
" B.P. Tilton Wounded severely in left thigh

COMPANY G
1st Sgt G. Crockett OK
Sgt J. McKenney OK
Corp. C. Knights Flesh wound in left thigh
" B. Lowell OK
" E. Somes Killed
" A. Farnham Killed
Prvt. J.O. Clark Wounded in abdomen-Taken prisoner
" C. Brookings Wounded slightly (Spent Ball) remained on duty
" B. Blinn OK
" A.Cunningham Wounded slightly in right hand-on duty
" E. Howard OK
" E. Light Wounded slightly in arm-now on duty
" N. Stewart OK
" Z. Young OK
" C. Howard Wounded severely in pelvis
" A Wright Mortally wounded in abdomen-Died Dec 20

COMPANY H
1st Sgt M. Long Mortally wounded in liver & left lung-Died Dec 18

Sgt. F. Ingalls Wounded slightly in right leg-On duty
Corp. G.F. Kane Wounded in foot
" M. Green Wounded severely in left arm
" Thos. Milan Wounded severely in both hands
" G.P. Wood OK
Prvt. D.M. Allen Wounded severely in head ,right arm & right side-Taken prisoner
" Geo. Cox OK
" S. Higgins OK
" H. Jellison Dangerously wounded in ling
" J. Jackson OK
" Amos Page Wounded in testes and right leg
" F.E. Sawyer OK
" F. Sherman Wounded in left leg
" H. Young Missing
" J. Webster Missing

COMPANY I
Sgt G. Knowlton Wounded and missing
" C.C. Gray OK
Corp. E. Lowell Wounded slightly in arm
" S. Carlton OK
" C.W. Gray OK
" Wm. Knowles OK
Prvt. M. Butler OK
" H.Calderwood OK
" A. Dickey OK
" G.H. Downes Wounded in left foot
" T.D. Eaton Wounded in right arm
" F. Forbes Taken Prisoner-Escaped following day
" S.M. Gray Killed
" H. Hinckley Wounded in left knee
" L. Jellison OK
" E.B. Moore OK
" J. Millano OK
" C. Parker Missing
" C.E. Phinney OK
" J. Towers Killed

" J. Ward Killed
" C.P. Whitton Killed

COMPANY K
1st Sgt A.B. Wooster OK
Sgt. Wm. Gardner OK
Corp. E. Hanning Missing
" S. Stuart Wounded severely in left lung
" J. Toothaker OK
" J. Doak OK
Prvt. S. Sleeper OK
" Benj. Burr Wounded slightly in right foot
" P.J. Carter OK
" J.E. Dean OK
" A. Hilton OK
" E.A. Gorden OK
" Saml. Young Wounded slightly in right breast
" M. Payne OK

Appendix Chapter 8

Casualties of Chancellorsville Campaign

2nd Lieut.	Sheridan F. Miller	Killed
1st "	Charles Conant	Wounded in rib
2nd "	Nathaniel Robbins	Wounded in hand
2nd "	Eben Harding	Wounded in foot

Prvt.	Ellis Bigelow	Shoulder slight
"	H. B. Surinous	Foot slight
"	Andrew Grindell	Foot slight
"	Ferdinand Sawyer	Foot slight
"	Isaiah Emuson	Leg slight
"	Simon B. Carlton	Knee severe
"	William Knowles	Side slight
"	Charles Phinney	Leg slight
Sgt.	David Carley	Breast slight
Prvt.	Orpheus Roberts	Leg slight
"	John Johnson	Arm amputated and prisoner
Sgt.	H. G. York	Shoulder
"	Joseph Hilt	Leg
Prvt.	Hosea Young	Leg and prisoner
"	F. L. Palmer	Breast severe taken prisoner
"	Leander Howard	Head
Sgt.	A. Merrithew	Face
Prvt.	Robert Green	Knee severe

Missing

Serg. Enoch Lurvey	Prvt. H. A. Collagin
Prvt. William Seavey	" Isaac Jordan
" S. B. Sylvester	" Isaac Witham
Prvt. James Seminous	Prvt. Joseph H. Bickford
" Bainbridge Poland	" Joseph E. Clark [1]

[1] Maine Archives Regimental File, Augusta, Maine.

Appendix Chapter 10

Participant and Casualty List
4th Maine at Gettysburg

Col. Elijah Walker Wounded Achilles tendon
Major Ebenezer Whitcomb Wounded, died Oct 5th
Adj. Charles Sawyer
Qtr Mstr. Isaac Abbott
Surg. Seth Hunkins
Sgt. Major William Gardner Prisoner
Hptl Steward Samuel Hersey
Qtr Mstr Sgt Henry Tibbetts
Comm. Sgt Lemuel Grant
Drum Major Fred Low
Fife Major John Singhi

Company A
2nd Lieut. Andrew Gray
Sgt. Marcian McManus Prisoner
" Henry Ladd Wounded leg
" Thomas Gurney Prisoner
" Tolford Durham Prisoner
Corp. Joseph Libby
" Michael Dorsey
" James Gall Wounded in hip on July 4th
" Timothy Abbott
" Jerry Denning Wounded hip
" Horace Speed
Pvts. Ephriam Allenwood Wounded in side
" Alpha Buker
" James Colly
" Stephen Curtis Prisoner
" Charles Doten
" Henry C. Hall Prisoner
" Hiram H. Hatch Prisoner died Belle Isle 12/27/63
" Llewellyn Lincoln

" Melvin Nichols
" Benjamin F. Philbrick
" George A. Russ
" Dennis Sweeney Wounded in hand
" George Sylvester Prisoner died Belle Isle 12/15/63
" Sanford Sylvester Prisoner
" Demetrius Bryant
" Melvin Cooley Prisoner
" William Crosby Prisoner
" Stephen Daggett
" Daniel O. Flye Prisoner
" Sylvanus Hatch Prisoner
" Melvin Law Prisoner
" Augustus S. Lord
" Lewis Ordway
" Albert Piper
" Manuel Sidelinger
" Andrew P Walker Wounded slight

Company B
Capt. Julius B. Litchfield Prisoner since July 2nd 1863
1st Lt. Arthur Libby
1st Sgt. Havilah Pease
Sgt. Henry O. Ripley Color bearer
" Edgar L. Mowry
Corp. Otis G. Spear
" Henry Mitchell Wounded Prisoner Died 12/17/63
" George E. Wall
" Thaddeus Pillsbury
" Wyman W. Ulmer Wounded shoulder and breast
" Charles W. Hopkins
Prvt. Ellis Bigdoll
" Andrew Gardiner
" Robert Grant
" Edward C. Megguier
" Levi A. Philbrook
" George F. Stetson Wounded shoulder and breast
" George F. Taylor

" Samuel Totman
" Alonzo Ulmer Wounded face
" Alden Wooster
" Dance Dow
" Albert Goodwin
" John J. Kallock
" Daniel Norris
" Josiah C. Spear
" Hanson B. Simmons Wounded face
" John W. Titus
" Charles A. Turner Wounded hand
" Aruna Willis
" Edward K. Waterman

Company C
1st Lt. Charles H. Conant
2nd Lt. Joseph R. Conant
1st Sgt. Kendall K. Rankin
Sgt. Charles H. Miller
" Rufus O. Fales Prisoner died Richmond 11/12/63
Corp. Warren W. Austin
" George G. Gardiner Killed
" John Colburn Wounded eye
Prvt. James M. Brown Prisoner
" Orlando F. Brown
" William J. Collins Prisoner Died Richmond 11/12/63
" Alfred W. Cunningham
" James A. Cain
" Thomas Kellar Prisoner died Richmond 1864
" Charles C. Perry
" Thomas E. Snowdeal Prisoner
" Benjamin F. Walter
" Alfred W. Cunningham Prisoner
" Ephriam K. Butler Prisoner
" William Caswell Prisoner died Richmond 11/1/63
" Austin Cunningham Prisoner
" Francis E. Knight
" Patrick Martin Wounded shoulder

" Andrew Pottle Prisoner
" John F. Walker
" Edwin Wade

Company D
Capt. Edwin Libby
Lt. George R. Abbott
1st Sgt. James McLaughlin
Sgt. William Fountain
" Samuel L Meservey
Corp. John Witham Killed
" William Perkins
" Levi G. Perry
" Edward Hall
Prvt. Joseph Dunbar Wounded Arm
" Abial B. Clark
" Charles A. Davis Wounded
" Anthony Fields Prisoner
" Charles Hodges Prisoner
" Henry P. Marshall
" John Morrissey
" Eben E. Pershon
" Almon Shepherd Wounded breast
" Appleton Townsend Wounded prisoner
" Joseph O. Trim Wounded leg
" John M. Clark Wounded leg trans. Invalid Corp
" Jacob C. Cunningham
" Isaiah V. Eaton Wounded died
" John S. Gray Wounded died July 28th
" Edward H. Joy
" Christopher Martin Wounded hand
" George Peasley Prisoner died Andersonville
" Horatio Richards Prisoner died Andersonville
" Alonzo H. Stickney Killed
" Simon Taylor Prisoner
" Jerome Watson Wounded face

Company E

1st Lt. Jason Carlisle
2nd Lt. Charles S. McCobb Killed
1st Sgt. Artemus Robinson
Sgt. Thomas B. Campbell
" Zuinglas Gowan Prisoner
Corp. Nathaniel B Waters
" Ira A. Waltz Prisoner
" William B. Perkins Wounded Leg
" Francis K. Chapman
" Willard Barstow Wounded died August 8th
" John P. Blake Wounded hand
Prvt. Albert W. Bryer
" Everett B. Chapman
" Isaac W. Fountain
" Oscar C. Gove
" Harlow M. Hall
" James H. Hodgkins
" Frank H, Lailer
" Thomas R. Perkins
" William M. Smith
" Charles C. Turner Prisoner
" Charles K. Chapman
" John C. Corey
" Harvey H. Giles
" Almond Hall
" Moses W. Hatch Wounded arm
" Jesse S. Kinney
" Joseph E. Mears
" John L. Thompson
" Isaac Waters
" John R. Skinner

Company F
Capt. George Davis Prisoner escaped Libby
1st Lt. Solomon Stearns Prisoner
2nd Lt. George M. Bragg Wounded died July 5th
1st Sgt. Albert H. Rose
Sgt. Henry Leach Prisoner

" Hiram G. York
" Francis O. J. S. Hill
" Joseph G. Hilt
Corp. Charles B. Parsons
" Rufus G. Bickford
" Freeman M. Roberts
" Winthrop H. Chick
" William C. Rowe Wounded side
" George R. Hall
Prvt. Elisha J. Barlow
" Albert D. Crocker
" Francis M. Forbes Prisoner
" Harrison Hall Wounded
" James M. Hollis Wounded Died 11/27/63 Richmond
" Daniel C. Nickerson Prisoner
" Nathan Patterson Prisoner
" Enoch F. Piper
" Frank Rowe Jr. Prisoner
" John F. Stone Wounded arm
" Thomas O. Whitcomb Prisoner
" Albert J. Condon
" Amos Evans
" John H. Gardiner Prisoner
" James H, Hines
" Edward Jackson
" Warren Overlock Wounded
" Daniel Pierce Jr.
" Charles H. Rowill
" John S. Shepherd Prisoner
" Ephriam D. Tasker Prisoner
" Charles A. Wood
" George Hall Killed
" Rufus Bickford Prisoner

Company G
1st Lt. William A. Barker
2nd Lt. George L. Crockett
Sgt. James F. McKenney

Corp. John R. Rittal Killed
" Crosby R. Brookings Wounded died August 10
" Bradford Lowell Prisoner
" Nathaniel Stewart
Prvt. Bradford H. Blinn Prisoner
" Joseph Erskine Prisoner died Richmond 11/22/63
" Daniel O. Howard Prisoner
" Leander Howard Prisoner
" Elwell Munsey Prisoner
" Alexander Nute
" James R. Piper Prisoner
" William Seavey Wounded in head
" George Tibbitts
" Timothy Call
" Peter Fredson Jr. Wounded in head
" Elijah Howard
" Leonard Jones
" Thomas J. McCorrison Wounded
" Joseph Nelson
" Eben Overlock Prisoner
" James R. Rittal Prisoner died 11/12/63
" Thomas Stewart
" Zealor Young

Company H
2nd Lt. Nathaniel Robbins Prisoner
1st Sgt. Thomas P. Ingalls Killed
Sgt. Joseph B. Babson
" George P. Wood
Corp. Daniel W. Barker Wounded Leg
" Horace C. Clough
" William H. Tripp
" John H. Thomas
" Jared R. Reed
Prvt. Charles W. Allen
" Charles W. Brackett Wounded arm
" Edwin J. Carter Wounded shoulder
" Patrick Crowley

" Joseph Farnham
" William D. Gilmore Prisoner
" Simon Higgins Wounded
" Silas Jones
" Daniel McMahon
" Edwin Mink
" Amos Page
" Thomas C. Saunders
" William H. Simmons
" Alexander Wallace
" Harrison Young Prisoner died Libby 1/19/64
" George L. Ames
" Alfred Blackington
" George Cox
" Andrew Emerton Captured Emmitsburg
" Samuel N Downes
" Abram J. Furbish
" Elijah H. Grindle
" Joel Jackson
" John Keefe
" Charles F. Moore
" James Noonan
" Charles Rose Wounded prisoner
" Frank A. Sherman
" Isaac Stahl
" Adolphus Whitney
" Morrison Young
" George W. Steele Captured Emmitsburg escaped

Company I
Capt. Robert H. Gray
2nd Lt. Orpheus Roberts Killed
1st Sgt. Christopher Gray
Sgt. Ivory W. Baird Prisoner
" Abiather Merrithew
" Daniel Carley Wounded hand
Corp. Clarenden W. Gray
" Moses H. Witham

" Elias B. Moore
Prvt. Augustus Burgin Wounded
" Henry D. Calderwood Prisoner
" John Donahue Prisoner
" Richard F. Fillmore
" John C. Fowler
" Edward E. Kent
" Charles P. Parker Prisoner
" Samuel D. Small Prisoner
" Alvah Staples
" Clifton Whittam Prisoner
" Chesbrook Burgin
" Nathan Chase Wounded died July 21st
" Thomas Doyle Wounded died July 5th
" Frank Forbes
" Lemuel B. Jefferson
" Jaun Millano
" Lewis E. Pendleton
" Wesley Rich Prisoner
" Rufus Sidelinger
" Benjamin F. Snow
" William S. Towers Wounded
" Charles Phinney Prisoner
Company K
Lt. George M. Bragg
1st Sgt. Amos B. Wooster Wounded face slight
Sgt. David H. Kimball
" John A. Toothaker Wounded died July 20th
Corp. Sears Nickerson
" Elisha Henning
" Dennis Moody
" Silas M. Perkins
" James E, Doak
" Henry E. Davis
Prvt. Edward Baker
" Charles Collins Prisoner
" Ephraim A. Gordon Wounded ankle
" Andrew Herrin Prisoner

"	George F. Johnson	Wounded died July 9th
"	Michael Rariden	Wounded died July 24th
"	John A. Robinson	
"	John H. Sawyer	Killed
"	Horace L. Ware	Missing prisoner
"	William L. Woodbury	Missing
"	Preston J. Carter	
"	James E. Deane	
"	Aurelius Hawkins	Wounded arm
"	Alvin Hilton	Wounded died July 9th
"	Isaiah B. Merrick	Wounded neck prisoner
"	Jacob D. Ray	Wounded hand
"	Frederick H. Rogers	Killed
"	John Shuman	Wounded died July 15th
"	Robert Whitehead	Wounded foot

Musicians
Frederick Dow
Eleazer J. Young

Bibliography

Maine Adjutant General Report, 1862. Elijah Walker.

Bicknell, George. History of the Fifth Maine Regiment. Portland, Maine : 5th Maine Museum, 1988.

Bigelow, John. Chancellorsville. New York : Smithmark Publishers, 1995

Catton, Bruce. A Stillness at Appomattox : New York : Doubleday, 1953.

Caski, John. The Army of the Potomac at Berkeley Plantation. The Harrison Landing Occupation of 1862. Richmond : Self Published, 1989.

Davis, William. Battle at Bull Run. Baton Rouge : Louisianna State University Press, 1977.

Fergurson, Ernest. Chancellorsville 1863, The Souls of the Brave. New York : Alfred A. Knopf, 1992.

Foote, Shelby. The Civil War, A Narrative. 3 vols. New York : Random House, 1963.

Gould, Edward K. Major-General Hiram G. Berry. Rockland, Maine : Courier-Gazette. 1899.

Haley, John W.. The Rebel Yell and the Yankee Hurrah. Camden, Maine : Downeast Books. 1985.

Harrison, Kathleen G. Our Principle Loss was in this Place. Action at the Slaughter Pen and at South End of Houck's Ridge. Gettysburg,

Pennsylvania. The Gettysburg Magazine. Vol. 1 : July 1989.

Haley, John. The Rebel Yell and the Yankee Hurrah. The Civil War Journal of a Maine Volunteer, Camden, Maine : Down East Books, 1985.

Hennessy, John. Return to Bull Run. The Campaign and Battle of Second Bull Run. New York : Simon and Shuster, 1993.

Hennessy, John. The First Battle Of Manassas. Lynchburg, Virginia : H. E. Howard, Inc., 1989.

Hiram G. Berry Correspondence. Larry Smith Collection. Wiscassett, Maine.

Howard, Oliver Otis. Autobiography of Oliver Otis Howard. Freeport, New York : Books for Libraries Press, 1971.

Hunt, Charles O. Escape from Camp Sorghum. Maine Commandery of the Order of the Loyal Legion of the Grand Army of the Republic. 4 Vols., 1912.

Libby, Abiel. Journal of Abiel Libby. Maine State Archives.

Longstreet, James. Battles and Leaders of the Civil War. New Jersey : Castle Publishers.

Lowry.Don. No Turning Back. New York : Hippocrene Books, 1992.

Luvas, Jay and Nelson, Harold. U. S. Army War College Guide to the Battles of Chancellorsville and Fredericksburg. New York : Harper and Row, 1988.

Maine Adjutant General Report, 1864-5. Vol I.

Maine Bugle, Campaign I, July 1894.Escape from Libby Prison. Rockland, Maine : Maine Association

Maine Gettysburg Commission. Maine at Gettysburg : Report of the Maine Commissioners. Portland, Me, : Lakeside Press, 1898.

Maine State Archives, Soldier Index. Augusta, Me.

Maine State Archives. Civil War Record Collection. Augusta, Me.

McClellan, George. The Civil War Papers of George B. McClellan.

McPherson, James. Battle Cry of Freedom. New York : Oxford University Press, 1988.

Official Records. The War of the Rebellion, 128 Vols. 1868 - 1927.

Pfantz, Harry W. Gettysburg. The Second Day. The University of North Carolina, 1987.

Rhea,.Gordon. The Battle of the Wilderness. May 5 - 6. 1864. Baton Rouge : Louisianna State University Press, 1994.

Robbins, 1895 Service Record. Maine State Archives.

Rockland Free Press. Rockland, Maine : 1861.

Sears, Stephen. To the Gates of Richmond. The Peninsula Campaign. New York : Ticnor and Fields, 1992.

Sifakis, . Who Was Who in the Civil War. New York : Facts on File Publications, 1988.

Smith, John Day. The History of the 19th Regiment of Maine Volunteer Infantry. Minneapolis : Great Western Printing Compant, 1909.

The Rockland Gazette Rockland, Maine : 1861 - 1864.

Trudeau, Bloody Roads South. The Wilderness to Cold Harbor, May to June 1864. New York : Fawcett Columbine, 1989.

Walker, Elijah. Historical Record from January 1st to November 1st, 1862. Maine State Archives.

Walker, Elijah. History of the Fourth Maine Infantry. Special Collections, University of Maine at Orono.

Walker, Elijah. Service Records, National Archives.

Wheeler,Richard. Lee's Terribel Swift Sword. From Antietam to Chancellorsville. New York : Harper Collins Publications, 1992

Wheeler, Richard. Sword Over Richmond An Eyewitness History of McClellans Peninsula Campaign. New York : Harper and Row, 1986.

Whitman, Maine in the War. Lewiston, Maine : Nelson Dingley, 1985